GATEWAY TO THE GREAT BOOKS

SYNGE	CARLYLE
O'NEILL	EMERSON
❧	HAWTHORNE
VOLUME 5	WHITMAN
VIRGINIA WOOLF	VIRGINIA WOOLF
ARNOLD	XENOPHON
SAINTE-BEUVE	PRESCOTT
BACON	LONG
HUME	PLINY
SCHOPENHAUER	TACITUS
SCHILLER	GUIZOT
SHELLEY	ADAMS
WHITMAN	BURY
HAZLITT	LUCIAN
LAMB	PAINE
JOHNSON	WASHINGTON
DE QUINCEY	JEFFERSON
T. S. ELIOT	FRANKLIN
❧	
VOLUME 6	
J. S. MILL	
TWAIN	LINCOLN
LA BRUYÈRE	❧

D1399971

GATEWAY
TO THE
GREAT BOOKS

Gateway
to the
Great Books

ROBERT M. HUTCHINS, MORTIMER J. ADLER
Editors in Chief

CLIFTON FADIMAN
Associate Editor

---

5 12877

CRITICAL

ESSAYS

Encyclopædia Britannica, Inc.

WILLIAM BENTON
Publisher

Chicago, London, Toronto, Geneva, Sydney, Tokyo, Manila

Portrait illustrations are by Fred Steffen

Contents
of Volume 5

VIRGINIA WOOLF 1
How Should One Read a Book? 5

MATTHEW ARNOLD 15
The Study of Poetry 19
Sweetness and Light 42

SAINTE-BEUVE 62
What Is a Classic? 65
Montaigne 76

SIR FRANCIS BACON 90
Of Beauty 94
Of Discourse 95
Of Studies 97

DAVID HUME 99
Of the Standard of Taste 103

ARTHUR SCHOPENHAUER   120

On Style   124

On Some Forms of Literature   137

*On the Comparative Place
of Interest and Beauty
in Works of Art*   143

FRIEDRICH SCHILLER   151

On Simple and Sentimental Poetry   155

PERCY BYSSHE SHELLEY   212

A Defence of Poetry   216

WALT WHITMAN   243

Preface to Leaves of Grass   247

WILLIAM HAZLITT   260

My First Acquaintance with Poets   264

On Swift   280

Of Persons One Would Wish to Have Seen 284

CHARLES LAMB   296

My First Play   300

Dream Children, a Reverie   304

Sanity of True Genius   308

SAMUEL JOHNSON   311

Preface to Shakespeare   316

THOMAS DE QUINCEY   354

*Literature of Knowledge
and Literature of Power*   358

On the Knocking at the Gate in Macbeth   362

THOMAS STEARNS ELIOT   367

Dante   371

Tradition and the Individual Talent   404

Virginia Woolf

1882–1941

Virginia Woolf was born at Kensington, January 25, 1882. She was the second daughter of Sir Leslie Stephen and his second wife. Sir Leslie was a well-known essayist and editor of the *Dictionary of National Biography*. Virginia Woolf was related to several famous Victorian families, including the Darwins. During her childhood many literary men of the day came to visit her father. Ruskin was one of these early acquaintances.

Delicate health kept Virginia from attending school, and her father educated her. He allowed her free run of his library; and, despite her lack of formal schooling, she was much better read than most women of her time.

In 1905, shortly after her father's death, Virginia, with her sister Vanessa and her brothers Adrian and Thoby, moved to a section of London called Bloomsbury. Their house was a popular meeting place for young writers and artists, who came to be known as the Bloomsbury Group.

In 1912 she married Leonard Sidney Woolf. Together they founded the Hogarth Press in 1917. Between periods of deep depression Virginia Woolf wrote novels and critical essays. Her first two novels, *The Voyage Out*, in 1915, and *Night and Day*, in 1919, were traditional in form. In her later novels, such as *Mrs. Dalloway*, in 1925, and *To the Lighthouse*, in 1927, she developed a characteristic style and experimented with various methods of representing the unspoken thoughts and feelings of her characters. *The Waves* was published in 1931.

Many of Virginia Woolf's critical essays were first published in the *Times Literary Supplement*. Two collections, *The Common Reader* and *The Common Reader, Second Series*, were published during her lifetime *How Should One Read a Book?* is from the second series.

On March 28, 1941, Virginia Woolf drowned herself in a river near the Woolfs' wartime home in Sussex.

The Bloomsbury Group was made up of young British intellectuals. The members prized wit and good manners and were strongly opposed to the utilitarianism which their Victorian parents had valued. They attached considerable importance to a delicate appreciation of art.

Many contemporary writers were critical of the group's aristocratic attitudes. D. H. Lawrence, for example, described the members as "beetles that sting like scorpions." But they also had many staunch defenders, including T. S. Eliot.

In her essays, Virginia Woolf appears to be addressing a larger Bloomsbury. She speaks to us as intellectual equals who share her passion for books and who are, or want to be, "creative readers" like herself.

The following essay, as noted above, is taken from *The Common Reader, Second Series*. The title comes from Samuel Johnson's *Life of Gray*. "I rejoice to concur with the common reader," says Dr. Johnson, "for by the common sense of readers . . . must be generally decided all claim to poetical honours."

Some critics have suggested that Mrs. Woolf's ideal reader is far from common. In a sense, this is true. She was herself an omnivorous and demanding reader, devouring and digesting hundreds of books, and bringing to the art of reading an uncommonly acute mind. But she was always concerned to discover and state those elements of the art which good readers have in common. In this sense, her essays are true to the title. And it is in this sense that the essay reprinted here must be understood.

She begins by pointing out that there can be no hard and fast

---

Notes from the artist: "Virginia Woolf seated before a window with a view of a lighthouse, a symbol in one of her most important ,novels . . . while the three 'footprints' across the page recall her fictional biography of 'Flush,' Elizabeth Barrett Browning's spaniel."

rules for reading, but she quickly goes on to say that liberty must not be interpreted as license. If reading is an art, it has principles. These are of particular importance, she suggests, in an age in which there are many books. You *cannot* read everything. What *should* you read?

Like many of the authors in this volume, she concludes that only the best books should be read. But how are we to discover them? One way is to write, she says. "Perhaps the quickest way to understand the elements of what a novelist is doing is not to read, but to write." Only then can you discover how difficult, and how magical, good writing is. It follows, too, that "you must be capable not only of great finesse of perception, but of great boldness of imagination if you are going to make use of all that the novelist—the great artist—gives." Reading is not a passive activity. One cannot do it, as it were, lying down. It is work.

It is rewarding. Nothing, Mrs. Woolf suggests, is more so. From novels we learn what it means to "be wrenched and uprooted." A great novel creates the world anew for a good reader. Biographies people the familiar world with characters who are more interesting than most of the people we know. When we read poetry, "our being for the moment is centred and constricted, as in any violent shock of personal emotion." Books, for the good reader, have a tremendous effect.

But, Mrs. Woolf says, "the first process, to receive impressions with the utmost understanding, is only half the process of reading; it must be completed, if we are to get the whole pleasure from the book, by another. We must pass judgment upon these multitudinous impressions." In other words, the good reader is a critic, too. His standards, she insists, must be very high.

These two points make the heart of the essay. The good reader must receive everything which the book gives him, and he must judge its worth. If he fails to do either—particularly, if he judges without first understanding—he has failed to do his best. The punishment is harsh and automatic. The bad reader is lost among good books. He lacks the highest pleasure available to man, according to Mrs. Woolf. If she is right, none but a fool would refuse to learn to read as well as he can.

How Should One Read a Book?

In the first place, I want to emphasize the note of interrogation at the end of my title. Even if I could answer the question for myself, the answer would apply only to me and not to you. The only advice, indeed, that one person can give another about reading is to take no advice, to follow your own instincts, to use your own reason, to come to your own conclusions. If this is agreed between us, then I feel at liberty to put forward a few ideas and suggestions because you will not allow them to fetter that independence which is the most important quality that a reader can possess. After all, what laws can be laid down about books? The battle of Waterloo was certainly fought on a certain day; but is *Hamlet* a better play than *Lear*? Nobody can say. Each must decide that question for himself. To admit authorities, however heavily furred and gowned, into our libraries and let them tell us how to read, what to read, what value to place upon what we read, is to destroy the spirit of freedom which is the breath of those sanctuaries. Everywhere else we may be bound by laws and conventions—there we have none.

But to enjoy freedom, if the platitude is pardonable, we have of course to control ourselves. We must not squander our powers, helplessly and ignorantly, squirting half the house in order to water a single rosebush; we must train them, exactly and powerfully, here on the very spot. This, it may be, is one of the first difficulties that faces us in a library. What is "the very spot"? There may well seem to be nothing but a conglomeration and huddle of confusion. Poems and novels, histories and memoirs, dictionaries and bluebooks; books written in all languages by men and women of all tempers, races, and ages jostle each other on the shelf. And outside the donkey brays, the women gossip at the pump, the colts gallop across the fields. Where are we to begin? How are we to bring order into this multitudinous chaos and get the deepest and widest pleasure from what we read?

It is simple enough to say that since books have classes—fiction, biography, poetry—we should separate them and take from each what it is right that each should give us. Yet few people ask from books what books can give us. Most commonly we come to books with blurred and divided minds, asking of fiction that it shall be true, of poetry that it shall be false, of biography that it shall be flattering, of history that it shall enforce our own prejudices. If we could banish all such preconceptions when we read, that would be an admirable beginning. Do not dictate to your author; try to become him. Be his fellow-worker and accomplice. If you hang back, and reserve and criticize at first, you are preventing yourself from getting the fullest possible value from what you read. But if you open your mind as widely as possible, then signs and hints of almost imperceptible fineness, from the twist and turn of the first sentences, will bring you into the presence of a human being unlike any other. Steep yourself in this, acquaint yourself with this, and soon you will find that your author is giving you, or attempting to give you, something far more definite. The thirty-two chapters of a novel—if we consider how to read a novel first—are an attempt to make something as formed and controlled as a building: but words are more impalpable than bricks; reading is a longer and more complicated process than seeing. Perhaps the quickest way to understand the elements of what a novelist is doing is not to read, but to write; to make your own experiment with the dangers and difficulties of words. Recall, then, some event that has left a distinct impression on you—how at the corner of the street, perhaps, you passed two people talking. A tree shook; an electric light danced; the tone of the talk was comic, but also tragic; a whole vision, an entire conception, seemed contained in that moment.

But when you attempt to reconstruct it in words, you will find that it breaks into a thousand conflicting impressions. Some must be subdued; others emphasized; in the process you will lose, probably, all grasp upon the emotion itself. Then turn from your blurred and littered pages to the opening pages of some great novelist—Defoe, Jane Austen, Hardy. Now you will be better able to appreciate their mastery. It is not merely that we are in the presence of a different person—Defoe, Jane Austen, or Thomas Hardy—but that we are living in a different world. Here, in *Robinson Crusoe,* we are trudging a plain high road; one thing happens after another; the fact and the order of the fact is enough. But if the open air and adventure mean everything to Defoe they mean nothing to Jane

Austen. Hers is the drawing-room, and people talking, and by the many mirrors of their talk revealing their characters. And if, when we have accustomed ourselves to the drawing-room and its reflections, we turn to Hardy, we are once more spun around. The moors are round us and the stars are above our heads. The other side of the mind is now exposed— the dark side that comes uppermost in solitude, not the light side that shows in company. Our relations are not towards people, but towards Nature and destiny. Yet different as these worlds are, each is consistent with itself. The maker of each is careful to observe the laws of his own perspective, and however great a strain they may put upon us they will never confuse us, as lesser writers so frequently do, by introducing two different kinds of reality into the same book. Thus to go from one great novelist to another—from Jane Austen to Hardy, from Peacock to Trollope, from Scott to Meredith—is to be wrenched and uprooted; to be thrown this way and then that. To read a novel is a difficult and complex art. You must be capable not only of great finesse of perception, but of great boldness of imagination if you are going to make use of all that the novelist—the great artist—gives you.

But a glance at the heterogeneous company on the shelf will show you that writers are very seldom "great artists"; far more often a book makes no claim to be a work of art at all. These biographies and autobiographies, for example, lives of great men, of men long dead and forgotten, that stand cheek by jowl with the novels and poems, are we to refuse to read them because they are not "art"? Or shall we read them, but read them in a different way, with a different aim? Shall we read them in the first place to satisfy that curiosity which possesses us sometimes when in the evening we linger in front of a house where the lights are lit and the blinds not yet drawn, and each floor of the house shows us a different section of human life in being? Then we are consumed with curiosity about the lives of these people—the servants gossiping, the gentlemen dining, the girl dressing for a party, the old woman at the window with her knitting. Who are they, what are they, what are their names, their occupations, their thoughts, and adventures?

Biographies and memoirs answer such questions, light up innumerable such houses; they show us people going about their daily affairs, toiling, failing, succeeding, eating, hating, loving, until they die. And sometimes as we watch, the house fades and the iron railings vanish and we are out at sea; we are hunting, sailing, fighting; we are among savages and soldiers; we are taking part in great campaigns. Or if we like to stay here in England, in London, still the scene changes; the street narrows; the house

becomes small, cramped, diamond-paned, and malodorous. We see a
poet, Donne, driven from such a house because the walls were so thin
that when the children cried their voices cut through them. We can follow him, through the paths that lie in the pages of books, to Twickenham;
to Lady Bedford's Park, a famous meeting-ground for nobles and poets;
and then turn our steps to Wilton, the great house under the downs, and
hear Sidney read the *Arcadia* to his sister; and ramble among the very
marshes and see the very herons that figure in that famous romance; and
then again travel north with that other Lady Pembroke, Anne Clifford,
to her wild moors, or plunge into the city and control our merriment at
the sight of Gabriel Harvey in his black velvet suit arguing about poetry
with Spenser. Nothing is more fascinating than to grope and stumble in
the alternate darkness and splendour of Elizabethan London. But there
is no staying there. The Temples and the Swifts, the Harleys and the St.
Johns beckon us on; hour upon hour can be spent disentangling their
quarrels and deciphering their characters; and when we tire of them we
can stroll on, past a lady in black wearing diamonds, to Samuel Johnson
and Goldsmith and Garrick; or cross the channel, if we like, and meet
Voltaire and Diderot, Madame du Deffand; and so back to England and
Twickenham—how certain places repeat themselves and certain names!
—where Lady Bedford had her Park once and Pope lived later, to Walpole's home at Strawberry Hill. But Walpole introduces us to such a
swarm of new acquaintances, there are so many houses to visit and
bells to ring that we may well hesitate for a moment, on the Miss Berrys'
doorstep, for example, when behold, up comes Thackeray; he is the
friend of the woman whom Walpole loved; so that merely by going from
friend to friend, from garden to garden, from house to house, we have
passed from one end of English literature to another and wake to find
ourselves here again in the present, if we can so differentiate this moment from all that have gone before. This, then, is one of the ways in
which we can read these lives and letters; we can make them light up
the many windows of the past; we can watch the famous dead in their
familiar habits and fancy sometimes that we are very close and can surprise their secrets, and sometimes we may pull out a play or a poem
that they have written and see whether it reads differently in the presence of the author. But this again rouses other questions. How far, we
must ask ourselves, is a book influenced by its writer's life—how far is it
safe to let the man interpret the writer? How far shall we resist or give
way to the sympathies and antipathies that the man himself rouses in us
—so sensitive are words, so receptive of the character of the author?

These are questions that press upon us when we read lives and letters, and we must answer them for ourselves, for nothing can be more fatal than to be guided by the preferences of others in a matter so personal.

But also we can read such books with another aim, not to throw light on literature, not to become familiar with famous people, but to refresh and exercise our own creative powers. Is there not an open window on the right hand of the bookcase? How delightful to stop reading and look out! How stimulating the scene is, in its unconsciousness, its irrelevance, its perpetual movement—the colts galloping round the field, the woman filling her pail at the well, the donkey throwing back his head and emitting his long, acrid moan. The greater part of any library is nothing but the record of such fleeting moments in the lives of men, women, and donkeys. Every literature, as it grows old, has its rubbish-heap, its records of vanished moments and forgotten lives told in faltering and feeble accents that have perished. But if you give yourself up to the delight of rubbish-reading you will be surprised, indeed you will be overcome, by the relics of human life that have been cast out to moulder. It may be one letter—but what a vision it gives! It may be a few sentences—but what vistas they suggest! Sometimes a whole story will come together with such beautiful humour and pathos and completeness that it seems as if a great novelist had been at work, yet it is only an old actor, Tate Wilkinson, remembering the strange story of Captain Jones; it is only a young subaltern serving under Arthur Wellesley and falling in love with a pretty girl at Lisbon; it is only Maria Allen letting fall her sewing in the empty drawing-room and sighing how she wishes she had taken Dr. Burney's good advice and had never eloped with her Rishy. None of this has any value; it is negligible in the extreme; yet how absorbing it is now and again to go through the rubbish-heaps and find rings and scissors and broken noses buried in the huge past and try to piece them together while the colt gallops round the field, the woman fills her pail at the well, and the donkey brays.

But we tire of rubbish-reading in the long run. We tire of searching for what is needed to complete the half-truth which is all that the Wilkinsons, the Bunburys, and the Maria Allens are able to offer us. They had not the artist's power of mastering and eliminating; they could not tell the whole truth even about their own lives; they have disfigured the story that might have been so shapely. Facts are all that they can offer us, and facts are a very inferior form of fiction. Thus the desire grows upon us to have done with half-statements and approximations; to cease from searching out the minute shades of human character, to enjoy the greater abstractness, the purer truth of fiction. Thus we create the mood, intense and generalized, unaware of detail, but stressed by some regular, recurrent beat, whose natural expression is poetry; and that is the time to read poetry when we are almost able to write it.

> Western wind, when wilt thou blow?
> The small rain down can rain.
> Christ, if my love were in my arms,
> And I in my bed again!

The impact of poetry is so hard and direct that for the moment there is no other sensation except that of the poem itself. What profound depths we visit then—how sudden and complete is our immersion! There is nothing here to catch hold of; nothing to stay us in our flight. The illusion of fiction is gradual; its effects are prepared; but who when they read these four lines stops to ask who wrote them, or conjures up the thought of Donne's house or Sidney's secretary; or enmeshes them in the intricacy of the past and the succession of generations? The poet is always our contemporary. Our being for the moment is centred and constricted, as in any violent shock of personal emotion. Afterwards, it is true, the sensation begins to spread in wider rings through our minds; remoter senses are reached; these begin to sound and to comment and we are aware of echoes and reflections. The intensity of poetry covers an immense range of emotion. We have only to compare the force and directness of

> I shall fall like a tree, and find my grave
> Only remembering that I grieve,

with the wavering modulation of

> Minutes are numbered by the fall of sands,
> As by an hour glass; the span of time
> Doth waste us to our graves, and we look on it;
> An age of pleasure, revelled out, comes home
> At last and ends in sorrow; but the life,
> Weary of riot, numbers every sand,
> Wailing in sighs, until the last drop down,
> So to conclude calamity in rest,

or place the meditative calm of

> whether we be young or old,
> Our destiny, our being's heart and home,

> Is with infinitude, and only there;
> With hope it is, hope that can never die,
> Effort, and expectation, and desire,
> And something evermore about to be,

beside the complete and inexhaustible loveliness of

> The moving Moon went up the sky,
> And no where did abide:
> Softly she was going up,
> And a star or two beside—

or the splendid fantasy of

> And the woodland haunter
> Shall not cease to saunter
>   When, far down some glade,
> Of the great world's burning,
> One soft flame upturning
> Seems, to his discerning,
> Crocus in the shade.

to bethink us of the varied art of the poet; his power to make us at once actors and spectators; his power to run his hand into character as if it were a glove, and be Falstaff or Lear; his power to condense, to widen, to state, once and for ever.

"We have only to compare"—with those words the cat is out of the bag, and the true complexity of reading is admitted. The first process, to receive impressions with the utmost understanding, is only half the process of reading; it must be completed, if we are to get the whole pleasure from a book, by another. We must pass judgment upon these multitudinous impressions; we must make of these fleeting shapes one that is hard and lasting. But not directly. Wait for the dust of reading to settle; for the conflict and the questioning to die down; walk, talk, pull the dead petals from a rose, or fall asleep. Then suddenly without our willing it, for it is thus that Nature undertakes these transitions, the book will return, but differently. It will float to the top of the mind as a whole. And the book as a whole is different from the book received currently in separate phrases. Details now fit themselves into their places. We see the shape from start to finish; it is a barn, a pigsty, or a cathedral. Now then we can compare book with book as we compare building with building. But this act of comparison means that our attitude has changed; we are no longer the friends of the writer, but his judges; and just as we cannot be too sympathetic as friends, so as judges we cannot be too severe. Are they not criminals, books that have wasted our time and sympathy; are they not the most insidious enemies of society, corrupters, defilers, the writers of false books, faked books, books that fill the air with decay and disease? Let us then be severe in our judgments; let us compare each book with the greatest of its kind. There they hang in the mind the shapes of the books we have read solidified by the judgments we have passed on them—*Robinson Crusoe, Emma, The Return of the Native.* Compare the novels with these—even the latest and least of novels has a right to be judged with the best. And so with poetry—when the intoxication of rhythm has died down and the splendour of words has faded a visionary shape will return to us and this must be compared with *Lear,* with *Phèdre,* with *The Prelude;* or if not with these, with whatever is the best or seems to us to be the best in its own kind. And we may be sure that the newness of new poetry and fiction is its most superficial quality and that we have only to alter slightly, not to recast, the standards by which we have judged the old.

It would be foolish, then, to pretend that the second part of reading, to judge, to compare, is as simple as the first—to open the mind wide to the fast flocking of innumerable impressions. To continue reading without the book before you, to hold one shadow-shape against another, to have read widely enough and with enough understanding to make such comparisons alive and illuminating—that is difficult; it is still more difficult to press further and to say, "Not only is the book of this sort, but it is of this value; here it fails; here it succeeds; this is bad; that is good." To carry out this part of a reader's duty needs such imagination, insight, and learning that it is hard to conceive any one mind sufficiently endowed; impossible for the most self-confident to find more than the seeds of such powers in himself. Would it not be wiser, then, to remit this part of reading and to allow the critics, the gowned and furred authorities of the library, to decide the question of the book's absolute value for us? Yet how impossible! We may stress the value of sympathy; we may try to sink our own identity as we read. But we know that we cannot sympathize wholly or immerse ourselves wholly; there is always a demon in us who whispers, "I hate, I love," and we cannot silence him. Indeed, it is precisely because we hate and we love that our relation with the poets and novelists is so intimate that we find the presence of another person intolerable. And even if the results are abhorrent and our judgments are wrong, still our taste, the nerve of sensation that sends shocks through us, is our chief illuminant; we learn through feeling; we cannot suppress our own idiosyncrasy without impoverishing it. But as time goes on perhaps we can train our taste; perhaps we can make it submit to some control. When it has fed greedily and lavishly upon books of all sorts—poetry, fiction, history, biography—and has stopped reading and looked for long spaces upon the variety, the incongruity of the living world, we shall find that it is changing a little; it is not so greedy, it is more reflective. It will begin to bring us not merely judgments on particular books, but it will tell us that there is a quality common to certain books. Listen, it will say, what shall we call *this?* And it will read us perhaps *Lear* and then perhaps *Agamemnon* in order to bring out that common quality. Thus, with our taste to guide us, we shall venture beyond the particular book in search of qualities that group books together; we shall give them names and thus frame a rule that brings order into our perceptions. We shall gain a further and a rarer pleasure from that discrimination. But as a rule only lives when it is perpetually broken by contact with the books themselves—nothing is easier and more stultifying than to make rules which exist out of touch with facts, in a vacuum—now at least, in order to steady ourselves in this difficult attempt, it may be well to turn to the very rare writers who are able to enlighten us upon literature as an art. Coleridge and Dryden and Johnson, in their considered criticism, the poets and novelists themselves in their unconsidered sayings, are often surprisingly relevant; they light up and solidify the vague ideas that have been tumbling in the misty depths of our minds. But they are only able to help us if we come to them laden with questions and suggestions won honestly in the course of our own reading. They can do nothing for us if we herd ourselves under their authority and lie down like sheep in the shade of a hedge. We can only understand their ruling when it comes in conflict with our own and vanquishes it.

If this is so, if to read a book as it should be read calls for the rarest qualities of imagination, insight, and judgment, you may perhaps conclude that literature is a very complex art and that it is unlikely that we shall be able, even after a lifetime of reading, to make any valuable contribution to its criticism. We must remain readers; we shall not put on the further glory that belongs to those rare beings who are also critics. But still we have our responsibilities as readers and even our importance. The standards we raise and the judgments we pass steal into the air and become part of the atmosphere which writers breathe as they work. An influence is created which tells upon them even if it never finds its way into print. And that influence, if it were well instructed, vigorous and individual and sincere, might be of great value now when criticism is necessarily in abeyance; when books pass in review like the procession of animals in a shooting gallery, and the critic has only one second in which to load and aim and shoot and may well be pardoned if he mistakes rabbits for tigers, eagles for barn-door fowls, or misses altogether and wastes his shot upon some peaceful sow grazing in a further field. If behind the erratic gunfire of the press the author felt that there was another kind of criticism, the opinion of people reading for the love of reading, slowly and unprofessionally, and judging with great sympathy and yet with great severity, might this not improve the quality of his work? And if by our means books were to become stronger, richer, and more varied, that would be an end worth reaching.

Yet who reads to bring about an end however desirable? Are there not some pursuits that we practise because they are good in themselves, and some pleasures that are final? And is not this among them? I have sometimes dreamt, at least, that when the Day of Judgment dawns and the great conquerors and lawyers and statesmen come to receive their rewards—their crowns, their laurels, their names carved indelibly upon imperishable marble—the Almighty will turn to Peter and will say, not without a certain envy when He sees us coming with our books under our arms, "Look, these need no reward. We have nothing to give them here. They have loved reading."

Matthew Arnold

1822–1888

M atthew Arnold was born in Middlesex, England, December 24, 1822. His father was the noted Dr. Thomas Arnold, headmaster of Rugby. Young Arnold went to Rugby and Balliol College, Oxford, where he took the Newdigate Prize for poetry. In the Lake District he walked, skated, and sailed a boat. He had "Olympian manners." When he visited the novelist George Sand in France, she said that he gave "the effect of a young Milton on his travels."

In 1847 he became private secretary to Lord Lansdowne. His first collection of verse, *The Strayed Reveller and Other Poems,* in 1849, and a second three years later, were published under the initial "A." He married Frances Lucy Wightman in 1851. Lansdowne had arranged an appointment for Arnold as an Inspector of Schools. He served in that department for thirty-five years. His work required almost continual travel in England, plus frequent inspection tours in Holland, Germany, Austria, Italy, and France.

Under his own name he published *Poems* in 1853 and *Poems: Second Series* two years later. The tragedy *Merope* appeared in 1858. Except for *New Poems* in 1867, most of his later work was devoted to the literature of ideas, criticism in particular. Much of this came out of his election in 1857 as professor of poetry at Oxford, a post he held for ten years. His inaugural address, *On the Modern Element in Literature,* and such lectures as *The Study of Poetry* (see below) and *On Translating Homer* belong among his most famous essays.

In 1868 the Arnold family moved to Harrow and in 1873 to Cobham, Surrey, Arnold's home for the rest of his life. *Culture and Anarchy* was much talked about, but *Literature and Dogma,* published in 1873, became his first best seller of sorts. His 1883–84 lecture tour in the United States was mildly successful. He made another visit two years later. As early as 1885 he had been troubled with angina pectoris. He continued to walk and skate a little. In the spring of 1888, he traveled to Liverpool to meet his daughter Lucy and his grandchild, inbound from America. Joyful at the reunion to come, he ran for a tram, leaped over a low fence, and fell dead. The date was April 15, 1888.

The *Study of Poetry* was first published in 1880 as an introduction to T. H. Ward's anthology, *The English Poets.* Like *Sweetness and Light,* its companion piece here, it shows us what a broad focus Arnold opened out on his time. At bottom, he was a poet-critic. Deliberately, he enlarged his viewpoint to take in the whole of society. He meant to deal with it in terms of those ideas—science, government, culture, history—by which, he felt, society was ordered; and this in turn required an expanded view of literature and of culture in general.

But he did not stop there. He was a reformer, at the topmost level. We recall his division of Englishmen into Barbarians (the upper class), Philistines (the middle class), and Populace (the working class). His mission, he felt, was to convert the heathen of the new middle class, swollen with industrial and financial power, and all but indifferent to any cultural demand that did not serve such power.

Thus he became a missionary politician of ideas, and most of his essays need to be understood first of all in that light. They are Epistles to the Philistines. He believed, as Lewis Mumford wrote nearly a hundred years later, that "an economy of abundance brings with it, not the duty to consume, but the readiness to create." And what was to be created was nothing less than the well-rounded and harmonious personality of man. Have we reached that goal yet? Insofar as we have not, and in the ways that we have not, Arnold still speaks to us as directly as he spoke to his contemporaries.

Notes from the artist: "Suggestions of two of his major poems are woven into the portrait of Matthew Arnold . . . at the left are shells and sea life recalling 'Dover Beach,' while above his head the protagonists of 'Sohrab and Rustum' are shown in combat."

Almost a century later, the first pages of *The Study of Poetry* can still shock us a little. "Without poetry," Arnold writes, "our science will appear incomplete; and most of what now passes with us for religion and philosophy will be replaced by poetry." But only "the best poetry" will do. And how shall we recognize and define "the best poetry"? This last question alone has occupied many minds for a score of centuries. Arnold makes it his principal subject.

Except as data, science leaves out the life of feeling that gives tone to everything we do. But feeling is the medium and combining agent in poetry. Thus the idea that science will "appear incomplete" without poetry and the other arts becomes an ordinary fact. But what are we to make of the prediction that much of Victorian religion and philosophy would be "replaced by poetry"? We know, at least, that it has not happened. Poetry can hardly be said to have taken the place of religion and philosophy in any significant way. And we gather from Arnold's other essays that he was a religious reformer rather than an agnostic.

But he makes an excellent case for the possible uses of poetry as a cultural agent. He begins by trying to tell us how to read poetry, and how to tell the good from the bad. This involves a revaluation of English poets from the beginning—rather too much for one essay. He quotes examples, to *show* us, rather than attempt to explain what good poetry is. (This approach, expanded to take in the whole poem as text, became the principal method of the American New Critics in the mid-twentieth century.) He takes his examples, not from English poetry alone, but from what he knows of European poetry in general.

Our second essay, *Sweetness and Light,* shows us Arnold as the missionary of culture marching boldly into the enemy camp. Armed with such slogans as "To make reason and the will of God prevail!" and "Perfection . . . consists in becoming something rather than in having something," he sets up his ideal of the harmonious man. Then, one by one, he attacks the enemy idols: wealth, the cult of bodily vigor and large families, Puritan religion, machinery, Bentham's utilitarianism and the rest. Culture, he asserts, is a democratic idea. It must be diffused "from one end of society to the other."

The Study
of Poetry

The future of poetry is immense, because in poetry, where it is worthy of its high destinies, our race, as time goes on, will find an ever surer and surer stay. There is not a creed which is not shaken, not an accredited dogma which is not shown to be questionable, not a received tradition which does not threaten to dissolve. Our religion has materialized itself in the fact, in the supposed fact; it has attached its emotion to the fact, and now the fact is failing it. But for poetry the idea is everything; the rest is a world of illusion, of divine illusion. Poetry attaches its emotion to the idea; the idea *is* the fact. The strongest part of our religion to-day is its unconscious poetry."

Let me be permitted to quote these words of my own, as uttering the thought which should, in my opinion, go with us and govern us in all our study of poetry. In the present work it is the course of one great contributory stream to the world-river of poetry that we are invited to follow. We are here invited to trace the stream of English poetry. But whether we set ourselves, as here, to follow only one of the several streams that make the mighty river of poetry, or whether we seek to know them all, our governing thought should be the same. We should conceive of poetry worthily, and more highly than it has been the custom to conceive of it. We should conceive of it as capable of higher uses, and called to higher destinies, than those which in general men have assigned to it hitherto. More and more mankind will discover that we have to turn to poetry to interpret life for us, to console us, to sustain us. Without poetry, our science will appear incomplete; and most of what now passes with us for religion and philosophy will be replaced by poetry. Science, I say, will appear incomplete without it. For finely and truly does Wordsworth call poetry "the impassioned expression which is in the countenance of all science"; and what is a countenance without its expression? Again,

Wordsworth finely and truly calls poetry "the breath and finer spirit of all knowledge": our religion, parading evidences such as those on which the popular mind relies now; our philosophy, pluming itself on its reasonings about causation and finite and infinite being; what are they but the shadows and dreams and false shows of knowledge? The day will come when we shall wonder at ourselves for having trusted to them, for having taken them seriously; and the more we perceive their hollowness, the more we shall prize "the breath and finer spirit of knowledge" offered to us by poetry.

But if we conceive thus highly of the destinies of poetry, we must also set our standard for poetry high, since poetry, to be capable of fulfilling such high destinies, must be poetry of a high order of excellence. We must accustom ourselves to a high standard and to a strict judgment. Sainte-Beuve relates that Napoleon one day said, when somebody was spoken of in his presence as a charlatan: "Charlatan as much as you please; but where is there *not* charlatanism?"—"Yes," answers Sainte-Beuve, "in politics, in the art of governing mankind, that is perhaps true. But in the order of thought, in art, the glory, the eternal honour is that charlatanism shall find no entrance; herein lies the inviolableness of that noble portion of man's being." It is admirably said, and let us hold fast to it. In poetry, which is thought and art in one, it is the glory, the eternal honour, that charlatanism shall find no entrance; that this noble sphere be kept inviolate and inviolable. Charlatanism is for confusing or obliterating the distinctions between excellent and inferior, sound and unsound or only half-sound, true and untrue or only half-true. It is charlatanism, conscious or unconscious, whenever we confuse or obliterate these. And in poetry, more than anywhere else, it is unpermissible to confuse or obliterate them. For in poetry the distinction between excellent and inferior, sound and unsound or only half-sound, true and untrue or only half-true, is of paramount importance. It is of paramount importance because of the high destinies of poetry. In poetry, as a criticism of life under the conditions fixed for such a criticism by the laws of poetic truth and poetic beauty, the spirit of our race will find, we have said, as time goes on and as other helps fail, its consolation and stay. But the consolation and stay will be of power in proportion to the power of the criticism of life. And the criticism of life will be of power in proportion as the poetry conveying it is excellent rather than inferior, sound rather than unsound or half-sound, true rather than untrue or half-true.

The best poetry is what we want; the best poetry will be found to have a power of forming, sustaining, and delighting us, as nothing else can.

A clearer, deeper sense of the best in poetry, and of the strength and joy to be drawn from it, is the most precious benefit which we can gather from a poetical collection such as the present. And yet in the very nature and conduct of such a collection there is inevitably something which tends to obscure in us the consciousness of what our benefit should be, and to distract us from the pursuit of it. We should therefore steadily set it before our minds at the outset, and should compel ourselves to revert constantly to the thought of it as we proceed.

Yes; constantly in reading poetry, a sense for the best, the really excellent, and of the strength and joy to be drawn from it should be present in our minds and should govern our estimate of what we read. But this real estimate, the only true one, is liable to be superseded, if we are not watchful, by two other kinds of estimate, the historic estimate and the personal estimate, both of which are fallacious. A poet or a poem may count to us historically, they may count to us on grounds personal to ourselves, and they may count to us really. They may count to us historically. The course of development of a nation's language, thought, and poetry is profoundly interesting; and by regarding a poet's work as a stage in this course of development we may easily bring ourselves to make it of more importance as poetry than in itself it really is, we may come to use a language of quite exaggerated praise in criticizing it; in short, to overrate it. So arises in our poetic judgments the fallacy caused by the estimate which we may call historic. Then, again, a poet or a poem may count to us on grounds personal to ourselves. Our personal affinities, likings, and circumstances have great power to sway our estimate of this or that poet's work, and to make us attach more importance to it as poetry than in itself it really possesses, because to us it is, or has been, of high importance. Here also we overrate the object of our interest, and apply to it a language of praise which is quite exaggerated. And thus we get the source of a second fallacy in our poetic judgments—the fallacy caused by an estimate which we may call personal.

Both fallacies are natural. It is evident how naturally the study of the history and development of a poetry may incline a man to pause over reputations and works once conspicuous but now obscure, and to quarrel with a careless public for skipping, in obedience to mere tradition and habit, from one famous name or work in its national poetry to another, ignorant of what it misses, and of the reason for keeping what it keeps, and of the whole process of growth in its poetry. The French have become diligent students of their own early poetry, which they long neglected; the study makes many of them dissatisfied with their so-called classical poetry, the court-tragedy of the seventeenth century, a poetry which Pellisson long ago reproached with its want of the true poetic stamp, with its *politesse stérile et rampante* [rampant and sterile polish], but which nevertheless has reigned in France as absolutely as if it had been the perfection of classical poetry indeed. The dissatisfaction is natural; yet a lively and accomplished critic, M. Charles d'Héricault, the editor of Clément Marot, goes too far when he says that "the cloud of glory playing round a classic is a mist as dangerous to the future of a literature as it is intolerable for the purposes of history." "It hinders," he goes on, "it hinders us from seeing more than one single point, the culminating and exceptional point; the summary, fictitious and arbitrary, of a thought and of a work. It substitutes a halo for a physiognomy, it puts a statue where there was once a man, and hiding from us all trace of the labour, the attempts, the weaknesses, the failures, it claims not study but veneration; it does not show us how the thing is done, it imposes upon us a model. Above all, for the historian this creation of classic personages is inadmissible; for it withdraws the poet from his time, from his proper life, it breaks historical relationships, it blinds criticism by conventional admiration, and renders the investigation of literary origins unacceptable. It gives us a human personage no longer, but a God seated immovable amidst His perfect work, like Jupiter on Olympus; and hardly will it be possible for the young student, to whom such work is exhibited at such a distance from him, to believe that it did not issue ready made from that divine head."

All this is brilliantly and tellingly said, but we must plead for a distinction. Everything depends on the reality of a poet's classic character. If he is a dubious classic, let us sift him; if he is a false classic, let us explode him. But if he is a real classic, if his work belongs to the class of the very best (for this is the true and right meaning of the word *classic, classical*), then the great thing for us is to feel and enjoy his work as deeply as ever we can, and to appreciate the wide difference between it and all work which has not the same high character. This is what is salutary, this is what is formative; this is the great benefit to be got from the study of poetry. Everything which interferes with it, which hinders it, is injurious. True, we must read our classic with open eyes, and not with eyes blinded with superstition; we must perceive when his work comes short, when it drops out of the class of the very best, and we must rate it, in such cases, at its proper value. But the use of this negative criticism is not in itself; it is entirely in its enabling us to have a clearer sense and a deeper enjoyment of what is truly excellent. To trace the labour, the attempts, the weaknesses, the failures of a genuine classic, to acquaint oneself with his

time and his life and his historical relationships, is mere literary dilettant-
ism unless it has that clear sense and deeper enjoyment for its end. It
may be said that the more we know about a classic the better we shall
enjoy him; and, if we lived as long as Methuselah and had all of us heads
of perfect clearness and wills of perfect steadfastness, this might be true
in fact as it is plausible in theory. But the case here is much the same as
the case with the Greek and Latin studies of our schoolboys. The elaborate
philological groundwork which we require them to lay is in theory an admirable preparation for appreciating the Greek and Latin authors worthily. The more thoroughly we lay the groundwork, the better we shall be
able, it may be said, to enjoy the authors. True, if time were not so short,
and schoolboys' wits not so soon tired and their power of attention exhausted; only, as it is, the elaborate philological preparation goes on, but
the authors are little known and less enjoyed. So with the investigator of
"historic origins" in poetry. He ought to enjoy the true classic all the
better for his investigations; he often is distracted from the enjoyment of
the best, and with the less good he overbusies himself, and is prone to
overrate it in proportion to the trouble which it has cost him.

The idea of tracing historic origins and historical relationships cannot
be absent from a compilation like the present. And naturally the poets to
be exhibited in it will be assigned to those persons for exhibition who are
known to prize them highly, rather than to those who have no special
inclination towards them. Moreover the very occupation with an author,
and the business of exhibiting him, disposes us to affirm and amplify his
importance. In the present work, therefore, we are sure of frequent
temptation to adopt the historic estimate, or the personal estimate, and to
forget the real estimate; which latter, nevertheless, we must employ if
we are to make poetry yield us its full benefit. So high is that benefit,
the benefit of clearly feeling and of deeply enjoying the really excellent,
the truly classic in poetry, that we do well, I say, to set it fixedly before
our minds as our object in studying poets and poetry, and to make the
desire of attaining it the one principle to which, as the *Imitation* says,
whatever we may read or come to know, we always return. *Cum multa
legeris et cognoveris, ad unum semper oportet redire principium.*

The historic estimate is likely in especial to affect our judgment and
our language when we are dealing with ancient poets; the personal
estimate when we are dealing with poets our contemporaries, or at any
rate modern. The exaggerations due to the historic estimate are not in
themselves, perhaps, of very much gravity. Their report hardly enters the
general ear; probably they do not always impose even on the literary
men who adopt them. But they lead to a dangerous abuse of language.

So we hear Caedmon, amongst our own poets, compared to Milton. I have already noticed the enthusiasm of one accomplished French critic for "historic origins." Another eminent French critic, M. Vitet, comments upon that famous document of the early poetry of his nation, the *Chanson de Roland*. It is indeed a most interesting document. The joculator or jongleur Taillefer, who was with William the Conqueror's army at Hastings, marched before the Norman troops, so said the tradition, singing "of Charlemagne and of Roland and of Oliver, and of the vassals who died at Roncevaux"; and it is suggested that in the *Chanson de Roland* by one Turoldus or Théroulde, a poem preserved in a manuscript of the twelfth century in the Bodleian Library at Oxford, we have certainly the matter, perhaps even some of the words, of the chant which Taillefer sang. The poem has vigour and freshness; it is not without pathos. But M. Vitet is not satisfied with seeing in it a document of some poetic value, and of very high historic and linguistic value; he sees in it a grand and beautiful work, a monument of epic genius. In its general design he finds the grandiose conception, in its details he finds the constant union of simplicity with greatness, which are the marks, he truly says, of the genuine epic, and distinguish it from the artificial epic of literary ages. One thinks of Homer; this is the sort of praise which is given to Homer, and justly given. Higher praise there cannot well be, and it is the praise due to epic poetry of the highest order only, and to no other. Let us try, then, the *Chanson de Roland* at its best. Roland, mortally wounded, lays himself down under a pine-tree, with his face turned towards Spain and the enemy—

> De plusurs choses à remembrer li prist,
> De tantes teres cume li bers cunquist,
> De dulce France, des humes de sun lign,
> De Charlemagne sun seignor ki l'nurrit.[1]

That is primitive work, I repeat, with an undeniable poetic quality of its own. It deserves such praise, and such praise is sufficient for it. But now turn to Homer—

> [*Hos phato; tous d'ede katechen physizoös aia*
> *en Lakedaimoni authi, phile en patridi gaie.*[2]]

---

1. "Then began he to call many things to remembrance—all the lands which his valour conquered, and pleasant France, and the men of his lineage, and Charlemagne his liege lord who nourished him."—*Chanson de Roland*, iii, 939–42.
2. So said she; they long since in Earth's soft arms were reposing,
   There, in their own dear land, their fatherland, Lacedaemon.
   —*Iliad*, iii, 243, 244 (translated by Dr. Hawtrey). [Cf. *Great Books of the Western World*, Vol. 4, p. 21 (Ed.).]

We are here in another world, another order of poetry altogether; here is rightly due such supreme praise as that which M. Vitet gives to the *Chanson de Roland*. If our words are to have any meaning, if our judgments are to have any solidity, we must not heap that supreme praise upon poetry of an order immeasurably inferior.

Indeed there can be no more useful help for discovering what poetry belongs to the class of the truly excellent, and can therefore do us most good, than to have always in one's mind lines and expressions of the great masters, and to apply them as a touchstone to other poetry. Of course we are not to require this other poetry to resemble them; it may be very dissimilar. But if we have any tact we shall find them, when we have lodged them well in our minds, an infallible touchstone for detecting the presence or absence of high poetic quality, and also the degree of this quality, in all other poetry which we may place beside them. Short passages, even single lines, will serve our turn quite sufficiently. Take the two lines which I have just quoted from Homer, the poet's comment on Helen's mention of her brothers; or take his

> [*Ha deilo, ti sphoi domen Pelei anakti thneta?*
> *Humeis d'eston agero t'athanato te.*
> *E hina dystinoisi met' andrasiv alge' echeton?*[3]]

the address of Zeus to the horses of Peleus; or take finally his

> [*Kai se, geron, to prin men akoumen olbion einai* [4]]

the words of Achilles to Priam, a suppliant before him. Take that incomparable line and a half of Dante, Ugolino's tremendous words—

> *Io no piangeva; sì dentro impietrai.*
> *Piangevan elli . . .*[5]

take the lovely words of Beatrice to Virgil—

> *Io son fatta da Dio, sua mercè, tale,*
> *Che la vostra miseria non mi tange,*
> *Nè fiamma d'esto incendio non m'assale . . .*[6]

---

3. Ah, unhappy pair, why gave we you to King Peleus, to a mortal? but ye are without old age, and immortal. Was it that with men born to misery ye might have sorrow? —*Iliad*, xvii, 443–45. [Cf. *Great Books of the Western World*, Vol. 4, p. 126 (Ed.).]
4. "Nay, and thou too, old man, in former days wast, as we hear, happy."—*Iliad*, xxiv, 543. [Cf. *Great Books of the Western World*, Vol. 4, p. 177 (Ed.).]
5. "I wailed not, so of stone grew I within;—*they* wailed."—*Inferno*, xxxiii, 39, 40. [Cf. *Great Books of the Western World*, Vol. 21, p. 50 (Ed.).]
6. "Of such sort hath God, thanked be His mercy, made me, that your misery toucheth me not, neither doth the flame of this fire strike me."—*Inferno*, ii, 91–93. [Cf. *Great Books of the Western World*, Vol. 21, p. 3 (Ed.).]

take the simple, but perfect, single line—

> *In la sua volontade è nostra pace.*[7]

Take of Shakespeare a line or two of Henry the Fourth's expostulation with sleep—

> Wilt thou upon the high and giddy mast
> Seal up the ship-boy's eyes, and rock his brains
> In cradle of the rude imperious surge . . .

and take, as well, Hamlet's dying request to Horatio—

> If thou didst ever hold me in thy heart,
> Absent thee from felicity awhile,
> And in this harsh world draw thy breath in pain
> To tell my story . . .

Take of Milton that Miltonic passage—

> Darken'd so, yet shone
> Above them all the archangel; but his face
> Deep scars of thunder had intrench'd, and care
> Sat on his faded cheek . . .

add two such lines as—

> And courage never to submit or yield
> And what is else not to be overcome . . .

and finish with the exquisite close to the loss of Proserpine, the loss

> . . . which cost Ceres all that pain
> To seek her through the world.

These few lines, if we have tact and can use them, are enough even of themselves to keep clear and sound our judgments about poetry, to save us from fallacious estimates of it, to conduct us to a real estimate.

The specimens I have quoted differ widely from one another, but they have in common this: the possession of the very highest poetical quality. If we are thoroughly penetrated by their power, we shall find that we have acquired a sense enabling us, whatever poetry may be laid before us, to feel the degree in which a high poetical quality is present or wanting there. Critics give themselves great labour to draw out what in the abstract constitutes the characters of a high quality of poetry. It is much

---

7. "In His will is our peace."—*Paradiso*, iii, 85. [Cf. *Great Books of the Western World*, Vol. 21, p. 110 (Ed.).]

better simply to have recourse to concrete examples—to take specimens of poetry of the high, the very highest quality, and to say: The characters of a high quality of poetry are what is expressed *there*. They are far better recognized by being felt in the verse of the master, than by being perused in the prose of the critic. Nevertheless if we are urgently pressed to give some critical account of them, we may safely, perhaps, venture on laying down, not indeed how and why the characters arise, but where and in what they arise. They are in the matter and substance of the poetry, and they are in its manner and style. Both of these, the substance and matter on the one hand, the style and manner on the other, have a mark, an accent, of high beauty, worth, and power. But if we are asked to define this mark and accent in the abstract, our answer must be: No, for we should thereby be darkening the question, not clearing it. The mark and accent are as given by the substance and matter of that poetry, by the style and manner of that poetry, and of all other poetry which is akin to it in quality.

Only one thing we may add as to the substance and matter of poetry, guiding ourselves by Aristotle's profound observation that the superiority of poetry over history consists in its possessing a higher truth and a higher seriousness [*philosophoteron kai spoudaioteron*]. Let us add, therefore, to what we have said, this: that the substance and matter of the best poetry acquire their special character from possessing, in an eminent degree, truth and seriousness. We may add yet further, what is in itself evident, that to the style and manner of the best poetry their special character, their accent, is given by their diction, and, even yet more, by their movement. And though we distinguish between the two characters, the two accents, of superiority, yet they are nevertheless vitally connected one with the other. The superior character of truth and seriousness, in the matter and substance of the best poetry, is inseparable from the superiority of diction and movement marking its style and manner. The two superiorities are closely related, and are in steadfast proportion one to the other. So far as high poetic truth and seriousness are wanting to a poet's matter and substance, so far also, we may be sure, will a high poetic stamp of diction and movement be wanting to his style and manner. In proportion as this high stamp of diction and movement, again, is absent from a poet's style and manner, we shall find, also, that high poetic truth and seriousness are absent from his substance and matter.

So stated, these are but dry generalities; their whole force lies in their application. And I could wish every student of poetry to make the application of them for himself. Made by himself, the application would impress itself upon his mind far more deeply than made by me. Neither will my limits allow me to make any full application of the generalities above propounded; but in the hope of bringing out, at any rate, some significance in them, and of establishing an important principle more firmly by their means, I will, in the space which remains to me, follow rapidly from the commencement the course of our English poetry with them in my view.

Once more I return to the early poetry of France, with which our own poetry, in its origins, is indissolubly connected. In the twelfth and thirteenth centuries, that seed-time of all modern language and literature, the poetry of France had a clear predominance in Europe. Of the two divisions of that poetry, its productions in the *langue d'oïl* and its productions in the *langue d'oc*, the poetry of the *langue d'oc*, of southern France, of the troubadours, is of importance because of its effect on Italian literature—the first literature of modern Europe to strike the true and grand note, and to bring forth, as in Dante and Petrarch it brought forth, classics. But the predominance of French poetry in Europe, during the twelfth and thirteenth centuries, is due to its poetry of the *langue d'oïl*, the poetry of northern France and of the tongue which is now the French language. In the twelfth century the bloom of this romance-poetry was earlier and stronger in England, at the court of our Anglo-Norman kings, than in France itself. But it was a bloom of French poetry; and as our native poetry formed itself, it formed itself out of this. The romance-poems which took possession of the heart and imagination of Europe in the twelfth and thirteenth centuries are French; "they are," as Southey justly says, "the pride of French literature, nor have we anything which can be placed in competition with them." Themes were supplied from all quarters; but the romance-setting which was common to them all, and which gained the ear of Europe, was French. This constituted for the French poetry, literature, and language, at the height of the Middle Ages, an unchallenged predominance. The Italian Brunetto Latini, the master of Dante, wrote his *Treasure* in French because, he says, *"la parleure en est plus délitable et plus commune à toutes gens"* [their speech is more charming and more commonly shared by the whole people]. In the same century, the thirteenth, the French romance-writer, Christian of Troyes, formulates the claims, in chivalry and letters, of France, his native country, as follows:

> *Or vous ert par ce livre apris,*
> *Que Gresse ot de chevalerie*
> *Le premier los et de clergie;*

Puis vint chevalerie à Rome,
Et de la clergie la some,
Qui ore est en France venue.
Diex doinst qu'ele i soit retenue,
Et que li lius li abelisse
Tant que de France n'isse
L'onor qui s'i est arestée!

Now by this book you will learn that first Greece had the renown for chivalry and letters; then chivalry and the primacy in letters passed to Rome, and now it is come to France. God grant it may be kept there; and that the place may please it so well, that the honour which has come to make stay in France may never depart thence!

Yet it is now all gone, this French romance-poetry, of which the weight of substance and the power of style are not unfairly represented by this extract from Christian of Troyes. Only by means of the historic estimate can we persuade ourselves now to think that any of it is of poetical importance.

But in the fourteenth century there comes an Englishman nourished on this poetry, taught his trade by this poetry, getting words, rhyme, metre from this poetry; for even of that stanza which the Italians used, and which Chaucer derived immediately from the Italians, the basis and suggestion was probably given in France. Chaucer (I have already named him) fascinated his contemporaries, but so too did Christian of Troyes and Wolfram of Eschenbach. Chaucer's power of fascination, however, is enduring; his poetical importance does not need the assistance of the historic estimate; it is real. He is a genuine source of joy and strength, which is flowing still for us and will flow always. He will be read, as time goes on, far more generally than he is read now. His language is a cause of difficulty for us; but so also, and I think in quite as great a degree, is the language of Burns. In Chaucer's case, as in that of Burns, it is a difficulty to be unhesitatingly accepted and overcome.

If we ask ourselves wherein consists the immense superiority of Chaucer's poetry over the romance-poetry—why it is that in passing from this to Chaucer we suddenly feel ourselves to be in another world, we shall find that his superiority is both in the substance of his poetry and in the style of his poetry. His superiority in substance is given by his large, free, simple, clear yet kindly view of human life—so unlike the total want, in the romance-poets, of all intelligent command of it. Chaucer has not their helplessness; he has gained the power to survey the world from a central, a truly human point of view. We have only to call to mind the Prologue to *The Canterbury Tales*. The right comment upon it is Dryden's: "It is sufficient to say, according to the proverb, that *here is God's plenty*." And again: "He is a perpetual fountain of good sense." It is by a large, free, sound representation of things that poetry, this high criticism of life, has truth of substance; and Chaucer's poetry has truth of substance.

Of his style and manner, if we think first of the romance-poetry and then of Chaucer's divine liquidness of diction, his divine fluidity of movement, it is difficult to speak temperately. They are irresistible, and justify all the rapture with which his successors speak of his "gold dew-drops of speech." Johnson misses the point entirely when he finds fault with Dryden for ascribing to Chaucer the first refinement of our numbers, and says that Gower also can show smooth numbers and easy rhymes. The refinement of our numbers means something far more than this. A nation may have versifiers with smooth numbers and easy rhymes, and yet may have no real poetry at all. Chaucer is the father of our splendid English poetry; he is our "well of English undefiled," because by the lovely charm of his diction, the lovely charm of his movement, he makes an epoch and founds a tradition. In Spenser, Shakespeare, Milton, Keats, we can follow the tradition of the liquid diction, the fluid movement, of Chaucer; at one time it is his liquid diction of which in these poets we feel the virtue, and at another time it is his fluid movement. And the virtue is irresistible.

Bounded as is my space, I must yet find room for an example of Chaucer's virtue, as I have given examples to show the virtue of the great classics. I feel disposed to say that a single line is enough to show the charm of Chaucer's verse; that merely one line like this—

O martyr souded [8] in virginitee!

has a virtue of manner and movement such as we shall not find in all the verse of romance-poetry; but this is saying nothing. The virtue is such as we shall not find, perhaps, in all English poetry, outside the poets whom I have named as the special inheritors of Chaucer's tradition. A single line, however, is too little if we have not the strain of Chaucer's verse well in our memory; let us take a stanza. It is from *The Prioress's Tale*, the story of the Christian child murdered in a Jewry—

My throte is cut unto my nekke-bone
Saidè this child, and as by way of kinde
I should have deyd, yea, longè time agone;

---

8. The French *soudé;* soldered, fixed fast.

> But Jesu Christ, as ye in bookès finde,
> Will that his glory last and be in minde,
> And for the worship of his mother dere
> Yet may I sing *O Alma* loud and clere.

Wordsworth has modernized this Tale, and to feel how delicate and evanescent is the charm of verse, we have only to read Wordsworth's first three lines of this stanza after Chaucer's—

> My throat is cut unto the bone, I trow,
> Said this young child, and by the law of kind
> I should have died, yea, many hours ago.

The charm is departed. It is often said that the power of liquidness and fluidity in Chaucer's verse was dependent upon a free, a licentious dealing with language, such as is now impossible; upon a liberty, such as Burns too enjoyed, of making words like *neck, bird,* into a dissyllable by adding to them, and words like *cause, rhyme,* into a dissyllable by sounding the *e* mute. It is true that Chaucer's fluidity is conjoined with this liberty, and is admirably served by it; but we ought not to say that it was dependent upon it. It was dependent upon his talent. Other poets with a like liberty do not attain to the fluidity of Chaucer; Burns himself does not attain to it. Poets, again, who have a talent akin to Chaucer's, such as Shakespeare or Keats, have known how to attain to his fluidity without the like liberty.

And yet Chaucer is not one of the great classics. His poetry transcends and effaces, easily and without effort, all the romance-poetry of Catholic Christendom; it transcends and effaces all the English poetry contemporary with it, it transcends and effaces all the English poetry subsequent to it down to the age of Elizabeth. Of such avail is poetic truth of substance, in its natural and necessary union with poetic truth of style. And yet, I say, Chaucer is not one of the great classics. He has not their accent. What is wanting to him is suggested by the mere mention of the name of the first great classic of Christendom, the immortal poet who died eighty years before Chaucer—Dante. The accent of such verse as

> *In la sua volontade è nostra pace . . .*

is altogether beyond Chaucer's reach; we praise him, but we feel that this accent is out of the question for him. It may be said that it was necessarily out of the reach of any poet in the England of that stage of growth. Possibly; but we are to adopt a real, not a historic, estimate of poetry. However we may account for its absence, something is wanting, then, to the poetry of Chaucer, which poetry must have before it can be placed in the glorious class of the best. And there is no doubt what that something is. It is the σπουδαιότης [*spoudaiotes;* seriousness] the high and excellent seriousness, which Aristotle assigns as one of the grand virtues of poetry. The substance of Chaucer's poetry, his view of things and his criticism of life, has largeness, freedom, shrewdness, benignity; but it has not this high seriousness. Homer's criticism of life has it, Dante's has it, Shakespeare's has it. It is this chiefly which gives to our spirits what they can rest upon; and with the increasing demands of our modern ages upon poetry, this virtue of giving us what we can rest upon will be more and more highly esteemed. A voice from the slums of Paris, fifty or sixty years after Chaucer, the voice of poor Villon out of his life of riot and crime, has at its happy moments (as, for instance, in the last stanza of "La Belle Heaulmière" [9]) more of this important poetic virtue of seriousness than all the productions of Chaucer. But its apparition in Villon, and in men like Villon, is fitful; the greatness of the great poets, the power of their criticism of life, is that their virtue is sustained.

To our praise, therefore, of Chaucer as a poet there must be this limitation; he lacks the high seriousness of the great classics, and therewith an important part of their virtue. Still, the main fact for us to bear in mind about Chaucer is his sterling value according to that real estimate which we firmly adopt for all poets. He has poetic truth of substance, though he has not high poetic seriousness, and corresponding to his truth of substance he has an exquisite virtue of style and manner. With him is born our real poetry.

For my present purpose I need not dwell on our Elizabethan poetry, or on the continuation and close of this poetry in Milton. We all of us profess to be agreed in the estimate of this poetry; we all of us recognize

---

9. The name *Heaulmière* is said to be derived from a headdress (helm) worn as a mark by courtesans. In Villon's ballad, a poor old creature of this class laments her days of youth and beauty. The last stanza of the ballad runs thus—

> *Ainsi le bon temps regretons*
> *Entre nous, pauvres vieilles sottes,*
> *Assises bas, à croppetons,*
> *Tout en ung tas comme pelottes;*
> *A petit feu de chenevottes*
> *Tost allumées, tost estainctes.*
> *Et jadis fusmes si mignottes!*
> *Ainsi en prend à maintz et maintes.*

Thus amongst ourselves we regret the good time, poor silly old things, low-seated on our heels, all in a heap like so many balls; by a little fire of hemp-stalks, soon lighted, soon spent. And once we were such darlings! So fares it with many and many a one

it as great poetry, our greatest, and Shakespeare and Milton as our poetical classics. The real estimate, here, has universal currency. With the next age of our poetry divergency and difficulty begin. An historic estimate of that poetry has established itself; and the question is, whether it will be found to coincide with the real estimate.

The age of Dryden, together with our whole eighteenth century which followed it, sincerely believed itself to have produced poetical classics of its own, and even to have made advance, in poetry, beyond all its predecessors. Dryden regards as not seriously disputable the opinion "that the sweetness of English verse was never understood or practised by our fathers." Cowley could see nothing at all in Chaucer's poetry. Dryden heartily admired it, and, as we have seen, praised its matter admirably; but of its exquisite manner and movement all he can find to say is that "there is the rude sweetness of a Scotch tune in it, which is natural and pleasing, though not perfect." Addison, wishing to praise Chaucer's numbers, compares them with Dryden's own. And all through the eighteenth century, and down even into our own times, the stereotyped phrase of approbation for good verse found in our early poetry has been, that it even approached the verse of Dryden, Addison, Pope, and Johnson.

Are Dryden and Pope poetical classics? Is the historic estimate, which represents them as such, and which has been so long established that it cannot easily give way, the real estimate? Wordsworth and Coleridge, as is well known, denied it; but the authority of Wordsworth and Coleridge does not weigh much with the young generation, and there are many signs to show that the eighteenth century and its judgments are coming into favour again. Are the favourite poets of the eighteenth century classics?

It is impossible within my present limits to discuss the question fully. And what man of letters would not shrink from seeming to dispose dictatorially of the claims of two men who are, at any rate, such masters in letters as Dryden and Pope; two men of such admirable talent, both of them, and one of them, Dryden, a man, on all sides, of such energetic and genial power? And yet, if we are to gain the full benefit from poetry, we must have the real estimate of it. I cast about for some mode of arriving, in the present case, at such an estimate without offence. And perhaps the best way is to begin, as it is easy to begin, with cordial praise.

When we find Chapman, the Elizabethan translator of Homer, expressing himself in his preface thus: "Though truth in her very nakedness sits in so deep a pit, that from Gades to Aurora and Ganges few eyes can sound her, I hope yet those few here will so discover and confirm that, the date being out of her darkness in this morning of our poet, he shall now gird his temples with the sun," we pronounce that such a prose is intolerable. When we find Milton writing: "And long it was not after, when I was confirmed in this opinion, that he, who would not be frustrate of his hope to write well hereafter in laudable things, ought himself to be a true poem," we pronounce that such a prose has its own grandeur, but that it is obsolete and inconvenient. But when we find Dryden telling us: "What Virgil wrote in the vigour of his age, in plenty and at ease, I have undertaken to translate in my declining years; struggling with wants, oppressed with sickness, curbed in my genius, liable to be misconstrued in all I write," then we exclaim that here at last we have the true English prose, a prose such as we would all gladly use if we only knew how. Yet Dryden was Milton's contemporary.

But after the Restoration the time had come when our nation felt the imperious need of a fit prose. So, too, the time had likewise come when our nation felt the imperious need of freeing itself from the absorbing preoccupation which religion in the Puritan age had exercised. It was impossible that this freedom should be brought about without some negative excess, without some neglect and impairment of the religious life of the soul; and the spiritual history of the eighteenth century shows us that the freedom was not achieved without them. Still, the freedom was achieved; the preoccupation, an undoubtedly baneful and retarding one if it had continued, was got rid of. And as with religion amongst us at that period, so it was also with letters. A fit prose was a necessity; but it was impossible that a fit prose should establish itself amongst us without some touch of frost to the imaginative life of the soul. The needful qualities for a fit prose are regularity, uniformity, precision, balance. The men of letters, whose destiny it may be to bring their nation to the attainment of a fit prose, must of necessity, whether they work in prose or in verse, give a predominating, an almost exclusive attention to the qualities of regularity, uniformity, precision, balance. But an almost exclusive attention to these qualities involves some repression and silencing of poetry.

We are to regard Dryden as the puissant and glorious founder, Pope as the splendid high priest, of our age of prose and reason, of our excellent and indispensable eighteenth century. For the purposes of their mission and destiny their poetry, like their prose, is admirable. Do you ask me whether Dryden's verse, take it almost where you will, is not good?

> A milk-white Hind, immortal and unchanged,
> Fed on the lawns and in the forest ranged.

I answer: Admirable for the purposes of the inaugurator of an age of prose and reason. Do you ask me whether Pope's verse, take it almost where you will, is not good?

> To Hounslow Heath I point, and Banstead Down;
> Thence comes your mutton, and these chicks my own.

I answer: Admirable for the purposes of the high priest of an age of prose and reason. But do you ask me whether such verse proceeds from men with an adequate poetic criticism of life, from men whose criticism of life has a high seriousness, or even, without that high seriousness, has poetic largeness, freedom, insight, benignity? Do you ask me whether the application of ideas to life in the verse of these men, often a powerful application, no doubt, is a powerful *poetic* application? Do you ask me whether the poetry of these men has either the matter or the inseparable manner of such an adequate poetic criticism; whether it has the accent of

> Absent thee from felicity awhile . . .

or of

> And what is else not to be overcome . . .

or of

> O martyr souded in virginitee!

I answer: It has not and cannot have them; it is the poetry of the builders of an age of prose and reason. Though they may write in verse, though they may in a certain sense be masters of the art of versification, Dryden and Pope are not classics of our poetry, they are classics of our prose.

Gray is our poetical classic of that literature and age; the position of Gray is singular, and demands a word of notice here. He has not the volume or the power of poets who, coming in times more favourable, have attained to an independent criticism of life. But he lived with the great poets, he lived, above all, with the Greeks, through perpetually studying and enjoying them; and he caught their poetic point of view for regarding life, caught their poetic manner. The point of view and the manner are not self-sprung in him, he caught them of others; and he had not the free and abundant use of them. But whereas Addison and Pope never had the use of them, Gray had the use of them at times. He is the scantiest and frailest of classics in our poetry, but he is a classic.

And now, after Gray, we are met, as we draw towards the end of the eighteenth century, we are met by the great name of Burns. We enter now on times where the personal estimate of poets begins to be rife, and where the real estimate of them is not reached without difficulty. But in spite of the disturbing pressures of personal partiality, of national partiality, let us try to reach a real estimate of the poetry of Burns.

By his English poetry Burns in general belongs to the eighteenth century, and has little importance for us.

> Mark ruffian Violence, distain'd with crimes,
> Rousing elate in these degenerate times;
> View unsuspecting Innocence a prey,
> As guileful Fraud points out the erring way;
> While subtle Litigation's pliant tongue
> The life-blood equal sucks of Right and Wrong!

Evidently this is not the real Burns, or his name and fame would have disappeared long ago. Nor is Clarinda's love-poet, Sylvander, the real Burns either. But he tells us himself: "These English songs gravel me to death. I have not the command of the language that I have of my native tongue. In fact, I think that my ideas are more barren in English than in Scotch. I have been at 'Duncan Gray' to dress it in English, but all I can do is desperately stupid." We English turn naturally, in Burns, to the poems in our own language, because we can read them easily; but in those poems we have not the real Burns.

The real Burns is of course in his Scotch poems. Let us boldly say that of much of this poetry, a poetry dealing perpetually with Scotch drink, Scotch religion, and Scotch manners, a Scotchman's estimate is apt to be personal. A Scotchman is used to this world of Scotch drink, Scotch religion, and Scotch manners; he has a tenderness for it; he meets its poet half-way. In this tender mood he reads pieces like the "Holy Fair" or "Halloween." But this world of Scotch drink, Scotch religion, and Scotch manners is against a poet, not for him, when it is not a partial countryman who reads him; for in itself it is not a beautiful world, and no one can deny that it is of advantage to a poet to deal with a beautiful world. Burns's world of Scotch drink, Scotch religion, and Scotch manners is often a harsh, a sordid, a repulsive world; even the world of his "Cotter's Saturday Night" is not a beautiful world. No doubt a poet's criticism of life may have such truth and power that it triumphs over its world and delights us. Burns may triumph over his world, often he does triumph over his world, but let us observe how and where. Burns is the first case we have had where the bias of the personal estimate tends to mislead; let us look at him closely, he can bear it.

Many of his admirers will tell us that we have Burns, convivial, genuine, delightful, here—

> Leeze me on drink! it gies us mair
> Than either school or college;
> It kindles wit, it waukens lair,
> It pangs us fou o' knowledge.
> Be 't whisky gill or penny wheep
> Or ony stronger potion,
> It never fails, on drinking deep,
> To kittle up our notion
> By night or day.

There is a great deal of that sort of thing in Burns, and it is unsatisfactory, not because it is bacchanalian poetry, but because it has not that accent of sincerity which bacchanalian poetry, to do it justice, very often has. There is something in it of bravado, something which makes us feel that we have not the man speaking to us with his real voice; something, therefore, poetically unsound.

With still more confidence will his admirers tell us that we have the genuine Burns, the great poet, when his strain asserts the independence, equality, dignity, of men, as in the famous song "For a' that and a' that"—

> A prince can mak' a belted knight,
> A marquis, duke, and a' that;
> But an honest man's aboon his might,
> Guid faith he mauna fa' that!
> For a' that, and a' that,
> Their dignities, and a' that,
> The pith o' sense, and pride o' worth,
> Are higher rank than a' that.

Here they find his grand, genuine touches; and still more, when this puissant genius, who so often set morality at defiance, falls moralizing—

> The sacred lowe o' weel-placed love
> Luxuriantly indulge it;
> But never tempt th' illicit rove,
> Tho' naething should divulge it.
> I waive the quantum o' the sin,
> The hazard o' concealing,
> But och! it hardens a' within,
> And petrifies the feeling.

Or in a higher strain—

> Who made the heart, 'tis He alone
>   Decidedly can try us;
> He knows each chord, its various tone;
>   Each spring, its various bias.
> Then at the balance let's be mute,
>   We never can adjust it;
> What's *done* we partly may compute,
>   But know not what's resisted.

Or in a better strain yet, a strain, his admirers will say, unsurpassable—

> To make a happy fireside clime
>   To weans and wife,
> That's the true pathos and sublime
>   Of human life.

There is a criticism of life for you, the admirers of Burns will say to us; there is the application of ideas to life! There is, undoubtedly. The doctrine of the last-quoted lines coincides almost exactly with what was the aim and end, Xenophon tells us, of all the teaching of Socrates. And the application is a powerful one; made by a man of vigorous understanding, and (need I say?) a master of language.

But for supreme poetical success more is required than the powerful application of ideas to life; it must be an application under the conditions fixed by the laws of poetic truth and poetic beauty. Those laws fix as an essential condition, in the poet's treatment of such matters as are here in question, high seriousness—the high seriousness which comes from absolute sincerity. The accent of high seriousness, born of absolute sincerity, is what gives to such verse as

> *In la sua volontade è nostra pace* . . .

to such criticism of life as Dante's, its power. Is this accent felt in the passages which I have been quoting from Burns? Surely not; surely, if our sense is quick, we must perceive that we have not in those passages a voice from the very inmost soul of the genuine Burns; he is not speaking to us from these depths, he is more or less preaching. And the compensation for admiring such passages less, from missing the perfect poetic accent in them, will be that we shall admire more the poetry where that accent is found.

No; Burns, like Chaucer, comes short of the high seriousness of the great classics, and the virtue of matter and manner which goes with that high seriousness is wanting to his work. At moments he touches it in a pro-

found and passionate melancholy, as in those four immortal lines taken by
Byron as a motto for *The Bride of Abydos,* but which have in them a
depth of poetic quality such as resides in no verse of Byron's own—

> Had we never loved sae kindly,
> Had we never loved sae blindly,
> Never met, or never parted,
> We had ne'er been broken-hearted.

But a whole poem of that quality Burns cannot make; the rest, in the
"Farewell to Nancy," is verbiage.

We arrive best at the real estimate of Burns, I think, by conceiving his
work as having truth of matter and truth of manner, but not the accent or
the poetic virtue of the highest masters. His genuine criticism of life,
when the sheer poet in him speaks, is ironic; it is not—

> Thou Power Supreme, whose mighty scheme
> These woes of mine fulfil,
> Here firm I rest, they must be best
> Because they are Thy will!

It is far rather: "Whistle owre the lave o't!" Yet we may say of him as of
Chaucer, that of life and the world, as they come before him, his view
is large, free, shrewd, benignant—truly poetic, therefore; and his manner
of rendering what he sees is to match. But we must note, at the same
time, his great difference from Chaucer. The freedom of Chaucer is
heightened, in Burns, by a fiery, reckless energy; the benignity of
Chaucer deepens, in Burns, into an overwhelming sense of the pathos
of things—of the pathos of human nature, the pathos, also, of non-human
nature. Instead of the fluidity of Chaucer's manner, the manner of Burns
has spring, bounding swiftness. Burns is by far the greater force, though
he has perhaps less charm. The world of Chaucer is fairer, richer, more
significant than that of Burns; but when the largeness and freedom of
Burns get full sweep, as in *Tam o' Shanter,* or still more in that puissant
and splendid production, *The Jolly Beggars,* his world may be what it will,
his poetic genius triumphs over it. In the world of *The Jolly Beggars*
there is more than hideousness and squalor, there is bestiality; yet the
piece is a superb poetic success. It has a breadth, truth, and power which
make the famous scene in Auerbach's Cellar, of Goethe's *Faust,* seem
artificial and tame beside it, and which are only matched by Shakespeare
and Aristophanes.

Here, where his largeness and freedom serve him so admirably, and
also in those poems and songs where to shrewdness he adds infinite arch-

ness and wit, and to benignity infinite pathos, where his manner is flawless, and a perfect poetic whole is the result—in things like the address to
the mouse whose home he had ruined, in things like "Duncan Gray,"
"Tam Glen," "Whistle and I'll come to you my Lad," "Auld Lang Syne"
(this list might be made much longer)—here we have the genuine Burns,
of whom the real estimate must be high indeed. Not a classic, nor with
the excellent σπουδαιότης [spoudaiotes] of the great classics, nor with a
verse rising to a criticism of life and a virtue like theirs; but a poet with
thorough truth of substance and an answering truth of style, giving us a
poetry sound to the core. We all of us have a leaning towards the pathetic, and may be inclined perhaps to prize Burns most for his touches
of piercing, sometimes almost intolerable, pathos; for verse like—

> We twa hae paidl't i' the burn
> From mornin' sun till dine;
> But seas between us braid hae roar'd
> Sin auld lang syne . . .

where he is as lovely as he is sound. But perhaps it is by the perfection of
soundness of his lighter and archer masterpieces that he is poetically
most wholesome for us. For the votary misled by a personal estimate of
Shelley, as so many of us have been, are, and will be—of that beautiful
spirit building his many-coloured haze of words and images

> Pinnacled dim in the intense inane—

no contact can be wholesomer than the contact with Burns at his archest
and soundest. Side by side with the

> On the brink of the night and the morning
> My coursers are wont to respire,
> But the Earth has just whispered a warning
> That their flight must be swifter than fire . . .

of *Prometheus Unbound,* how salutary, how very salutary, to place this
from "Tam Glen"—

> My minnie does constantly deave me
> And bids me beware o' young men;
> They flatter, she says, to deceive me;
> But wha can think sae o' Tam Glen?

But we enter on burning ground as we approach the poetry of times
so near to us—poetry like that of Byron, Shelley, and Wordsworth—of
which the estimates are so often not only personal, but personal with

passion. For my purpose, it is enough to have taken the single case of Burns, the first poet we come to of whose work the estimate formed is evidently apt to be personal, and to have suggested how we may proceed, using the poetry of the great classics as a sort of touchstone, to correct this estimate, as we had previously corrected by the same means the historic estimate where we met with it. A collection like the present, with its succession of celebrated names and celebrated poems, offers a good opportunity to us for resolutely endeavouring to make our estimates of poetry real. I have sought to point out a method which will help us in making them so, and to exhibit it in use so far as to put any one who likes in a way of applying it for himself.

At any rate the end to which the method and the estimate are designed to lead, and from leading to which, if they do lead to it, they get their whole value—the benefit of being able clearly to feel and deeply to enjoy the best, the truly classic, in poetry—is an end, let me say it once more at parting, of supreme importance. We are often told that an era is opening in which we are to see multitudes of a common sort of readers, and masses of a common sort of literature; that such readers do not want and could not relish anything better than such literature, and that to provide it is becoming a vast and profitable industry. Even if good literature entirely lost currency with the world, it would still be abundantly worth-while to continue to enjoy it by oneself. But it never will lose currency with the world, in spite of momentary appearances; it never will lose supremacy. Currency and supremacy are insured to it, not indeed by the world's delicate and conscious choice, but by something far deeper—by the instinct of self-preservation in humanity.

Sweetness
and Light

The disparagers of culture make its motive curiosity; sometimes, indeed, they make its motive mere exclusiveness and vanity. The culture which is supposed to plume itself on a smattering of Greek and Latin is a culture which is begotten by nothing so intellectual as curiosity; it is valued either out of sheer vanity and ignorance, or else as an engine of social and class distinction, separating its holder, like a badge or title, from other people who have not got it. No serious man would call this *culture*, or attach any value to it, as culture, at all. To find the real ground for the very differing estimate which serious people will set upon culture, we must find some motive for culture in the terms of which may lie a real ambiguity; and such a motive the word *curiosity* gives us.

I have before now pointed out that we English do not, like the foreigners, use this word in a good sense as well as in a bad sense. With us the word is always used in a somewhat disapproving sense. A liberal and intelligent eagerness about the things of the mind may be meant by a foreigner when he speaks of curiosity, but with us the word always conveys a certain notion of frivolous and unedifying activity. In the *Quarterly Review*, some little time ago, was an estimate of the celebrated French critic, M. Sainte-Beuve, and a very inadequate estimate it in my judgment was. And its inadequacy consisted chiefly in this: that in our English way it left out of sight the double sense really involved in the word *curiosity*, thinking enough was said to stamp M. Sainte-Beuve with blame if it was said that he was impelled in his operations as a critic by curiosity, and omitting either to perceive that M. Sainte-Beuve himself, and many other people with him, would consider that this was praiseworthy and not blameworthy, or to point out why it ought really to be accounted worthy of blame and not of praise. For as there is a curiosity about intellectual matters which is futile, and merely a disease, so there is certainly a curiosity—a desire after the things of the mind simply for their own sakes and for the pleasure of seeing them as they are—which is, in an intelligent being, natural and laudable. Nay, and the very desire to see things as they are implies a balance and regulation of mind which is not often attained without fruitful effort, and which is the very opposite of the blind and diseased impulse of mind which is what we mean to blame when we blame curiosity. Montesquieu says: "The first motive which ought to impel us to study is the desire to augment the excellence of our nature, and to render an intelligent being yet more intelligent." This is the true ground to assign for the genuine scientific passion, however manifested, and for culture, viewed simply as a fruit of this passion; and it is a worthy ground, even though we let the term *curiosity* stand to describe it.

But there is of culture another view, in which not solely the scientific passion, the sheer desire to see things as they are, natural and proper in an intelligent being, appears as the ground of it. There is a view in which all the love of our neighbour, the impulses towards action, help, and beneficence, the desire for removing human error, clearing human confusion, and diminishing human misery, the noble aspiration to leave the world better and happier than we found it—motives eminently such as are called social—come in as part of the grounds of culture, and the main and pre-eminent part. Culture is then properly described not as having its origin in curiosity, but as having its origin in the love of perfection; it is *a study of perfection*. It moves by the force, not merely or primarily of the scientific passion for pure knowledge, but also of the moral and social passion for doing good. As, in the first view of it, we took for its worthy motto Montesquieu's words: "To render an intelligent being yet more intelligent!" so, in the second view of it, there is no better motto which it can have than these words of Bishop Wilson: "To make reason and the will of God prevail!"

Only, whereas the passion for doing good is apt to be over-hasty in determining what reason and the will of God say, because its turn is for acting rather than thinking, and it wants to be beginning to act; and whereas it is apt to take its own conceptions, which proceed from its own state of development and share in all the imperfections and immaturities of this, for a basis of action; what distinguishes culture is that it is possessed by the scientific passion as well as by the passion of doing good; that it demands worthy notions of reason and the will of God, and does not readily suffer its own crude conceptions to substitute themselves for them. And knowing that no action or institution can be salutary and

stable which is not based on reason and the will of God, it is not so bent
on acting and instituting, even with the great aim of diminishing human
error and misery ever before its thoughts, but that it can remember that
acting and instituting are of little use, unless we know how and what
we ought to act and to institute.

This culture is more interesting and more far-reaching than that other,
which is founded solely on the scientific passion for knowing. But it
needs times of faith and ardour, times when the intellectual horizon is
opening and widening all round us, to flourish in. And is not the close and
bounded intellectual horizon within which we have long lived and
moved now lifting up, and are not new lights finding free passage to shine
in upon us? For a long time there was no passage for them to make their
way in upon us, and then it was of no use to think of adapting the
world's action to them. Where was the hope of making reason and the
will of God prevail among people who had a routine which they had
christened reason and the will of God, in which they were inextricably
bound, and beyond which they had no power of looking? But now the
iron force of adhesion to the old routine—social, political, religious—has
wonderfully yielded; the iron force of exclusion of all which is new has
wonderfully yielded. The danger now is, not that people should obstinately refuse to allow anything but their old routine to pass for reason and
the will of God, but either that they should allow some novelty or other to
pass for these too easily, or else that they should underrate the importance of them altogether, and think it enough to follow action for its own
sake, without troubling themselves to make reason and the will of God
prevail therein. Now, then, is the moment for culture to be of service,
culture which believes in making reason and the will of God prevail, believes in perfection, is the study and pursuit of perfection, and is no longer
debarred, by a rigid invincible exclusion of whatever is new, from getting
acceptance for its ideas, simply because they are new.

The moment this view of culture is seized, the moment it is regarded
not solely as the endeavour to see things as they are, to draw towards a
knowledge of the universal order which seems to be intended and aimed
at in the world, and which it is a man's happiness to go along with or his
misery to go counter to—to learn, in short, the will of God—the moment,
I say, culture is considered not merely as the endeavour to *see* and
learn this, but as the endeavour, also, to make it *prevail*, the moral, social,
and beneficent character of culture becomes manifest. The mere endeavour to see and learn the truth for our own personal satisfaction is indeed

a commencement for making it prevail, a preparing the way for this, which always serves this, and is wrongly, therefore, stamped with blame absolutely in itself and not only in its caricature and degeneration. But perhaps it has got stamped with blame, and disparaged with the dubious title of curiosity, because in comparison with this wider endeavour of such great and plain utility it looks selfish, petty, and unprofitable.

And religion, the greatest and most important of the efforts by which the human race has manifested its impulse to perfect itself—religion, that voice of the deepest human experience—does not only enjoin and sanction the aim which is the great aim of culture, the aim of setting ourselves to ascertain what perfection is and to make it prevail; but also, in determining generally in what human perfection consists, religion comes to a conclusion identical with that which culture—culture seeking the determination of this question through *all* the voices of human experience which have been heard upon it, of art, science, poetry, philosophy, history, as well as of religion, in order to give a greater fullness and certainty to its solution—likewise reaches. Religion says: *The kingdom of God is within you;* and culture, in like manner, places human perfection in an *internal* condition, in the growth and predominance of our humanity proper, as distinguished from our animality. It places it in the ever-increasing efficacy and in the general harmonious expansion of those gifts of thought and feeling which make the peculiar dignity, wealth, and happiness of human nature. As I have said on a former occasion: "It is in making endless additions to itself, in the endless expansion of its powers, in endless growth in wisdom and beauty, that the spirit of the human race finds its ideal. To reach this ideal, culture is an indispensable aid, and that is the true value of culture." Not a having and a resting, but a growing and a becoming, is the character of perfection as culture conceives it; and here, too, it coincides with religion.

And because men are all members of one great whole, and the sympathy which is in human nature will not allow one member to be indifferent to the rest or to have a perfect welfare independent of the rest, the expansion of our humanity, to suit the idea of perfection which culture forms, must be a *general* expansion. Perfection, as culture conceives it, is not possible while the individual remains isolated. The individual is required, under pain of being stunted and enfeebled in his own development if he disobeys, to carry others along with him in his march towards perfection, to be continually doing all he can to enlarge and increase the volume of the human stream sweeping thitherward. And here, once

more, culture lays on us the same obligation as religion, which says, as
Bishop Wilson has admirably put it, that "to promote the kingdom of
God is to increase and hasten one's own happiness."

But, finally, perfection—as culture, from a thorough disinterested study
of human nature and human experience learns to conceive it—is a harmonious expansion of *all* the powers which make the beauty and worth of
human nature, and is not consistent with the over-development of any
one power at the expense of the rest. Here culture goes beyond religion,
as religion is generally conceived by us.

If culture, then, is a study of perfection, and of harmonious perfection,
general perfection, and perfection which consists in becoming something rather than in having something, in an inward condition of the
mind and spirit, not in an outward set of circumstances, it is clear that
culture, instead of being the frivolous and useless thing which Mr. Bright,
and Mr. Frederic Harrison, and many other Liberals are apt to call it,
has a very important function to fulfil for mankind. And this function is
particularly important in our modern world, of which the whole civilization is, to a much greater degree than the civilization of Greece and
Rome, mechanical and external, and tends constantly to become more so.
But above all in our own country has culture a weighty part to perform,
because here that mechanical character, which civilization tends to take
everywhere, is shown in the most eminent degree. Indeed nearly all the
characters of perfection, as culture teaches us to fix them, meet in this
country with some powerful tendency which thwarts them and sets them
at defiance. The idea of perfection as an *inward* condition of the mind
and spirit is at variance with the mechanical and material civilization in
esteem with us, and nowhere, as I have said, so much in esteem as with
us. The idea of perfection as a *general* expansion of the human family is
at variance with our strong individualism, our hatred of all limits to the
unrestrained swing of the individual's personality, our maxim of "every
man for himself." Above all the idea of perfection as a *harmonious* expansion of human nature is at variance with our want of flexibility, with our
inaptitude for seeing more than one side of a thing, with our intense energetic absorption in the particular pursuit we happen to be following.
So culture has a rough task to achieve in this country. Its preachers
have, and are likely long to have, a hard time of it, and they will much
oftener be regarded, for a great while to come, as elegant or spurious
Jeremiahs, than as friends and benefactors. That, however, will not prevent their doing in the end good service if they persevere. And meanwhile, the mode of action they have to pursue, and the sort of habits they

must fight against, ought to be made quite clear for every one to see who may be willing to look at the matter attentively and dispassionately.

Faith in machinery is, I said, our besetting danger; often in machinery most absurdly disporportioned to the end which this machinery, if it is to do any good at all, is to serve; but always in machinery, as if it had a value in and for itself. What is freedom but machinery? What is population but machinery? What is coal but machinery? What are railroads but machinery? What is wealth but machinery? What are, even, religious organizations but machinery? Now almost every voice in England is accustomed to speak of these things as if they were precious ends in themselves, and therefore had some of the characters of perfection indisputably joined to them. I have before now noticed Mr. Roebuck's stock argument for proving the greatness and happiness of England as she is, and for quite stopping the mouths of all gainsayers. Mr. Roebuck is never weary of reiterating this argument of his, so I do not know why I should be weary of noticing it. "May not every man in England say what he likes?" Mr. Roebuck perpetually asks; and that, he thinks, is quite sufficient, and when every man may say what he likes, our aspirations ought to be satisfied. But the aspirations of culture, which is the study of perfection, are not satisfied, unless what men say, when they may say what they like, is worth saying—has good in it, and more good than bad. In the same way the *Times*, replying to some foreign strictures on the dress, looks, and behaviour of the English abroad, urges that the English ideal is that every one should be free to do and to look just as he likes. But culture indefatigably tries, not to make what each raw person may like, the rule by which he fashions himself; but to draw ever nearer to a sense of what is indeed beautiful, graceful, and becoming, and to get the raw person to like that.

And in the same way with respect to railroads and coal. Every one must have observed the strange language current during the late discussions as to the possible failure of our supplies of coal. Our coal, thousands of people were saying, is the real basis of our national greatness; if our coal runs short, there is an end of the greatness of England. But what *is* greatness?—culture makes us ask. Greatness is a spiritual condition worthy to excite love, interest, and admiration; and the outward proof of possessing greatness is that we excite love, interest, and admiration. If England were swallowed up by the sea to-morrow, which of the two, a hundred years hence, would most excite the love, interest, and admiration of mankind—would most, therefore, show the evidences of having possessed greatness—the England of the last twenty years, or the England of Elizabeth, of a time of splendid spiritual effort, but when our coal, and our industrial operations depending on coal, were very little developed? Well, then, what an unsound habit of mind it must be which makes us talk of things like coal or iron as constituting the greatness of England, and how salutary a friend is culture, bent on seeing things as they are, and thus dissipating delusions of this kind and fixing standards of perfection that are real!

Wealth, again, that end to which our prodigious works for material advantage are directed—the commonest of commonplaces tells us how men are always apt to regard wealth as a precious end in itself; and certainly they have never been so apt thus to regard it as they are in England at the present time. Never did people believe anything more firmly, than nine Englishmen out of ten at the present day believe that our greatness and welfare are proved by our being so very rich. Now, the use of culture is that it helps us, by means of its spiritual standard of perfection, to regard wealth as but machinery, and not only to say as a matter of words that we regard wealth as but machinery, but really to perceive and feel that it is so. If it were not for this purging effect wrought upon our minds by culture, the whole world, the future as well as the present, would inevitably belong to the Philistines. The people who believe most that our greatness and welfare are proved by our being very rich, and who most give their lives and thoughts to becoming rich, are just the very people whom we call Philistines. Culture says: "Consider these people, then, their way of life, their habits, their manners, the very tones of their voice; look at them attentively; observe the literature they read, the things which give them pleasure, the words which come forth out of their mouths, the thoughts which make the furniture of their minds; would any amount of wealth be worth having with the condition that one was to become just like these people by having it?" And thus culture begets a dissatisfaction which is of the highest possible value in stemming the common tide of men's thoughts in a wealthy and industrial community, and which saves the future, as one may hope, from being vulgarized, even if it cannot save the present.

Population, again, and bodily health and vigour, are things which are nowhere treated in such an unintelligent, misleading, exaggerated way as in England. Both are really machinery; yet how many people all around us do we see rest in them and fail to look beyond them! Why, one has heard people, fresh from reading certain articles of the *Times* on the Registrar-General's returns of marriages and births in this country, who would talk of our large English families in quite a solemn strain, as if they had something in itself beautiful, elevating, and meritorious in them; as if the British Philistine would have only to present himself before the Great Judge with his twelve children, in order to be received among the sheep as a matter of right!

But bodily health and vigour, it may be said, are not to be classed with wealth and population as mere machinery; they have a more real and essential value. True; but only as they are more intimately connected with a perfect spiritual condition than wealth or population are. The moment we disjoin them from the idea of a perfect spiritual condition, and pursue them, as we do pursue them, for their own sake and as ends in themselves, our worship of them becomes as mere worship of machinery, as our worship of wealth or population, and as unintelligent and vulgarizing a worship as that is. Every one with anything like an adequate idea of human perfection has distinctly marked this subordination to higher and spiritual ends of the cultivation of bodily vigour and activity. "Bodily exercise profiteth little; but godliness is profitable unto all things," says the author of the Epistle to Timothy. And the utilitarian Franklin says just as explicitly: "Eat and drink such an exact quantity as suits the constitution of thy body, *in reference to the services of the mind.*" But the point of view of culture, keeping the mark of human perfection simply and broadly in view, and not assigning to this perfection, as religion or utilitarianism assign to it, a special and limited character— this point of view, I say, of culture is best given by these words of Epictetus: "It is a sign of *aphuia,*" says he, that is, of a nature not finely tempered, "to give yourselves up to things which relate to the body; to make, for instance, a great fuss about exercise, a great fuss about eating, a great fuss about drinking, a great fuss about walking, a great fuss about riding. All these things ought to be done merely by the way: the formation of the spirit and character must be our real concern." This is admirable; and, indeed, the Greek word *euphuia,* a finely tempered nature, gives exactly the notion of perfection as culture brings us to conceive it: a harmonious perfection, a perfection in which the characters of beauty and intelligence are both present, which unites "the two noblest of things," as Swift, who of one of the two, at any rate, had himself all too little, most happily calls them in his *Battle of the Books,* "the two noblest of things, *sweetness and. light.*" The *euphues* is the man who tends towards sweetness and light; the *aphues,* on the other hand, is our Philistine. The immense spiritual significance of the Greeks is due to their having been inspired with this central and happy idea of the essential character of human perfection; and Mr. Bright's misconception of culture, as a smattering of Greek and Latin, comes itself, after all, from this wonderful significance of the Greeks having affected the very machinery of our education, and is in itself a kind of homage to it.

In thus making sweetness and light to be characters of perfection, culture is of like spirit with poetry, follows one law with poetry. Far more than on our freedom, our population, and our industrialism, many amongst us rely upon our religious organizations to save us. I have called religion a yet more important manifestation of human nature than poetry, because it has worked on a broader scale for perfection, and with greater masses of men. But the idea of beauty and of a human nature perfect on all its sides, which is the dominant idea of poetry, is a true and invaluable idea, though it has not yet had the success that the idea of conquering the obvious faults of our animality, and of a human nature perfect on the moral side—which is the dominant idea of religion—has been enabled to have; and it is destined, adding to itself the religious idea of a devout energy, to transform and govern the other.

The best art and poetry of the Greeks, in which religion and poetry are one, in which the idea of beauty and of a human nature perfect on all sides adds to itself a religious and devout energy, and works in the strength of that, is on this account of such surpassing interest and instructiveness for us, though it was—as, having regard to the human race in general, and, indeed, having regard to the Greeks themselves, we must own—a premature attempt, an attempt which for success needed the moral and religious fibre in humanity to be more braced and developed than it had yet been. But Greece did not err in having the idea of beauty, harmony, and complete human perfection, so present and paramount. It is impossible to have this idea too present and paramount; only, the moral fibre must be braced too. And we, because we have braced the moral fibre, are not on that account in the right way, if at the same time the idea of beauty, harmony, and complete human perfection is wanting or misapprehended amongst us; and evidently it *is* wanting or misapprehended at present. And when we rely as we do on our religious organizations, which in themselves do not and cannot give us this idea, and think we have done enough if we make them spread and prevail, then, I say, we fall into our common fault of overvaluing machinery.

Nothing is more common than for people to confound the inward peace and satisfaction which follows the subduing of the obvious faults of our animality with what I may call absolute inward peace and satisfaction— the peace and satisfaction which are reached as we draw near to complete spiritual perfection, and not merely to moral perfection, or rather to relative moral perfection. No people in the world have done more and struggled more to attain this relative moral perfection than our English race has. For no people in the world has the command to *resist the devil*, to *overcome the wicked one*, in the nearest and most obvious sense of those words, had such a pressing force and reality. And we have had our reward, not only in the great worldly prosperity which our obedience to this command has brought us, but also, and far more, in great inward peace and satisfaction. But to me few things are more pathetic than to see people, on the strength of the inward peace and satisfaction which their rudimentary efforts towards perfection have brought them, employ, concerning their incomplete perfection and the religious organizations within which they have found it, language which properly applies only to complete perfection, and is a far-off echo of the human soul's prophecy of it. Religion itself, I need hardly say, supplies them in abundance with this grand language. And very freely do they use it; yet it is really the severest criticism of such an incomplete perfection as alone we have yet reached through our religious organizations.

The impulse of the English race towards moral development and self-conquest has nowhere so powerfully manifested itself as in Puritanism. Nowhere has Puritanism found so adequate an expression as in the religious organization of the Independents. The modern Independents have a newspaper, the *Nonconformist*, written with great sincerity and ability. The motto, the standard, the profession of faith which this organ of theirs carries aloft, is: "The Dissidence of Dissent and the Protestantism of the Protestant religion." There is sweetness and light, and an ideal of complete harmonious human perfection! One need not go to culture and poetry to find language to judge it. Religion, with its instinct for perfection, supplies language to judge it, language too which is in our mouths every day. "Finally, be of one mind, united in feeling," says St. Peter. There is an ideal which judges the Puritan ideal: "The Dissidence of Dissent and the Protestantism of the Protestant religion!" And religious organizations like this are what people believe in, rest in, would give their lives for! Such, I say, is the wonderful virtue of even the beginnings of perfection, of having conquered even the plain faults of our animality, that the religious organization which has helped us to do it can seem to us something precious, salutary, and to be propagated, even when it wears such a brand of imperfection on its forehead as this. And men have got such a habit of giving to the language of religion a special application, of making it a mere jargon, that for the condemnation which religion itself passes on the shortcomings of their religious organizations they have no ear; they are sure to cheat themselves and to explain this condemnation away. They can only be reached by the criticism which culture, like poetry, speaking a language not to be sophisticated, and resolutely testing these organizations by the ideal of a human perfection complete on all sides, applies to them.

But men of culture and poetry, it will be said, are again and again failing, and failing conspicuously, in the necessary first stage to a harmonious perfection, in the subduing of the great obvious faults of our animality, which it is the glory of these religious organizations to have helped us to subdue. True, they do often so fail. They have often been without the virtues as well as the faults of the Puritan; it has been one of their dangers that they so felt the Puritan's faults that they too much neglected the practice of his virtues. I will not, however, exculpate them at the Puritan's expense. They have often failed in morality, and morality is indispensable. And they have been punished for their failure, as the Puritan has been rewarded for his performance. They have been punished wherein they erred; but their ideal of beauty, of sweetness and light, and a human nature complete on all its sides, remains the true ideal of perfection still; just as the Puritan's ideal of perfection remains narrow and inadequate, although for what he did well he has been richly rewarded. Notwithstanding the mighty results of the Pilgrim Fathers' voyage, they and their standard of perfection are rightly judged when we figure to ourselves Shakespeare or Virgil—souls in whom sweetness and light, and all that in human nature is most humane, were eminent—accompanying them on their voyage, and think what intolerable company Shakespeare and Virgil would have found them! In the same way let us judge the religious organizations which we see all around us. Do not let us deny the good and the happiness which they have accomplished; but do not let us fail to see clearly that their idea of human perfection is narrow and inadequate, and that the Dissidence of Dissent and the Protestantism of the Protestant religion will never bring humanity to its true goal. As I said with regard to wealth: Let us look at the life of those who live in and for it—so I say with regard to the religious organizations. Look at the life imaged in such a newspaper as the *Nonconformist*—a life of jealousy of the Establishment, disputes, tea-meetings, openings of chapels, sermons; and then think of it as an ideal of a human life completing itself on all sides, and aspiring with all its organs after sweetness, light, and perfection!

Another newspaper, representing, like the *Nonconformist,* one of the religious organizations of this country, was a short time ago giving an account of the crowd at Epsom on the Derby day, and of all the vice and hideousness which was to be seen in that crowd; and then the writer turned suddenly round upon Professor Huxley, and asked him how he proposed to cure all this vice and hideousness without religion. I confess I felt disposed to ask the asker this question: and how do you propose to cure it with such a religion as yours? How is the ideal of a life so unlovely, so unattractive, so incomplete, so narrow, so far removed from a true and satisfying ideal of human perfection, as is the life of your religious organization as you yourself reflect it, to conquer and transform all this vice and hideousness? Indeed, the strongest plea for the study of perfection as pursued by culture, the clearest proof of the actual inadequacy of the idea of perfection held by the religious organizations—expressing, as I have said, the most wide-spread effort which the human race has yet made after perfection—is to be found in the state of our life and society with these in possession of it, and having been in possession of it I know not how many hundred years. We are all of us included in some religious organization or other; we all call ourselves, in the sublime and aspiring language of religion which I have before noticed, *children of God*. Children of God;—it is an immense pretension!—and how are we to justify it? By the works which we do, and the words which we speak. And the work which we collective children of God do, our grand centre of life, our *city* which we have builded for us to dwell in, is London! London, with its unutterable external hideousness, and with its internal canker of *publicè egestas, privatim opulentia* [public want, private opulence]—to use the words which Sallust puts into Cato's mouth about Rome—unequalled in the world! The word, again, which we children of God speak, the voice which most hits our collective thought, the newspaper with the largest circulation in England, nay, with the largest circulation in the whole world, is the *Daily Telegraph!* I say that when our religious organizations—which I admit to express the most considerable effort after perfection that our race has yet made—land us in no better result than this, it is high time to examine carefully their idea of perfection, to see whether it does not leave out of account sides and forces of human nature which we might turn to great use; whether it would not be more operative if it were more complete. And I say that the English reliance on our religious organizations and on their ideas of human perfection just as they stand is like our reliance on freedom, on muscular Christianity, on population, on coal, on wealth—mere belief in machinery, and unfruitful; and that it is wholesomely counteracted by culture, bent on seeing things as they are, and on drawing the human race onwards to a more complete, a harmonious perfection.

Culture, however, shows its single-minded love of perfection, its desire simply to make reason and the will of God prevail, its freedom from fanaticism, by its attitude towards all this machinery, even while it insists that it *is* machinery. Fanatics, seeing the mischief men do themselves by their blind belief in some machinery or other—whether it is wealth and industrialism, or whether it is the cultivation of bodily strength and activity, or whether it is a political organization—or whether it is a religious organization—oppose with might and main the tendency to this or that political and religious organization, or to games and athletic exercises, or to wealth and industrialism, and try violently to stop it. But the flexibility which sweetness and light give, and which is one of the rewards of culture pursued in good faith, enables a man to see that a tendency may be necessary, and even, as a preparation for something in the future, salutary, and yet that the generations or individuals who obey this tendency are sacrificed to it, that they fall short of the hope of perfection by following it; and that its mischiefs are to be criticized, lest it should take too firm a hold and last after it has served its purpose.

Mr. Gladstone well pointed out, in a speech at Paris—and others have pointed out the same thing—how necessary is the present great movement towards wealth and industrialism, in order to lay broad foundations of material well-being for the society of the future. The worst of these justifications is, that they are generally addressed to the very people engaged, body and soul, in the movement in question; at all events, that they are always seized with the greatest avidity by these people, and taken by them as quite justifying their life; and that thus they tend to harden them in their sins. Now, culture admits the necessity of the movement towards fortune-making and exaggerated industrialism, readily allows that the future may derive benefit from it; but insists, at the same time, that the passing generations of industrialists—forming, for the most part, the stout main body of Philistinism—are sacrificed to it. In the same way, the result of all the games and sports which occupy the passing generation of boys and young men may be the establishment of a better and sounder physical type for the future to work with. Culture does not set itself against the games and sports; it congratulates the future, and hopes it will make a good use of its improved physical basis; but it points out that our passing generation of boys and young men is, meantime, sacrificed. Puritanism was perhaps necessary to develop the moral fibre of the English race, Nonconformity to break the yoke of ecclesiastical domination over men's minds and to prepare the way for freedom of thought in the distant future; still, culture points out that the harmonious perfection of generations of Puritans and Nonconformists has been, in consequence, sacrificed. Freedom of speech may be necessary for the society of the future, but the young lions of the *Daily Telegraph* in the meanwhile are sacrificed. A voice for every man in his country's government may be necessary for the society of the future, but meanwhile Mr. Beales and Mr. Bradlaugh are sacrificed.

Oxford, the Oxford of the past, has many faults; and she has heavily paid for them in defeat, in isolation, in want of hold upon the modern world. Yet we in Oxford, brought up amidst the beauty and sweetness of that beautiful place, have not failed to seize one truth: the truth that beauty and sweetness are essential characters of a complete human perfection. When I insist on this, I am all in the faith and tradition of Oxford. I say boldly that this our sentiment for beauty and sweetness, our sentiment against hideousness and rawness, has been at the bottom of our attachment to so many beaten causes, of our opposition to so many triumphant movements. And the sentiment is true, and has never been wholly defeated, and has shown its power even in its defeat. We have not won our political battles, we have not carried our main points, we have not stopped our adversaries' advance, we have not marched victoriously with the modern world; but we have told silently upon the mind of the country, we have prepared currents of feeling which sap our adversaries' position when it seems gained, we have kept up our own communications with the future. Look at the course of the great movement which shook Oxford to its centre some thirty years ago! It was directed, as any one who reads Dr. Newman's *Apology* may see, against what in one word may be called "Liberalism." Liberalism prevailed; it was the appointed force to do the work of the hour; it was necessary, it was inevitable that it should prevail. The Oxford movement was broken, it failed; our wrecks are scattered on every shore:

Quæ regio in terris nostri non plena laboris?

[What place on earth is not full of our labours?]

But what was it, this Liberalism, as Dr. Newman saw it, and as it really broke the Oxford movement? It was the great middle-class Liberalism, which had for the cardinal points of its belief the Reform Bill of 1832, and local self-government, in politics; in the social sphere, free trade, unrestricted competition, and the making of large industrial fortunes; in the religious sphere, the Dissidence of Dissent and the Protestantism of the Protestant religion. I do not say that other and more intelligent forces than this were not opposed to the Oxford movement: but this was the force which really beat it; this was the force which Dr. Newman felt himself fighting with; this was the force which till only the other day seemed to be the paramount force in this country, and to be in possession of the future; this was the force whose achievements fill Mr. Lowe with such inexpressible admiration, and whose rule he was so horror-struck to see threatened. And where is this great force of Philistinism now? It is thrust into the second rank, it is become a power of yesterday, it has lost the future. A new power has suddenly appeared, a power which it is impossible yet to judge fully, but which is certainly a wholly different force from middle-class Liberalism; different in its cardinal points of belief, different in its tendencies in every sphere. It loves and admires neither the legislation of middle-class Parliaments, nor the local self-government of middle-class vestries, nor the unrestricted competition of middle-class industrialists, nor the dissidence of middle-class Dissent and the Protestantism of middle-class Protestant religion. I am not now praising this new force, or saying that its own ideals are better; all I say is, that they are wholly different. And who will estimate how much the currents of feeling created by Dr. Newman's movement, the keen desire for beauty and sweetness which it nourished, the deep aversion it manifested to the hardness and vulgarity of middle-class Liberalism, the strong light it turned on the hideous and grotesque illusions of middle-class Protestantism—who will estimate how much all these contributed to swell the tide of secret dissatisfaction which has mined the ground under the self-confident Liberalism of the last thirty years, and has prepared the way for its sudden collapse and supersession? It is in this manner that the sentiment of Oxford for beauty and sweetness conquers, and in this manner long may it continue to conquer!

In this manner it works to the same end as culture, and there is plenty of work for it yet to do. I have said that the new and more democratic force which is now superseding our old middle-class Liberalism cannot yet be rightly judged. It has its main tendencies still to form. We hear promises of its giving us administrative reform, law reform, reform of education, and I know not what; but those promises come rather from its advocates, wishing to make a good plea for it and to justify it for superseding middle-class Liberalism, than from clear tendencies which it has itself yet developed. But meanwhile it has plenty of well-intentioned friends against whom culture may with advantage continue to uphold steadily its ideal of human perfection; that this is *an inward spiritual activity, having for its characters increased sweetness, increased light, increased life, increased sympathy.* Mr. Bright, who has a foot in both worlds, the world of middle-class Liberalism and the world of democracy, but who brings most of his ideas from the world of middle-class Liberalism in which he was bred, always inclines to inculcate that faith in machinery to which, as we have seen, Englishmen are so prone, and which has been the bane of middle-class Liberalism. He complains with a sorrowful indignation of people who "appear to have no proper estimate of the value of the franchise"; he leads his disciples to believe—what the Englishman is always too ready to believe—that the having a vote, like the having a large family, or a large business, or large muscles, has in itself some edifying and perfecting effect upon human nature. Or else he cries out to the democracy—"the men," as he calls them, "upon whose shoulders the greatness of England rests"—he cries out to them: "See what you have done! I look over this country and see the cities you have built, the railroads you have made, the manufactures you have produced, the cargoes which freight the ships of the greatest mercantile navy the world has ever seen! I see that you have converted by your labours what was once a wilderness, these islands, into a fruitful garden; I know that you have created this wealth, and are a nation whose name is a word of power throughout all the world." Why, this is just the very style of laudation with which Mr. Roebuck or Mr. Lowe debauch the minds of the middle classes, and make such Philistines of them. It is the same fashion of teaching a man to value himself not on what he *is*, not on his progress in sweetness and light, but on the number of the railroads he has constructed, or the bigness of the tabernacle he has built. Only the middle classes are told they have done it all with their energy, self-reliance, and capital, and the democracy are told they have done it all with their hands and sinews. But teaching the democracy to put its trust in achievements of this kind is merely training them to be Philistines to take the place of the Philistines whom they are superseding; and they too, like the middle class, will be encouraged to sit down at the banquet of the future without having on a wedding garment, and nothing excellent can then come from them. Those who know their besetting faults, those who have watched them and listened to them, or those who will read the instructive account recently given of them by one of themselves, the *Journeyman Engineer*, will agree that the idea which culture sets before us of perfection—an increased spiritual activity, having for its characters increased sweetness, increased light, increased life, increased sympathy—is an idea which the new democracy needs far more than the idea

of the blessedness of the franchise, or the wonderfulness of its own industrial performances.

Other well-meaning friends of this new power are for leading it, not
in the old ruts of middle-class Philistinism, but in ways which are naturally alluring to the feet of democracy, though in this country they are
novel and untried ways. I may call them the ways of Jacobinism. Violent
indignation with the past, abstract systems of renovation applied whole-
sale, a new doctrine drawn up in black and white for elaborating down
to the very smallest details a rational society for the future—these are the
ways of Jacobinism. Mr. Frederic Harrison and other disciples of Comte
—one of them, Mr. Congreve, is an old friend of mine, and I am glad to
have an opportunity of publicly expressing my respect for his talents
and character—are among the friends of democracy who are for leading
it in paths of this kind. Mr. Frederic Harrison is very hostile to culture,
and from a natural enough motive; for culture is the eternal opponent of
the two things which are the signal marks of Jacobinism—its fierceness,
and its addiction to an abstract system. Culture is always assigning to
system-makers and systems a smaller share in the bent of human destiny
than their friends like. A current in people's minds sets towards new
ideas; people are dissatisfied with their old narrow stock of Philistine
ideas, Anglo-Saxon ideas, or any other; and some man, some Bentham or
Comte, who has the real merit of having early and strongly felt and
helped the new current, but who brings plenty of narrowness and mistakes of his own into his feeling and help of it, is credited with being
the author of the whole current, the fit person to be entrusted with its
regulation and to guide the human race.

The excellent German historian of the mythology of Rome, Preller, relating the introduction at Rome under the Tarquins of the worship of
Apollo, the god of light, healing, and reconciliation, will have us observe
that it was not so much the Tarquins who brought to Rome the new worship of Apollo, as a current in the mind of the Roman people which set
powerfully at that time towards a new worship of this kind, and away
from the old run of Latin and Sabine religious ideas. In a similar way,
culture directs our attention to the natural current there is in human affairs, and to its continual working, and will not let us rivet our faith upon
any one man and his doings. It makes us see, not only his good side, but
also how much in him was of necessity limited and transient; nay, it even
feels a pleasure, a sense of an increased freedom and of an ampler future, in so doing.

I remember, when I was under the influence of a mind to which I feel
the greatest obligations, the mind of a man who was the very incarnation

of sanity and clear sense, a man the most considerable, it seems to me, whom America has yet produced—Benjamin Franklin—I remember the relief with which, after long feeling the sway of Franklin's imperturbable common sense, I came upon a project of his for a new version of the Book of Job, to replace the old version, the style of which, says Franklin, has become obsolete, and thence less agreeable. "I give," he continues, "a few verses, which may serve as a sample of the kind of version I would recommend." We all recollect the famous verse in our translation: "Then Satan answered the Lord and said: 'Doth Job fear God for nought?'" Franklin makes this: "Does Your Majesty imagine that Job's good conduct is the effect of mere personal attachment and affection?" I well remember how when first I read that, I drew a deep breath of relief, and said to myself: "After all, there is a stretch of humanity beyond Franklin's victorious good sense!" So, after hearing Bentham cried loudly up as the renovator of modern society, and Bentham's mind and ideas proposed as the rulers of our future, I open the *Deontology*. There I read: "While Xenophon was writing his history and Euclid teaching geometry, Socrates and Plato were talking nonsense under pretence of talking wisdom and morality. This morality of theirs consisted in words; this wisdom of theirs was the denial of matters known to every man's experience." From the moment of reading that, I am delivered from the bondage of Bentham! the fanaticism of his adherents can touch me no longer; I feel the inadequacy of his mind and ideas for supplying the rule of human society, for perfection.

Culture tends always thus to deal with the men of a system, of disciples, of a school; with men like Comte or, the late Mr. Buckle, or Mr. Mill. However much it may find to admire in these personages, or in some of them, it nevertheless remembers the text: "Be not ye called Rabbi!" and it soon passes on from any Rabbi. But Jacobinism loves a Rabbi; it does not want to pass on from its Rabbi in pursuit of a future and still unreached perfection; it wants its Rabbi and his ideas to stand for perfection, that they may with the more authority recast the world; and for Jacobinism, therefore, culture, eternally passing onwards and seeking, is an impertinence and an offence. But culture, just because it resists this tendency of Jacobinism to impose on us a man with limitations and errors of his own along with the true ideas of which he is the organ, really does the world and Jacobinism itself a service.

So, too, Jacobinism, in its fierce hatred of the past and of those whom it makes liable for the sins of the past, cannot away with the inexhaustible indulgence proper to culture, the consideration of circumstances, the severe judgment of actions joined to the merciful judgment of persons.

"The man of culture is in politics," cries Mr. Frederic Harrison, "one of the poorest mortals alive!" Mr. Frederic Harrison wants to be doing business, and he complains that the man of culture stops him with a "turn for small fault-finding, love of selfish ease, and indecision in action." Of what use is culture, he asks, except for "a critic of new books or a professor of *belles lettres?*" Why, it is of use because, in presence of the fierce exasperation which breathes, or rather, I may say, hisses, through the whole production in which Mr. Frederic Harrison asks that question, it reminds us that the perfection of human nature is sweetness and light. It is of use because, like religion, that other effort after perfection, it testifies that, where bitter envying and strife are, there is confusion and every evil work.

The pursuit of perfection, then, is the pursuit of sweetness and light. He who works for sweetness works in the end for light also; he who works for light works in the end for sweetness also. But he who works for sweetness and light united works to make reason and the will of God prevail. He who works for machinery, he who works for hatred, works only for confusion. Culture looks beyond machinery, culture hates hatred; culture has one great passion, the passion for sweetness and light. It has one even yet greater! the passion for making them *prevail*. It is not satisfied till we *all* come to a perfect man; it knows that the sweetness and light of the few must be imperfect until the raw and unkindled masses of humanity are touched with sweetness and light. If I have not shrunk from saying that we must work for sweetness and light, so neither have I shrunk from saying that we must have a broad basis, must have sweetness and light for as many as possible. Again and again I have insisted how those are the happy moments of humanity, how those are the marking epochs of a people's life, how those are the flowering times for literature and art and all the creative power of genius, when there is a *national* glow of life and thought, when the whole of society is in the fullest measure permeated by thought, sensible to beauty, intelligent and alive. Only it must be *real* thought and *real* beauty; *real* sweetness and *real* light. Plenty of people will try to give the masses, as they call them, an intellectual food prepared and adapted in the way they think proper for the actual condition of the masses. The ordinary popular literature is an example of this way of working on the masses. Plenty of people will try to indoctrinate the masses with the set of ideas and judgments constituting the creed of their own profession or party. Our religious and political organizations give an example of this way of working on the masses. I condemn neither way; but culture works differently. It does not try to teach down to the level of inferior classes; it does not try to win them for this or that sect of its own, with ready-made judgments and watchwords. It seeks to do away with classes; to make the best that has been thought and known in the world current everywhere; to make all men live in an atmosphere of sweetness and light, where they may use ideas, as it uses them itself, freely—nourished and not bound by them.

This is the *social idea;* and the men of culture are the true apostles of equality. The great men of culture are those who have had a passion for diffusing, for making prevail, for carrying from one end of society to the other, the best knowledge, the best ideas of their time; who have laboured to divest knowledge of all that was harsh, uncouth, difficult, abstract, professional, exclusive; to humanize it, to make it efficient outside the clique of the cultivated and learned, yet still remaining the *best* knowledge and thought of the time, and a true source, therefore, of sweetness and light. Such a man was Abelard in the Middle Ages, in spite of all his imperfections; and thence the boundless emotion and enthusiasm which Abelard excited. Such were Lessing and Herder in Germany, at the end of the last century; and their services to Germany were in this way inestimably precious. Generations will pass, and literary monuments will accumulate, and works far more perfect than the works of Lessing and Herder will be produced in Germany; and yet the names of these two men will fill a German with a reverence and enthusiasm such as the names of the most gifted masters will hardly awaken. And why? Because they *humanized* knowledge; because they broadened the basis of life and intelligence; because they worked powerfully to diffuse sweetness and light, to make reason and the will of God prevail. With Saint Augustine they said: "Let us not leave Thee alone to make in the secret of thy knowledge, as thou didst before the creation of the firmament, the division of light from darkness; let the children of thy spirit, placed in their firmament, make their light shine upon the earth, mark the division of night and day, and announce the revolution of the times; for the old order is passed, and the new arises; the night is spent, the day is come forth; and thou shalt crown the year with thy blessing, when thou shalt send forth labourers into thy harvest sown by other hands than theirs; when thou shalt send forth new labourers to new seedtimes, whereof the harvest shall be not yet."

The foregoing consists of Chapter I of Arnold's CULTURE AND ANARCHY.

Sainte-Beuve

1804–1869

Charles Augustin Sainte-Beuve was born on December 23, 1804, at Boulogne-sur-Mer, France. His father, a commissioner of taxes, died before Charles's birth, leaving his mother little money. Until the boy was fourteen, he was educated at Boulogne. Then he went to the Collège Charlemagne in Paris.

In 1823 Sainte-Beuve began to study medicine, but from 1824 on he combined literary journalism with his medical studies. After 1827 he gave up medicine altogether and devoted all his time to literature. He became a regular critic for several Paris reviews.

Sainte-Beuve's essays were sympathetic to the writers of his own generation. These young Frenchmen—Flaubert, Mérimée, and others—had been fired by the ideas of Schiller, Goethe, and the English Romantic poets. Sainte-Beuve was one of their earliest champions.

Sainte-Beuve was especially friendly with Victor Hugo and his wife, until he fell passionately in love with Mme Hugo. This brought an end to the friendship and marked the beginning of deep spiritual and intellectual unrest for Sainte-Beuve.

In addition to literary criticism, he wrote poems and one novel, *Volupté*. Sainte-Beuve was elected to the French Academy in 1844. He lectured at Lausanne and at Liège, where he was professor of French literature for a time. In 1854 he was appointed professor of Latin poetry at the Collège de France; but, because of his pro-government political beliefs, the students refused to hear his lectures and he was forced to resign the post.

Sainte-Beuve was appointed a member of the Senate in 1865. He died in Paris on October 13, 1869. On his instructions, he was buried without any religious ceremony.

Sainte-Beuve has been called the father of modern criticism. He believed that criticism was itself an art rather than simply a means of commenting on art.

Two ideas characterize Sainte-Beuve's view of criticism. Both place him as an articulate spokesman of his time. He held that because literature reflects its time and place, the evaluation of any work necessarily varies according to the reader's background. He championed the "romantic" literature of his age against the "classical" style favored by older critics.

But even though he was, on the whole, a defender of the "romantics" against the "classical" writers, his definition of a classic work includes both. "A true classic," he writes, ". . . is an author who has enriched the human mind, increased its treasure, and caused it to advance a step; who has discovered some moral and not equivocal truth, or revealed some eternal passion in that heart where all seemed known and discovered." The emphasis is thus on the classic author's knowledge and insight, not on his style. A classic can be expressed, he says, "in no matter what form, only provided it be broad and great, refined and sensible, sane and beautiful in itself." It speaks "to all in (its) own peculiar style, a style which is found to be also that of the whole world, a style new without neologism, new and old, easily contemporary with all time."

This definition, which contains much food for thought, is clearly very far from being applicable only to the writers of one or another epoch. It does not exalt Wordsworth and Coleridge (typical "romantics") above Pope and Dr. Johnson (typical "classical" writers). It includes all great authors. It demands only that they be great.

"There is no receipt for making classics," Sainte-Beuve writes. "With regard to classics the least expected prove the best and greatest." He does not mean that originality is the highest virtue of great literature. Virgil "imitated" Homer; yet both are classics. And Dante imitated Virgil. Their spontaneity lies in the freshness of what they added. Though Virgil and Dante had models which they followed, they are at the same time always new. Classics are always new; but they are also deeply bedded in the common stock of human knowledge and experience. A work that was entirely new could hardly be a classic. It would share nothing of importance with its readers.

Sainte-Beuve peoples an imaginary "temple of taste" with writers whom he believes to be classics. The immense variety in his choices proves that there is no one characteristic or set of characteristics which makes a classic. The only true test is whether a book gives us "that sensation of serenity and amenity . . . which reconciles us with mankind and with ourselves." The best books, he says, are our best friends.

Montaigne was, for Sainte-Beuve, a classic author. In the second essay reprinted below, we see Sainte-Beuve's philosophy of criticism put into practice. Following his tenet that a book should be studied at least partly through its author, he tells us a good deal about Montaigne and leaves the judgment of individual works to us.

Both in Montaigne's time and in Sainte-Beuve's, France was in political turmoil. The critic, writing three hundred years after the essayist, admires the personal traits that served Montaigne so well in time of crisis. Montaigne was moderate, orderly, witty, optimistic, fair, humble, and courageous, says Sainte-Beuve. Such a man is good to have around in time of trouble.

As to trouble itself, Sainte-Beuve concludes that Montaigne's most pertinent advice may be not to anticipate it. The man who looks for trouble does not generally have to look far.

Sainte-Beuve's essays were titled, in the original, *Causeries*. The French word means "talks" or "chats." There is no question that the tone of the following essays is chatty and informal. This is one of the best things about them. Sainte-Beuve is a critic who is easy to read. He is entertaining. But that, he says, is one of the criteria of a classic author—that he entertain. By this token, Sainte-Beuve is himself a classic.

What Is a Classic?

A delicate question, to which somewhat diverse solutions might be given according to times and seasons. An intelligent man suggests it to me, and I intend to try, if not to solve it, at least to examine and discuss it face to face with my readers, were it only to persuade them to answer it for themselves, and, if I can, to make their opinion and mine on the point clear. And why, in criticism, should we not, from time to time, venture to treat some of those subjects which are not personal, in which we no longer speak of some one but of some thing? Our neighbours, the English, have well succeeded in making of it a special division of literature under the modest title of "Essays." It is true that in writing of such subjects, always slightly abstract and moral, it is advisable to speak of them in a season of quiet, to make sure of our own attention and of that of others, to seize one of those moments of calm moderation and leisure seldom granted our amiable France; even when she is desirous of being wise and is not making revolutions, her brilliant genius can scarcely tolerate them.

A classic, according to the usual definition, is an old author canonized by admiration, and an authority in his particular style. The word *classic* was first used in this sense by the Romans. With them not all the citizens of the different classes were properly called *classici*, but only those of the chief class, those who possessed an income of a certain fixed sum. Those who possessed a smaller income were described by the term *infra classem*, below the pre-eminent class. The word *classicus* was used in a figurative sense by Aulus Gellius, and applied to writers: a writer of worth and distinction, *classicus assiduusque scriptor*, a writer who is of account, has real property, and is not lost in the proletariate crowd. Such an expression implies an age sufficiently advanced to have already made some sort of valuation and classification of literature.

At first the only true classics for the moderns were the ancients. The Greeks, by peculiar good fortune and natural enlightenment of mind, had no classics but themselves. They were at first the only classical authors for the Romans, who strove and contrived to imitate them. After the great periods of Roman literature, after Cicero and Virgil, the Romans in their turn had their classics, who became almost exclusively the classical authors of the centuries which followed. The Middle Ages, which were less ignorant of Latin antiquity than is believed, but which lacked proportion and taste, confused the ranks and orders. Ovid was placed above Homer, and Boetius seemed a classic equal to Plato. The revival of learning in the fifteenth and sixteenth centuries helped to bring this long chaos to order, and then only was admiration rightly proportioned. Thenceforth the true classical authors of Greek and Latin antiquity stood out in a luminous background, and were harmoniously grouped on their two heights.

Meanwhile modern literatures were born, and some of the more precocious, like the Italian, already possessed the style of antiquity. Dante appeared, and, from the very first, posterity greeted him as a classic. Italian poetry has since shrunk into far narrower bounds; but, whenever it desired to do so, it always found again and preserved the impulse and echo of its lofty origin. It is no indifferent matter for a poetry to derive its point of departure and classical source in high places; for example, to spring from Dante rather than to issue laboriously from Malherbe.

Modern Italy had her classical authors, and Spain had every right to believe that she also had hers at a time when France was yet seeking hers. A few talented writers endowed with originality and exceptional animation, a few brilliant efforts, isolated, without following, interrupted and recommenced, did not suffice to endow a nation with a solid and imposing basis of literary wealth. The idea of a classic implies something that has continuance and consistence, and which produces unity and tradition, fashions and transmits itself, and endures. It was only after the glorious years of Louis XIV that the nation felt with tremor and pride that such good fortune had happened to her. Every voice informed Louis XIV of it with flattery, exaggeration, and emphasis, yet with a certain sentiment of truth. Then arose a singular and striking contradiction: those men of whom Perrault was the chief, the men who were most smitten with the marvels of the age of Louis the Great, who even went the length of sacrificing the ancients to the moderns, aimed at exalting and canonizing even those whom they regarded as inveterate opponents and adversaries. Boileau avenged and angrily upheld the ancients against Perrault, who extolled the moderns—that is to say, Corneille, Molière, Pascal, and the eminent men of his age, Boileau, one of the first, included.

Kindly La Fontaine, taking part in the dispute in behalf of the learned Huet, did not perceive that, in spite of his defects, he was in his turn on the point of being held as a classic himself.

Example is the best definition. From the time France possessed her age of Louis XIV and could contemplate it at a little distance, she knew, better than by any arguments, what to be classical meant. The eighteenth century, even in its medley of things, strengthened this idea through some fine works, due to its four great men. Read Voltaire's *Age of Louis XIV*, Montesquieu's *Greatness and Fall of the Romans*, Buffon's *Epochs of Nature*, the beautiful pages of reverie and natural description of Rousseau's *Savoyard Vicar*, and say if the eighteenth century, in these memorable works, did not understand how to reconcile tradition with freedom of development and independence. But at the beginning of the present century and under the Empire, in sight of the first attempts of a decidedly new and somewhat adventurous literature, the idea of a classic in a few resisting minds, more sorrowful than severe, was strangely narrowed and contracted. The first Dictionary of the Academy (1694) merely defined a classical author as "a much-approved ancient writer, who is an authority as regards the subject he treats." The Dictionary of the Academy of 1835 narrows that definition still more, and gives precision and even limit to its rather vague form. It describes classical authors as those "who have become *models* in any language whatever," and in all the articles which-follow, the expressions, *models, fixed rules* for composition and style, *strict rules* of art to which men must conform, continually recur. That definition of *classic* was evidently made by the respectable Academicians, our predecessors, in face and sight of what was then called *romantic*—that is to say, in sight of the enemy. It seems to me time to renounce those timid and restrictive definitions and to free our mind of them.

A true classic, as I should like to hear it defined, is an author who has enriched the human mind, increased its treasure, and caused it to advance a step; who has discovered some moral and not equivocal truth, or revealed some eternal passion in that heart where all seemed known and discovered; who has expressed his thought, observation, or invention, in no matter what form, only provided it be broad and great, refined and sensible, sane and beautiful in itself; who has spoken to all in his own peculiar style, a style which is found to be also that of the whole world, a style new without neologism, new and old, easily contemporary with all time.

Such a classic may for a moment have been revolutionary; it may at least have seemed so, but it is not; it only lashed and subverted whatever prevented the restoration of the balance of order and beauty.

If it is desired, names may be applied to this definition which I wish to make purposely majestic and fluctuating, or in a word, all-embracing. I should first put there Corneille of the *Polyeucte, Cinna,* and *Horace.* I should put Molière there, the fullest and most complete poetic genius we have ever had in France. Goethe, the king of critics, said: "Molière is so great that he astonishes us afresh every time we read him. He is a man apart; his plays border on the tragic, and no one has the courage to try and imitate him. His *Avare,* where vice destroys all affection between father and son, is one of the most sublime works, and dramatic in the highest degree. In a drama every action ought to be important in itself, and to lead to an action greater still. In this respect *Tartuffe* is a model. What a piece of exposition the first scene is! From the beginning everything has an important meaning, and causes something much more important to be foreseen. The exposition in a certain play of Lessing that might be mentioned is very fine, but the world only sees that of *Tartuffe* once. It is the finest of the kind we possess. Every year I read a play of Molière, just as from time to time I contemplate some engraving after the great Italian masters."

I do not conceal from myself that the definition of the classic I have just given somewhat exceeds the notion usually ascribed to the term. It should, above all, include conditions of uniformity, wisdom, moderation, and reason, which dominate and contain all the others. Having to praise M. Royer-Collard, M. de Rémusat said: "If he derives purity of taste, propriety of terms, variety of expression, attentive care in suiting the diction to the thought, from our classics, he owes to himself alone the distinctive character he gives it all." It is here evident that the part allotted to classical qualities seems mostly to depend on harmony and *nuances* of expression, on graceful and temperate style: such is also the most general opinion. In this sense the pre-eminent classics would be writers of a middling order, exact, sensible, elegant, always clear, yet of noble feeling and airily veiled strength. Marie-Joseph Chénier has described the poetics of those temperate and accomplished writers in lines where he shows himself their happy disciple: "It is good sense, reason which does all— virtue, genius, soul, talent, and taste. What is virtue? reason put in practice; talent? reason expressed with brilliance; soul? reason delicately put forth; and genius is sublime reason."

While writing those lines he was evidently thinking of Pope, Boileau, and Horace, the master of them all. The peculiar characteristic of the theory which subordinated imagination and feeling itself to reason, of which Scaliger perhaps gave the first sign among the moderns, is, properly speaking, the *Latin* theory, and for a long time it was also by preference the *French* theory. If it is used appositely, if the term *reason* is not abused, that theory possesses some truth; but it is evident that it is abused, and that if, for instance, reason can be confounded with poetic genius and make one with it in a moral epistle, it cannot be the same thing as the genius, so varied and so diversely creative in its expression of the passions, of the drama or the epic. Where will you find reason in the fourth book of the *Aeneid* and the transports of Dido? Be that as it may, the spirit which prompted the theory caused writers who ruled their inspiration, rather than those who abandoned themselves to it, to be placed in the first rank of classics; to put Virgil there more surely than Homer, Racine in preference to Corneille. The masterpiece to which the theory likes to point, which in fact brings together all conditions of prudence, strength, tempered boldness, moral elevation, and grandeur, is *Athalie*. Turenne in his two last campaigns and Racine in *Athalie* are the great examples of what wise and prudent men are capable of when they reach the maturity of their genius and attain their supremest boldness.

Buffon, in his *Discourse on Style,* insisting on the unity of design, arrangement, and execution, which are the stamps of true classical works, said: "Every subject is one, *and however vast it is, it can be comprised in a single treatise.* Interruptions, pauses, subdivisions should only be used when many subjects are treated, when, having to speak of great, intricate, and dissimilar things, the march of genius is interrupted by the multiplicity of obstacles, and contracted by the necessity of circumstances: otherwise, far from making a work more solid, a great number of divisions destroys the unity of its parts; the book appears clearer to the view, but the author's design remains obscure." And he continues his criticism, having in view Montesquieu's *Spirit of Laws,* an excellent book at bottom, but subdivided: the famous author, worn out before the end, was unable to infuse inspiration into all his ideas, and to arrange all his matter. However, I can scarcely believe that Buffon was not also thinking, by way of contrast, of Bossuet's *Discourse on Universal History,* a subject vast indeed, and yet of such a unity that the great orator was able to comprise it in a single treatise. When we open the first edition, that of 1681, before the division into chapters, which was introduced later, passed from the margin into the text, everything is developed in a single series, almost in one breath. It might be said that the orator has here acted like the nature of which Buffon speaks, that "he has worked on an eternal plan from which he has nowhere departed," so deeply does he seem to have entered into the familiar counsels and designs of providence.

Are *Athalie* and the *Discourse on Universal History* the greatest masterpieces that the strict classical theory can present to its friends as well as to its enemies? In spite of the admirable simplicity and dignity in the achievement of such unique productions, we should like, nevertheless, in the interests of art, to expand that theory a little, and to show that it is possible to enlarge it without relaxing the tension. Goethe, whom I like to quote on such a subject, said: "I call the classical *healthy*, and the romantic *sickly*. In my opinion the Nibelungen song is as much a classic as Homer. Both are healthy and vigorous. The works of the day are romantic, not because they are new, but because they are weak, ailing, or sickly. Ancient works are classical not because they are old, but because they are powerful, fresh, and healthy. If we regarded romantic and classical from those two points of view we should soon all agree."

Indeed, before determining and fixing the opinions on that matter, I should like every unbiased mind to take a voyage round the world and devote itself to a survey of different literatures in their primitive vigour and infinite variety. What would be seen? Chief of all a Homer, the father of the classical world, less a single distinct individual than the vast living expression of a whole epoch and a semi-barbarous civilization. In order to make him a true classic, it was necessary to attribute to him later a design, a plan, literary invention, qualities of atticism and urbanity of which he had certainly never dreamed in the luxuriant development of his natural inspirations. And who appear by his side? August, venerable ancients, the Aeschyluses and the Sophocles, mutilated, it is true, and only there to present us with a *débris* of themselves, the survivors of many others as worthy, doubtless, as they to survive, but who have succumbed to the injuries of time. This thought alone would teach a man of impartial mind not to look upon the whole of even classical literatures with a too narrow and restricted view; he would learn that the exact and well-proportioned order which has since so largely prevailed in our admiration of the past was only the outcome of artificial circumstances.

And in reaching the modern world, how would it be? The greatest names to be seen at the beginning of literatures are those which disturb and run counter to certain fixed ideas of what is beautiful and appropriate in poetry. For example, is Shakespeare a classic? Yes, now, for England and the world; but in the time of Pope he was not considered so. Pope and his friends were the only pre-eminent classics; directly after their death they seemed so for ever. At the present time they are still classics, as they deserve to be, but they are only of the second order, and are forever subordinated and relegated to their rightful place by him who has again come to his own on the height of the horizon.

It is not, however, for me to speak ill of Pope or his great disciples, above all, when they possess pathos and naturalness like Goldsmith: after the greatest they are perhaps the most agreeable writers and the poets best fitted to add charm to life. Once when Lord Bolingbroke was writing to Swift, Pope added a postscript, in which he said, "I think some advantage would result to our age, if we three spent three years together." Men who, without boasting, have the right to say such things must never be spoken of lightly; the fortunate ages, when men of talent could propose such things, then no chimera, are rather to be envied. The ages called by the name of Louis XIV or of Queen Anne are, in the dispassionate sense of the word, the only true classical ages, those which offer protection and a favourable climate to real talent. We know only too well how in our untrammelled times, through the instability and storminess of the age, talents are lost and dissipated. Nevertheless, let us acknowledge our age's part and superiority in greatness. True and sovereign genius triumphs over the very difficulties that cause others to fail: Dante, Shakespeare, and Milton were able to attain their height and produce their imperishable works in spite of obstacles, hardships, and tempests. Byron's opinion of Pope has been much discussed, and the explanation of it sought in the kind of contradiction by which the singer of *Don Juan* and *Childe Harold* extolled the purely classical school and pronounced it the only good one, while himself acting so differently. Goethe spoke the truth on that point when he remarked that Byron, great by the flow and source of poetry, feared that Shakespeare was more powerful than himself in the creation and realization of his characters. "He would have liked to deny it; the elevation so free from egoism irritated him; he felt when near it that he could not display himself at ease. He never denied Pope, because he did not fear him; he knew that Pope was only a *low wall* by his side."

If, as Byron desired, Pope's school had kept the supremacy and a sort of honorary empire in the past, Byron would have been the first and only poet in his particular style; the height of Pope's wall shuts out Shakespeare's great figure from sight, whereas when Shakespeare reigns and rules in all his greatness, Byron is only second.

In France there was no great classic before the age of Louis XIV; the Dantes and Shakespeares, the early authorities to whom, in times of emancipation, men sooner or later return, were wanting. There were mere sketches of great poets, like Mathurin Régnier, like Rabelais, without any ideal, without the depth of emotion and the seriousness which canonizes. Montaigne was a kind of premature classic, of the family of Horace; but for want of worthy surroundings, like a spoiled child, he gave himself up to the unbridled fancies of his style and humour. Hence it happened that France, less than any other nation, found in her old authors a right to demand vehemently at a certain time literary liberty and freedom, and that it was more difficult for her, in enfranchising herself, to remain classical. However, with Molière and La Fontaine among her classics of the great period, nothing could justly be refused to those who possessed courage and ability.

The important point now seems to me to be to uphold, while extending, the idea and belief. There is no receipt for making classics; this point should be clearly recognized. To believe that an author will become a classic by imitating certain qualities of purity, moderation, accuracy, and elegance, independently of the style and inspiration, is to believe that after Racine the father there is a place for Racine the son; dull and estimable role, the worst in poetry. Further, it is hazardous to take too quickly and without opposition the place of a classic in the sight of one's contemporaries; in that case there is a good chance of not retaining the position with posterity. Fontanes in his day was regarded by his friends as a pure classic; see how at twenty-five years' distance his star has set. How many of these precocious classics are there who do not endure, and who are so only for a while! We turn round one morning and are surprised not to find them standing behind us. Madame de Sévigné would wittily say they possessed but an *evanescent colour*. With regard to classics, the least expected prove the best and greatest: seek them rather in the vigorous genius born immortal and flourishing forever. Apparently the least classical of the four great poets of the age of Louis XIV was Molière; he was then applauded far more than he was esteemed; men took delight in him without understanding his worth. After him, La Fontaine seemed the least classical: observe after two centuries what is the result for both. Far above Boileau, even above Racine, are they not now unanimously considered to possess in the highest degree the characteristics of an all-embracing morality?

Meanwhile there is no question of sacrificing or depreciating anything. I believe the temple of taste is to be rebuilt; but its reconstruction is merely a matter of enlargement, so that it may become the home of all noble human beings, of all who have permanently increased the sum of the mind's delights and possessions. As for me, who cannot, obviously, in any degree pretend to be the architect or designer of such a temple, I shall confine myself to expressing a few earnest wishes, to submit, as it were, my designs for the edifice. Above all I should desire not to exclude anyone among the worthy, each should be in his place there, from Shakespeare, the freest of creative geniuses, and the greatest of classics without knowing it, to Andrieux, the last of classics in little. "There is more than one chamber in the mansions of my Father"; that should be as true of the kingdom of the beautiful here below, as of the kingdom of Heaven. Homer, as always and everywhere, should be first, likest a god; but behind him, like the procession of the three wise kings of the East, would be seen the three great poets, the three Homers, so long ignored by us, who wrote epics for the use of the old peoples of Asia, the poets Valmiki, Vyasa of the Hindus, and Firdousi of the Persians; in the domain of taste it is well to know that such men exist, and not to divide the human race. Our homage paid to what is recognized as soon as perceived, we must not stray further; the eye should delight in a thousand pleasing or majestic spectacles, should rejoice in a thousand varied and surprising combinations, whose apparent confusion would never be without concord and harmony. The oldest of the wise men and poets, those who put human morality into maxims, and those who in simple fashion sung it, would converse together in rare and gentle speech, and would not be surprised at understanding each other's meaning at the very first word. Solon, Hesiod, Theognis, Job, Solomon, and why not Confucius, would welcome the cleverest moderns, La Rochefoucauld and La Bruyère, who, when listening to them, would say "they knew all that we know, and in repeating life's experiences, we have discovered nothing." On the hill, most easily discernible, and of most accessible ascent, Virgil, surrounded by Menander, Tibullus, Terence, Fénelon, would occupy himself in discoursing with them with great charm and divine enchantment: his gentle countenance would shine with an inner light, and be tinged with modesty; as on the day when entering the theatre at Rome, just as they finished reciting his verses, he saw the people rise with a unanimous movement and pay to him the same homage as to Augustus. Not far from him, regretting the separation from so dear a friend, Horace, in his turn, would preside (as far as so accomplished and wise a poet could preside) over the group of poets of social life who could talk although they sang— Pope, Boileau, the one become less irritable, the other less faultfinding. Montaigne, a true poet, would be among them, and would give the finishing touch that should deprive that delightful corner of the air of a literary school. There would La Fontaine forget himself, and becoming less volatile would wander no more. Voltaire would be attracted by it, but while finding pleasure in it would not have patience to remain. A little lower down, on the same hill as Virgil, Xenophon, with simple bearing, looking in no way like a general, but rather resembling a priest of the Muses, would be seen gathering round him the Attics of every tongue and of every nation, the Addisons, Pellissons, Vauvenargues—all who feel the value of an easy persuasiveness, an exquisite simplicity, and a gentle negligence mingled with ornament. In the centre of the place, in the portico of the principal temple (for there would be several in the enclosure), three great men would like to meet often, and when they were together, no fourth, however great, would dream of joining their discourse or their silence. In them would be seen beauty, proportion in greatness, and that perfect harmony which appears but once in the full youth of the world. Their three names have become the ideal of art—Plato, Sophocles, and Demosthenes. Those demi-gods honoured, we see a numerous and familiar company of choice spirits who follow, the Cervantes and Molières, practical painters of life, indulgent friends who are still the first of benefactors, who laughingly embrace all mankind, turn man's experience to gaiety, and know the powerful workings of a sensible, hearty, and legitimate joy. I do not wish to make this description, which if complete would fill a volume, any longer. In the Middle Ages, believe me, Dante would occupy the sacred heights: at the feet of the singer of Paradise all Italy would be spread out like a garden; Boccaccio and Ariosto would there disport themselves, and Tasso would find again the orange groves of Sorrento. Usually a corner would be reserved for each of the various nations, but the authors would take delight in leaving it, and in their travels would recognize, where we should least expect it, brothers or masters. Lucretius, for example, would enjoy discussing the origin of the world and the reducing of chaos to order with Milton. But both arguing from their own point of view, they would only agree as regards divine pictures of poetry and nature.

Such are our classics; each individual imagination may finish the sketch and choose the group preferred. For it is necessary to make a choice, and the first condition of taste, after obtaining knowledge of all, lies not in continual travel, but in rest and cessation from wandering. Nothing blunts and destroys taste so much as endless journeyings; the poetic spirit is not the Wandering Jew. However, when I speak of resting and making choice, my meaning is not that we are to imitate those who charm us most among our masters in the past. Let us be content to know them, to penetrate them, to admire them; but let us, the late-comers, endeavour to be ourselves. Let us have the sincerity and naturalness of our own thoughts, of our own feelings; so much is always possible. To that let us add what is more difficult, elevation, an aim, if possible, towards an exalted goal; and while speaking our own language, and submitting to the conditions of the times in which we live, whence we derive our strength and our defects, let us ask from time to time, our brows lifted towards the heights and our eyes fixed on the group of honoured mortals: *what would they say of us?*

But why speak always of authors and writings? Maybe an age is coming when there will be no more writing. Happy those who read and read again, those who in their reading can follow their unrestrained inclination! There comes a time in life when, all our journeys over, our experiences ended, there is no enjoyment more delightful than to study and thoroughly examine the things we know, to take pleasure in what we feel, and in seeing and seeing again the people we love: the pure joys of our maturity. Then it is that the word classic takes its true meaning, and is defined for every man of taste by an irresistible choice. Then taste is formed, it is shaped and definite; then good sense, if we are to possess it at all, is perfected in us. We have neither more time for experiments, nor a desire to go forth in search of pastures new. We cling to our friends, to those proved by a long intercourse. Old wine, old books, old friends. We say to ourselves with Voltaire in these delightful lines: "Let us enjoy, let us write, let us live, my dear Horace! . . . I have lived longer than you: my verse will not last so long. But on the brink of the tomb I shall make it my chief care—to follow the lessons of your philosophy—to despise death in enjoying life—to read your writings full of charm and good sense—as we drink an old wine which revives our senses."

In fact, be it Horace or another who is the author preferred, who reflects our thoughts in all the wealth of their maturity, of some one of those excellent and antique minds shall we request an interview at every moment; of some one of them shall we ask a friendship which never deceives, which could not fail us; to some one of them shall we appeal for that sensation of serenity and amenity (we have often need of it) which reconciles us with mankind and with ourselves.

Montaigne

While the good ship France is taking a somewhat haphazard course, getting into unknown seas, and preparing to double what the pilots (if there is a pilot) call the Stormy Cape, while the look-out at the mast-head thinks he sees the spectre of the giant Adamastor rising on the horizon, many honourable and peaceable men continue their work and studies all the same, and follow out to the end, or as far as they can, their favourite hobbies. I know, at the present time, a learned man who is collating more carefully than has ever yet been done the different early editions of Rabelais—editions, mark you, of which only one copy remains, of which a second is not to be found: from the careful collation of the texts some literary and maybe philosophical result will be derived with regard to the genius of the French Lucian-Aristophanes. I know another scholar whose devotion and worship is given to a very different man—to Bossuet: he is preparing a complete, exact, detailed history of the life and works of the great bishop. And as tastes differ, and *"human fancy is cut* into a thousand shapes" (Montaigne said that), Montaigne also has his devotees, he who, himself, was so little of one: a sect is formed round him. In his lifetime he had Mademoiselle de Gournay, his daughter of *alliance,* who was solemnly devoted to him; and his disciple, Charron, followed him closely, step by step, only striving to arrange his thoughts with more order and method. In our time amateurs, intelligent men, practise the religion under another form: they devote themselves to collecting the smallest traces of the author of the *Essays,* to gathering up the slightest relics, and Dr. Payen may be justly placed at the head of the group. For years he has been preparing a book on Montaigne, of which the title will be: "MICHEL DE MONTAIGNE, a collection of unedited or little known facts about the author of the *Essays,* his book, and his other writings, about his family, his friends, his admirers, his detractors."

While awaiting the conclusion of the book, the occupation and amusement of a lifetime, Dr. Payen keeps us informed in short pamphlets of the various works and discoveries made about Montaigne.

If we separate the discoveries made during the last five or six years from the jumble of quarrels, disputes, cavilling, quackery, and lawsuits (for there have been all those), they consist in this—

In 1846 M. Macé found in the (then) Royal Library, amongst the "Collection Du Puys," a letter of Montaigne, addressed to the king, Henri IV, September 2, 1590.

In 1847 M. Payen printed a letter, or a fragment of a letter of Montaigne of February 16, 1588, a letter corrupt and incomplete, coming from the collection of the Comtesse Boni de Castellane.

But, most important of all, in 1848, M. Horace de Viel-Castel found in London, at the British Museum, a remarkable letter of Montaigne, May 22, 1585, when Mayor of Bordeaux, addressed to M. de Matignon, the king's lieutenant in the town. The great interest of the letter is that it shows Montaigne for the first time in the full discharge of his office with all the energy and vigilance of which he was capable. The pretended idler was at need much more active than he was ready to own.

M. Detcheverry, keeper of the records to the mayoralty of Bordeaux, found and published (1850) a letter of Montaigne, while mayor, to the jurats, or aldermen of the town, July 30, 1585.

M. Achille Jubinal found among the manuscripts of the National Library, and published (1850), a long, remarkable letter from Montaigne to the king, Henri IV, January 18, 1590, which happily coincides with that already found by M. Macé.

Lastly, to omit nothing and to do justice to all, in a "Visit to Montaigne's Château in Périgord," of which the account appeared in 1850, M. Bertrand de Saint-Germain described the place and pointed out the various Greek and Latin inscriptions that may still be read in Montaigne's tower in the third-story chamber (the ground floor counting as the first), which the philosopher made his library and study.

M. Payen, collecting together and criticizing in his last pamphlet the various notices and discoveries, not all of equal importance, allowed himself to be drawn into some little exaggeration of praise; but we cannot blame him. Admiration, when applied to such noble, perfectly innocent, and disinterested subjects, is truly a spark of the sacred fire: it produces research that a less ardent zeal would quickly leave aside, and sometimes leads to valuable results. However, it would be well for those who, following M. Payen's example, intelligently understand and greatly admire

Montaigne, to remember, even in their ardour, the advice of the wise man and the master. "There is more to do," said he, speaking of the commentators of his time, "in interpreting the interpretations than in interpreting the things themselves; and more books about books than on any other subject. We do nothing, but everything swarms with commentators; of authors there is a great rarity." Authors are of great price and very scarce at all times—that is to say, authors who really increase the sum of human knowledge. I should like all who write on Montaigne, and give us the details of their researches and discoveries, to imagine one thing—Montaigne himself reading and criticizing them. "What would he think of me and of the manner in which I am going to speak of him to the public?" If such a question was put, how greatly it would suppress useless phrases and shorten idle discussions! M. Payen's last pamphlet was dedicated to a man who deserves equally well of Montaigne— M. Gustave Brunet, of Bordeaux. He, speaking of M. Payen, in a work in which he pointed out interesting and various corrections of Montaigne's text, said: "May he soon decide to publish the fruits of his researches: he will have left nothing for future *Montaignologues*." *Montaignologues!* Great Heaven! what would Montaigne say of such a word coined in his honour? You who occupy yourselves so meritoriously with him, but who have, I think, no claim to appropriate him to yourselves, in the name of him whom you love, and whom we all love by a greater or lesser title, never, I beg of you, use such words; they smack of the brotherhood and the sect, of pedantry and of the chatter of the schools—things utterly repugnant to Montaigne.

Montaigne had a simple, natural, affable mind, and a very happy disposition. Sprung from an excellent father, who, though of no great education, entered with real enthusiasm into the movement of the Renaissance and all the *liberal* novelties of his time, the son corrected the excessive enthusiasm, vivacity, and tenderness he inherited by a great refinement and justness of reflection; but he did not abjure the original groundwork. It is scarcely more than thirty years ago that whenever the sixteenth century was mentioned it was spoken of as a barbarous epoch, Montaigne only excepted: therein lay error and ignorance. The sixteenth century was a great century, fertile, powerful, learned, refined in parts, although in some aspects it was rough, violent, and seemingly coarse. What it particularly lacked was taste, if by taste is meant the faculty of clear and perfect selection, the extrication of the elements of the beautiful. But in the succeeding centuries taste quickly became distaste. If, however, in literature it was crude, in the arts properly so-called, in those of the hand and the chisel, the sixteenth century, even in France, is, in the quality of taste, far greater than the two succeeding centuries: it is neither meagre nor massive, heavy nor distorted. In art its taste is rich and of fine quality—at once unrestrained and complex, ancient and modern, special to itself and original. In the region of morals it is unequal and mixed. It was an age of contrasts, of contrasts in all their crudity, an age of philosophy and fanaticism, of scepticism and strong faith. Everything was at strife and in collision; nothing was blended and united. Everything was in ferment; it was a period of chaos; every ray of light caused a storm. It was not a gentle age, or one we can call an age of light, but an age of struggle and combat. What distinguished Montaigne and made a phenomenon of him was that in such an age he should have possessed moderation, caution, and order.

Born on the last day of February, 1533, taught the ancient languages as a game while still a child, waked even in his cradle by the sound of musical instruments, he seemed less fitted for a rude and violent epoch than for the commerce and *sanctuary of the Muses*. His rare good sense corrected what was too ideal and poetical in his early education; but he preserved the happy faculty of saying everything with freshness and wit. Married, when past thirty, to an estimable woman who was his companion for twenty-eight years, he seems to have put passion only into friendship. He immortalized his love for Étienne de la Boëtie, whom he lost after four years of the sweetest and closest intimacy. For some time counsellor in the Parliament of Bordeaux, Montaigne, before he was forty, retired from public life and flung away ambition to live in his tower of Montaigne, enjoying his own society and his own intellect, entirely given up to his own observations and thoughts, and to the busy idleness of which we know all the sports and fancies. The first edition of the *Essays* appeared in 1580, consisting of only two books, and in a form representing only the first rough draft of what we have in the later editions. The same year Montaigne set out on a voyage to Switzerland and Italy. It was during that voyage that the aldermen of Bordeaux elected him mayor of their town. At first he refused and excused himself, but warned that it would be well to accept, and enjoined by the king, he took the office, "the more beautiful," he said, "that there was neither renunciation nor gain other than the honour of its performance." He filled the office for four years, from July 1582 to July 1586, being re-elected after the first two years. Thus Montaigne, at the age of fifty, and a little against his will, re-entered public life when the country was on the eve of civil disturbances which, quieted and lulled to sleep for a while, broke out more violently at the cry of the League. Although, as a rule, lessons serve for nothing, since the art of wisdom and happiness cannot be taught, let us not deny ourselves the pleasure of listening to Montaigne; let us look on his wisdom and happiness; let him speak of public affairs, of revolutions and disturbances, and of his way of conducting himself with regard to them. We do not put forward a model, but we offer our readers an agreeable recreation.

Although Montaigne lived in so agitated and stormy a time, a period that a man who had lived through the Terror (M. Daunou) called the *most tragic century in all history*, he by no means regarded his age as the worst of ages. He was not of those prejudiced and afflicted persons, who, measuring everything by their visual horizon, valuing everything according to their present sensations, always declare that the disease they suffer from is worse than any ever before experienced by a human being. He was like Socrates, who did not consider himself a citizen of one city but of the world; with his broad and full imagination he embraced the universality of countries and of ages; he even judged more equitably the very evils of which he was witness and victim. "Who is it," he said, "that, seeing the bloody havoc of these civil wars of ours, does not cry out that the machine of the world is near dissolution, and that the day of judgment is at hand, without considering that many worse revolutions have been seen, and that, in the meantime, people are being merry in a thousand other parts of the earth for all this? For my part, considering the licence and impunity that always attend such commotions, I admire they are so moderate, and that there is not more mischief done. To him who feels the hailstones patter about his ears, the whole hemisphere appears to be in storm and tempest." And raising his thoughts higher and higher, reducing his own suffering to what it was in the immensity of nature, seeing there not only himself but whole kingdoms as mere specks in the infinite, he added in words which foreshadowed Pascal, in words whose outline and salient points Pascal did not disdain to borrow: "But whoever shall represent to his fancy, as in a picture, that great image of our mother nature, portrayed in her full majesty and lustre, whoever in her face shall read so general and so constant a variety, whoever shall observe himself in that figure, and not himself but a whole kingdom, no bigger than the least touch or prick of a pencil in comparison of the whole, that man alone is able to value things according to their true estimate and grandeur."

Thus Montaigne gives us a lesson, a useless lesson, but I state it all the same, because among the many unprofitable ones that have been written down, it is perhaps of greater worth than most. I do not mean to underrate the gravity of the circumstances in which France is just now involved, for I believe there is pressing need to bring together all the energy, prudence, and courage she possesses in order that the country may come out with honour. However, let us reflect, and remember that, leaving aside the Empire, which as regards internal affairs was a period of calm, and before 1812 of prosperity, we who utter such loud complaints lived in peace from 1815 to 1830, fifteen long years; that the three days of July only inaugurated another order of things that for eighteen years guaranteed peace and industrial prosperity; in all, thirty-two years of repose. Stormy days came; tempests burst, and will doubtless burst again. Let us learn how to live through them, but do not let us cry out every day, as we are disposed to do, that never under the sun were such storms known as we are enduring. To get away from the present state of feeling, to restore lucidity and proportion to our judgments, let us read every evening a page of Montaigne.

A criticism of Montaigne on the men of his day struck me, and it bears equally well on those of ours. Our philosopher says somewhere that he knows a fair number of men possessing various good qualities—one, intelligence; another, heart; another, address, conscience or knowledge, or skill in languages; each has his share: "but of a great man as a whole, having so many good qualities together, or one with such a degree of excellence that we ought to admire him, or compare him with those we honour in the past, my fortune has never shown me one." He afterwards made an exception in favour of his friend Étienne de la Boëtie, but he belonged to the company of great men dead before attaining maturity, and showing promise without having time to fulfil it. Montaigne's criticism called up a smile. He did not see a true and wholly great man in his time, the age of L'Hôpital, Coligny, and the Guises. Well! How does ours seem to you? We have as many great men as in Montaigne's time, one distinguished for his intellect, another for his heart, a third for skill, some (a rare thing) for conscience, many for knowledge and language. But we too lack the perfect man, and he is greatly to be desired. One of the most intelligent observers of our day recognized and proclaimed it some years ago: "Our age," said M. de Rémusat, "is wanting in great men."

How did Montaigne conduct himself in his duties as first magistrate of a great city? If we take him literally and on a hasty first glance, we should believe he discharged them slackly and languidly. Did not Horace, doing the honours to himself, say that in war he one day let his shield fall (*relicta non bene parmula*)? We must not be in too great a hurry to take too literally the men of taste who have a horror of overestimating themselves. Minds of a fine quality are more given to vigilance and to action than they are apt to confess. The man who boasts and makes a great noise, will, I am almost sure, be less brave in the combat than Horace, and less vigilant at the council board than Montaigne.

On entering office Montaigne was careful to warn the aldermen of Bordeaux not to expect to find in him more than there really was; he presented himself to them without affectation. "I represented to them faithfully and conscientiously all that I felt myself to be—a man without memory, without vigilance, without experience, and without energy; but also, without hate, without ambition, without avarice, and without violence." He should be sorry, while taking the affairs of the town in hand, that his feelings should be so strongly affected as those of his worthy father had been, who in the end had lost his place and health. *The eager and ardent pledge to satisfy an impetuous desire* was not his method. His opinion was "that you must lend yourself to others, and only give yourself to yourself." And repeating his thought, according to his custom in all kinds of metaphors and picturesque forms, he said again that if he sometimes allowed himself to be urged to the management of other men's affairs, he promised to take them in hand, not "into my lungs and liver." We are thus forewarned, we know what to expect. The mayor and Montaigne were two distinct persons; under his role and office he reserved to himself a certain freedom and secret security. He continued to judge things in his own fashion and impartially, although acting loyally for the cause confided to him. He was far from approving or even excusing all he saw in his party, and he could judge his adversaries and say of them: "He did that thing wickedly, and this virtuously." "I would have," he added, "matters go well on our side; but if they do not, I shall not run mad. I am heartily for the right party; but I do not affect to be taken notice of for an especial enemy to others." And he entered into some details and applications which at that time were piquant. Let us remark, however, in order to explain and justify his somewhat extensive profession of impartiality, that the chiefs of the party then in evidence, the three Henris, were famous and considerable men on several counts: Henri, Duke of Guise, head of the League; Henri, King of Navarre, leader of the Opposition; and the King Henri III in whose name Montaigne was mayor, who wavered between the two. When parties have neither chief nor head, when they are known by the body only, that is to say in their hideous and brutal reality, it is more difficult and also more hazardous to be just towards them and to assign to each its share of action.

The principle which guided him in his administration was to look only at the fact, at the result, and to grant nothing to noise and outward show: "How much more a good effect makes a noise, so much I abate of the goodness of it." For it is always to be feared that it was more performed for the sake of the noise than upon the account of goodness: "Being exposed upon the stall, 'tis half sold." That was not Montaigne's way: he made no show; he managed men and affairs as quietly as he could; he employed in a manner useful to all alike the gifts of sincerity and conciliation; the personal attraction with which nature endowed him was a quality of the highest value in the management of men. He preferred to warn men of evil rather than to take on himself the honour of repressing it: "Is there anyone who desires to be sick that he may see his physician's practice? And would not that physician deserve to be whipped who should wish the plague amongst us that he might put his art into practice?" Far from desiring that trouble and disorder in the affairs of the city should rouse and honour his government, he had ever willingly, he said, contributed all he could to their tranquillity and ease. He is not of those whom municipal honours intoxicate and elate, those "dignities of office" as he called them, and of which all the noise "goes from one cross-road to another." If he was a man desirous of fame, he recognized that it was of a kind greater than that. I do not know, however, if even in a vaster field he would have changed his method and manner of proceeding. To do good for the public imperceptibly would always seem to him the ideal of skill and the culminating point of happiness. "He who will not thank me," he said, "for the order and quiet calm that has accompanied my administration, cannot, however, deprive me of the share that belongs to me by the title of my good fortune." And he is inexhaustible in describing in lively and graceful expressions the kinds of effective and imperceptible services he believed he had rendered— services greatly superior to noisy and glorious deeds: "Actions which come from the workman's hand carelessly and noiselessly have most charm, that some honest man chooses later and brings from their obscurity to thrust them into the light for their own sake." Thus fortune served Montaigne to perfection, and even in his administration of affairs, in difficult conjunctures, he never had to belie his maxim, nor to step very far out of the way of life he had planned: "For my part I commend a gliding, solitary, and silent life." He reached the end of his magistracy almost satisfied with himself, having accomplished what he had promised himself, and much more than he had promised others.

The letter lately discovered by M. Horace de Vieil-Castel corroborates the chapter in which Montaigne exhibits and criticizes himself in the period of his public life. "That letter," says M. Payen, "is entirely on affairs. Montaigne is mayor; Bordeaux, lately disturbed, seems threatened by fresh agitations; the king's lieutenant is away. It is Wednesday, May 22, 1585; it is night, Montaigne is wakeful, and writes to the governor of the province." The letter, which is of too special and local an interest to be inserted here, may be summed up in these words: Montaigne regretted the absence of Marshal de Matignon, and feared the consequences of its prolongation; he was keeping, and would continue to keep, him acquainted with all that was going on, and begged him to return as soon as his circumstances would permit. "We are looking after our gates and guards, and a little more carefully in your absence. . . . If anything important and fresh occurs, I shall send you a messenger immediately, so that if you hear no news from me, you may consider that nothing has happened." He begs M. de Matignon to remember, however, that he might not have time to warn him, "entreating you to consider that such movements are usually so sudden, that if they do occur they will take me by the throat without any warning." Besides, he will do everything to ascertain the march of events beforehand. "I will do what I can to hear news from all parts, and to that end shall visit and observe the inclinations of all sorts of men." Lastly, after keeping the marshal informed of everything, of the least rumours abroad in the city, he pressed him to return, assuring him "that we spare neither our care, nor, if need be, our lives to preserve everything in obedience to the king." Montaigne was never prodigal of protestations and praises, and what with others was a mere form of speech, was with him a real undertaking and the truth.

Things, however, became worse and worse: civil war broke out; friendly or hostile parties (the difference was not great) infested the country. Montaigne, who went to his country house as often as he could, whenever the duties of his office, which was drawing near its term, did not oblige him to be in Bordeaux, was exposed to every sort of insult and outrage. "I underwent," he said, "the inconveniences that moderation brings along with it in such a disease. I was pitied on all hands; to the Ghibelline I was a Guelph, and to the Guelph a Ghibelline." In the midst of his personal grievances he could disengage and raise his thoughts to reflections on the public misfortunes and on the degradation of men's characters. Considering closely the disorder of parties, and all the abject and wretched things which developed so quickly, he was ashamed to see leaders of renown stoop and debase themselves by cowardly complacency; for in those circumstances we know, like him, "that in the word

of command to march, draw up, wheel, and the like, we obey him indeed; but all the rest is dissolute and free." "It pleases me," said Montaigne ironically, "to observe how much pusillanimity and cowardice
there is in ambition; by how abject and servile ways it must arrive at
its end." Despising ambition as he did, he was not sorry to see it un-
masked by such practices and degraded in his sight. However, his goodness of heart overcoming his pride and contempt, he adds sadly, "it
displeases me to see good and generous natures, and that are capable
of justice, every day corrupted in the management and command of this
confusion. . . . We had ill-contrived souls enough without spoiling those
that were generous and good." He rather sought in that misfortune an
opportunity and motive for fortifying and strengthening himself. Attacked one by one by many disagreeables and evils, which he would
have endured more cheerfully in a heap—that is to say, all at once—
pursued by war, disease, by all the plagues (July 1585), in the course
things were taking, he already asked himself to whom he and his could
have recourse, of whom he could ask shelter and subsistence for his
old age; and having looked and searched thoroughly all around, he found
himself actually destitute and ruined. For, "to let a man's self fall plumb
down, and from so great a height, it ought to be in the arms of a solid,
vigorous, and fortunate friendship. They are very rare, if there be any."
Speaking in such a manner, we perceive that La Boëtie had been some
time dead. Then he felt that he must after all rely on himself in his distress, and must gain strength; now or never was the time to put into
practice the lofty lessons he spent his life in collecting from the books
of the philosophers. He took heart again, and attained all the height of
his virtue: "In an ordinary and quiet time, a man prepares himself for
moderate and common accidents; but in the confusion wherein we have
been for these thirty years, every Frenchman, whether in particular or in
general, sees himself every hour upon the point of the total ruin and over-
throw of his fortune." And far from being discouraged and cursing fate
for causing him to be born in so stormy an age, he suddenly congratulated
himself: "Let us thank fortune that has not made us live in an effeminate,
idle, and languishing age." Since the curiosity of wise men seeks the past
for disturbances in states in order to learn the secrets of history, and,
as we should say, the whole physiology of the body social, "so does my
curiosity," he declares, "make me in some sort please myself with seeing
with my own eyes this notable spectacle of our public death, its forms
and symptoms; and, seeing I could not hinder it, am content to be destined to assist in it, and thereby to instruct myself." I shall not suggest

a consolation of that sort to most people; the greater part of mankind does not possess the heroic and eager curiosity of Empedocles and the elder Pliny, the two intrepid men who went straight to the volcanoes and the disturbances of nature to examine them at close quarters, at the risk of destruction and death. But to a man of Montaigne's nature, the thought of that stoical observation gave him consolation even amid real evils. Considering the condition of false peace and doubtful truce, the *régime* of dull and profound corruption which had preceded the last disturbances, he almost congratulated himself on seeing their cessation; for "it was," he said of the *régime* of Henri III, "a universal juncture of particular members, rotten to emulation of one another, and the most of them with inveterate ulcers, that neither required nor admitted of any cure. This conclusion therefore did really more animate than depress me." Note that his health, usually delicate, is here raised to the level of his morality, although what it had suffered through the various disturbances might have been enough to undermine it. He had the satisfaction of feeling that he had some hold against fortune, and that it would take a greater shock still to crush him.

Another consideration, humbler and more humane, upheld him in his troubles, the consolation arising from a common misfortune, a misfortune shared by all, and the sight of the courage of others. The people, especially the real people, they who are victims and not robbers, the peasants of his district, moved him by the manner in which they endured the same, or even worse, troubles than his. The disease or plague which raged at that time in the country pressed chiefly on the poor; Montaigne learned from them resignation and the practice of philosophy. "Let us look down upon the poor people that we see scattered upon the face of the earth, prone and intent upon their business, that neither know Aristotle nor Cato, example nor precept. Even from these does nature every day extract effects of constancy and patience, more pure and manly than those we so inquisitively study in the schools." And he goes on to describe them working to the bitter end, even in their grief, even in disease, until their strength failed them. "He that is now digging in my garden has this morning buried his father, or his son. . . . They never keep their beds but to die." The whole chapter is fine, pathetic, to the point, evincing noble, stoical elevation of mind, and also the cheerful and affable disposition which Montaigne said, with truth, was his by inheritance, and in which he had been nourished. There could be nothing better as regards "consolation in public calamities," except a chapter of some not more human, but of some truly divine, book, in which the hand of God should be everywhere visible, not perfunctorily, as with Montaigne, but actually and lovingly present. In fact, the consolation Montaigne gives himself and others is perhaps as lofty and beautiful as human consolation without prayer can be.

He wrote the chapter, the twelfth of the third book, in the midst of the evils he described, and before they were ended. He concluded it in his graceful and poetical way with a collection of examples, "a heap of foreign flowers," to which he furnished only the thread for fastening them together.

There is Montaigne to the life; no matter how seriously he spoke, it was always with the utmost charm. To form an opinion on his style you have only to open him indifferently at any page and listen to his talk on any subject; there is none that he did not enliven and make suggestive. In the chapter "Of Liars," for instance, after enlarging on his lack of memory and giving a list of reasons by which he might console himself, he suddenly added this fresh and delightful reason, that, thanks to his faculty for forgetting, "the places I revisit, and the books I read over again, always smile upon me with a fresh novelty." It is thus that on every subject he touched he was continually new, and created sources of freshness.

Montesquieu, in a memorable exclamation, said: "The four great poets, Plato, Malebranche, Shaftesbury, Montaigne!" How true it is of Montaigne! No French writer, including the poets proper, had so lofty an idea of poetry as he had. "From my earliest childhood," he said, "poetry had power over me to transport and transpierce me." He considered, and therein shows penetration, that "we have more poets than judges and interpreters of poetry. It is easier to write than to understand." In itself and its pure beauty his poetry defies definition; whoever desired to recognize it at a glance and discern of what it actually consisted would see no more than "the brilliance of a flash of lightning." In the constitution and continuity of his style, Montaigne is a writer very rich in animated, bold similes, naturally fertile in metaphors that are never detached from the thought, but that seize it in its very centre, in its interior, that join and bind it. In that respect, fully obeying his own genius, he has gone beyond and sometimes exceeded the genius of language. His concise, vigorous, and always forcible style, by its poignancy, emphasizes and repeats the meaning. It may be said of his style that it is a continual epigram, or an ever-renewed metaphor, a style that has only been successfully employed by the French once, by Montaigne himself. If we wanted to imitate him, supposing we had the power and were naturally fitted for it—if we de-

sired to write with his severity, exact proportion, and diverse continuity
of figures and turns—it would be necessary to force our language to be
more powerful, and poetically more complete, than is usually our custom.
Style *à la* Montaigne, consistent, varied in the series and assortment of the
metaphors, exacts the creation of a portion of the tissue itself to hold
them. It is absolutely necessary that in places the woof should be enlarged and extended, in order to weave into it the metaphor; but in defining him I come almost to write like him. The French language, French
prose, which in fact always savours more or less of conversation, does
not, naturally, possess the resources and the extent of canvas necessary
for a continued picture: by the side of an animated metaphor it will often
exhibit a sudden lacuna and some weak places. In filling this by boldness
and invention as Montaigne did, in creating, in imagining the expression
and locution that is wanting, our prose should appear equally finished.
Style *à la* Montaigne would, in many respects, be openly at war with that
of Voltaire. It could only come into being and flourish in the full freedom
of the sixteenth century, in a frank, ingenious, jovial, keen, brave, and
refined mind, of a unique stamp, that even for that time seemed free and
somewhat licentious, and that was inspired and emboldened, but not intoxicated by the pure and direct spirit of ancient sources.

Such as he is, Montaigne is the French Horace; he is Horatian in the
groundwork, often in the form and expression, although in that he sometimes approaches Seneca. His book is a treasurehouse of moral observations and of experience; at whatever page it is opened, and in whatever
condition of mind, some wise thought expressed in a striking and enduring fashion is certain to be found. It will at once detach itself and en-
grave itself on the mind, a beautiful meaning in full and forcible words,
in one vigorous line, familiar or great. The whole of his book, said Étienne
Pasquier, is a real *seminary* of beautiful and remarkable sentences, and
they come in so much the better that they run and hasten on without
thrusting themselves into notice. There is something for every age, for
every hour of life: you cannot read in it for any time without having the
mind filled and lined as it were, or, to put it better, fully armed and
clothed. We have just seen how much useful counsel and actual consolation it contains for an honourable man, born for private life, and fallen
on times of disturbance and revolution. To this I shall add the counsel he
gave those who, like myself and many men of my acquaintance, suffer
from political disturbances without in any way provoking them, or believing ourselves capable of averting them. Montaigne, as Horace would
have done, counsels them, while apprehending everything from afar off,

not to be too much preoccupied with such matters in advance; to take advantage to the end of pleasant moments and bright intervals. Stroke on stroke come his piquant and wise similes, and he concludes, to my thinking, with the most delightful one of all, and one, besides, entirely appropriate and seasonable: it is folly and fret, he said, "to take out your furred gown at Saint John because you will want it at Christmas."

The foregoing two essays were translated
by Elizabeth Lee.

Sir Francis Bacon

1561–1626

Francis Bacon was born on January 22, 1561, in London, England. His father, Sir Nicholas Bacon, was Lord Keeper of the Seal to Queen Elizabeth I.

In 1573 Bacon entered Trinity College, Cambridge. He left, in 1576, and went abroad with the ambassador to France to learn the arts of diplomacy. When his father died suddenly, in 1579, he returned to England. There he studied law and was admitted to the bar in 1582.

The Earl of Essex befriended Bacon and tried to help him in his career. Later, when Essex was tried for treason, Bacon took a leading role in the prosecution and helped to bring about Essex' execution. This action has never been entirely understood.

When James I came to the throne, Bacon's career advanced rapidly. He became Attorney General in 1613, Lord Keeper of the Seal in 1617, and Lord Chancellor in 1618. He was made Baron Verulam in 1618 and Viscount St. Albans in 1621. Bacon defended the King's policies against Parliament, which brought him into conflict with the great lawyer Sir Edward Coke.

In 1621 Bacon was accused of taking bribes in his position as Lord Chancellor. The practice of receiving gifts was an old one, to which Bacon pleaded guilty. He claimed, however, that his judgment was

---

Notes from the artist: "A bold, forceful approach was used to present Bacon as the last of the 'all-round' intellectual giants. . . . In the background, a university; at right, the servant who accompanied Bacon to record his observations and thoughts."

not swayed by the gifts. Bacon was sentenced to prison, heavily fined, and disqualified from holding office. The prison sentence and fine were not enforced, but Bacon spent the rest of his life in writing and scientific research rather than in public office.

Because of Bacon's insistence that scientists should reach conclusions solely by experiment, he is considered one of the founders of the modern scientific method.

Bacon's philosophical writings are in the two completed parts of what he planned as a huge work, the *Instauratio magna,* or "Great Reconstruction of Philosophy." His *Essays,* published in 1597, are famous for their shrewdness and epigrammatic style. He died on April 9, 1626, after catching a cold while trying to see if meat could be preserved in snow.

Francis Bacon was a master of the aphorism. The first sentences of his essays are often particularly brilliant and memorable. People have been quoting them for three hundred years.

"Virtue is like a rich stone, best plain set," the essay *Of Beauty* begins. It is not only a trenchant phrase. It also sets the tone and makes the point of the entire essay. Physical beauty is, in itself, nothing to be proud of, Bacon is saying. "Beauty is as summer fruits, which are easy to corrupt, and cannot last," he writes. True beauty is inside, where virtue is; true beauty is in action, not in seeming. But Bacon also says that "virtue is best in a body that is comely, though not of delicate features." Virtue and beauty together make a fine package.

The advice Bacon gives in *Of Discourse* is as good as we are likely to find on the subject anywhere. Above all, do not be a bore, he says, and do not be rude. There are some subjects that should not be joked about, especially if it is done only to exhibit our own wit. It is both useful and polite to ask questions, but they should be chosen to put the other person in a good light rather than to expose his lack of knowledge. Perhaps the best advice of all is this: "Speech of a man's self ought to be seldom."

Of Studies contains some of Bacon's most famous sentences. For example: "Crafty men contemn studies, simple men admire them, and wise men use them." There is much truth in that. Again: "Some books are to be tasted, others to be swallowed, and some few to be chewed and digested." This is often quoted without the explanation that follows. "That is," Bacon says, "some books are to be read only in part; others to be read, but not curiously (*i.e.*, carefully); and some few to be read wholly, and with diligence and attention." [1]

Less famous, but perhaps even more interesting, is the sentence: "Reading maketh a full man; conference a ready man; and writing an exact man." Each part of this statement deserves a full discourse. We do not really know our own thoughts unless we can write them down. Quickness of wit (which Bacon calls readiness) comes from conversation. The silent man is too often slow of mind. And without the ability and willingness to read, we are empty things. So much of the world is closed to us without books.

The style of Bacon's essays is special and quite unique to him, though others have attempted to imitate it. Not a word is wasted. His entire output in the form—some fifty-eight essays—would, if closely printed, fill hardly a hundred pages. Yet those hundred pages would contain as much wisdom as most libraries. The cold, piercing brain of this distant, unknowable man saw through to the realities. We may not always like him and what he says, but we cannot deny that what he says is largely true, and relevant to our own concerns.

---

[1] Compare what Virginia Woolf has to say on this point in Vol. 5, pp. 5–14, in this set.

Of Beauty

Virtue is like a rich stone, best plain set; and surely virtue is best in a body that is comely, though not of delicate features; and that hath rather dignity of presence, than beauty of aspect. Neither is it almost seen, that very beautiful persons are otherwise of great virtue; as if nature were rather busy not to err, than in labour to produce excellency. And therefore they prove accomplished, but not of great spirit; and study rather behaviour than virtue. But this holds not always: for Augustus Caesar, Titus Vespasianus, Philip le Bel of France, Edward the Fourth of England, Alcibiades of Athens, Ismail the Sophy of Persia were all high and great spirits; and yet the most beautiful men of their times. In beauty, that of favour is more than that of colour; and that of decent and gracious motion more than that of favour. That is the best part of beauty, which a picture cannot express; no nor the first sight of life. There is no excellent beauty that hath not some strangeness in the proportion. A man cannot tell whether Apelles or Albert Dürer were the more trifler; whereof the one would make a personage by geometrical proportions; the other, by taking the best parts out of divers faces, to make one excellent. Such personages, I think, would please nobody but the painter that made them. Not but I think a painter may make a better face than ever was; but he must do it by a kind of felicity (as a musician that maketh an excellent air in music) and not by rule. A man shall see faces, that if you examine them part by part, you shall find never a good; and yet altogether do well.

If it be true that the principal part of beauty is in decent motion, certainly it is no marvel though persons in years seem many times more amiable—*pulchrorum autumnus pulcher* [autumn is the beauty of beauties] —for no youth can be comely but by pardon, and considering the youth as to make up the comeliness. Beauty is as summer fruits, which are easy to corrupt, and cannot last; and for the most part it makes a dissolute youth, and an age a little out of countenance; but yet certainly again, if it light well, it maketh virtue shine, and vices blush.

Of Discourse

Some in their discourse desire rather commendation of wit, in being able to hold all arguments, than of judgment, in discerning what is true; as if it were a praise to know what might be said, and not what should be thought. Some have certain common places and themes wherein they are good, and want variety; which kind of poverty is for the most part tedious, and when it is once perceived, ridiculous. The honourablest part of talk is to give the occasion; and again to moderate and pass to somewhat else; for then a man leads the dance. It is good, in discourse and speech of conversation, to vary and intermingle speech of the present occasion with arguments, tales with reasons, asking of questions with telling of opinions, and jest with earnest: for it is a dull thing to tire, and, as we say now, to jade, any thing too far. As for jest, there be certain things which ought to be privileged from it; namely, religion, matters of state, great persons, any man's present business of importance, and any case that deserveth pity. Yet there be some that think their wits have been asleep, except they dart out somewhat that is piquant, and to the quick. This is a vein which should be bridled: *Parce, puer, stimulis, et fortius utere loris* [Spare the spurs, lad, and more vigorously use the reins]. And generally, men ought to find the difference between saltness and bitterness. Certainly, he that hath a satirical vein, as he maketh others afraid of his wit, so he had need be afraid of others' memory.

He that questioneth much shall learn much, and content much; but especially if he apply his questions to the skill of the persons whom he asketh; for he shall give them occasion to please themselves in speaking, and himself shall continually gather knowledge. But let his questions not be troublesome; for that is fit for a poser. And let him be sure to leave other men their turns to speak. Nay, if there be any that would reign and take up all the time, let him find means to take them off, and to bring

95

others on; as musicians use to do with those that dance too long galliards. If you dissemble sometimes your knowledge of that you are thought to know, you shall be thought another time to know that you know not.

Speech of a man's self ought to be seldom, and well chosen. I knew one was wont to say in scorn, "He must needs be a wise man, he speaks so much of himself": and there is but one case wherein a man may commend himself with good grace; and that is in commending virtue in another; especially if it be such a virtue whereunto himself pretendeth. Speech of touch towards others should be sparingly used; for discourse ought to be as a field, without coming home to any man. I knew two noblemen, of the west part of England, whereof the one was given to scoff, but kept ever royal cheer in his house; the other would ask of those that had been at the other's table, "Tell truly, was there never a flout or dry blow given?" To which the guest would answer, "Such and such a thing passed." The lord would say, "I thought he would mar a good dinner." Discretion of speech is more than eloquence; and to speak agreeably to him with whom we deal is more than to speak in good words or in good order. A good continued speech, without a good speech of interlocution, shows slowness; and a good reply or second speech, without a good settled speech, showeth shallowness and weakness. As we see in beasts, that those that are weakest in the course are yet nimblest in the turn; as it is betwixt the greyhound and the hare. To use too many circumstances ere one come to the matter is wearisome; to use none at all is blunt.

Of Studies

Studies serve for delight, for ornament, and for ability. Their chief use for delight is in privateness and retiring; for ornament, is in discourse; and for ability, in the judgment and disposition of business. For expert men can execute, and perhaps judge of particulars, one by one; but the general counsels, and the plots and marshalling of affairs, come best from those that are learned. To spend too much time in studies is sloth; to use them too much for ornament is affectation; to make judgment wholly by their rules is the humour of a scholar. They perfect nature, and are perfected by experience: for natural abilities are like natural plants, that need pruning by study; and studies themselves do give forth directions too much at large, except they be bounded in by experience. Crafty men contemn studies, simple men admire them, and wise men use them; for they teach not their own use; but that is a wisdom without them, and above them, won by observation. Read not to contradict and confute; nor to believe and take for granted; nor to find talk and discourse; but to weigh and consider.

Some books are to be tasted, others to be swallowed, and some few to be chewed and digested; that is, some books are to be read only in parts; others to be read, but not curiously; and some few to be read wholly, and with diligence and attention. Some books also may be read by deputy, and extracts made of them by others; but that would be only in the less important arguments, and the meaner sort of books; else distilled books are like common distilled waters, flashy things. Reading maketh a full man; conference a ready man; and writing an exact man. And therefore, if a man write little, he had need have a great memory; if he confer little, he had need have a present wit: and if he read little, he had need have much cunning, to seem to know that he doth not. Histories make men wise; poets witty; the mathematics subtile; natural philosophy deep; moral grave; logic and rhetoric able to contend. *Abeunt studia in mores* [studies develop into habits]. Nay there is no stond or impediment in the wit but may be wrought out by fit studies: like as dis- eases of the body may have appropriate exercises.

Bowling is good for the stone and reins; shooting for the lungs and breast; gentle walking for the stomach; riding for the head; and the like. So if a man's wit be wandering, let him study the mathematics; for in demonstrations, if his wit be called away never so little, he must begin again. If his wit be not apt to distinguish or find differences, let him study the schoolmen; for they are *cymini sectores* [hairsplitters, literally cumin- seed sorters]. If he be not apt to beat over matters, and to call up one thing to prove and illustrate another, let him study the lawyers' cases. So every defect of the mind may have a special receipt.

The foregoing essays
are from a collection of Bacon's essays entitled
ESSAYS: CIVIL AND MORAL

David Hume

1711–1776

The Homes or Humes were minor Scottish gentry. David Hume was born in Edinburgh, April 26 (Old Style), 1711. He left Edinburgh University about 1726. Like Congreve, Burke, and others, he tried the law and did not like it. A turn at business helped him to work off a slight nervous disorder. He went to France, where he wrote *A Treatise of Human Nature*. The three-volume work was published in England in 1739–40.

It got little notice. The first two volumes of his *Essays Moral and Political* were somewhat better received. He took various positions— tutor to a mad marquess, aide-de-camp to General James Sinclair in Vienna and Turin—in order to earn money for writing. More essays, a rewriting of Book I of the *Treatise* (this later became *Enquiry concerning Human Understanding*), and *An Enquiry concerning the Principles of Morals* were all published in 1751.

The next year he became keeper of the Advocates' Library in Edinburgh. There, by 1762, he had finished the *Four Dissertations* and his six-volume *History of England*. He was famous. How great that fame was he did not know until he went to Paris in 1763 as Acting Secretary of the British Embassy under the Earl of Hertford. The King gave him a reception. The great hostesses fought over him. He became a public idol, as Franklin did later.

Hume returned to London in 1766. He took Jean Jacques Rousseau along and found him a house in Staffordshire. But the disturbed Rousseau imagined a plot and fled back to France, where he accused Hume of betraying him. Hume served a year as Undersecretary of State. Then he retired to the company of Adam Smith and other friends in Edinburgh. Boswell, who had called him "the greatest writer in Britain," visited him just before his death. Would Hume admit to a belief in immortality? No, said Hume, and fended him off with his usual clearheaded good nature. He died on August 25, 1776.

Some writers give us trouble by using too many difficult words. In Hume's case we might almost say that the reverse is true. *Of the Standard of Taste* is a good example. Its very simplicity of statement, on first reading, makes it a little hard to grasp. Hume does not define his terms. What is "taste"? If we are patient, we shall see that the whole essay becomes a definition. And what is a "sentiment"? We go to the dictionary and find a meaning that seems closest to Hume's sense: "mental attitude, thought or judgment permeated or prompted by feeling."

He begins by attacking head on the main difficulty in regard to taste: its great variety, and the variety of standards and points of view this implies. *Chacun à son goût,* says the French proverb, meaning "everyone to his taste." Is this cynicism, or mere intellectual courtesy, or the final wisdom of the matter? In any case, Hume would not have been content with it. If we understand what he is doing, we shall be well on the way to understanding his argument. He is not defining taste per se, though it comes to that. He is examining the various factors that have a bearing on it in order to set up a standard of taste. He does this by giving us a point-by-point description of the qualities requisite to a man of taste.

Often we are principally conscious of the difference between the standards of his time, in which he shared, and ours. For example, "blame" is a term we might apply to a hunting dog that failed to make a good point, not to a work of art or its creator. The distinction goes beyond vocabulary. The men of the eighteenth century spread moral judgment like a blanket over every aspect of human life. In the same way, Hume extends the operation of taste over theology, philosophy, ethics, science, poetry, and the other arts.

Notes from the artist: "Hume the man, as he saw himself in the quotation from Enquiry concerning Human Understanding, *was the theme of this portrait. The gay figures in the background, suggesting music and dance, are taken from a Greek vase."*

David Hume

Be a philosopher; but amidst all your philosophy,
be still a man.

Sometimes, as in the discussion of the characters in Homer and
Fénelon, we find it difficult to guess whether a moral judgment or a
judgment of taste is implied. Perhaps Hume is suggesting that they
are close to being the same thing.

But in his discussion of the qualities that distinguish the man of
taste, Hume stands on high and solid ground. We may disagree here
and there, as, for example, in regard to his view that the object
of poetry is "to please, by means of the passions and the imagination." Shelley and Whitman, among others, give it a different
character. But we can hardly fail to concur with Hume's requirements for "a true judge in the finer arts." He tells us that "strong
sense, united to delicate sentiment, improved by practice, perfected
by comparison, and cleared of all prejudice, can alone entitle critics
to this valuable character; and the joint verdict of such, wherever
they are to be found, is the true standard of taste and beauty."
In the two centuries or more since Hume wrote, we have hardly
bettered that judgment.

Of the Standard
of Taste

T he great variety of Taste, as well as of opinion, which prevails
in the world, is too obvious not to have fallen under every one's observation. Men of the most confined knowledge are able to remark a difference
of taste in the narrow circle of their acquaintance, even where the persons
have been educated under the same government, and have early im-
bibed the same prejudices. But those who can enlarge their view to contemplate distant nations and remote ages, are still more surprised at the
great inconsistence and contrariety. We are apt to call barbarous whatever departs widely from our own taste and apprehension; but soon find
the epithet of reproach retorted on us. And the highest arrogance and
self-conceit is at last startled, on observing an equal assurance on all sides,
and scruples, amidst such a contest of sentiment, to pronounce positively
in its own favour.

As this variety of taste is obvious to the most careless inquirer, so will
it be found, on examination, to be still greater in reality than in appearance. The sentiments of men often differ with regard to beauty and deformity of all kinds, even while their general discourse is the same. There
are certain terms in every language which import blame, and others
praise; and all men who use the same tongue must agree in their application of them. Every voice is united in applauding elegance, propriety,
simplicity, spirit in writing; and in blaming fustian, affectation, coldness,
and a false brilliancy. But when critics come to particulars, this seeming
unanimity vanishes; and it is found that they had affixed a very different
meaning to their expressions. In all matters of opinion and science, the
case is opposite; the difference among men is there oftener found to lie
in generals than in particulars, and to be less in reality than in appearance. An explanation of the terms commonly ends the controversy: and

the disputants are surprised to find that they had been quarrelling, while at bottom they agreed in their judgment.

Those who found morality on sentiment, more than on reason, are inclined to comprehend ethics under the former observation, and to maintain that, in all questions which regard conduct and manners, the difference among men is really greater than at first sight it appears. It is indeed obvious, that writers of all nations and all ages concur in applauding justice, humanity, magnanimity, prudence, veracity; and in blaming the opposite qualities. Even poets and other authors, whose compositions are chiefly calculated to please the imagination, are yet found, from Homer down to Fénelon, to inculcate the same moral precepts, and to bestow their applause and blame on the same virtues and vices. This great unanimity is usually ascribed to the influence of plain reason, which, in all these cases, maintains similar sentiments in all men, and prevents those controversies to which the abstract sciences are so much exposed. So far as the unanimity is real, this account may be admitted as satisfactory. But we must also allow that some part of the seeming harmony in morals may be accounted for from the very nature of language. The word virtue, with its equivalent in every tongue, implies praise, as that of vice does blame; and no one, without the most obvious and grossest impropriety, could affix reproach to a term, which in general acceptation is understood in a good sense: or bestow applause, where the idiom requires disapprobation. Homer's general precepts, where he delivers any such, will never be controverted; but it is obvious that, when he draws particular pictures of manners, and represents heroism in Achilles, and prudence in Ulysses, he intermixes a much greater degree of ferocity in the former, and of cunning and fraud in the latter, than Fénelon would admit of. The sage Ulysses, in the Greek poet, seems to delight in lies and fictions, and often employs them without any necessity, or even advantage. But his more scrupulous son, in the French epic writer, exposes himself to the most imminent perils, rather than depart from the most exact line of truth and veracity.

The admirers and followers of the Alcoran insist on the excellent moral precepts interspersed throughout that wild and absurd performance. But it is to be supposed, that the Arabic words, which correspond to the English, equity, justice, temperance, meekness, charity, were such as, from the constant use of that tongue, must always be taken in a good sense: and it would have argued the greatest ignorance, not of morals, but of language, to have mentioned them with any epithets, besides those of applause and approbation. But would we know, whether the pretended prophet had really attained a just sentiment of morals, let us attend to his narration, and we shall soon find, that he bestows praise on such instances of treachery, inhumanity, cruelty, revenge, bigotry, as are utterly incompatible with civilized society. No steady rule of right seems there to be attended to; and every action is blamed or praised, so far only as it is beneficial or hurtful to the true believers.

The merit of delivering true general precepts in ethics is indeed very small. Whoever recommends any moral virtues, really does no more than is implied in the terms themselves. That people who invented the word charity, and used it in a good sense, inculcated more clearly, and much more efficaciously, the precept, Be charitable, than any pretended legislator or prophet who should insert such a maxim in his writings. Of all expressions, those which, together with their other meaning, imply a degree either of blame or approbation, are the least liable to be perverted or mistaken.

It is natural for us to seek a Standard of Taste; a rule by which the various sentiments of men may be reconciled; at least a decision afforded confirming one sentiment, and condemning another.

There is a species of philosophy which cuts off all hopes of success in such an attempt, and represents the impossibility of ever attaining any standard of taste. The difference, it is said, is very wide between judgment and sentiment. All sentiment is right; because sentiment has a reference to nothing beyond itself, and is always real, wherever a man is conscious of it. But all determinations of the understanding are not right; because they have a reference to something beyond themselves, to wit, real matter of fact; and are not always conformable to that standard. Among a thousand different opinions which different men may entertain of the same subject, there is one, and but one, that is just and true: and the only difficulty is to fix and ascertain it. On the contrary, a thousand different sentiments, excited by the same object, are all right; because no sentiment represents what is really in the object. It only marks a certain conformity or relation between the object and the organs or faculties of the mind; and if that conformity did not really exist, the sentiment could never possibly have being. Beauty is no quality in things themselves: it exists merely in the mind which contemplates them; and each mind perceives a different beauty. One person may even perceive deformity, where another is sensible of beauty; and every individual ought to acquiesce in his own sentiment, without pretending to regulate those of others. To seek the real beauty, or real deformity, is as fruitless an inquiry as to pretend to ascertain the real sweet or real bitter. According to the disposition of the organs, the same object may be both sweet and bitter; and the proverb has justly determined it to be fruitless to dispute concerning tastes. It is very natural, and even quite necessary, to extend this axiom to mental, as well as bodily taste; and thus common sense, which is so often at variance with philosophy, especially with the sceptical kind, is found, in one instance at least, to agree in pronouncing the same decision.

But though this axiom, by passing into a proverb, seems to have attained the sanction of common sense, there is certainly a species of common sense which opposes it, at least serves to modify and restrain it. Whoever would assert an equality of genius and elegance between Ogilby and Milton, or Bunyan and Addison, would be thought to defend no less an extravagance, than if he had maintained a mole-hill to be as high as Tenerife, or a pond as extensive as the ocean. Though there may be found persons who give the preference to the former authors, no one pays attention to such a taste; and we pronounce, without scruple, the sentiment of these pretended critics to be absurd and ridiculous. The principle of the natural equality of tastes is then totally forgot, and while we admit it on some occasions, where the objects seem near an equality, it appears an extravagant paradox, or rather a palpable absurdity, where objects so disproportioned are compared together.

It is evident that none of the rules of composition are fixed by reasonings a priori, or can be esteemed abstract conclusions of the understanding, from comparing those habitudes and relations of ideas which are eternal and immutable. Their foundation is the same with that of all the practical sciences, experience; nor are they any thing but general observations, concerning what has been universally found to please in all countries and in all ages. Many of the beauties of poetry, and even of eloquence, are founded on falsehood and fiction, on hyperboles, metaphors, and an abuse or perversion of terms from their natural meaning. To check the sallies of the imagination, and to reduce every expression to geometrical truth and exactness, would be the most contrary to the laws of criticism; because it would produce a work, which, by universal experience, has been found the most insipid and disagreeable. But though poetry can never submit to exact truth, it must be confined by rules of art, discovered to the author either by genius or observation. If some negligent or irregular writers have pleased, they have not pleased by their transgressions of rule or order, but in spite of these transgressions: they have possessed other beauties, which were conformable to just criticism; and the force of these beauties has been able to overpower censure, and give the mind a satisfaction superior to the disgust arising from the blemishes. Ariosto pleases; but not by his monstrous and improbable fictions, by his bizarre mixture of the serious and comic styles, by the want of coherence in his stories, or by the continual interruptions of his narration. He charms by the force and clearness of his expression, by the readiness and variety of his inventions, and by his natural pictures of the passions, especially those of the gay and amorous kind: and, however his faults may diminish our satisfaction, they are not able entirely to destroy it. Did our pleasure really arise from those parts of his poem which we denominate faults, this would be no objection to criticism in general: it would only be an objection to those particular rules of criticism which would establish such circumstances to be faults, and would represent them as universally blamable. If they are found to please, they cannot be faults, let the pleasure which they produce be ever so unexpected and unaccountable.

But though all the general rules of art are founded only on experience, and on the observation of the common sentiments of human nature, we must not imagine that, on every occasion, the feelings of men will be conformable to these rules. Those finer emotions of the mind are of a very tender and delicate nature, and require the concurrence of many favourable circumstances to make them play with facility and exactness, according to their general and established principles. The least exterior hindrance to such small springs, or the least internal disorder, disturbs their motion, and confounds the operations of the whole machine. When we would make an experiment of this nature, and would try the force of any beauty or deformity, we must choose with care a proper time and place, and bring the fancy to a suitable situation and disposition. A perfect serenity of mind, a recollection of thought, a due attention to the object; if any of these circumstances be wanting, our experiment will be fallacious, and we shall be unable to judge of the catholic and universal beauty. The relation, which nature has placed between the form and the sentiment, will at least be more obscure; and it will require greater accuracy to trace and discern it. We shall be able to ascertain its influence, not so much from the operation of each particular beauty as from the durable admiration which attends those works that have survived all the caprices of mode and fashion, all the mistakes of ignorance and envy.

The same Homer who pleased at Athens and Rome two thousand years ago is still admired at Paris and at London. All the changes of climate, government, religion, and language have not been able to obscure his glory. Authority or prejudice may give a temporary vogue to a bad poet or orator; but his reputation will never be durable or general. When his compositions are examined by posterity or by foreigners, the enchantment is dissipated, and his faults appear in their true colours. On the contrary, a real genius, the longer his works endure, and the more wide they are spread, the more sincere is the admiration which he meets with. Envy and jealousy have too much place in a narrow circle; and even familiar acquaintance with his person may diminish the applause due to his performances: but when these obstructions are removed, the beauties, which are naturally fitted to excite agreeable sentiments, immediately display their energy; and while the world endures, they maintain their authority over the minds of men.

It appears, then, that amidst all the variety and caprice of taste, there are certain general principles of approbation or blame, whose influence a careful eye may trace in all operations of the mind. Some particular forms or qualities, from the original structure of the internal fabric are calculated to please, and others to displease; and if they fail of their effect in any particular instance, it is from some apparent defect or imperfection in the organ. A man in a fever would not insist on his palate as able to decide concerning flavours; nor would one affected with the jaundice pretend to give a verdict with regard to colours. In each creature there is a sound and a defective state; and the former alone can be supposed to afford us a true standard of taste and sentiment. If, in the sound state of the organ, there be an entire or a considerable uniformity of sentiment among men, we may thence derive an idea of the perfect beauty; in like manner as the appearance of objects in daylight, to the eye of a man in health, is denominated their true and real colour, even while colour is allowed to be merely a phantasm of the senses.

Many and frequent are the defects in the internal organs, which prevent or weaken the influence of those general principles, on which depends our sentiment of beauty or deformity. Though some objects, by the structure of the mind, be naturally calculated to give pleasure, it is not to be expected that in every individual the pleasure will be equally felt. Particular incidents and situations occur, which either throw a false light on the objects, or hinder the true from conveying to the imagination the proper sentiment and perception.

One obvious cause why many feel not the proper sentiment of beauty is the want of that delicacy of imagination which is requisite to convey a sensibility of those finer emotions. This delicacy every one pretends to: every one talks of it; and would reduce every kind of taste or sentiment to its standard. But as our intention in this Essay is to mingle some light of the understanding with the feelings of sentiment, it will be proper to give a more accurate definition of delicacy than has hitherto been attempted. And not to draw our philosophy from too profound a source, we shall have recourse to a noted story in *Don Quixote*.

It is with good reason, says Sancho to the squire with the great nose, that I pretend to have a judgment in wine: this is a quality hereditary in our family. Two of my kinsmen were once called to give their opinion of a hogshead, which was supposed to be excellent, being old and of a good vintage. One of them tastes it, considers it; and, after mature reflection, pronounces the wine to be good, were it not for a small taste of leather which he perceived in it. The other, after using the same precautions, gives also his verdict in favour of the wine; but with the reserve of a taste of iron, which he could easily distinguish. You cannot imagine how much they were both ridiculed for their judgment. But who laughed in the end? On emptying the hogshead, there was found at the bottom an old key with a leathern thong tied to it.

The great resemblance between mental and bodily taste will easily teach us to apply this story. Though it be certain that beauty and deformity, more than sweet and bitter, are not qualities in objects, but belong entirely to the sentiment, internal or external, it must be allowed, that there are certain qualities in objects which are fitted by nature to produce those particular feelings. Now, as these qualities may be found in a small degree, or may be mixed and confounded with each other, it often happens that the taste is not affected with such minute qualities, or is not able to distinguish all the particular flavours, amidst the disorder in which they are presented. Where the organs are so fine as to allow nothing to escape them, and at the same time so exact as to perceive every ingredient in the composition, this we call delicacy of taste, whether we employ these terms in the literal or metaphorical sense. Here then the general rules of beauty are of use, being drawn from established models, and from the observation of what pleases or displeases, when presented singly and in a high degree; and if the same qualities, in a continued composition, and in a smaller degree, affect not the organs with a sensible delight or uneasiness, we exclude the person from all pretensions to this delicacy. To produce these general rules or avowed patterns of composition is like finding the key with the leathern thong, which justified the verdict of Sancho's kinsmen, and confounded those pretended judges who had condemned them. Though the hogshead had never been emptied, the taste of the one was still equally delicate, and that of the other equally dull and languid; but it would have been more difficult to have proved the superiority of the former, to the conviction of every bystander. In like manner, though the beauties of writing had never been methodized, or reduced to general principles; though no excellent models had ever been acknowledged, the different degrees of taste would still have subsisted, and the judgment of one man been preferable to that of another; but it would not have been so easy to silence the bad critic, who might always insist upon his particular sentiment, and refuse to submit to his antagonist. But when we show him an avowed principle of art; when we illustrate this principle by examples, whose operation, from his own particular taste, he acknowledges to be conformable to the principle; when we prove that the same principle may be applied to the present case, where he did not perceive or feel its influence: he must conclude, upon the whole, that the fault lies in himself, and that he wants the delicacy which is requisite to make him sensible of every beauty and every blemish in any composition or discourse.

It is acknowledged to be the perfection of every sense or faculty, to perceive with exactness its most minute objects, and allow nothing to escape its notice and observation. The smaller the objects are which become sensible to the eye, the finer is that organ, and the more elaborate its make and composition. A good palate is not tried by strong flavours, but by a mixture of small ingredients, where we are still sensible of each part, notwithstanding its minuteness and its confusion with the rest. In like manner, a quick and acute perception of beauty and deformity must be the perfection of our mental taste; nor can a man be satisfied with himself while he suspects that any excellence or blemish in a discourse has passed him unobserved. In this case, the perfection of the man, and the perfection of the sense of feeling, are found to be united. A very delicate palate, on many occasions, may be a great inconvenience both to a man himself and to his friends. But a delicate taste of wit or beauty must always be a desirable quality, because it is the source of all the finest and most innocent enjoyments of which human nature is susceptible. In this decision the sentiments of all mankind are agreed. Wherever you can ascertain a delicacy of taste, it is sure to meet with approbation; and the best way of ascertaining it is to appeal to those models and principles which have been established by the uniform consent and experience of nations and ages.

But though there be naturally a wide difference, in point of delicacy, between one person and another, nothing tends further to increase and improve this talent, than practice in a particular art, and the frequent survey or contemplation of a particular species of beauty. When objects of any kind are first presented to the eye or imagination, the sentiment which attends them is obscure and confused; and the mind is, in a great measure, incapable of pronouncing concerning their merits or defects. The taste cannot perceive the several excellences of the performance, much less distinguish the particular character of each excellency and ascertain its quality and degree. If it pronounce the whole in general to be beautiful or deformed, it is the utmost that can be expected; and even this judgment a person so unpractised will be apt to deliver with great hesitation and reserve. But allow him to acquire experience in those objects, his feeling becomes more exact and nice: he not only perceives the beauties and defects of each part, but marks the distinguishing species of each quality, and assigns it suitable praise or blame. A clear and distinct sentiment attends him through the whole survey of the objects; and he discerns that very degree and kind of approbation or displeasure which each part is naturally fitted to produce. The mist dissipates which seemed formerly to hang over the object; the organ acquires greater perfection in its operations, and can pronounce, without danger of mistake, concerning the merits of every performance. In a word, the same address and dexterity which practice gives to the execution of any work, is also acquired by the same means in the judging of it.

So advantageous is practice to the discernment of beauty that, before we can give judgment on any work of importance, it will even be requisite that that very individual performance be more than once perused by us, and be surveyed in different lights with attention and deliberation. There is a flutter or hurry of thought which attends the first perusal of any piece, and which confounds the genuine sentiment of beauty. The relation of the parts is not discerned: the true characters of style are little distinguished. The several perfections and defects seem wrapped up in a species of confusion, and present themselves indistinctly to the imagination. Not to mention that there is a species of beauty, which, as it is florid and superficial, pleases at first, but being found incompatible with a just expression either of reason or passion, soon palls upon the taste, and is then rejected with disdain, at least rated at a much lower value.

It is impossible to continue in the practice of contemplating any order of beauty, without being frequently obliged to form comparisons between the several species and degrees of excellence, and estimating their proportion to each other. A man who has had no opportunity of comparing the different kinds of beauty is indeed totally unqualified to pronounce an opinion with regard to any object presented to him. By comparison

alone we fix the epithets of praise or blame, and learn how to assign
the due degree of each. The coarsest daubing contains a certain lustre of
colours and exactness of imitation, which are so far beauties, and would
affect the mind of a peasant or Indian with the highest admiration. The
most vulgar ballads are not entirely destitute of harmony or nature; and
none but a person familiarized to superior beauties would pronounce their
members harsh, or narration uninteresting. A great inferiority of beauty
gives pain to a person conversant in the highest excellence of the kind,
and is for that reason pronounced a deformity; as the most finished object
with which we are acquainted is naturally supposed to have reached the
pinnacle of perfection, and to be entitled to the highest applause. One
accustomed to see, and examine, and weigh the several performances,
admired in different ages and nations, can alone rate the merits of a
work exhibited to his view, and assign its proper rank among the productions of genius.

But to enable a critic the more fully to execute this undertaking, he
must preserve his mind free from all prejudice, and allow nothing to
enter into his consideration, but the very object which is submitted
to his examination. We may observe that every work of art, in order to
produce its due effect on the mind, must be surveyed in a certain point of
view, and cannot be fully relished by persons whose situation, real or
imaginary, is not conformable to that which is required by the performance. An orator addresses himself to a particular audience, and must have
a regard to their particular genius, interests, opinions, passions, and
prejudices; otherwise he hopes in vain to govern their resolutions, and
inflame their affections. Should they even have entertained some pre-
possessions against him, however unreasonable, he must not overlook
this disadvantage: but, before he enters upon the subject, must endeavour
to conciliate their affection, and acquire their good graces. A critic of a
different age or nation, who should peruse this discourse, must have all
these circumstances in his eye, and must place himself in the same situation as the audience, in order to form a true judgment of the oration.
In like manner, when any work is addressed to the public, though I
should have a friendship or enmity with the author, I must depart from
this situation, and, considering myself as a man in general, forget, if
possible, my individual being, and my peculiar circumstances. A person
influenced by prejudice complies not with this condition, but obstinately
maintains his natural position, without placing himself in that point of
view which the performance supposes. If the work be addressed to persons of a different age or nation, he makes no allowance for their

peculiar views and prejudices; but, full of the manners of his own age and country, rashly condemns what seemed admirable in the eyes of those for whom alone the discourse was calculated. If the work be executed for the public, he never sufficiently enlarges his comprehension, or forgets his interest as a friend or enemy, as a rival or commentator. By this means his sentiments are perverted; nor have the same beauties and blemishes the same influence upon him, as if he had imposed a proper violence on his imagination, and had forgotten himself for a moment. So far his taste evidently departs from the true standard, and of consequence loses all credit and authority.

It is well known that, in all questions submitted to the understanding, prejudice is destructive of sound judgment, and perverts all operations of the intellectual faculties: it is no less contrary to good taste; nor has it less influence to corrupt our sentiment of beauty. It belongs to good sense to check its influence in both cases; and in this respect, as well as in many others, reason, if not an essential part of taste, is at least requisite to the operations of this latter faculty. In all the nobler productions of genius, there is a mutual relation and correspondence of parts; nor can either the beauties or blemishes be perceived by him whose thought is not capacious enough to comprehend all those parts, and compare them with each other, in order to perceive the consistence and uniformity of the whole. Every work of art has also a certain end or purpose for which it is calculated; and is to be deemed more or less perfect, as it is more or less fitted to attain this end. The object of eloquence is to persuade, of history to instruct, of poetry to please, by means of the passions and the imagination. These ends we must carry constantly in our view when we peruse any performance; and we must be able to judge how far the means employed are adapted to their respective purposes. Besides, every kind of composition, even the most poetical, is nothing but a chain of propositions and reasonings; not always, indeed, the justest and most exact, but still plausible and specious, however disguised by the colouring of the imagination. The persons introduced in tragedy and epic poetry must be represented as reasoning, and thinking, and concluding, and acting, suitably to their character and circumstances; and without judgment, as well as taste and invention, a poet can never hope to succeed in so delicate an undertaking. Not to mention that the same excellence of faculties which contributes to the improvement of reason, the same clearness of conception, the same exactness of distinction, the same vivacity of apprehension, are essential to the operations of true taste, and are its infallible concomitants. It seldom or never happens that a man of sense, who has experience in any art, cannot judge of its beauty; and it is no less rare to meet with a man who has a just taste without a sound understanding.

Thus, though the principles of taste be universal, and nearly, if not entirely, the same in all men, yet few are qualified to give judgment on any work of art, or establish their own sentiment as the standard of beauty. The organs of internal sensation are seldom so perfect as to allow the general principles their full play, and produce a feeling correspondent to those principles. They either labour under some defect, or are vitiated by some disorder; and by that means excite a sentiment, which may be pronounced erroneous. When the critic has no delicacy, he judges without any distinction, and is only affected by the grosser and more palpable qualities of the object: the finer touches pass unnoticed and disregarded. Where he is not aided by practice, his verdict is attended with confusion and hesitation. Where no comparison has been employed, the most frivolous beauties, such as rather merit the name of defects, are the object of his admiration. Where he lies under the influence of prejudice, all his natural sentiments are perverted. Where good sense is wanting, he is not qualified to discern the beauties of design and reasoning, which are the highest and most excellent. Under some or other of these imperfections, the generality of men labour; and hence a true judge in the finer arts is observed, even during the most polished ages, to be so rare a character: strong sense, united to delicate sentiment, improved by practice, perfected by comparison, and cleared of all prejudice, can alone entitle critics to this valuable character; and the joint verdict of such, wherever they are to be found, is the true standard of taste and beauty.

But where are such critics to be found? By what marks are they to be known? How distinguish them from pretenders? These questions are embarrassing, and seem to throw us back into the same uncertainty from which, during the course of this Essay, we have endeavoured to extricate ourselves.

But if we consider the matter aright, these are questions of fact, not of sentiment. Whether any particular person be endowed with good sense and a delicate imagination, free from prejudice, may often be the subject of dispute, and be liable to great discussion and inquiry: but that such a character is valuable and estimable, will be agreed in by all mankind. Where these doubts occur, men can do no more than in other disputable questions which are submitted to the understanding: they must produce the best arguments that their invention suggests to them; they must acknowledge a true and decisive standard to exist somewhere, to wit, real existence and matter of fact; and they must have indulgence to such as differ from them in their appeals to this standard. It is sufficient for our present purpose, if we have proved that the taste of all individuals is not upon an equal footing, and that some men in general, however difficult to be particularly pitched upon, will be acknowledged by universal sentiment to have a preference above others.

But, in reality, the difficulty of finding, even in particulars, the standard of taste, is not so great as it is represented. Though in speculation we may readily avow a certain criterion in science, and deny it in sentiment, the matter is found in practice to be much more hard to ascertain in the former case than in the latter. Theories of abstract philosophy, systems of profound theology, have prevailed during one age; in a successive period these have been universally exploded, their absurdity has been detected, other theories and systems have supplied their place, which again gave place to their successors, and nothing has been experienced more liable to the revolutions of chance and fashion than these pretended decisions of science. The case is not the same with the beauties of eloquence and poetry. Just expressions of passion and nature are sure, after a little time, to gain public applause, which they maintain for ever. Aristotle and Plato and Epicurus and Descartes may successively yield to each other: but Terence and Virgil maintain an universal, undisputed empire over the minds of men. The abstract philosophy of Cicero has lost its credit: the vehemence of his oratory is still the object of our admiration.

Though men of delicate taste be rare, they are easily to be distinguished in society by the soundness of their understanding, and the superiority of their faculties above the rest of mankind. The ascendant which they acquire gives a prevalence to that lively approbation with which they receive any productions of genius, and renders it generally predominant. Many men, when left to themselves, have but a faint and dubious perception of beauty, who yet are capable of relishing any fine stroke which is pointed out to them. Every convert to the admiration of the real poet or orator is the cause of some new conversion. And though prejudices may prevail for a time, they never unite in celebrating any rival to the true genius, but yield at last to the force of nature and just sentiment. Thus, though a civilized nation may easily be mistaken in the choice of their admired philosopher, they never have been found long to err in their affection for a favourite epic or tragic author.

But notwithstanding all our endeavours to fix a standard of taste, and reconcile the discordant apprehensions of men, there still remain two sources of variation, which are not sufficient indeed to confound all the boundaries of beauty and deformity, but will often serve to produce a difference in the degrees of our approbation or blame. The one is the different humours of particular men; the other, the particular manners and opinions of our age and country. The general principles of taste are uniform in human nature: where men vary in their judgments, some defect or perversion in the faculties may commonly be remarked, proceeding either from prejudice, from want of practice, or want of delicacy: and there is just reason for approving one taste, and condemning another. But where there is such a diversity in the internal frame or external situation as is entirely blameless on both sides, and leaves no room to give one the preference above the other; in that case a certain degree of diversity in judgment is unavoidable, and we seek in vain for a standard, by which we can reconcile the contrary sentiments.

A young man, whose passions are warm, will be more sensibly touched with amorous and tender images than a man more advanced in years, who takes pleasure in wise, philosophical reflections, concerning the conduct of life, and moderation of the passions. At twenty, Ovid may be the favourite author, Horace at forty, and perhaps Tacitus at fifty. Vainly would we, in such cases, endeavour to enter into the sentiments of others, and divest ourselves of those propensities which are natural to us. We choose our favourite author as we do our friend, from a conformity of humour and disposition. Mirth or passion, sentiment or reflection, whichever of these most predominates in our temper, it gives us a peculiar sympathy with the writer who resembles us.

One person is more pleased with the sublime, another with the tender, a third with raillery. One has a strong sensibility to blemishes, and is extremely studious of correctness; another has a more lively feeling of beauties, and pardons twenty absurdities and defects for one elevated or pathetic stroke. The ear of this man is entirely turned towards conciseness and energy; that man is delighted with a copious, rich, and harmonious expression. Simplicity is affected by one; ornament by another. Comedy, tragedy, satire, odes, have each its partisans, who prefer that particular species of writing to all others. It is plainly an error in a critic, to confine his approbation to one species or style of writing, and condemn all the rest. But it is almost impossible not to feel a predilection for that which suits our particular turn and disposition. Such performances are innocent and unavoidable, and can never reasonably be the object of dispute, because there is no standard by which they can be decided.

For a like reason, we are more pleased, in the course of our reading, with pictures and characters that resemble objects which are found in our own age and country, than with those which describe a different set of customs. It is not without some effort that we reconcile ourselves to the simplicity of ancient manners, and behold princesses carrying water from the spring, and kings and heroes dressing their own victuals. We may allow in general, that the representation of such manners is no fault in the author, nor deformity in the piece; but we are not so sensibly touched with them. For this reason, comedy is not easily transferred from one age or nation to another. A Frenchman or Englishman is not pleased with the *Andria* of Terence, or *Clizia* of Machiavelli; where the fine lady, upon whom all the play turns, never once appears to the spectators, but is always kept behind the scenes, suitably to the reserved humour of the ancient Greeks and modern Italians. A man of learning and reflection can make allowance for these peculiarities of manners; but a common audience can never divest themselves so far of their usual ideas and sentiments as to relish pictures which nowise resemble them.

But here there occurs a reflection, which may, perhaps, be useful in examining the celebrated controversy concerning ancient and modern learning; where we often find the one side excusing any seeming absurdity in the ancients from the manners of the age, and the other refusing to admit this excuse, or at least admitting it only as an apology for the author, not for the performance. In my opinion, the proper boundaries in this subject have seldom been fixed between the contending parties. Where any innocent peculiarities of manners are represented, such as those above mentioned, they ought certainly to be admitted; and a man who is shocked with them gives an evident proof of false delicacy and refinement. The poet's "monument more durable than brass," must fall to the ground like common brick or clay, were men to make no allowance for the continual revolutions of manners and customs, and would admit of nothing but what was suitable to the prevailing fashion. Must we throw aside the pictures of our ancestors, because of their ruffs and farthingales? But where the ideas of morality and decency alter from one age to another, and where vicious manners are described, without being marked with the proper characters of blame and disapprobation, this must be allowed to disfigure the poem, and to be a real deformity. I cannot, nor is it proper I should, enter into such sentiments; and however I may excuse the poet, on account of the manners of his age, I can never relish the composition. The want of humanity and of decency, so conspicuous in the characters drawn by several of the ancient poets, even sometimes by Homer and the Greek tragedians, diminishes considerably the merit of their noble performances, and gives modern authors an advantage over them. We are not interested in the fortunes and sentiments of such rough heroes; we are displeased to find the limits of vice and virtue so much confounded; and whatever indulgence we may give to the writer on account of his prejudices, we cannot prevail on ourselves to enter into his sentiments, or bear an affection to characters which we plainly discover to be blamable.

The case is not the same with moral principles as with speculative opinions of any kind. These are in continual flux and revolution. The son embraces a different system from the father. Nay, there scarcely is any man who can boast of great constancy and uniformity in this particular. Whatever speculative errors may be found in the polite writings of any age or country, they detract but little from the value of those compositions. There needs but a certain turn of thought or imagination to make us enter into all the opinions which then prevailed, and relish the sentiments or conclusions derived from them. But a very violent effort is requisite to change our judgment of manners, and excite sentiments of approbation or blame, love or hatred, different from those to which the mind, from long custom, has been familiarized. And where a man is confident of the rectitude of that moral standard by which he judges, he is justly jealous of it, and will not pervert the sentiments of his heart for a moment in complaisance to any writer whatsoever.

Of all speculative errors, those which regard religion are the most excusable in compositions of genius; nor is it ever permitted to judge of the civility or wisdom of any people, or even of single persons, by the grossness or refinement of their theological principles. The same good sense that directs men in the ordinary occurrences of life is not hearkened to in religious matters, which are supposed to be placed altogether above the cognizance of human reason. On this account, all the absurdities of the pagan system of theology must be overlooked by every critic who would pretend to form a just notion of ancient poetry; and our posterity, in their turn, must have the same indulgence to their forefathers. No religious principles can ever be imputed as a fault to any poet while they remain merely principles, and take not such strong possession of his heart as to lay him under the imputation of bigotry or superstition. Where that happens, they confound the sentiments of morality, and alter the natural boundaries of vice and virtue. They are therefore eternal blemishes, according to the principle above mentioned; nor are the prejudices and false opinions of the age sufficient to justify them.

It is essential to the Roman Catholic religion to inspire a violent hatred of every other worship, and to represent all pagans, Mohammedans, and heretics as the objects of divine wrath and vengeance. Such sentiments, though they are in reality very blamable, are considered as virtues by the zealots of that communion, and are represented in their tragedies and epic poems as a kind of divine heroism. This bigotry has disfigured two very fine tragedies of the French theatre, *Polyeucte* and *Athalie;* where an intemperate zeal for particular modes of worship is set off with all the pomp imaginable, and forms the predominant character of the heroes. "What is this," says the sublime Joad to Josabeth, finding her in discourse with Mathan the priest of Baal, "Does the daughter of David speak to this traitor? Are you not afraid lest the earth should open, and pour forth flames to devour you both? Or lest these holy walls should fall and crush you together? What is his purpose? Why comes that enemy of God hither to poison the air, which we breathe, with his horrid presence?" Such sentiments are received with great applause on the theatre of Paris; but at London the spectators would be full as much pleased to hear Achilles tell Agamemnon that he was a dog in his forehead, and a deer in his heart; or Jupiter threaten Juno with a sound drubbing, if she will not be quiet.

Religious principles are also a blemish in any polite composition, when they rise up to superstition, and intrude themselves into every sentiment, however remote from any connection with religion. It is no excuse for the poet that the customs of his country had burdened life with so many religious ceremonies and observances, that no part of it was exempt from that yoke. It must for ever be ridiculous in Petrarch to compare his mistress, Laura, to Jesus Christ. Nor is it less ridiculous in that agreeable libertine, Boccaccio, very seriously to give thanks to God Almighty and the ladies, for their assistance in defending him against his enemies.

---

*"Of the Standard of Taste" is from a collection
of Hume's essays entitled*
ESSAYS MORAL, POLITICAL AND LITERARY.

Arthur Schopenhauer

1788–1860

Arthur Schopenhauer was born in Danzig on February 22, 1788. His father, Heinrich, was a well-to-do merchant who had strongly liberal political opinions and broad cultural interests. His mother, Johanna, was a very intelligent woman and a successful novelist. Heinrich Schopenhauer's dislike of authoritarian government caused him to move the family to Hamburg in 1793 when Danzig surrendered to Prussia.

At an early age young Arthur's exceptional intelligence became evident. He studied at Hamburg, and in England and France, and then went into business at Hamburg. After his father's sudden death, probably by suicide, in 1805, Arthur took up his studies again, concentrating on classical literature, medicine, and philosophy. At the University of Berlin, from 1811 to 1813, he attended lectures by J. G. Fichte, of whose philosophy he became very scornful. He determined to work out his own philosophy, taking off from the ideas of Immanuel Kant.

Schopenhauer's doctoral thesis, *On the Fourfold Root of the Principle of Sufficient Reason*, was published in 1813. He went to live with his mother in Weimar, where, in her salon, he met many stimulating thinkers, including Goethe.

After a quarrel with his mother, Schopenhauer left Weimar for

Notes from the artist: "Schopenhauer as a young man together with a porcupine, illustrating the quotation from Parerga und Paralipomena, *a remarkably modern parable of coexistence."*

Arthur Schopenhauer.

A company of porcupines crowded themselves very
close together one cold winter's day so as to profit by one another's warmth and so save themselves from being frozen to
death. But soon they felt one another's quills, which induced
them to separate again. And now, when the need for warmth
brought them nearer together again, the second evil arose once
more. So that they were driven backwards and forwards from
one trouble to the other, until they had discovered a mean distance at which they could most tolerably exist.

Dresden in 1814. There he wrote his major work, *The World as Will and Idea*. He expected that this would be immediately accepted as an important, even revolutionary, philosophical work, but what little attention it attracted was unfavorable.

Schopenhauer began lecturing at the University of Berlin in 1820, but here too he failed. Hegel was the most highly thought of philosopher in Berlin at the time, and Schopenhauer's outspoken scorn for him was unpopular. From 1822 to 1831 Schopenhauer went from Italy to Munich and back to Berlin, traveling and living in isolation, a sick and resentful man. Finally, in 1831, he settled in Frankfurt-am-Main, where he lived in bitter solitude, continuing his attack on Hegel in occasional essays.

The apparent pessimism of Schopenhauer's philosophy—based on the idea that will is the foundation of the universe and that will is basically evil—was out of tune with his time. By 1850, however, the world mood had altered somewhat and Schopenhauer began to acquire some fame, especially in England, Russia, and the United States. He died at Frankfurt on September 21, 1860.

There is one aspect of Schopenhauer's personality and writing that most often comes to mind whenever his name is mentioned—his pessimism. It is difficult, however, if not dangerous, to accept such pigeonholing of so complex a person as Schopenhauer. His "pessimism" may be only a matter of point of view. His philosophy admits no possibility of free will. We cannot hope to improve our lot by our own efforts because we have no control over events—that is the province of Will. What we can hope for is not progress but quiet. This may appear a dismal state. But E. F. J. Payne, a translator of Schopenhauer, suggests in an introduction that it is no more pessimistic than the teachings of Brahmanism, Buddhism, and Christianity, which preach that the highest goal is the deliverance from earthly existence. Nietzsche, in an essay about Schopenhauer, goes even further and suggests that the philosopher is actually "joyful" for having faced a somber truth squarely and conquered it.

There is one point, however, on which all readers of Schopenhauer agree, whether or not they find his philosophy congenial. He is a fine writer. The clear beauty of his style makes his work a pleasure to read.

Like many good workmen, Schopenhauer is impatient with people who abuse his craft. He is as irked as Virginia Woolf with mediocre writing, but he does not use her ladylike restraint in expressing his impatience. In *On Style* he dismisses Fichte and the Hegelians as "miserable dunces." Their complicated style, he says, is only a cover-up for paucity of ideas.

This outspoken, often angry, frankness works on us sometimes as a sudden bang does on a person dropping off to sleep. It startles us to a sharp awareness, sometimes to agree with him, sometimes to argue.

Schopenhauer uses his shock tactics to good advantage in *On Some Forms of Literature*. From the first arbitrary statement that drama is the most perfect reflection of human existence, we know that we are reading a man who has strong opinions and does not hesitate to state them boldly. About the novel he says that insight, not incident, is the important thing. "The business of the novelist," he says, "is not to relate great events, but to make small ones interesting." He lists the four greatest novels. It is interesting to guess what his opinion would be of contemporary novelists. Using his own criteria, would he approve, for example, of Mann, Gide, Joyce, and Virginia Woolf? Would he disapprove of Hemingway?

Dealing a sarcastic blow at conventional historians—"History has always been the favorite study of those who wish to learn something without having to face the effort demanded by any branch of real knowledge, which taxes the intelligence"—he goes on to describe the acceptable historian. After a few additional shocks to complacency, Schopenhauer concludes that "a high degree of culture leads us to seek entertainment almost wholly from books and not from men."

On the Comparative Place of Interest and Beauty in Works of Art has fewer bald statements of opinion presented as inarguable fact, but just as many stimulating ideas. By getting our agreement to a series of carefully reasoned premises, Schopenhauer brings us, as Plato does, to agree in conclusion to a proposition about which we might have argued in the beginning.

On Style

Style is the physiognomy of the mind, and a safer index to character than the face. To imitate another man's style is like wearing a mask, which, be it never so fine, is not long in arousing disgust and abhorrence, because it is lifeless; so that even the ugliest living face is better. Hence those who write in Latin and copy the manner of ancient authors may be said to speak through a mask; the reader, it is true, hears what they say, but he cannot observe their physiognomy too; he cannot see their *style*. With the Latin works of writers who think for themselves, the case is different, and their style is visible; writers, I mean, who have not condescended to any sort of imitation, such as Scotus Erigena, Petrarch, Bacon, Descartes, Spinoza, and many others. An affectation in style is like making grimaces. Further, the language in which a man writes is the physiognomy of the nation to which he belongs; and here there are many hard and fast differences, beginning from the language of the Greeks down to that of the Caribbean islanders.

To form a provincial estimate of the value of a writer's productions, it is not directly necessary to know the subject on which he has thought, or what it is that he has said about it; that would imply a perusal of all his works. It will be enough, in the main, to know *how* he has thought. This, which means the essential temper or general quality of his mind, may be precisely determined by his style. A man's style shows the formal nature of all his thoughts—the formal nature which can never change, be the subject or the character of his thoughts what it may: it is, as it were, the dough out of which all the contents of his mind are kneaded. When Eulenspiegel was asked how long it would take to walk to the next village, he gave the seemingly incongruous answer: *Walk*. He wanted to find out by the man's pace the distance he would cover in a given time. In the same way, when I have read a few pages of an author, I know fairly well how far he can bring me.

Every mediocre writer tries to mask his own natural style, because in his heart he knows the truth of what I am saying. He is thus forced, at the outset, to give up any attempt at being frank or naïve—a privilege which is thereby reserved for superior minds, conscious of their own worth, and therefore sure of themselves. What I mean is that these everyday writers are absolutely unable to resolve upon writing just as they think; because they have a notion that, were they to do so, their work might possibly look very childish and simple. For all that, it would not be without its value. If they would only go honestly to work, and say, quite simply, the things they have really thought, and just as they have thought them, these writers would be readable and, within their own proper sphere, even instructive.

But instead of that, they try to make the reader believe that their thoughts have gone much further and deeper than is really the case. They say what they have to say in long sentences that wind about in a forced and unnatural way; they coin new words and write prolix periods which go round and round the thought and wrap it up in a sort of disguise. They tremble between the two separate aims of communicating what they want to say and of concealing it. Their object is to dress it up so that it may look learned or deep, in order to give people the impression that there is very much more in it than for the moment meets the eye. They either jot down their thoughts bit by bit, in short, ambiguous, and paradoxical sentences, which apparently mean much more than they say—of this kind of writing Schelling's treatises on natural philosophy are a splendid instance; or else they hold forth with a deluge of words and the most intolerable diffusiveness, as though no end of fuss were necessary to make the reader understand the deep meaning of their sentences, whereas it is some quite simple if not actually trivial idea, examples of which may be found in plenty in the popular works of Fichte, and the philosophical manuals of a hundred other miserable dunces not worth mentioning; or, again, they try to write in some particular style which they have been pleased to take up and think very grand, a style, for example, par excellence profound and scientific, where the reader is tormented to death by the narcotic effect of long-spun periods without a single idea in them—such as are furnished in a special measure by those most impudent of all mortals, the Hegelians; or it may be that it is an intellectual style they have striven after, where it seems as though their object were to go crazy altogether; and so on in many other cases. All these endeavors to put off the *nascetur ridiculus mus* [birth of a ridiculous mouse born of the mountains' labor]—to avoid showing the funny little creature that is born after such mighty throes—often make it difficult to know what it is that they really mean. And then, too, they write down words, nay, even whole sentences, without attaching any meaning to them themselves, but in the hope that someone else will get sense out of them.

And what is at the bottom of all this? Nothing but the untiring effort to sell words for thoughts; a mode of merchandise that is always trying to make fresh openings for itself, and by means of odd expressions, turns of phrase, and combinations of every sort, whether new or used in a new sense, to produce the appearance of intellect in order to make up for the very painfully felt lack of it.

It is amusing to see how writers with this object in view will attempt first one mannerism and then another, as though they were putting on the mask of intellect! This mask may possibly deceive the inexperienced for a while, until it is seen to be a dead thing, with no life in it at all; it is then laughed at and exchanged for another. Such an author will at one moment write in a dithyrambic vein, as though he were tipsy; at another, nay, on the very next page, he will be pompous, severe, profoundly learned and prolix, stumbling on in the most cumbrous way and chopping up everything very small; like the late Christian Wolf, only in a modern dress. Longest of all lasts the mask of unintelligibility; but this is only in Germany, whither it was introduced by Fichte, perfected by Schelling, and carried to its highest pitch in Hegel—always with the best results.

And yet nothing is easier than to write so that no one can understand; just as contrarily, nothing is more difficult than to express deep things in such a way that everyone must necessarily grasp them. All the arts and tricks I have been mentioning are rendered superfluous if the author really has any brains; for that allows him to show himself as he is, and confirms to all time Horace's maxim that good sense is the source and origin of good style:

Scribendi recte sapere est et principium et fons.

[Wisdom is the beginning and source of good writing.]

But those authors I have named are like certain workers in metal, who try a hundred different compounds to take the place of gold—the only metal which can never have any substitute. Rather than do that, there is nothing against which a writer should be more upon his guard than the manifest endeavor to exhibit more intellect than he really has; because this makes the reader suspect that he possesses very little; since it is always the case that if a man affects anything, whatever it may be, it is just there that he is deficient.

That is why it is praise to an author to say that he is naïve; it means that he need not shrink from showing himself as he is. Generally speaking, to be naïve is to be attractive; while lack of naturalness is everywhere repulsive. As a matter of fact, we find that every really great writer tries to express his thoughts as purely, clearly, definitely and shortly as possible. Simplicity has always been held to be a mark of truth; it is also a mark of genius. Style receives its beauty from the thought it expresses; but with sham-thinkers the thoughts are supposed to be fine because of the style. Style is nothing but the mere silhouette of thought; and an obscure or bad style means a dull or confused brain.

The first rule, then, for a good style is that *the author should have something to say;* nay, this is in itself almost all that is necessary. Ah, how much it means! The neglect of this rule is a fundamental trait in the philosophical writing, and, in fact, in all the reflective literature, of my country, more especially since Fichte. These writers all let it be seen that they want to appear as though they had something to say; whereas they have nothing to say. Writing of this kind was brought in by the pseudo-philosophers at the Universities, and now it is current everywhere, even among the first literary notabilities of the age. It is the mother of that strained and vague style, where there seem to be two or even more meanings in the sentence; also of that prolix and cumbrous manner of expression, called *le style empesé;* again, of that mere waste of words which consists in pouring them out like a flood; finally, of that trick of concealing the direst poverty of thought under a farrago of never-ending chatter, which clacks away like a windmill and quite stupefies one—stuff which a man may read for hours together without getting hold of a single clearly expressed and definite idea. However, people are easygoing, and they have formed the habit of reading page upon page of all sorts of such verbiage, without having any particular idea of what the author really means. They fancy it is all as it should be, and fail to discover that he is writing simply for writing's sake.

On the other hand, a good author, fertile in ideas, soon wins his reader's confidence that, when he writes, he has really and truly *something to say;* and this gives the intelligent reader patience to follow him with attention. Such an author, just because he really has something to say, will never fail to express himself in the simplest and most straightforward manner; because his object is to awake the very same thought in the reader that he has in himself, and no other. So he will be able to af-

firm with Boileau that his thoughts are everywhere open to the light of
the day, and that his verse always says something, whether it says it well
or ill:

> *Ma pensée au grand jour partout s'offre et s'expose,*
> *Et mon vers, bien ou mal, dit toujours quelque chose:*

while of the writers previously described it may be asserted, in the words
of the same poet, that they talk much and never say anything at all—*qui
parlant beaucoup ne disent jamais rien.*

Another characteristic of such writers is that they always avoid a positive assertion wherever they can possibly do so, in order to leave a loop-
hole for escape in case of need. Hence they never fail to choose the more
abstract way of expressing themselves; whereas intelligent people use
the more *concrete*, because the latter brings things more within the
range of actual demonstration, which is the source of all evidence.

There are many examples proving this preference for abstract expression; and a particularly ridiculous one is afforded by the use of the verb
to condition in the sense of *to cause* or *to produce*. People say *to condition something* instead of *to cause it,* because being abstract and indefinite
it says less; it affirms that A cannot happen without B, instead of that A
is caused by B. A back door is always left open; and this suits people
whose secret knowledge of their own incapacity inspires them with a
perpetual terror of all positive assertion; while with other people it is
merely the effect of that tendency by which everything that is stupid in
literature or bad in life is immediately imitated—a fact proved in either
case by the rapid way in which it spreads. The Englishman uses his own
judgment in what he writes as well as in what he does; but there is no
nation of which this eulogy is less true than of the Germans. The consequence of this state of things is that the word *cause* has of late almost
disappeared from the language of literature, and people talk only of *condition.* The fact is worth mentioning because it is so characteristically
ridiculous.

The very fact that these commonplace authors are never more than
half-conscious when they write would be enough to account for their dullness of mind and the tedious things they produce. I say they are only half-
conscious, because they really do not themselves understand the meaning
of the words they use: they take words ready-made and commit them to
memory. Hence when they write, it is not so much words as whole phrases
that they put together—*phrases banales.* This is the explanation of that
palpable lack of clearly expressed thought in what they say. The fact is

that they do not possess the die to give this stamp to their writing;
clear thought of their own is just what they have not got. And what do
we find in its place?—a vague, enigmatical intermixture of words, current
phrases, hackneyed terms, and fashionable expressions. The result is that
the foggy stuff they write is like a page printed with very old type.

On the other hand, an intelligent author really speaks to us when he
writes, and that is why he is able to rouse our interest and commune with
us. It is the intelligent author alone who puts individual words together
with a full consciousness of their meaning, and chooses them with deliberate design. Consequently, his discourse stands to that of the writer described above, much as a picture that has been really painted, to one that
has been produced by the use of a stencil. In the one case, every word,
every touch of the brush, has a special purpose; in the other, all is done
mechanically. The same distinction may be observed in music. For just as
Lichtenberg says that Garrick's soul seemed to be in every muscle in his
body, so it is the omnipresence of intellect that always and everywhere
characterizes the work of genius.

I have alluded to the tediousness which marks the works of these writers, and in this connection it is to be observed, generally, that tediousnes
is of two kinds: objective and subjective. A work is objectively tediou
when it contains the defect in question; that is to say, when its author ha
no perfectly clear thought or knowledge to communicate. For if a ma
has any clear thought or knowledge in him, his aim will be to commun
cate it, and he will direct his energies to this end; so that the ideas he fu
nishes are everywhere clearly expressed. The result is that he is neith
diffuse, nor unmeaning, nor confused, and consequently not tedious.
such a case, even though the author is at bottom in error, the error is
any rate clearly worked out and well thought over, so that it is at lea
formally correct; and thus some value always attaches to the work. But f
the same reason a work that is objectively tedious is at all times devc
of any value whatever.

The other kind of tediousness is only relative: a reader may find a wc
dull because he has no interest in the question treated of in it, and t
means that his intellect is restricted. The best work may, therefore,
tedious subjectively, tedious, I mean, to this or that particular person; j
as, contrarily, the worst work may be subjectively engrossing to this
that particular person who has an interest in the question treated of, oi
the writer of the book.

It would generally serve writers in good stead if they would see tl
while a man should, if possible, think like a great genius, he should t

the same language as everyone else. Authors should use common words to say uncommon things. But they do just the opposite. We find them trying to wrap up trivial ideas in grand words, and to clothe their very ordinary thoughts in the most extraordinary phrases, the most farfetched, unnatural, and out-of-the-way expressions. Their sentences perpetually stalk about on stilts. They take so much pleasure in bombast, and write in such a high-flown, bloated, affected, hyperbolical and acrobatic style that their prototype is Ancient Pistol, whom his friend Falstaff once impatiently told to say what he had to say like a man of this world.[1]

There is no expression in any other language exactly answering to the French *style empesé;* but the thing itself exists all the more often. When associated with affectation, it is in literature what assumption of dignity, grand airs and primness are in society, and equally intolerable. Dullness of mind is fond of donning this dress; just as in ordinary life it is stupid people who like being demure and formal.

An author who writes in the prim style resembles a man who dresses himself up in order to avoid being confounded or put on the same level with a mob——a risk never run by the gentleman, even in his worst clothes. The plebeian may be known by a certain showiness of attire and a wish to have everything spick-and-span; and in the same way, the commonplace person is betrayed by his style.

Nevertheless, an author follows a false aim if he tries to write exactly as he speaks. There is no style of writing but should have a certain trace of kinship with the epigraphic or monumental style, which is, indeed, the ancestor of all styles. For an author to write as he speaks is just as reprehensible as the opposite fault, to speak as he writes; for this gives a pedantic effect to what he says, and at the same time makes him hardly intelligible.

An obscure and vague manner of expression is always and everywhere a very bad sign. In ninety-nine cases out of a hundred it comes from vagueness of thought; and this again almost always means that there is something radically wrong and incongruous about the thought itself—in a word, that it is incorrect. When a right thought springs up in the mind, it strives after expression and is not long in reaching it, for clear thought easily finds words to fit it. If a man is capable of thinking anything at all, he is also always able to express it in clear, intelligible, and unambiguous terms. Those writers who construct difficult, obscure, involved,

---

1. *King Henry IV,* Part II, Act v, Sc. 3. [See *Great Books of the Western World,* Vol. 26, p. 500 (Ed.).]

and equivocal sentences most certainly do not know aright what it is that they want to say: they have only a dull consciousness of it, which is still in the stage of struggle to shape itself as thought. Often, indeed, their desire is to conceal from themselves and others that they really have nothing at all to say. They wish to appear to know what they do not know, to think what they do not think, to say what they do not say. If a man has some real communication to make, which will he choose—an indistinct or a clear way of expressing himself? Even Quintilian remarks that things which are said by a highly educated man are often easier to understand and much clearer; and that the less educated a man is, the more obscurely he will write—*plerumque accidit ut faciliora sint ad intelligendum et lucidiora multo quae a doctissimo quoque dicuntur . . . . Erit ergo etiam obscurior quo quisque deterior.*

An author should avoid enigmatical phrases; he should know whether he wants to say a thing or does not want to say it. It is this indecision of style that makes so many writers insipid. The only case that offers an exception to this rule arises when it is necessary to make a remark that is in some way improper.

As exaggeration generally produces an effect the opposite of that aimed at, so words, it is true, serve to make thought intelligible—but only up to a certain point. If words are heaped up beyond it, the thought becomes more and more obscure again. To find where the point lies is the problem of style, and the business of the critical faculty; for a word too much always defeats its purpose. This is what Voltaire means when he says that *the adjective is the enemy of the substantive.* But, as we have seen, many people try to conceal their poverty of thought under a flood of verbiage.

Accordingly let all redundancy be avoided, all stringing together of remarks which have no meaning and are not worth perusal. A writer must make a sparing use of the reader's time, patience and attention, so as to lead him to believe that his author writes what is worth careful study, and will reward the time spent upon it. It is always better to omit something good than to add that which is not worth saying at all. This is the right application of Hesiod's maxim, *pleon hemisy pantos* [2]—the half is more than the whole. *Le secret pour être ennuyeux, c'est de tout dire* [The secret of being tedious is to tell everything]. Therefore, if possible, the quintessence only! Mere leading thoughts! Nothing that the reader would

---

2. *Works and Days*, 40.

think for himself. To use many words to communicate few thoughts is everywhere the unmistakable sign of mediocrity. To gather much thought into few words stamps the man of genius.

Truth is most beautiful undraped; and the impression it makes is deep in proportion as its expression has been simple. This is so partly because it then takes unobstructed possession of the hearer's whole soul, and leaves him no by-thought to distract him; partly, also, because he feels that here he is not being corrupted or cheated by the arts of rhetoric, but that all the effect of what is said comes from the thing itself. For instance, what declamation on the vanity of human existence could ever be more telling than the words of Job? "Man that is born of a woman hath but a short time to live and is full of misery. He cometh up, and is cut down, like a flower; he fleeth as it were a shadow, and never continueth in one stay."

For the same reason Goethe's naïve poetry is incomparably greater than Schiller's rhetoric. It is this, again, that makes many popular songs so affecting. As in architecture an excess of decoration is to be avoided, so in the art of literature a writer must guard against all rhetorical finery, all useless amplification, and all superfluity of expression in general; in a word, he must strive after chastity of style. Every word that can be spared is hurtful if it remains. The law of simplicity and naïveté holds good of all fine art, for it is quite possible to be at once simple and sublime.

True brevity of expression consists in everywhere saying only what is worth saying, and in avoiding tedious detail about things which everyone can supply for himself. This involves correct discrimination between what is necessary and what is superfluous. A writer should never be brief at the expense of being clear, to say nothing of being grammatical. It shows lamentable want of judgment to weaken the expression of a thought, or to stunt the meaning of a period, for the sake of using a few words less. But this is the precise endeavor of that false brevity nowadays so much in vogue, which proceeds by leaving out useful words and even by sacrificing grammar and logic. It is not only that such writers spare a word by making a single verb or adjective do duty for several different periods, so that the reader, as it were, has to grope his way through them in the dark; they also practice, in many other respects, an unseeming economy of speech in the effort to effect what they foolishly take to be brevity of expression and conciseness of style. By omitting something that might have thrown a light over the whole sentence, they turn it into a conundrum, which the reader tries to solve by going over it again and again.

It is wealth and weight of thought, and nothing else, that gives brevity to style, and makes it concise and pregnant. If a writer's ideas are important, luminous, and generally worth communicating, they will necessarily furnish matter and substance enough to fill out the periods which give them expression, and make these in all their parts both grammatically and verbally complete; and so much will this be the case that no one will ever find them hollow, empty or feeble. The diction will everywhere be brief and pregnant, and allow the thought to find intelligible and easy expression, and even unfold and move about with grace.

Therefore instead of contracting his words and forms of speech, let a writer enlarge his thoughts. If a man has been thinned by illness and finds his clothes too big, it is not by cutting them down but by recovering his usual bodily condition that he ought to make them fit him again.

Let me here mention an error of style, very prevalent nowadays, and, in the degraded state of literature and the neglect of ancient languages, always on the increase; I mean *subjectivity*. A writer commits this error when he thinks it enough if he himself knows what he means and wants to say, and takes no thought for the reader, who is left to get at the bottom of it as best he can. This is as though the author were holding a monologue, whereas, it ought to be a dialogue; and a dialogue, too, in which he must express himself all the more clearly inasmuch as he cannot hear the questions of his interlocutor.

Style should for this very reason never be subjective, but *objective;* and it will not be objective unless the words are so set down that they directly force the reader to think precisely the same thing as the author thought when he wrote them. Nor will this result be obtained unless the author has always been careful to remember that thought so far follows the law of gravity that it travels from head to paper much more easily than from paper to head; so that he must assist the latter passage by every means in his power. If he does this, a writer's words will have a purely objective effect, like that of a finished picture in oils; while the subjective style is not much more certain in its working than spots on the wall, which look like figures only to one whose phantasy has been accidentally aroused by them; other people see nothing but spots and blurs. The difference in question applies to literary method as a whole; but it is often established also in particular instances. For example, in a recently published work I found the following sentence: "I have not written in order to increase the number of existing books." This means just the opposite of what the writer wanted to say, and is nonsense as well.

He who writes carelessly confesses thereby at the very outset that he does not attach much importance to his own thoughts. For it is only where a man is convinced of the truth and importance of his thoughts that he feels the enthusiasm necessary for an untiring and assiduous effort to find the clearest, finest, and strongest expression for them, just as for sacred relics or priceless works of art there are provided silver or golden receptacles. It was this feeling that led ancient authors, whose thoughts, expressed in their own words, have lived thousands of years, and therefore bear the honored title of *classics*, always to write with care. Plato, indeed, is said to have written the introduction to his *Republic* seven times over in different ways.[3]

As neglect of dress betrays want of respect for the company a man meets, so a hasty, careless, bad style shows an outrageous lack of regard for the reader, who then rightly punishes it by refusing to read the book. It is especially amusing to see reviewers criticizing the works of others in their own most careless style—the style of a hireling. It is as though a judge were to come into court in dressing gown and slippers! If I see a man badly and dirtily dressed, I feel some hesitation, at first, in entering into conversation with him; and when, on taking up a book, I am struck at once by the negligence of its style, I put it away.

Good writing should be governed by the rule that a man can think only one thing clearly at a time; and, therefore, that he should not be expected to think two or even more things in one and the same moment. But this is what is done when a writer breaks up his principal sentence into little pieces for the purpose of pushing into the gaps thus made two or three other thoughts by way of parenthesis, thereby unnecessarily and wantonly confusing the reader. And here it is again my own countrymen who are chiefly at fault. That German lends itself to this way of writing makes the thing possible, but does not justify it. No prose reads more easily or pleasantly than French, because, as a rule, it is free from the error in question. The Frenchman strings his thoughts together, as far as he can, in the most logical and natural order, and so lays them before his reader one after the other for convenient deliberation, so that every one of them may receive undivided attention. The German, on the other hand, weaves them together into a sentence which he twists and crosses, and crosses and twists again; because he wants to say six things all at once, instead of advancing them one by one. His aim should be to attract and hold the reader's attention; but, above and beyond neglect of this aim, he demands from the reader that he shall set the above-mentioned rule at defiance, and think three or four different thoughts at one and the same time; or since that is

---

3. *Translator's Note.*—It is a fact worth mentioning that the first twelve words of the *Republic* are placed in the exact order which would be natural in English.

impossible, that his thoughts shall succeed each other as quickly as the vibrations of a cord. In this way an author lays the foundation of his *style empesé,* which is then carried to perfection by the use of high-flown, pompous expressions to communicate the simplest things, and other artifices of the same kind.

In those long sentences rich in involved parenthesis, like a box of boxes one within another, and padded out like roast geese stuffed with apples, it is really the memory that is chiefly taxed; while it is the understanding and the judgment which should be called into play, instead of having their activity thereby actually hindered and weakened. This kind of sentence furnishes the reader with mere half-phrases, which he is then called upon to collect carefully and store up in his memory, as though they were the pieces of a torn letter, afterwards to be completed and made sense of by the other halves to which they respectively belong. He is expected to go on reading for a little without exercising any thought, nay, exerting only his memory, in the hope that, when he comes to the end of the sentence, he may see its meaning and so receive something to think about; and he is thus given a great deal to learn by heart before obtaining anything to understand. This is manifestly wrong and an abuse of the reader's patience.

The ordinary writer has an unmistakable preference for this style, because it causes the reader to spend time and trouble in understanding that which he would have understood in a moment without it; and this makes it look as though the writer had more depth and intelligence than the reader. This is, indeed, one of those artifices referred to above, by means of which mediocre authors unconsciously, and as it were by instinct, strive to conceal their poverty of thought and give an appearance of the opposite. Their ingenuity in this respect is really astounding.

It is manifestly against all sound reason to put one thought obliquely on top of another, as though both together formed a wooden cross. But this is what is done where a writer interrupts what he has begun to say for the purpose of inserting some quite alien matter, thus depositing with the reader a meaningless half-sentence, and bidding him keep it until the completion comes. It is much as though a man were to treat his guests by handing them an empty plate in the hope of something appearing upon it. And commas used for a similar purpose belong to the same family as notes at the foot of the page and parenthesis in the middle of the text; nay, all three differ only in degree. If Demosthenes and Cicero occasionally inserted words by ways of parenthesis, they would have done better to have refrained.

But this style of writing becomes the height of absurdity when the parenthesis are not even fitted into the frame of the sentence but wedged in so as directly to shatter it. If, for instance, it is an impertinent thing to interrupt another person when he is speaking, it is no less impertinent to interrupt oneself. But all bad, careless, and hasty authors, who scribble with the bread actually before their eyes, use this style of writing six times on a page, and rejoice in it. It consists in—it is advisable to give rule and example together, wherever it is possible—breaking up one phrase in order to glue in another. Nor is it merely out of laziness that they write thus. They do it out of stupidity; they think there is a charming *légèreté* about it; that it gives life to what they say. No doubt there are a few rare cases where such a form of sentence may be pardonable.

Few write in the way in which an architect builds, who, before he sets to work, sketches out his plan, and thinks it over down to its smallest details. Nay, most people write only as though they were playing dominoes; and, as in this game, the pieces are arranged half by design, half by chance, so it is with the sequence and connection of their sentences. They only have an idea of what the general shape of their work will be, and of the aim they set before themselves. Many are ignorant even of this, and write as the coral insects build; period joins to period, and the Lord only knows what the author means.

Life nowadays goes at a gallop; and the way in which this affects literature is to make it extremely superficial and slovenly.

On Some Forms
of Literature

In the drama, which is the most perfect reflection of human existence, there are three stages in the presentation of the subject, with a corresponding variety in the design and scope of the piece.

At the first, which is also the most common, stage, the drama is never anything more than merely interesting. The persons gain our attention by following their own aims, which resemble ours; the action advances by means of intrigue and the play of character and incident; while wit and railery season the whole.

At the second stage, the drama becomes *sentimental*. Sympathy is roused with the hero and, indirectly, with ourselves. The action takes a pathetic turn, but the end is peaceful and satisfactory.

The climax is reached with the third stage, which is the most difficult. There the drama aims at being *tragic*. We are brought face to face with great suffering and the storm and stress of existence; and the outcome of it is to show the vanity of all human effort. Deeply moved, we are either directly prompted to disengage our will from the struggle of life, or else a chord is struck in us which echoes a similar feeling.

The beginning, it is said, is always difficult. In the drama it is just the contrary; for these the difficulty always lies in the end. This is proved by countless plays which promise very well for the first act or two, and then become muddled, stick, or falter—notoriously so in the fourth act—and finally conclude in a way that is either forced or unsatisfactory or else long foreseen by everyone. Sometimes, too, the end is positively revolting, as in Lessing's *Emilia Galotti,* which sends the spectators home in a temper.

This difficulty in regard to the end of a play arises partly because it is everywhere easier to get things into a tangle than to get them out again; partly also because at the beginning we give the author carte blanche to do as he likes, but, at the end, make certain definite demands upon him. Thus we ask for a conclusion that shall be either quite happy or else quite tragic, whereas human affairs do not easily take so decided a turn; and then we expect that it shall be natural, fit and proper, unlabored, and at the same time foreseen by no one.

These remarks are also applicable to an epic and to a novel; but the more compact nature of the drama makes the difficulty plainer by increasing it.

E nihilo nihil fit. That nothing can come from nothing is a maxim true in fine art as elsewhere. In composing an historical picture, a good artist will use living men as a model, and take the groundwork of the faces from life; and then proceed to idealize them in point of beauty or expression. A similar method, I fancy, is adopted by good novelists. In drawing a character they take a general outline of it from some real person of their acquaintance, and then idealize and complete it to suit their purpose.

A novel will be of a high and noble order the more it represents of inner, and the less it represents of outer, life; and the ratio between the two will supply a means of judging any novel, of whatever kind, from *Tristram Shandy* down to the crudest and most sensational tale of knight or robber. *Tristram Shandy* has, indeed, as good as no action at all; and there is not much in *La Nouvelle Héloïse* and *Wilhelm Meister.* Even *Don Quixote* has relatively little, and what there is, very unimportant, and introduced merely for the sake of fun. And these four are the best of all existing novels.

Consider, further, the wonderful romances of Jean Paul, and how much inner life is shown on the narrowest basis of actual event. Even in Walter Scott's novels there is a great preponderance of inner over outer life, and incident is never brought in except for the purpose of giving play to thought and emotion; whereas in bad novels incident is there on its own account. Skill consists in setting the inner life in motion with the smallest possible array of circumstance, for it is this inner life that really excites our interest.

The business of the novelist is not to relate great events, but to make small ones interesting.

History, which I like to think of as the contrary of poetry [*historou-menon* (investigated)—*pepoiemenon* (invented)], is for time what geography is for space; and it is no more to be called a science, in any strict sense of the word, than is geography, because it does not deal with universal truths but only with particular details. History has always been the favorite study of those who wish to learn something without having to face the effort demanded by any branch of real knowledge, which taxes the intelligence. In our time history is a favorite pursuit, as witness the numerous books upon the subject which appear every year.

If the reader cannot help thinking, with me, that history is merely the constant recurrence of similar things, just as in a kaleidoscope the same bits of glass are represented, but in different combinations, he will not be able to share all this lively interest; nor, however, will he censure it. But there is a ridiculous and absurd claim, made by many people, to regard history as a part of philosophy, nay, as philosophy itself; they imagine that history can take its place.

The preference shown for history by the greater public in all ages may be illustrated by the kind of conversation which is so much in vogue everywhere in society. It generally consists in one person relating something and then another person relating something else; so that in this way everyone is sure of receiving attention. Both here and in the case of history it is plain that the mind is occupied with particular details. But as in science, so also in every worthy conversation, the mind rises to the consideration of some general truth.

This objection does not, however, deprive history of its value. Human life is short and fleeting, and many millions of individuals share in it, who are swallowed by that monster of oblivion which is waiting for them with ever open jaws. It is thus a very thankworthy task to try to rescue something—the memory of interesting and important events, or the leading features and personages of some epoch—from the general shipwreck of the world.

From another point of view, we might look upon history as the sequel to zoology; for while with all other animals it is enough to observe the species, with man individuals, and therefore individual events, have to be studied; because every man possesses a character as an individual. And since individuals and events are without number or end, an essential imperfection attaches to history. In the study of it, all that a man learns never contributes to lessen that which he has still to learn. With any real science, a perfection of knowledge is, at any rate, conceivable.

When we gain access to the histories of China and of India, the endlessness of the subject matter will reveal to us the defects in the study, and force our historians to see that the object of science is to recognize the many in the one, to perceive the rules in any given example, and to apply to the life of nations a knowledge of mankind; not to go on counting up facts ad infinitum.

There are two kinds of history; the history of politics and the history of literature and art. The one is the history of the will; the other, that of the intellect. The first is a tale of woe, even of terror: it is a record of agony, struggle, fraud, and horrible murder en masse. The second is everywhere pleasing and serene, like the intellect when left to itself, even though its path be one of error. Its chief branch is the history of philosophy. This is, in fact, its fundamental bass, and the notes of it are heard even in the other kind of history. These deep tones guide the formation of opinion, and opinion rules the world. Hence philosophy, rightly understood, is a material force of the most powerful kind, though very slow in its working. The philosophy of a period is thus the fundamental base of its history.

The newspaper is the second hand in the clock of history; and it is not only made of baser metal than those which point to the minute and the hour, but it seldom goes right.

The so-called leading article is the chorus to the drama of passing events.

Exaggeration of every kind is as essential to journalism as it is to the dramatic art, for the object of journalism is to make events go as far as possible. Thus it is that all journalists are, in the very nature of their calling, alarmists; and this is their way of giving interest to what they write. Herein they are like little dogs; if anything stirs, they immediately set up a shrill bark.

Therefore, let us carefully regulate the attention to be paid to this trumpet of danger so that it may not disturb our digestion. Let us recognize that a newspaper is at best but a magnifying glass, and very often merely a shadow on the wall.

The pen is to thought what the stick is to walking; but you walk most easily when you have no stick, and you think with the greatest perfection when you have no pen in your hand. It is only when a man begins to be old that he likes to use a stick and is glad to take up his pen.

When a hypothesis has once come to birth in the mind, or gained a footing there, it leads a life so far comparable with the life of an organism, as that it assimilates matter from the outer world only when it is like in kind with it and beneficial; and when, contrarily, such matter is not like in kind but hurtful, the hypothesis, equally with the organism, throws it off, or, if forced to take it, gets rid of it again entire.

To gain immortality an author must possess so many excellences that while it will not be easy to find anyone to understand and appreciate them all, there will be men in every age who are able to recognize and value some of them. In this way the credit of his book will be maintained throughout the long course of centuries, in spite of the fact that human interests are always changing.

An author like this, who has a claim to the continuance of his life even with posterity, can only be a man who, over the wide earth, will seek his like in vain, and offer a palpable contrast with everyone else in virtue of his unmistakable distinction. Nay, more: were he, like the wandering Jew, to live through several generations, he would still remain in the same superior position. If this were not so, it would be difficult to see why his thoughts should not perish like those of other men.

Metaphors and similes are of great value, in so far as they explain an unknown relation by a known one. Even the more detailed simile which grows into a parable or an allegory is nothing more than the exhibition of some relation in its simplest, most visible and palpable form. The growth of ideas rests, at bottom, upon similes, because ideas arise by a process of combining the similarities and neglecting the differences between things. Further, intelligence, in the strict sense of the word, ultimately consists in a seizing of relations; and a clear and pure grasp of relations is all the more often attained when the comparison is made between cases that lie wide apart from one another, and between things of quite different nature. As long as a relation is known to me as existing only in a single case, I have but an individual idea of it—in other words, only an intuitive knowledge of it; but as soon as I see the same relation in two different cases, I have a general idea of its whole nature, and this is a deeper and more perfect knowledge.

Since, then, similes and metaphors are such a powerful engine of knowledge, it is a sign of great intelligence in a writer if his similes are unusual and, at the same time, to the point. Aristotle also observes that by far the most important thing to a writer is to have this power of metaphor, for it is a gift which cannot be acquired, and it is a mark of genius.

As regards reading, to require that a man shall retain everything he has ever read is like asking him to carry about with him all he has ever eaten. The one kind of food has given him bodily, and the other mental, nourishment; and it is through these two means that he has grown to be what he is. The body assimilates only that which is like it; and so a man retains in his mind only that which interests him, in other words, that which suits his system of thought or his purposes in life.

If a man wants to read good books, he must make a point of avoiding bad ones; for life is short, and time and energy limited.

Repetitio est mater studiorum [Repetition is the mother of learning]. Any book that is at all important ought to be at once read through twice; partly because, on a second reading, the connection of the different portions of the book will be better understood, and the beginning comprehended only when the end is known; and partly because we are not in the same temper and disposition on both readings. On the second perusal we get a new view of every passage and a different impression of the whole book, which then appears in another light.

A man's works are the quintessence of his mind, and even though he may possess very great capacity, they will always be incomparably more valuable than his conversation. Nay, in all essential matters his works will not only make up for the lack of personal intercourse with him, but they will far surpass it in solid advantages. The writings even of a man of moderate genius may be edifying, worth reading, and instructive, because they are his quintessence—the result and fruit of all his thought and study; while conversation with him may be unsatisfactory.

So it is that we can read books by men in whose company we find nothing to please, and that a high degree of culture leads us to seek entertainment almost wholly from books and not from men.

On the Comparative Place
of Interest and Beauty in Works
# of Art

In the productions of poetic genius, especially of the epic and dramatic kind, there is, apart from Beauty, another quality which is attractive: I mean Interest.

The beauty of a work of art consists in the fact that it holds up a clear mirror to certain ideas inherent in the world in general; the beauty of a work of poetic art in particular is that it renders the ideas inherent in mankind, and thereby leads it to a knowledge of these ideas. The means which poetry uses for this end are the exhibition of significant characters and the invention of circumstances which will bring about significant situations, giving occasion to the characters to unfold their peculiarities and show what is in them; so that by some such representation a clearer and fuller knowledge of the many-sided idea of humanity may be attained. Beauty, however, in its general aspect, is the inseparable characteristic of the idea when it has become known. In other words, everything is beautiful in which an idea is revealed, for to be beautiful means no more than clearly to express an idea.

Thus we perceive that beauty is always an affair of knowledge, and that it appeals to the knowing subject and not to the will; nay, it is a fact that the apprehension of beauty on the part of the subject involves a complete suppression of the will.

On the other hand, we call drama or descriptive poetry interesting when it represents events and actions of a kind which necessarily arouse concern or sympathy, like that which we feel in real events involving our own person. The fate of the person represented in them is felt in just the same fashion as our own: we await the development of events with anxiety; we eagerly follow their course; our hearts quicken when the hero is threatened; our pulse falters as the danger reaches its acme, and throbs again when he is suddenly rescued. Until we reach the end of the story we cannot put the book aside; we lie awake far into the night sympathizing with our hero's troubles as though they were our own. Nay, instead of finding pleasure and recreation in such representations, we should feel all the pain which real life often inflicts upon us, or at least the kind which pursues us in our uneasy dreams, if in the act of reading or looking at the stage we had not the firm ground of reality always beneath our feet. As it is, in the stress of a too violent feeling, we can find relief from the illusion of the moment, and then give way to it again at will. Moreover, we can gain this relief without any such violent transition as occurs in a dream, when we rid ourselves of its terrors only by the act of awaking.

It is obvious that what is affected by poetry of this character is our will, and not merely our intellectual powers pure and simple. The word interest means, therefore, that which arouses the concern of the individual will, *quod nostra interest;* and here it is that beauty is clearly distinguished from interest. The one is an affair of the intellect, and that, too, of the purest and simplest kind. The other works upon the will. Beauty, then, consists in an apprehension of ideas; and knowledge of this character is beyond the range of the principle that nothing happens without a cause. Interest, on the other hand, has its origin nowhere but in the course of events; that is to say, in the complexities which are possible only through the action of this principle in its different forms.

We have now obtained a clear conception of the essential difference between the beauty and the interest of a work of art. We have recognized that beauty is the true end of every art and therefore, also, of the poetic art. It now remains to raise the question whether the interest of a work of art is a second end, or a means to the exhibition of its beauty; or whether the interest of it is produced by its beauty as an essential concomitant, and comes of itself as soon as it is beautiful; or whether interest is at any rate compatible with the main end of art; or, finally whether it is a hindrance to it.

In the first place, it is to be observed that the interest of a work of art is confined to works of poetic art. It does not exist in the case of fine art, or of music or architecture. Nay, with these forms of art it is not even conceivable, unless, indeed, the interest be of an entirely personal character, and confined to one or two spectators; as, for example, where a picture is a portrait of someone whom we love or hate; the building, my house or my prison; the music, my wedding dance, or the tune to which I marched to the war. Interest of this kind is clearly quite foreign to the essence and purpose of art; it disturbs our judgment in so far as it makes the purely artistic attitude impossible. It may be, indeed, that to a smaller extent this is true of all interest.

Now, since the interest of a work of art lies in the fact that we have the same kind of sympathy with a poetic representation as with reality, it is obvious that the representation must deceive us for the moment; and this it can do only by its truth. But truth is an element in perfect art. A picture, a poem, should be as true as nature itself; but at the same time it should lay stress on whatever forms the unique character of its subject by drawing out all its essential manifestations, and by rejecting everything that is unessential and accidental. The picture or the poem will thus emphasize its idea, and give us that ideal truth which is superior to nature.

Truth, then, forms the point that is common both to interest and beauty in a work of art, as it is its truth which produces the illusion. The fact that the truth of which I speak is ideal truth might, indeed, be detrimental to the illusion, since it is just here that we have the general difference between poetry and reality, art and nature. But since it is possible for reality to coincide with the ideal, it is not actually necessary that this difference should destroy the illusion. In the case of fine arts there is, in the range of the means which art adopts, a certain limit, and beyond it illusion is impossible. Sculpture, that is to say, gives us mere colorless form; its figures are without eyes and without movement; and painting provides us with no more than a single view, enclosed within strict limits, which separate the picture from the adjacent reality. Here, then, there is no room for illusion, and consequently none for that interest or sympathy which resembles the interest we have in reality; the will is at once excluded, and the object alone is presented to us in a manner that frees it from any personal concern.

It is a highly remarkable fact that a spurious kind of fine art oversteps these limits, produces an illusion of reality, and arouses our interest; but at the same time it destroys the effect which fine art produces, and serves as nothing but a mere means of exhibiting the beautiful, that is, of communicating a knowledge of the ideas which it embodies. I refer to waxwork. Here, we might say, is the dividing line which separates it from the province of fine art. When waxwork is properly executed, it produces a perfect illusion; but for that very reason we approach a wax figure as we approach a real man, who, as such, is for the moment an object presented to our will. That is to say, he is an object of interest; he arouses the will, and consequently stills the intellect. We come up to a wax figure with the same reserve and caution as a real man would inspire in us: our will is excited; it waits to see whether he is going to be friendly to us, or the reverse, fly from us, or attack us; in a word, it expects some action of him. But as the figure, nevertheless, shows no sign of life, it produces the impression which is so very disagreeable, namely, of a corpse. This is a case where the interest is of the most complete kind, and yet where there is no work of art at all. In other words, interest is not in itself a real end of art.

The same truth is illustrated by the fact that even in poetry it is only the dramatic and descriptive kind to which interest attaches; for if interest were, with beauty, the aim of art, poetry of the lyrical kind would, for that very reason, not take half so great a position as the other two.

In the second place, if interest were a means in the production of beauty, every interesting work would also be beautiful. That, however, is by no means the case. A drama or a novel may often attract us by its interest, and yet be so utterly deficient in any kind of beauty that we are afterwards ashamed of having wasted our time on it. This applies to many a drama which gives no true picture of the real life of man, which contains characters very superficially drawn, or so distorted as to be actual monstrosities, such as are not to be found in nature; but the course of events and the play of the action are so intricate, and we feel so much for the hero in the situation in which he is placed, that we are not content until we see the knot untangled and the hero rescued. The action is so cleverly governed and guided in its course that we remain in a state of constant curiosity as to what is going to happen, and we are utterly unable to form a guess; so that between eagerness and surprise our interest is kept active; and as we are pleasantly entertained, we do not notice the lapse of time. Most of Kotzebue's plays are of this character. For the mob this is the right thing: it looks for amusement, something to pass the time, not for intellectual perception. Beauty is an affair of such perception; hence sensibility to beauty varies as much as the intellectual faculties themselves. For the inner truth of a representation, and its correspondence with the real nature of humanity, the mob has no sense at all. What is flat and superficial it can grasp, but the depths of human nature are opened to it in vain.

It is also to be observed that dramatic representations which depend for their value on their interest lose by repetition, because they are no longer able to arouse curiosity as to their course, since it is already known. To see them often makes them stale and tedious. On the other hand, works of which the value lies in their beauty gain by repetition, as they are then more and more understood.

Most novels are on the same footing as dramatic representations of this character. They are creatures of the same sort of imagination as we see in the storyteller of Venice and Naples, who lays a hat on the ground and waits until an audience is assembled. Then he spins a tale which so captivates his hearers that, when he gets to the catastrophe, he makes a round of the crowd, hat in hand, for contributions, without the least fear that his hearers will slip away. Similar storytellers ply their trade in this country, though in a less direct fashion. They do it through the agency of publishers and circulating libraries. Thus they can avoid going about in rags, like their colleagues elsewhere; they can offer the children of their imagination to the public under the title of novels, short stories, romantic poems, fairy tales, and so on; and the public, in a dressing gown by the fireside, sits down more at its ease, but also with a greater amount of patience, to the enjoyment of the interest which they provide.

How very little aesthetic value there generally is in productions of this sort is well known; and yet it cannot be denied that many of them are interesting; or else how could they be so popular?

We see, then, in reply to our second question, that interest does not necessarily involve beauty; and, conversely, it is true that beauty does not necessarily involve interest. Significant characters may be represented that open up the depths of human nature, and it may all be expressed in actions and sufferings of an exceptional kind, so that the real nature of humanity and the world may stand forth in the picture in the clearest and most forcible lines; and yet no high degree of interest may be excited in the course of events by the continued progress of the action, or by the complexity and unexpected solution of the plot. The immortal masterpieces of Shakespeare contain little that excites interest; the action does not go forward in one straight line, but falters, as in *Hamlet,* all through the play; or else it spreads out in breadth, as in *The Merchant of Venice,* whereas length is the proper dimension of interest; or the scenes hang loosely together, as in *Henry IV.* Thus it is that Shakespeare's dramas produce no appreciable effect on the mob.

The dramatic requirement stated by Aristotle, and more particularly the unity of action, have in view the interest of the piece rather than its artistic beauty. It may be said, generally, that these requirements are drawn up in accordance with the principle of sufficient reason to which I have referred above. We know, however, that the idea, and, consequently, the beauty of a work of art, exist only for the perceptive intelligence which has freed itself from the domination of that principle. It is just here that we find the distinction between interest and beauty, as it is obvious that interest is part and parcel of the mental attitude which is governed by the principle, whereas beauty is always beyond its range. The best and most striking refutation of the Aristotelian unities is Manzoni's. It may be found in the preface to his dramas.

What is true of Shakespeare's dramatic works is true also of Goethe's. Even *Egmont* makes little effect on the public, because it contains scarcely any complication or development; and if *Egmont* fails, what are we to say of *Tasso* or *Iphigenia?* That the Greek tragedians did not look to interest as a means of working upon the public is clear from the fact that the material of their masterpieces was almost always known to everyone: they selected events which had often been treated dramatically before. This shows us how sensitive was the Greek public to the beautiful, as it did not require the interest of unexpected events and new stories to season its enjoyment.

Neither does the quality of interest often attach to masterpieces of descriptive poetry. Father Homer lays the world and humanity before us in its true nature, but he takes no trouble to attract our sympathy by a complexity of circumstance, or to surprise us by unexpected entanglements. His pace is lingering; he stops at every scene; he puts one picture after another tranquilly before us, elaborating it with care. We experience no passionate emotion in reading him; our demeanor is one of pure perceptive intelligence; he does not arouse our will, but sings it to rest; and it costs us no effort to break off in our reading, for we are not in condition of eager curiosity. This is all still more true of Dante, whose work is not, in the proper sense of the word, an epic, but a descriptive poem. The same thing may be said of the four immortal romances: *Don Quixote, Tristram Shandy, La Nouvelle Héloïse,* and *Wilhelm Meister. To* arouse our interest is by no means the chief aim of these works; in *Tristram Shandy* the hero, even at the end of the book, is only eight years of age.

On the other hand, we must not venture to assert that the quality of interest is not to be found in masterpieces of literature. We have it in Schiller's dramas in an appreciable degree, and consequently they are popular; also in the *Oedipus Rex* of Sophocles. Among masterpieces of description, we find it in Ariosto's *Orlando Furioso;* nay, an example of a high degree of interest, bound up with the beautiful, is afforded in an excellent novel by Walter Scott—*The Heart of Midlothian.* This is the most interesting work of fiction that I know, where all the effects due to interest, as I have given them generally in the preceding remarks, may be most clearly observed. At the same time it is a very beautiful romance throughout; it shows the most varied pictures of life, drawn with striking truth; and it exhibits highly different characters with great justice and fidelity.

Interest, then, is certainly compatible with beauty. That was our third question. Nevertheless, a comparatively small admixture of the element of interest may well be found to be most advantageous as far as beauty is concerned; for beauty is and remains the end of art. Beauty is in twofold opposition with interest; firstly, because it lies in the perception of the idea, and such perception takes its object entirely out of the range of the forms enunciated by the principle of sufficient reason; whereas interest has its sphere mainly in circumstance, and it is out of this principle that the complexity of circumstance arises. Secondly, interest works by exciting the will; whereas beauty exists only for the pure perceptive intelligence, which has no will. However, with dramatic and descriptive literature an admixture of interest is necessary, just as a volatile and gaseous substance requires a material basis if it is to be preserved and transferred. The admixture is necessary, partly, indeed, because interest is itself created by the events which have to be devised in order to set the characters in motion; partly because our minds would be weary of watching scene after scene if they had no concern for us, or of passing from one significant picture to enother if we were not drawn on by some secret thread. It is this that we call interest; it is the sympathy which the event in itself forces us to feel, and which, by riveting our attention, makes the mind obedient to the poet, and able to follow him into all the parts of his story.

If the interest of a work of art is sufficient to achieve this result, it does all that can be required of it; for its only service is to connect the pictures by which the poet desires to communicate a knowledge of the idea, as if they were pearls, and interest were the thread that holds them together, and makes an ornament out of the whole. But interest is prejudicial to beauty as soon as it oversteps this limit; and this is the case if we are so led away by the interest of a work that whenever we come to any detailed description in a novel, or any lengthy reflection on the part of a character in a drama, we grow impatient and want to put spurs to our author, so that we may follow the development of events with greater speed. Epic and dramatic writings, where beauty and interest are both present in a high degree, may be compared to the working of a watch, where interest is the spring which keeps all the wheels in motion. If it worked unhindered, the watch would run down in a few minutes. Beauty, holding us in the spell of description and reflection, is like the barrel which checks its movement.

Or we may say that interest is the body of a poetic work, and beauty the soul. In the epic and the drama, interest, as a necessary quality of the action, is the matter; and beauty, the form that requires the matter in order to be visible.

The foregoing three essays were translated by T. Bailey Saunders.

Friedrich Schiller

1759–1805

Johann Christoph Friedrich Schiller was born on November 10, 1759, at Marbach in Württemberg. His mother was the daughter of a small-town innkeeper, his father an army surgeon. Later, however, Schiller's father served as superintendent of forests and nurseries on the estates of the duke Karl Eugen of Württemberg. The Duke entered Friedrich in "Solitude," a military school he had founded. There young Schiller was forced to study law, although he had hoped to prepare for the church. When the school moved to Stuttgart, Schiller was allowed to take up the study of medicine. In 1780 he was appointed by the Duke as a regimental surgeon at Stuttgart.

Schiller was upset by the tyranny of both the school and the Duke and attracted by the revolutionary authors of the period. In 1781 he published a play, *Die Räuber* ("The Robbers"). It was produced the next year at Mannheim, and Schiller stole away to attend the performance. It was so successful that he began to work on another tragedy. The Duke, however, hearing of a second visit by Schiller to Mannheim, had him placed under military arrest. The Duke forbade him to write any more and insisted that he not leave Württemberg. In 1782 Schiller fled from the duchy.

After some weeks of extreme poverty and hunger, he finally found refuge in the home of a mother of a school friend at Bauerbach in Thuringia. Here he finished two plays, *Fiesco* and *Kabale und Liebe* ("Intrigue and Love").

He was appointed dramatist to the Mannheim Theater, but his contract was not renewed and Schiller stayed on in Mannheim for a while. Then, in 1785, he accepted the invitation of some admirers to visit Leipzig. For the next two years he was the guest of one of them, C. G. Körner, in Leipzig and Dresden. In 1787 he finished *Don Carlos,* written in blank verse. He also, at this time, wrote joyful poems, including *An die Freude* ("Ode to Joy"), the basis of the last movement of Beethoven's Ninth Symphony.

Schiller went to Weimar in 1787. Two years later he was appointed honorary professor of history at Jena—following the publication of the first volume of a history of the revolt of the Netherlands—a position which he held until 1793. During this time he met and married Charlotte von Lengefeld. He became a friend of Goethe, who had an important influence on his thought and work. In 1799 he took up permanent residence in Weimar, partly to be near Goethe. He continued to write very successful historical dramas. During his last years he was plagued with ill-health. Schiller died at Weimar on May 9, 1805.

Schiller was a Romantic. He was a German. In the first role he was a vigorous spokesman for his time. In the second, he was, and has often been since, an inspiration to his fellow nationals.

There were three phases of Schiller's career. At first he wrote *Sturm und Drang* ("Storm and Stress") poetry and plays of social criticism. The ideas of this literary school, largely influenced by Rousseau, were concerned with individual rights and scorn for convention. These ideas had a great appeal to young Schiller, newly out of the clutches of the dictatorial Duke and hence in revolt against authority of all sorts.

In the second stage of his writing life, he concentrated on history and philosophy, largely influenced by Kant. In the third, he wrote poetic dramas which exemplified his aesthetic ideas.

On Simple and Sentimental Poetry is Schiller's definition of his aesthetic principles and at the same time a statement of his ethics.

The several pairs of concepts which Schiller talks of here repre-

Notes from the artist: "Schiller contemplating the bust of Goethe, his friend and source of inspiration. On Schiller's head is an apple, nearby the hat of the tyrant Gessler, both suggesting Wilhelm Tell."

sent the differences between himself and Goethe—Goethe's classic naïveté and his own Romantic sentimentalism.

Schiller eulogizes the *natural* or *simple,* in typically Rousseau fashion. Children and childlike people (as different from *childish* people) have this simplicity to a high degree, he says—or, as Wordsworth put it, they are "trailing clouds of glory." Further, he says that true genius is necessarily simple—that is, modest rather than decent; intelligent rather than cunning; faithful from natural necessity rather than principles.

Schiller notes the dangers of growing out of this state of childlike simplicity. People may become burdened with troubles. They may become disillusioned "with the artifices, offended by the abuses . . . in social life." Then, he says, the moral man must be careful to remain pure in the midst of impurities. It is fruitless and wrong then to yearn for lost innocence; there is no chance, and no sense in trying, to go back to a state of naïveté. "But when you have consoled yourself for having lost the happiness of nature," he says, "let its perfection be a model to your heart."

Reasonable men have free will, he says. And, in the loss of naïve innocence, they must depend on that free will to be moral persons.

Schiller explains the difference this way: the poet *is* nature, or he *seeks* nature. In the former case, he is a simple poet; in the second case a sentimental poet. The ideal, to Schiller, would be a perfect synthesis, each side keeping the other from excess.

The title of this essay is almost paradoxical in its modesty. For "simple" read "Goethe and classic." For "sentimental" read "Schiller and modern." For "poetry" read "life." Then the scope of the essay begins to be apparent.

On Simple
and Sentimental Poetry

There are moments in life when nature inspires us with a sort of love and respectful emotion, not because she is pleasing to our senses or because she satisfies our mind or our taste (it is often the very opposite that happens), but merely because she is nature. This feeling is often elicited when nature is considered in her plants, in the mineral kingdom, in rural districts; also in the case of human nature, in the case of children, and in the manners of country people and of the primitive races. Every man of refined feeling, provided he has a soul, experiences this feeling when he walks out under the open sky, when he lives in the country, or when he stops to contemplate the monuments of early ages; in short, when escaping from factitious situations and relations, he finds himself suddenly face to face with nature. This interest, which is often exalted in us so as to become a want, is the explanation of many of our fancies for flowers and for animals, our preference for gardens laid out in a natural style, our love of walks, of the country and those who live there, of a great number of objects proceeding from a remote antiquity, etc. It is taken for granted that no affectation exists in the matter, and moreover that no accidental interest comes into play. But this sort of interest which we take in nature is only possible under two conditions. First the object that inspires us with this feeling must be really nature, or something we take for nature; secondly, this object must be in the full sense of the word simple, that is, presenting the entire contrast of nature with art, all the advantage remaining on the side of nature. Directly this second condition is united to the first, but no sooner, nature assumes the character of simplicity.

Considered thus, nature is for us nothing but existence in all its freedom; it is the constitution of things taken in themselves; it is existence itself according to its proper and immutable laws.

It is strictly necessary that we should have this idea of nature to take an interest in phenomena of this kind. If we conceive an artificial flower so perfectly imitated that it has all the appearance of nature and would produce the most complete illusion, or if we imagine the imitation of simplicity carried out to the extremest degree, the instant we discover it is only an imitation, the feeling of which I have been speaking is completely destroyed. It is, therefore, quite evident that this kind of satisfaction which nature causes us to feel is not a satisfaction of the aesthetical taste, but a satisfaction of the moral sense; for it is produced by means of a conception and not immediately by the single fact of intuition: accordingly it is by no means determined by the different degrees of beauty in forms. For, after all, is there anything so specially charming in a flower of common appearance, in a spring, a moss-covered stone, the warbling of birds, or the buzzing of bees, etc.? What is it that can give these objects a claim to our love? It is not these objects in themselves; it is an idea represented by them that we love in them. We love in them life and its latent action, the effects peacefully produced by beings of themselves, existence under its proper laws, the inmost necessity of things, the eternal unity of their nature.

These objects which captivate us are what we were, what we must be again some day. We were nature as they are; and culture, following the way of reason and of liberty, must bring us back to nature. Accordingly these objects are an image of our infancy irrevocably past—of our infancy which will remain eternally very dear to us, and thus they infuse a certain melancholy into us; they are also the image of our highest perfection in the ideal world whence they excite a sublime emotion in us.

But the perfection of these objects is not a merit that belongs to them, because it is not the effect of their free choice. Accordingly they procure quite a peculiar pleasure for us, by being our models without having anything humiliating for us. It is like a constant manifestation of the divinity surrounding us, which refreshes without dazzling us. The very feature that constitutes their character is precisely what is lacking in ours to make it complete; and what distinguishes us from them is precisely what they lack to be divine. We are free and they are necessary; we change, and they remain identical. Now it is only when these two conditions are united, when the will submits freely to the laws of necessity, and when, in the midst of all the changes of which the imagination is susceptible, reason maintains its rule—it is only then that the divine or the ideal is manifested. Thus we perceive eternally in them that which we have not, but which we are continually forced to strive after; that which we can never reach, but which we can hope to approach by continual progress. And we perceive in ourselves an advantage which they lack, but in which some of them—the beings deprived of reason—cannot absolutely share, and in which the others, such as children, can only one day have a share by following our way. Accordingly, they procure us the most delicious feeling of our human nature, as an idea, though in relation to each determinate state of our nature they cannot fail to humble us.

As this interest in nature is based on an idea, it can only manifest itself in a soul capable of ideas, that is, in a moral soul. For the immense majority it is nothing more than pure affectation; and this taste of sentimentality so widely diffused in our day, manifesting itself, especially since the appearance of certain books, by sentimental excursions and journeys, by sentimental gardens and other fancies akin to these—this taste by no means proves that true refinement of sense has become general. Nevertheless it is certain that nature will always produce something of this impression, even on the most insensible hearts, because all that is required for this is the moral disposition or aptitude, which is common to all men. For all men, however contrary their acts may be to simplicity and to the truth of nature, are brought back to it in their ideas. This sensibility in connection with nature is specially and most strongly manifested, in the greater part of persons, in connection with those sorts of objects which are closely related to us, and which, causing us to look closer into ourselves, show us more clearly what in us departs from nature; for example, in connection with children, or with nations in a state of infancy. It is an error to suppose that it is only the idea of their weakness that, in certain moments, makes us dwell with our eyes on children with so much emotion. This may be true with those who, in the presence of a feeble being, are used to feel nothing but their own superiority. But the feeling of which I speak is only experienced in a very peculiar moral disposition, nor must it be confounded with the feeling awakened in us by the joyous activity of children. The feeling of which I speak is calculated rather to humble than to flatter our self-love; and if it gives us the idea of some advantage, this advantage is at all events not on our side.

We are moved in the presence of childhood, but it is not because from the height of our strength and of our perfection we drop a look of pity on it; it is, on the contrary, because from the depths of our impotence, of which the feeling is inseparable from that of the real and determinate state to which we have arrived, we raise our eyes to the child's determinableness and pure innocence. The feeling we then experience is too evidently mingled with sadness for us to mistake its source. In the child all is disposition and destination; in us all is in the state of a completed, finished thing, and the completion always remains infinitely below the destination. It follows that the child is to us like a representation of the ideal; not, indeed, of the ideal as we have realized it, but such as our destination admitted; and, consequently, it is not at all the idea of its indigence, of its hindrances, that makes us experience emotion in the child's presence; it is, on the contrary, the idea of its pure and free force, of the integrity, the infinity of its being. This is the reason why, in the sight of every moral and sensible man, the child will always be a sacred thing; I mean an object which, by the grandeur of an idea, reduces to nothingness all grandeur realized by experience; an object which, in spite of all it may lose in the judgment of the understanding, regains largely the advantage before the judgment of reason.

Now it is precisely this contradiction between the judgment of reason and that of the understanding which produces in us this quite special phenomenon, this mixed feeling, called forth in us by the sight of the simple—I mean the simple in the manner of thinking. It is at once the idea of a childlike simplicity and of a childish simplicity. By what it has of childish simplicity it exposes a weak side to the understanding, and provokes in us that smile by which we testify our superiority (an entirely speculative superiority). But directly we have reason to think that childish simplicity is at the same time a childlike simplicity—that it is not consequently a want of intelligence, an infirmity in a theoretical point of view, but a superior force (practically), a heart full of truth and innocence which is its source, a heart that has despised the help of art because it was conscious of its real and internal greatness—directly this is understood, the understanding no longer seeks to triumph. Then raillery, which was directed against simpleness, makes way for the admiration inspired by noble simplicity. We feel ourselves obliged to esteem this object, which at first made us smile, and directing our eye to ourselves, to feel ourselves unhappy in not resembling it. Thus is produced that very special phenomenon of a feeling in which good-natured raillery, respect, and sadness are confounded. It is the condition of the simple that nature should triumph over art, either unconsciously to the individual and against his inclination, or with his full and entire cognizance. In the former case it is simplicity as a surprise, and the impression resulting from it is one of gaiety; in the second case it is simplicity of feeling, and we are moved.

With regard to simplicity as a surprise, the person must be morally capable of denying nature. In simplicity of feeling the person may be morally incapable of this, but we must not think him physically incapable, in order that it may make upon us the impression of the simple. This is the reason why the acts and words of children only produce the impression of simplicity upon us when we forget that they are physically incapable of artifice, and in general only when we are exclusively impressed by the contrast between their natural character and what is artificial in us. Simplicity is a childlike ingenuousness which is encountered when it is not expected; and it is for this very reason that, taking the word in its strictest sense, simplicity could not be attributed to childhood properly speaking.

But in both cases, in simplicity as a surprise and simplicity as a feeling, nature must always have the upper hand, and art succumb to her.

Until we have established this distinction we can only form an incomplete idea of simplicity. The affections are also something natural, and the rules of decency are artificial; yet the triumph of the affections over decency is anything but simple. But when affection triumphs over artifice, over false decency, over dissimulation we shall have no difficulty in applying the word simple to this. Nature must therefore triumph over art, not by its blind and brutal force as a dynamical power, but in virtue of its form as a moral magnitude; in a word, not as a want, but as an internal necessity. It must not be insufficiency but the inopportune character of the latter that gives nature her victory; for insufficiency is only a want and a defect, and nothing that results from a want or defect could produce esteem. No doubt in the simplicity resulting from surprise, it is always the predominance of affection and a want of reflection that causes us to appear natural. But this want and this predominance do not by any means suffice to constitute simplicity; they merely give occasion to nature to obey without let or hindrance her moral constitution, that is, the law of harmony.

The simplicity resulting from surprise can only be encountered in man, and that only in as far as at the moment he ceases to be a pure and innocent nature. This sort of simplicity implies a will that is not in harmony with that which nature does of her own accord. A person simple after this fashion, when recalled to himself, will be the first to be alarmed at what he is; on the other hand, a person in whom simplicity is found as a feeling will only wonder at one thing, that is, at the way in which men feel astonishment. As it is not the moral subject as a person, but only his natural character set free by affection, that confesses the truth, it follows from this that we shall not attribute this sincerity to man as a merit, and that we shall be entitled to laugh at it, our raillery not being held in check by any personal esteem for his character. Nevertheless, as it is still the sincerity of nature which, even in the simplicity caused by surprise, pierces suddenly through the veil of dissimulation, a satisfaction of a superior order is mixed with the mischievous joy we feel in having caught any one in the act. This is because nature, opposed to affectation, and truth, opposed to deception, must in every case inspire us with esteem. Thus we experience, even in the presence of simplicity originating in surprise, a really moral pleasure, though it be not in connection with a moral object.

I admit that in simplicity proceeding from surprise, we always experience a feeling of esteem for nature, because we must esteem truth; whereas in the simplicity of feeling we esteem the person himself, enjoying in this way not only a moral satisfaction, but also a satisfaction of which the object is moral. In both cases nature is right, since she speaks the truth; but in the second case not only is nature right, but there is also an act that does honour to the person. In the first case the sincerity of nature always puts the person to the blush, because it is involuntary; in the second it is always a merit which must be placed to the credit of the person, even when what he confesses is of a nature to cause a blush.

We attribute simplicity of feeling to a man when, in the judgments he pronounces on things, he passes without seeing them over all the factitious and artificial sides of an object, to keep exclusively to simple nature. We require of him all the judgments that can be formed of things without departing from a sound nature; and we only hold him entirely free in what presupposes a departure from nature, in his mode of thinking or feeling.

If a father relates to his son that such and such a person is dying of hunger, and if the child goes and carries the purse of his father to this unfortunate being, this is a simple action. It is in fact a healthy nature that acts in the child; and in a world where healthy nature would be the law, he would be perfectly right to act so. He only sees the misery of his neighbour and the speediest means of relieving him. The extension given to the right of property, in consequence of which part of the human race might perish, is not based on mere nature. Thus the act of this child puts to shame real society, and this is acknowledged by our heart in the pleasure it experiences from this action.

If a good-hearted man, inexperienced in the ways of the world, confides his secrets to another, who deceives him, but who is skilful in disguising his perfidy, and if by his very sincerity he furnishes him with the means of doing him injury, we find his conduct simple. We laugh at him, yet we cannot avoid esteeming him, precisely on account of his simplicity. This is because his trust in others proceeds from the rectitude of his own heart; at all events, there is simplicity here only as far as this is the case.

Simplicity in the mode of thinking cannot then ever be the act of a depraved man; this quality belongs only to children, and to men who are children in heart. It often happens to these in the midst of the artificial relations of the great world to act or to think in a simple manner. Being themselves of a truly good and humane nature, they forget that they have to do with a depraved world; and they act, even in the courts of kings, with an ingenuousness and an innocence that are only found in the world of pastoral idylls.

Nor is it always such an easy matter to distinguish exactly childish candour from childlike candour, for there are actions that are on the skirts of both. Is a certain act foolishly simple, and must we laugh at it? Or is it nobly simple, and must we esteem the actors the higher on that account? It is difficult to know which side to take in some cases. A very remarkable example of this is found in the history of the government of Pope Adrian VI, related by Mr. [J. M.] Schröckh with all the solidity and the spirit of practical truth which distinguish him. Adrian, a Netherlander by birth, exerted the pontifical sway at one of the most critical moments for the hierarchy—at a time when an exasperated party laid bare without any scruple all the weak sides of the Roman Church, while the opposite party was interested in the highest degree in covering them over. I do not entertain the question how a man of a truly simple character ought to act in such a case, if such a character were placed in the papal chair. But, we ask, how could this simplicity of feeling be compatible with the part of a pope? This question gave indeed very little embarrassment to the predecessors and successors of Adrian. They followed uniformly the system adopted once for all by the court of Rome, not to make any concessions anywhere. But Adrian had preserved the upright character of his nation and the innocence of his previous condition. Issuing from the humble sphere of literary men to rise to this eminent position, he did not belie at that elevation the primitive simplicity of his character. He was moved by the abuses of the Roman Church, and he was much too sincere to dissimulate publicly what he confessed privately. It was in consequence of this manner of thinking that, in his instruction to his legate in Germany, he allowed himself to be drawn into avowals hitherto unheard of in a sovereign pontiff, and diametrically contrary to the principles of that court: "We know well," he said among other things, "that for many years many abominable things have taken place in this holy chair; it is not therefore astonishing that the evil has been propagated from the head to the members, from the pope to the prelates. We have all gone astray from the good road, and for a long time there is none of us, not one, who has done anything good." Elsewhere he orders his legate to declare in his name "that he, Adrian, cannot be blamed for what other popes have done before him; that he himself, when he occupied a comparatively mediocre position, had always condemned these excesses." It may easily be conceived how such simplicity in a pope must have been received by the Roman clergy. The smallest crime of which he was accused was that of betraying the Church and delivering it over to heretics. Now this proceeding, supremely imprudent in a pope, would yet deserve our esteem and admiration if we could believe it was real simplicity; that is that Adrian, without fear of consequences, had made such an avowal, moved by his natural sincerity, and that he would have persisted in acting thus, though he had understood all the drift of his clumsiness. Unhappily we have some reason to believe that he did not consider his conduct as altogether impolitic, and that in his candour he went so far as to flatter himself that he had served very usefully the interests of his Church by his indulgence to his adversaries. He did not even imagine that he ought to act thus in his quality as an honest man, he thought also as a pope to be able to justify himself, and forgetting that the most artificial of structures could only be supported by continuing to deny the truth, he committed the unpardonable fault of having recourse to means of safety, excellent perhaps in a natural situation, but here applied to entirely contrary circumstances. This necessarily modifies our judgment very much, and although we cannot refuse our esteem for the honesty of heart in which the act originates, this esteem is greatly lessened when we reflect that nature on this occasion was too easily mistress of art, and that the heart too easily overruled the head.

True genius is of necessity simple, or it is not genius. Simplicity alone gives it this character, and it cannot belie in the moral order what it is in the intellectual and aesthetical order. It does not know those rules, the crutches of feebleness, those pedagogues which prop up slippery spirits; it is only guided by nature and instinct, its guardian angel; it walks with a firm, calm step across all the snares of false taste, snares in which the man without genius, if he have not the prudence to avoid them the moment he detects them, remains infallibly imbedded. It is therefore the part only of genius to issue from the known without ceasing to be at home, or to enlarge the circle of nature without overstepping it. It does indeed sometimes happen that a great genius oversteps it; but only because geniuses have their moments of frenzy, when nature, their protector, abandons them, because the force of example impels them, or because the corrupt taste of their age leads them astray.

The most intricate problems must be solved by genius with simplicity, without pretension, with ease; the egg of Christopher Columbus is the emblem of all the discoveries of genius. It only justifies its character as genius by triumphing through simplicity over all the complications of art. It does not proceed according to known principles, but by feelings and inspiration; the sallies of genius are the inspirations of a God (all that healthy nature produces is divine); its feelings are laws for all time, for all human generations.

This childlike character imprinted by genius on its works is also shown by it in its private life and manners. It is modest, because nature is always so; but it is not decent, because corruption alone is decent. It is intelligent, because nature cannot lack intelligence; but it is not cunning, because art only can be cunning. It is faithful to its character and inclinations, but this is not so much because it has principles as because nature, notwithstanding all its oscillations, always returns to its equilibrium, and brings back the same wants. It is modest and even timid, because genius remains always a secret to itself; but it is not anxious, because it does not know the dangers of the road in which it walks. We know little of the private life of the greatest geniuses; but the little that we know of it—what tradition has preserved, for example, of Sophocles, of Archimedes, of Hippocrates, and in modern times of Ariosto, of Dante, of Tasso, of Raphael, of Albrecht Dürer, of Cervantes, of Shakespeare, of Fielding, of Sterne, etc.—confirms this assertion.

Nay, more; though this admission seems more difficult to support, even the greatest philosophers and great commanders, if great by their genius, have simplicity in their character. Among the ancients I need only name Julius Caesar and Epaminondas; among the moderns Henry IV in France, Gustavus Adolphus in Sweden, and the Czar Peter the Great. The Duke of Marlborough, Turenne, and Vendôme all present this character. With regard to the other sex, nature proposes to it simplicity of character as the supreme perfection to which it should reach. Accordingly, the love of pleasing in women strives after nothing so much as the appearance of simplicity; a sufficient proof, if it were the only one, that the greatest power of the sex reposes in this quality. But, as the principles that prevail in the education of women are perpetually struggling with this character, it is as difficult for them in the moral order to reconcile this magnificent gift of nature with the advantages of a good education as it is difficult for men to preserve them unchanged in the intellectual order; and the woman who knows how to join a knowledge of the world to this sort of simplicity in manners is as deserving of respect as a scholar who joins to the strictness of scholastic rules the freedom and originality of thought.

Simplicity in our mode of thinking brings with it of necessity simplicity in our mode of expression, simplicity in terms as well as movement; and it is in this that grace especially consists. Genius expresses its most sublime and its deepest thoughts with this simple grace; they are the divine oracles that issue from the lips of a child; while the scholastic spirit, always anxious to avoid error, tortures all its words, all its ideas, and makes them pass through the crucible of grammar and logic, hard and rigid, in order to keep from vagueness, and uses few words in order not to say too much, enervates and blunts thought in order not to wound the reader who is not on his guard—genius gives to its expression, with a single and happy stroke of the brush, a precise, firm, and yet perfectly free form. In the case of grammar and logic, the sign and the thing signified are always heterogeneous, and strangers to each other: with genius, on the contrary, the expression gushes forth spontaneously from the idea, the language and the thought are one and the same; so that even though the expression thus gives it a body, the spirit appears as if disclosed in a nude state. This fashion of expression, when the sign disappears entirely in the thing signified, when the tongue, so to speak, leaves the thought it translates naked, while the other mode of expression cannot represent thought without veiling it at the same time: this is what is called originality and inspiration in style.

This freedom, this natural mode by which genius expresses itself in works of intellect, is also the expression of the innocence of heart in the intercourse of life. Every one knows that in the world men have departed from simplicity, from the rigorous veracity of language, in the same proportion as they have lost the simplicity of feelings. The guilty conscience easily wounded, the imagination easily seduced, made an anxious decency necessary. Without telling what is false, people often speak differently from what they think; we are obliged to make circumlocutions to say certain things, which however, can never afflict any but a sickly self-love, and that have no danger except for a depraved imagination. The ignorance of these laws of propriety (conventional laws), coupled with a natural sincerity which despises all kinds of bias and all appearance of falsity (sincerity I mean, not coarseness, for coarseness dispenses with forms because it is hampered), gives rise in the intercourse of life to a simplicity of expression that consists in naming things by their proper name without circumlocution. This is done because we do not venture to

designate them as they are, or only to do so by artificial means. The ordinary expressions of children are of this kind. They make us smile because they are in opposition to received manners; but men would always
agree in the bottom of their hearts that the child is right.

It is true that simplicity of feeling cannot properly be attributed to the
child any more than to the man—that is, to a being not absolutely subject
to nature, though there is still no simplicity, except on the condition that
it is pure nature that acts through him. But by an effort of the imagination, which likes to poetize things, we often carry over these attributes
of a rational being to beings destitute of reason. It is thus that, on seeing
an animal, a landscape, a building, and nature in general, from opposition
to what is arbitrary and fantastic in the conceptions of man, we often
attribute to them a simple character. But that implies always that in our
thought we attribute a will to these things that have none, and that we are
struck to see it directed rigorously according to the laws of necessity. Discontented as we are that we have ill employed our own moral freedom,
and that we no longer find moral harmony in our conduct, we are easily
led to a certain disposition of mind, in which we willingly address ourselves to a being destitute of reason, as if it were a person. And we
readily view it as if it had really had to struggle against the temptation
of acting otherwise, and proceed to make a merit of its eternal uniformity,
and to envy its peaceable constancy. We are quite disposed to consider
in those moments reason, this prerogative of the human race, as a perni-
cious gift and as an evil; we feel so vividly all that is imperfect in our conduct that we forget to be just to our destiny and to our aptitudes.

We see, then, in nature, destitute of reason, only a sister who, more
fortunate than ourselves, has remained under the maternal roof, while in
the intoxication of our freedom we have fled from it to throw ourselves
into a stranger world. We regret this place of safety, we earnestly long to
come back to it as soon as we have begun to feel the bitter side of civilization, and in the totally artificial life in which we are exiled we hear in
deep emotion the voice of our mother. While we were still only children
of nature we were happy, we were perfect: we have become free, and
we have lost both advantages. Hence a twofold and very unequal longing
for nature: the longing for happiness and the longing for the perfection
that prevails there. Man, as a sensuous being, deplores sensibly the loss
of the former of these goods; it is only the moral man who can be afflicted
at the loss of the other.

Therefore, let the man with a sensible heart and a loving nature question himself closely. Is it your indolence that longs for its repose, or your

wounded moral sense that longs for its harmony? Ask yourself well, when, disgusted with the artifices, offended by the abuses that you discover in social life, you feel yourself attracted towards inanimate nature, in the midst of solitude ask yourself what impels you to fly the world. Is it the privation from which you suffer, its loads, its troubles? Or is it the moral anarchy, the caprice, the disorder that prevail there? Your heart ought to plunge into these troubles with joy, and to find in them the compensation in the liberty of which they are the consequence. You can, I admit, propose as your aim, in a distant future, the calm and the happiness of nature, but only that sort of happiness which is the reward of your dignity. Thus, then, let there be no more complaint about the loads of life, the inequality of conditions, or the hampering of social relations, or the uncertainty of possession, ingratitude, oppression, and persecution. You must submit to all these evils of civilization with a free resignation; it is the natural condition of good, par excellence, of the only good, and you ought to respect it under this head. In all these evils you ought only to deplore what is morally evil in them, and you must do so not with cowardly tears only. Rather watch to remain pure yourself in the midst of these impurities, free amidst this slavery, constant with yourself in the midst of these capricious changes, a faithful observer of the law amidst this anarchy. Be not frightened at the disorder that is without you, but at the disorder which is within; aspire after unity, but seek it not in uniformity; aspire after repose, but through equilibrium, and not by suspending the action of your faculties. This nature which you envy in the being destitute of reason deserves no esteem: it is not worth a wish. You have passed beyond it; it ought to remain forever behind you. The ladder that carried you having given way under your foot, the only thing for you to do is to seize again on the moral law freely, with a free consciousness, a free will, or else to roll down, hopeless of safety, into a bottomless abyss.

But when you have consoled yourself for having lost the happiness of nature, let its perfection be a model to your heart. If you can issue from the circle in which art keeps you enclosed and find nature again, if it shows itself to you in its greatness and in its calm, in its simple beauty, in its childlike innocence and simplicity, oh! then pause before its image, cultivate this feeling lovingly. It is worthy of you, and of what is noblest in man. Let it no more come into your mind to change with it; rather embrace it, absorb it into your being, and try to associate the infinite advantage it has over you with that infinite prerogative that is peculiar to you, and let the divine issue from this sublime union. Let nature breathe around you like a lovely idyll, where far from artifice and its wanderings you may always find yourself again, where you may go to draw fresh courage, a new confidence, to resume your course, and kindle again in your heart the flame of the ideal, so readily extinguished amidst the tempests of life.

If we think of that beautiful nature which surrounded the ancient Greeks, if we remember how intimately that people, under its blessed sky, could live with that free nature; how their mode of imagining, and of feeling, and their manners approached far nearer than ours to the simplicity of nature, how faithfully the works of their poets express this; we must necessarily remark, as a strange fact, that so few traces are met among them of that sentimental interest that we moderns ever take in the scenes of nature and in natural characters. I admit that the Greeks are superiorly exact and faithful in their descriptions of nature. They reproduce their details with care, but we see that they take no more interest in them and no more heart in them than in describing a vestment, a shield, armour, a piece of furniture, or any production of the mechanical arts. In their love for the object it seems that they make no difference between what exists in itself and what owes its existence to art, to the human will. It seems that nature interests their minds and their curiosity more than moral feeling. They do not attach themselves to it with that depth of feeling, with that gentle melancholy, that characterize the moderns. Nay, more, by personifying nature in its particular phenomena, by deifying it, by representing its effects as the acts of free beings, they take from it that character of calm necessity which is precisely what makes it so attractive to us. Their impatient imagination only traverses nature to pass beyond it to the drama of human life. It only takes pleasure in the spectacle of what is living and free; it requires characters, acts, the accidents of fortune and of manners; and while it happens with us, at least in certain moral dispositions, to curse our prerogative, this free will, which exposes us to so many combats with ourselves, to so many anxieties and errors, and to wish to exchange it for the condition of beings destitute of reason, for that fatal existence that no longer admits of any choice, but which is so calm in its uniformity—while we do this, the Greeks, on the contrary, only have their imagination occupied in retracing human nature in the inanimate world, and in giving to the will an influence where blind necessity rules.

Whence can arise this difference between the spirit of the ancients and the modern spirit? How comes it that, being, for all that relates to nature, incomparably below the ancients, we are superior to them precisely on this point, that we render a more complete homage to nature; that we have a closer attachment to it; and that we are capable of embracing even the inanimate world with the most ardent sensibility. It is because nature, in our time, is no longer in man, and that we no longer encounter it in its primitive truth except out of humanity, in the inanimate world. It is not because we are more conformable to nature—quite the contrary; it is because in our social relations, in our mode of existence, in our manners, we are in opposition with nature. This is what leads us, when the instinct of truth and of simplicity is awakened—this instinct which, like the moral aptitude from which it proceeds, lives incorruptible and indelible in every human heart—to procure for it in the physical world the satisfaction which there is no hope of finding in the moral order. This is the reason why the feeling that attaches us to nature is connected so closely with that which makes us regret our infancy, forever flown, and our primitive innocence. Our childhood is all that remains of nature in humanity, such as civilization has made it, of untouched, unmutilated nature. It is, therefore, not wonderful, when we meet out of us the impress of nature, that we are always brought back to the idea of our childhood.

It was quite different with the Greeks in antiquity. Civilization with them did not degenerate, nor was it carried to such an excess that it was necessary to break with nature. The entire structure of their social life reposed on feelings, and not on a factitious conception, on a work of art. Their very theology was the inspiration of a simple spirit, the fruit of a joyous imagination, and not, like the ecclesiastical dogmas of modern nations, subtle combinations of the understanding. Since, therefore, the Greeks had not lost sight of nature in humanity, they had no reason, when meeting it out of man, to be surprised at their discovery, and they would not feel very imperiously the need of objects in which nature could be retraced. In accord with themselves, happy in feeling themselves men, they would of necessity keep to humanity as to what was greatest to them, and they must needs try to make all the rest approach it; while we, who are not in accord with ourselves—we who are discontented with the experience we have made of our humanity—have no more pressing interest than to fly out of it and to remove from our sight a so ill-fashioned form. The feeling of which we are treating here is, therefore, not that which was known by the ancients; it approaches far more nearly that which we ourselves experience for the ancients. The ancients felt naturally; we, on our part, feel what is natural. It was certainly a very different inspiration that filled the soul of Homer, when he depicted his divine cowherd giving hospitality to Ulysses, from that which agitated the soul of the young Werther at the moment when he read the *Odyssey* on issuing from an assembly in which he had only found tedium. The feeling we experience for nature resembles that of a sick man for health.

As soon as nature gradually vanishes from human life—that is, in proportion as it ceases to be experienced as a subject (active and passive) —we see it dawn and increase in the poetical world in the guise of an idea and as an object. The people who have carried furthest the want of nature, and at the same time the reflections on that matter, must needs have been the people who at the same time were most struck with this phenomenon of the simple, and gave it a name. If I am not mistaken, this people was the French. But the feeling of the simple, and the interest we take in it, must naturally go much farther back, and it dates from the time when the moral sense and the aesthetical sense began to be corrupt. This modification in the manner of feeling is exceedingly striking in Euripides, for example, if compared with his predecessors, especially Aeschylus; and yet Euripides was the favourite poet of his time. The same revolution is perceptible in the ancient historians. Horace, the poet of a cultivated and corrupt epoch, praises, under the shady groves of Tibur, the calm and happiness of the country, and he might be termed the true founder of this sentimental poetry, of which he has remained the unsurpassed model. In Propertius, Virgil, and others we find also traces of this mode of feeling; less of it is found in Ovid, who would have required for that more abundance of heart, and who in his exile at Tomis sorrowfully regrets the happiness that Horace so readily dispensed with in his villa at Tibur.

It is in the fundamental idea of poetry that the poet is everywhere the guardian of nature. When he can no longer entirely fill this part, and has already in himself suffered the deleterious influence of arbitrary and factitious forms, or has had to struggle against this influence, he presents himself as the witness of nature and as its avenger. The poet will, therefore, be the expression of nature itself, or his part will be to seek it, if men have lost sight of it. Hence arise two kinds of poetry, which embrace and exhaust the entire field of poetry. All poets—I mean those who are really so—will belong, according to the time when they flourish, according to the accidental circumstances that have influenced their education generally, and the different dispositions of mind through which they pass, will belong, I say, to the order of the sentimental poetry or to simple poetry.

The poet of a young world, simple and inspired, as also the poet who at an epoch of artificial civilization approaches nearest to the primitive bards, is austere and prudish, like the virginal Diana in her forests. Wholly unconfiding, he hides himself from the heart that seeks him, from the desire that wishes to embrace him. It is not rare for the dry truth with which he treats his subject to resemble insensibility. The whole object possesses him, and to reach his heart it does not suffice, as with metals of little value, to stir up the surface; as with pure gold, you must go down to the lowest depths. Like the Deity behind this universe, the simple poet hides himself behind his work; he is himself his work, and his work is himself. A man must be no longer worthy of the work, nor understand it, or be tired of it, to be even anxious to learn who is its author.

Such appear to us, for instance, Homer in antiquity and Shakespeare among moderns: two natures infinitely different and separated in time by an abyss, but perfectly identical as to this trait of character. When, at a very youthful age, I became first acquainted with Shakespeare, I was displeased with his coldness, with his insensibility, which allows him to jest even in the most pathetic moments, to disturb the impression of the most harrowing scenes in *Hamlet*, in *King Lear*, and in *Macbeth*, etc., by mixing with them the buffooneries of a madman. I was revolted by his insensibility, which allowed him to pause sometimes at places where my sensibility would bid me hasten and bear me along, and which sometimes carried him away with indifference when my heart would be so happy to pause. Though I was accustomed, by the practice of modern poets, to seek at once the poet in his works, to meet his heart, to reflect with him in his theme—in a word, to see the object in the subject—I could not bear that the poet could in Shakespeare never be seized, that he would never give me an account of himself. For some years Shakespeare had been the object of my study and of all my respect, before I had learnt to love his personality. I was not yet able to comprehend nature at first hand. All that my eyes could bear was its image only, reflected by the understanding and arranged by rules; and on this score the sentimental poetry of the French, or that of the Germans of 1750 to 1780, was what suited me best. For the rest, I do not blush at this childish judgment; adult critics pronounced in that day in the same way, and carried their simplicity so far as to publish their decisions to the world.

The same thing happened to me in the case of Homer, with whom I made acquaintance at a later date. I remember now that remarkable passage of the sixth book of the *Iliad*, where Glaucus and Diomed meet each other in the strife, and then, recognizing each other as host and guest, exchange presents.[1] With this touching picture of the piety with which the laws of hospitality were observed even in war, may be com-

---

1. See *Great Books of the Western World*, Vol. 4, pp. 41–42.

pared a picture of chivalrous generosity in Ariosto. The knights, rivals in love, Ferragus and Rinaldo—the former a Saracen, the latter a Christian —after having fought to extremity, all covered with wounds, make peace together, and mount the same horse to go and seek the fugitive Angelica. These two examples, however different in other respects, are very similar with regard to the impression produced on our heart; both represent the noble victory of moral feeling over passion, and touch us by the simplicity of feeling displayed in them. But what a difference in the way in which the two poets go to work to describe two such analogous scenes! Ariosto, who belongs to an advanced epoch, to a world where simplicity of manners no longer existed, in relating this trait cannot conceal the astonishment, the admiration, he feels at it. He measures the distance from those manners to the manners of his own age, and this feeling of astonishment is too strong for him. He abandons suddenly the painting of the object, and comes himself on the scene in person. This beautiful stanza [*Orlando Furioso,* canto i, stanza 22] is well known, and has been always specially admired at all times:

> Oh nobleness, oh generosity of the ancient manners of chivalry! These were rivals, separated by their faith, suffering bitter pain throughout their frames in consequence of a desperate combat; and, without any suspicion, behold them riding in company along dark and winding paths. Stimulated by four spurs, the horse hastens his pace till they arrive at the place where the road divides.

Now let us turn to old Homer. Scarcely has Diomed learnt by the story of Glaucus, his adversary, that the latter has been, from the time of their fathers, the host and friend of his family, when he drives his lance into the ground, converses familiarly with him, and both agree henceforth to avoid each other in the strife. But let us hear Homer himself:

> "Henceforth, however, I must be your host in middle Argos, and you mine in Lycia, if I should ever go there; let us avoid one another's spears even during a general engagement; there are many noble Trojans and allies whom I can kill, if I overtake them and heaven delivers them into my hand; so again with yourself, there are many Achaeans whose lives you may take if you can; we two, then, will exchange armour, that all present may know of the old ties that subsist between us."
>
> With these words they sprang from their chariots, grasped one another's hands, and plighted friendship.

It would have been difficult for a modern poet (at least to one who would be modern in the moral sense of the term) even to wait as long as this before expressing his joy in the presence of such an action. We should pardon this in him the more easily, because we also, in reading it, feel that our heart makes a pause here, and readily turns aside from the object to bring back its thoughts on itself. But there is not the least trace of this in Homer. As if he had been relating something that is seen every day—nay, more, as if he had no heart beating in his breast—he continues, with his dry truthfulness:

> But the son of Saturn made Glaucus take leave of his wits, for he exchanged golden armour for bronze, the worth of a hundred head of cattle for the worth of nine.

The poets of this order—the genuinely simple poets, are scarcely any longer in their place in this artificial age. Accordingly they are scarcely possible in it, or at least they are only possible on the condition of traversing their age, like scared persons, at a running pace, and of being preserved by a happy star from the influence of their age, which would mutilate their genius. Never, for aye and forever, will society produce these poets; but out of society they still appear sometimes at intervals, rather, I admit, as strangers who excite wonder, or as ill-trained children of nature who give offence. These apparitions, so very comforting for the artist who studies them, and for the real connoisseur who knows how to appreciate them, are, as a general conclusion, in the age when they are begotten, to a very small degree prosperous. The seal of empire is stamped on their brow, and we, we ask the Muses to cradle us, to carry us in their arms. The critics, as regular constables of art, detest these poets as disturbers of rules or of limits. Homer himself may have been only indebted to the testimony of ten centuries for the reward these aristarchs are kindly willing to concede him. Moreover, they find it a hard matter to maintain their rules against his example, or his authority against their rules.

SENTIMENTAL POETRY

I have previously remarked that the poet is nature, or he seeks nature. In the former case, he is a simple poet; in the second case, a sentimental poet.

The poetic spirit is immortal, nor can it disappear from humanity; it can only disappear with humanity itself, or with the aptitude to be a man, a human being. And actually, though man by the freedom of his imagination and of his understanding departs from simplicity, from truth, from the necessity of nature, not only a road always remains open to him to return to it, but, moreover, a powerful and indestructible instinct, the moral instinct, brings him incessantly back to nature; and it is precisely the poetical faculty that is united to this instinct by the ties of the closest relationship. Thus man does not lose the poetic faculty directly he parts with the simplicity of nature; only this faculty acts out of him in another direction.

Even at present, nature is the only flame that kindles and warms the poetic soul. From nature alone it obtains all its force; to nature alone it speaks in the artificial culture-seeking man. Any other form of displaying its activity is remote from the poetic spirit. Accordingly it may be remarked that it is incorrect to apply the expression poetic to any of the so-styled productions of wit, though the high credit given to French literature has led people for a long period to class them in that category. I repeat that at present, even in the existing phase of culture, it is still nature that powerfully stirs up the poetic spirit, only its present relation to nature is of a different order from formerly.

As long as man dwells in a state of pure nature (I mean pure and not coarse nature), all his being acts at once like a simple sensuous unity, like a harmonious whole. The senses and reason, the receptive faculty and the spontaneously active faculty, have not been as yet separated in their respective functions; a fortiori they are not yet in contradiction with each other. Then the feelings of man are not the formless play of chance; nor are his thoughts an empty play of the imagination, without any value. His feelings proceed from the law of necessity, his thoughts from reality. But when man enters the state of civilization, and art has fashioned him, this sensuous harmony which was in him disappears, and henceforth he can only manifest himself as a moral unity, that is, as aspiring to unity. The harmony that existed as a fact in the former state, the harmony of feeling and thought, only exists now in an ideal state. It is no longer in him, but out of him; it is a conception of thought which he must begin by realizing in himself; it is no longer a fact, a reality of his life. Well, now let us take the idea of poetry, which is nothing else than expressing humanity as completely as possible, and let us apply this idea to these two states. We shall be brought to infer that on the one hand, in the state of natural simplicity, when all the faculties of man are exerted together, his being still manifests itself in a harmonious unity, where, consequently, the totality of his nature expresses itself in reality itself, the part of the poet is necessarily to imitate the real as completely as is possible. In the state of civilization, on the contrary, when this harmonious competition of the whole of human nature is no longer anything but an idea, the part of the poet is necessarily to raise reality to the ideal, or, what amounts to the same thing, to represent the ideal. And actually, these are the only two ways in which, in general, the poetic genius can manifest itself. Their great difference is quite evident, but though there be great opposition between them, a higher idea exists that embraces both, and there is no cause to be astonished if this idea coincides with the very idea of humanity.

This is not the place to pursue this thought any further, as it would require a separate discussion to place it in its full light. But if we only compare the modern and ancient poets together, not according to the accidental forms which they may have employed, but according to their spirit, we shall be easily convinced of the truth of this thought. The thing that touches us in the ancient poets is nature; it is the truth of sense, it is a present and a living reality: modern poets touch us through the medium of ideas.

The path followed by modern poets is, moreover, that necessarily followed by man generally, individuals as well as the species. Nature reconciles man with himself; art divides and disunites him; the ideal brings him back to unity. Now, the ideal being an infinite that he never succeeds in reaching, it follows that civilized man can never become perfect in his kind, while the man of nature can become so in his. Accordingly in relation to perfection one would be infinitely below the other, if we only considered the relation in which they are both to their own kind and to their maximum. If, on the other hand, it is the kinds that are compared together, it is ascertained that the end to which man tends by civilization is infinitely superior to that which he reaches through nature. Thus one has his reward, because having for object a finite magnitude, he completely reaches this object: the merit of the other is to approach an object that is of infinite magnitude. Now, as there are only degrees, and as there is only progress in the second of these evolutions, it follows that the relative merit of the man engaged in the ways of civilization is never determinable in general, though this man, taking the individuals separately, is necessarily at a disadvantage compared with the man in whom nature acts in all its perfection. But we know also that humanity cannot reach its final end except by progress, and that the man of nature cannot make progress save through culture, and consequently by passing himself through the way of civilization. Accordingly there is no occasion to ask with which of the two the advantage must remain, considering this last end.

All that we say here of the different forms of humanity may be applied equally to the two orders of poets who correspond to them.

Accordingly it would have been desirable not to compare at all the ancient and the modern poets, the simple and the sentimental poets, or only to compare them by referring them to a higher idea (since there is really only one) which embraces both. For, sooth to say, if we begin by forming a specific idea of poetry, merely from the ancient poets, nothing is easier, but also nothing is more vulgar, than to depreciate the moderns by this comparison. If persons wish to confine the name of poetry to that which has in all times produced the same impression in simple nature, this places them in the necessity of contesting the title of poet in the moderns precisely in that which constitutes their highest beauties, their greatest originality and sublimity; for precisely in the points where they excel the most, it is the child of civilization whom they address, and they have nothing to say to the simple child of nature.

To the man who is not disposed beforehand to issue from reality in order to enter the field of the ideal, the richest and most substantial poetry is an empty appearance, and the sublimest flights of poetic inspiration are an exaggeration. Never will a reasonable man think of placing alongside Homer, in his grandest episodes, any of our modern poets; and it has a discordant and ridiculous effect to hear Milton or Klopstock honoured with the name of a "new Homer." But take in modern poets what characterizes them, what makes their special merit, and try to compare any ancient poet with them in this point, they will not be able to support the comparison any better, and Homer less than any other. I should express it thus: the power of the ancients consists in compressing objects into the finite, and the moderns excel in the art of the infinite.

What we have said here may be extended to the fine arts in general, except certain restrictions that are self-evident. If then the strength of the artists of antiquity consists in determining and limiting objects, we must no longer wonder that in the field of the plastic arts the ancients remain so far superior to the moderns, nor especially that poetry and the plastic arts with the moderns, compared respectively with what they were among the ancients, do not offer the same relative value. This is because an object that addresses itself to the eyes is only perfect in proportion as the object is clearly limited in it; while a work that is addressed to the imagination can also reach the perfection which is proper to it by means of the ideal and the infinite. This is why the superiority of the moderns in what relates to ideas is not of great aid to them in the plastic arts, where it is necessary for them to determine in space, with the greatest precision, the image which their imagination has conceived, and where they must therefore measure themselves with the ancient artist just on a point where his superiority cannot be contested. In the matter of poetry it is another affair, and if the advantage is still with the ancients on that ground, as respects the simplicity of forms—all that can be represented by sensuous features, all that is something bodily—yet, on the other hand, the moderns have the advantage over the ancients as regards fundamental wealth, and all that can neither be represented nor translated by sensuous signs, in short, for all that is called mind and idea in the works of art.

From the moment that the simple poet is content to follow simple nature and feeling, that he is contented with the imitation of the real world, he can only be placed, with regard to his subject, in a single relation. And in this respect he has no choice as to the manner of treating it. If simple poetry produces different impressions—I do not, of course, speak of the impressions that are connected with the nature of the subject, but only of those that are dependent on poetic execution—the whole difference is in the degree; there is only one way of feeling, which varies from more to less; even the diversity of external forms changes nothing in the quality of aesthetic impressions. Whether the form be lyric or epic, dramatic or descriptive, we can receive an impression either stronger or weaker, but if we remove what is connected with the nature of the subject, we shall always be affected in the same way. The feeling we experience is absolutely identical; it proceeds entirely from one single and the same element to such a degree that we are unable to make any distinction. The very difference of tongues and that of times does not here occasion any diversity, for their strict unity of origin and of effect is precisely a characteristic of simple poetry.

It is quite different with sentimental poetry. The sentimental poet reflects on the impression produced on him by objects; and it is only on this reflection that his poetic force is based. It follows that the sentimental poet is always concerned with two opposite forces, has two modes of representing objects to himself and of feeling them; these are the real or limited, and the ideal or infinite; and the mixed feeling that he will awaken will always testify to this duality of origin. Sentimental poetry thus admitting more than one principle, it remains to know which of the two will be predominant in the poet, both in his fashion of feeling and in that of representing the object; and consequently a difference in the mode of treating it is possible. Here, then, a new subject is presented: shall the poet attach himself to the real or the ideal? to the real as an object of aversion and of disgust, or to the ideal as an object of inclination? The poet will therefore be able to treat the same subject either in its satirical aspect or in its elegiac aspect—taking these words in a larger sense, which will be explained in the sequel: every sentimental poet will of necessity become attached to one or the other of these two modes of feeling.

SATIRICAL POETRY

The poet is a satirist when he takes as subject the distance at which things are from nature, and the contrast between reality and the ideal: as regards the impression received by the soul, these two subjects blend into the same. In the execution he may place earnestness and passion, or jests and levity, according as he takes pleasure in the domain of the will or in that of the understanding. In the former case it is avenging and pathetic satire; in the second case it is sportive, humorous, and mirthful satire.

Properly speaking, the object of poetry is not compatible either with the tone of punishment or that of amusement. The former is too grave for play, which should be the main feature of poetry; the latter is too trifling for seriousness, which should form the basis of all poetic play. Our mind is necessarily interested in moral contradictions, and these deprive the mind of its liberty. Nevertheless, all personal interest, and reference to a personal necessity, should be banished from poetic feeling. But mental contradictions do not touch the heart; nevertheless, the poet deals with the highest interests of the heart—nature and the ideal. Accordingly, it is a hard matter for him not to violate the poetic form in pathetic satire, because this form consists in the liberty of movement; and in sportive satire he is very apt to miss the true spirit of poetry, which ought to be the infinite. The problem can only be solved in one way: by the pathetic satire assuming the character of the sublime, and the playful satire acquiring poetic substance by enveloping the theme in beauty.

In satire the real as imperfection is opposed to the ideal, considered as the highest reality. In other respects it is by no means essential that the ideal should be expressly represented, provided the poet knows how to awaken it in our souls, but he must in all cases awaken it, otherwise he will exert absolutely no poetic action. Thus reality is here a necessary object of aversion; but it is also necessary, for the whole question centres here, that this aversion should come necessarily from the ideal, which is opposed to reality. To make this clear—this aversion might proceed from a purely sensuous source, and repose only on a want of which the satisfaction finds obstacles in the real. How often, in fact, we think we feel against society a moral discontent, while we are simply soured by the obstacles that it opposes to our inclination. It is this entirely material interest that the vulgar satirist brings into play; and as by this road he never fails to call forth in us movements connected with the affections, he fancies that he holds our heart in his hand, and thinks he has graduated in the pathetic. But all pathos derived from this source is unworthy of poetry, which ought only to move us through the medium of ideas, and reach our heart only by passing through the reason. Moreover, this impure and material pathos will never have its effect on minds, except by over-exciting the affective faculties, and by occupying our hearts with painful feelings; in this it differs entirely from the truly poetic pathos which raises in us the feeling of moral independence, and which is recognized by the freedom of our mind persisting in it even while it is in the state of affection. And, in fact, when the emotion emanates from the ideal opposed to the real, the sublime beauty of the ideal corrects all impression of restraint; and the grandeur of the idea with which we are imbued raises us above all the limits of experience. Thus in the representation of some revolting reality, the essential thing is that the necessary be the foundation on which the poet or the narrator places the real: that he know how to dispose our mind for ideas. Provided the point from which we see and judge be elevated, it matters little if the object be low and far beneath us. When the historian Tacitus depicts the profound decadence of the Romans of the first century, it is a great soul which from a loftier position lets his looks drop down on a low object; and the disposition in which he places us is truly poetic, because it is the height where he is himself placed, and where he has succeeded in raising us, which alone renders so perceptible the baseness of the object.

Accordingly the satire of pathos must always issue from a mind deeply imbued with the ideal. It is nothing but an impulsion towards harmony that can give rise to that deep feeling of moral opposition and that ardent indignation against moral obliquity which amounted to the fullness of enthusiasm in Juvenal, Swift, Rousseau, Haller, and others. These same poets would have succeeded equally well in forms of poetry relating to all that is tender and touching in feeling, and it was only the accidents of life in their early days that diverted their minds into other walks. Nay, some amongst them actually tried their hand successfully in these other branches of poetry. The poets whose names have been just mentioned lived either at a period of degeneracy, and had scenes of painful moral obliquity presented to their view, or personal troubles had combined to fill their souls with bitter feelings. The strictly austere spirit in which Rousseau, Haller, and others paint reality is a natural result, moreover, of the philosophical mind, when with rigid adherence to laws of thought it separates the mere phenomenon from the substance of things. Yet these outer and contingent influences, which always put restraint on the mind, should never be allowed to do more than decide the direction taken by enthusiasm, nor should they ever give the material for it. The substance ought always to remain unchanged, emancipated from all external motion or stimulus, and it ought to issue from an ardent impulsion towards the ideal, which forms the only true motive that can be put forth for satirical poetry, and indeed for all sentimental poetry.

While the satire of pathos is only adapted to elevated minds, playful satire can only be adequately represented by a heart imbued with beauty. The former is preserved from triviality by the serious nature of the theme; but the latter, whose proper sphere is confined to the treatment of subjects of morally unimportant nature, would infallibly adopt the form of frivolity, and be deprived of all poetic dignity, were it not that the substance is ennobled by the form, and did not the personal dignity of the poet compensate for the insignificance of the subject. Now, it is only given to mind imbued with beauty to impress its character, its entire image, on each of its manifestations, independently of the object of its manifestations. A sublime soul can only make itself known as such by single victories over the rebellion of the senses, only in certain moments of exaltation, and by efforts of short duration. In a mind imbued with beauty, on the contrary, the ideal acts in the same manner as nature, and therefore continuously; accordingly it can manifest itself in it in a state of repose. The deep sea never appears more sublime than when it is agitated; the true beauty of a clear stream is in its peaceful course.

The question has often been raised as to the comparative preference to be awarded to tragedy or comedy. If the question is confined merely to their respective themes, it is certain that tragedy has the advantage. But if our inquiry be directed to ascertain which has the more important personality, it is probable that a decision may be given in favour of comedy. In tragedy the theme in itself does great things; in comedy the object does nothing and the poet all. Now, as in the judgments of taste, no account must be kept of the matter treated of, it follows naturally that the aesthetic value of these two kinds will be in an inverse ratio to the proper importance of their themes.

The tragic poet is supported by the theme, while the comic poet, on the contrary, has to keep up the aesthetic character of his theme by his own individual influence. The former may soar, which is not a very difficult matter, but the latter has to remain one and the same in tone; he has to be in the elevated region of art, where he must be at home, but where the tragic poet has to be projected and elevated by a bound. And this is precisely what distinguishes a soul of beauty from a sublime soul. A soul of beauty bears in itself by anticipation all great ideas; they flow without constraint and without difficulty from its very nature—an infinite nature, at least in potency, at whatever point of its career you seize it. A sublime soul can rise to all kinds of greatness, but by an effort; it can tear itself from all bondage, to all that limits and constrains it, but only by strength of will. Consequently the sublime soul is only free by broken efforts; the other with ease and always.

The noble task of comedy is to produce and keep up in us this freedom of mind, just as the end of tragedy is to re-establish in us this freedom of mind by aesthetic ways, when it has been violently suspended by passion. Consequently it is necessary that in tragedy the poet, as if he made an experiment, should artificially suspend our freedom of mind, since tragedy shows its poetic virtue by re-establishing it; in comedy, on the other hand, care must be taken that things never reach this suspension of freedom.

It is for this reason that the tragic poet invariably treats his theme in a practical manner, and the comic poet in a theoretic manner, even when the former, as happened with Lessing in his *Nathan*, should have the curious fancy to select a theoretical, and the latter should have that of choosing a practical subject. A piece is constituted a tragedy or a comedy not by the sphere from which the theme is taken, but by the tribunal before which it is judged. A tragic poet ought never to indulge in tranquil reasoning, and ought always to gain the interest of the heart; but the comic poet ought to shun the pathetic and bring into play the understanding. The former displays his art by creating continual excitement, the latter by perpetually subduing his passion; and it is natural that the art in both cases should acquire magnitude and strength in proportion as the theme of one poet is abstract, and that of the other pathetic in character. Accordingly, if tragedy sets out from a more exalted place, it must be allowed, on the other hand, that comedy aims at a more important end; and if this end could be actually attained it would make all tragedy not only unnecessary, but impossible. The aim that comedy has in view is the same as that of the highest destiny of man, and this consists in liberating himself from the influence of violent passions, and taking a calm and lucid survey of all that surrounds him, and also of his own being, and of seeing everywhere occurrence rather than fate or hazard, and ultimately rather smiling at the absurdities than shedding tears and feeling anger at sight of the wickedness of man.

It frequently happens in human life that facility of imagination, agreeable talents, a good-natured mirthfulness are taken for ornaments of the mind. The same fact is discerned in the case of poetical displays.

Now, public taste scarcely if ever soars above the sphere of the agreeable, and authors gifted with this sort of elegance of mind and style do not find it a difficult matter to usurp a glory which is or ought to be the reward of so much real labour. Nevertheless, an infallible test exists to enable us to discriminate a natural facility of manner from ideal gentleness, and qualities that consist in nothing more than natural virtue from genuine moral worth of character. This test is presented by trials such as those presented by difficulty and events offering great opportunities. Placed in positions of this kind, the genius whose essence is elegance is sure infallibly to fall into platitudes, and that virtue which only results from natural causes drops down to a material sphere. But a mind imbued with true and spiritual beauty is in cases of the kind we have supposed sure to be elevated to the highest sphere of character and of feeling. So long as Lucian merely furnishes absurdity, as in his *Wishes*, in the *Lapithas*, in *Jupiter Tragoedus*, etc., he is only a humorist, and gratifies us by his sportive humour; but he changes character in many passages in his *Nigrinus*, his *Timon*, and his *Alexander*, when his satire directs its shafts against moral depravity. Thus he begins in his *Nigrinus* his picture of the degraded corruption of Rome at that time in this way: "Wretch, why didst thou quit Greece, the sunlight, and that free and happy life? Why didst thou come here into this turmoil of splendid slavery, of service and festivals, of sycophants, flatterers, poisoners, orphan-robbers, and false friends?" It is on such occasions that the poet ought to show the lofty earnestness of soul which has to form the basis of all plays, if a poetical character is to be attained by them. A serious intention may even be detected under the malicious jests with which Lucian and Aristophanes pursue Socrates. Their purpose is to avenge truth against sophistry, and to do combat for an ideal which is not always prominently put forward. There can be no doubt that Lucian has justified this character in his Diogenes and Demonax. Again, among modern writers how grave and beautiful is the character depicted on all occasions by Cervantes in his Don Quixote! How splendid must have been the ideal that filled the mind of a poet who created a Tom Jones and a Sophonisba! How deeply and strongly our hearts are moved by the jests of Yorick when he pleases! I detect this seriousness also in our own Wieland: even the wanton sportiveness of his humour is elevated and impeded by the goodness of his heart; it has an influence even on his rhythm; nor does he ever lack elastic power, when it is his wish, to raise us up to the most elevated planes of beauty and of thought.

The same judgment cannot be pronounced on the satire of Voltaire. No doubt, also, in his case, it is the truth and simplicity of nature which here and there make us experience poetic emotions, whether he really encounters nature and depicts it in a simple character, as many times in his *Ingénu;* or whether he seeks it and avenges it as in his *Candide* and elsewhere. But when neither one nor the other takes place, he can doubtless amuse us with his fine wit, but he assuredly never touches us as a poet. There is always rather too little of the serious under his raillery, and this is what makes his vocation as poet justly suspicious. You always meet his intelligence only; never his feelings. No ideal can be detected under this light gauze envelope; scarcely can anything absolutely fixed be found under this perpetual movement. His prodigious diversity of externals and forms, far from proving anything in favour of the inner fullness of his inspiration, rather testifies to the contrary; for he has exhausted all forms without finding a single one on which he has succeeded in impressing his heart. We are almost driven to fear that in the case of his rich talent the poverty of heart alone determined his choice of satire. And how could we otherwise explain the fact that he could pursue so long a road without ever issuing from its narrow rut? Whatever may be the variety of matter and of external forms, we see the inner form return everywhere with its sterile and eternal uniformity, and in spite of his so productive career, he never accomplished in himself the circle of humanity, that circle which we see joyfully traversed throughout by the satirists previously named.

ELEGIAC POETRY

When the poet opposes nature to art, and the ideal to the real, so that nature and the ideal form the principal object of his pictures, and that the pleasure we take in them is the dominant impression, I call him an elegiac poet. In this kind, as well as in satire, I distinguish two classes. Either nature and the ideal are objects of sadness, when one is represented as lost to man and the other as unattained; or both are objects of joy, being represented to us as reality. In the first case it is elegy in the narrower sense of the term; in the second case it is the idyll in its most extended acceptation.

Indignation in the pathetic and ridicule in mirthful satire are occasioned by an enthusiasm which the ideal has excited; and thus also sadness should issue from the same source in elegy. It is this, and this only, that gives poetic value to elegy, and any other origin for this description of poetical effusion is entirely beneath the dignity of poetry. The elegiac poet seeks after nature, but he strives to find her in her beauty, and not only in her mirth; in her agreement with conceptions, and not merely in her facile disposition towards the requirements and demands of sense. Melancholy at the privation of joys, complaints at the disappearance of the world's golden age, or at the vanished happiness of youth, affection, etc., can only become the proper themes for elegiac poetry if those conditions implying peace and calm in the sphere of the senses can moreover be portrayed as states of moral harmony. On this account I cannot bring myself to regard as poetry the complaints of Ovid, which he transmitted from his place of exile by the Black Sea; nor would they appear so to me however touching and however full of passages of the highest poetry they might be. His suffering is too devoid of spirit, and nobleness. His lamentations display a want of strength and enthusiasm; though they may not reflect the traces of a vulgar soul, they display a low and sensuous condition of a noble spirit that has been trampled into the dust by its hard destiny. If, indeed, we call to mind that his regrets are directed to Rome in the Augustan age, we forgive him the pain he suffers; but even Rome in all its splendour, except it be transfigured by the imagination, is a limited greatness, and therefore a subject unworthy of poetry, which, raised above every trace of the actual, ought only to mourn over what is infinite.

Thus the object of poetic complaint ought never to be an external object, but only an internal and ideal object; even when it deplores a real loss, it must begin by making it an ideal loss. The proper work of the poet consists in bringing back the finite object to the proportions of the infinite. Consequently, the external matter of elegy, considered in itself, is always indifferent, since poetry can never employ it as it finds it, and because it is only by what it makes of it that it confers on it a poetic dignity. The elegiac poet seeks nature, but nature as an idea, and in a degree of perfection that it has never reached in reality, although he weeps over this perfection as something that has existed and is now lost. When Ossian speaks to us of the days that are no more, and of the heroes that have disappeared, his imagination has long since transformed these pictures represented to him by his memory into a pure ideal, and changed these heroes into gods. The different experiences of such or such a life in particular have become extended and confounded in the universal idea of transitoriness, and the bard, deeply moved, pursued by the increase of ruin everywhere present, takes his flight towards heaven, to find there in the course of the sun an emblem of what does not pass away.

I turn now to the elegiac poets of modern times. Rousseau, whether considered as a poet or a philosopher, always obeys the same tendency: to seek nature or to avenge it by art. According to the state of his heart, whether he prefers to seek nature or to avenge it, we see him at one time roused by elegiac feelings, at others showing the tone of the satire of Juvenal, and again, as in his Julia, delighting in the sphere of the idyll. His compositions have undoubtedly a poetic value, since their object is ideal; only he does not know how to treat it in a poetic fashion. No doubt his serious character prevents him from falling into frivolity; but this seriousness also does not allow him to rise to poetic play. Sometimes absorbed by passion, at others by abstractions, he seldom if ever reaches aesthetic freedom, which the poet ought to maintain in spite of his material before his object, and in which he ought to make the reader share. Either he is governed by his sickly sensibility and his impressions become a torture, or the force of thought chains down his imagination and destroys by its strictness of reasoning all the grace of his pictures. These two faculties, whose reciprocal influence and intimate union are what properly make the poet, are found in this writer in an uncommon degree, and he lacks only one thing—it is that the two qualities should manifest themselves actually united; it is that the proper activity of thought should show itself mixed more with feeling, and the sensuous more with thought. Accordingly, even in the ideal which he has made of human nature, he is too much taken up with the limits of this nature, and not enough with its capabilities; he always betrays a want of physical repose rather than want of moral harmony. His passionate sensuousness must be blamed when, to finish as quickly as possible that struggle in humanity which offends him, he prefers to carry man back to the unintelligent uniformity of his primitive condition, rather than see that struggle carried out in the intellectual harmony of perfect cultivation, when, rather than await the fulfilment of art he prefers not to let it begin; in short, when he prefers to place the aim nearer the earth, and to lower the ideal in order to reach it the sooner and the safer.

Among the poets of Germany who belong to this class, I shall mention here only Haller, Kleist, and Klopstock. The character of their poetry is sentimental; it is by the ideal that they touch us, not by sensuous reality; and that not so much because they are themselves nature as because they know how to fill us with enthusiasm for nature. However, what is true in general, as well of these three poets as of every sentimental poet, does not evidently exclude the faculty of moving us, in particular, by beauties of the simple genus; without this they would not be poets. I only mean that it is not their proper and dominant characteristic to receive the impression of objects with a calm feeling, simple, easy, and to give forth in like manner the impression received. Involuntarily the imagination in them anticipates intuition, and reflection is in play before the sensuous nature has done its function; they shut their eyes and stop their ears to plunge into internal meditations. Their souls could not be touched by any impression without observing immediately their own movements, without placing before their eyes and outside themselves what takes place in them. It follows from this that we never see the object itself, but what the intelligence and reflection of the poet have made of the object; and even if this object be the person itself of the poet, even when he wishes to represent to us his own feelings, we are not informed of his state immediately or at first hand; we only see how this state is reflected in his mind, and what he has thought of it in the capacity of spectator of himself. When Haller deplores the death of his wife—every one knows this beautiful elegy—and begins in the following manner:

> If I must needs sing of thy death,
> O Marian, what a song it would be!
> When sighs strive against words,
> And idea follows fast on idea,

we feel that this description is strictly true, but we feel also that the poet does not communicate to us, properly speaking, his feelings, but the thoughts that they suggest to him. Accordingly, the emotion we feel on hearing him is much less vivid; people remark that the poet's mind must have been singularly cooled down, to become thus a spectator of his own emotion.

Haller treated scarcely any subjects but the supersensuous, and part of the poems of Klopstock are also of this nature: this choice itself excludes them from the simple kind. Accordingly, in order to treat these supersensuous themes in a poetic fashion, as no body could be given to them, and they could not be made the objects of sensuous intuition, it was necessary to make them pass from the finite to the infinite, and raise them to the state of objects of spiritual intuition. In general, it may be said that it is only in this sense that a didactic poetry can be conceived without involving contradiction; for, repeating again what has been so often said, poetry has only two fields, the world of sense and the ideal world, since in the sphere of conceptions, in the world of the understanding, it cannot absolutely thrive. I confess that I do not know as yet any didactic poem, either among the ancients or among the moderns, where the subject is completely brought down to the individual, or purely and completely raised to the ideal. The most common case, in the most happy essays, is where the two principles are used together; the abstract idea predominates, and the imagination, which ought to reign over the whole domain of poetry, has merely the permission to serve the understanding. A didactic poem in which thought itself would be poetic and would remain so is a thing which we must still wait to see.

What we say here of didactic poems in general is true in particular of the poems of Haller. The thought itself of these poems is not poetical, but the execution becomes so sometimes, occasionally by the use of images, at other times by a flight towards the ideal. It is from this last quality only that the poems of Haller belong to this class. Energy, depth, a pathetic earnestness—these are the traits that distinguish this poet. He has in his soul an ideal that enkindles it, and his ardent love of truth seeks in the peaceful valleys of the Alps that innocence of the first ages that the world no longer knows. His complaint is deeply touching; he retraces in an energetic and almost bitter satire the wanderings of the mind and of the heart, and he lovingly portrays the beautiful simplicity of nature. Only, in his pictures as well as in his soul, abstraction prevails too much, and the sensuous is overweighted by the intellectual. He constantly teaches rather than paints; and even in his paintings his brush is more energetic than lovable. He is great, bold, full of fire, sublime; but he rarely and perhaps never attains to beauty.

For the solidity and depth of ideas, Kleist is far inferior to Haller; in point of grace, perhaps, he would have the advantage—if, as happens occasionally, we did not impute to him as a merit, on the one side, that which really is a want on the other. The sensuous soul of Kleist takes especial delight at the sight of country scenes and manners; he withdraws gladly from the vain jingle and rattle of society, and finds in the heart of inanimate nature the harmony and peace that are not offered to him by the moral world. How touching is his "Aspiration after Repose"! How much truth and feeling there is in these verses!

> O world, thou art the tomb of true life!
> Often a generous instinct attracts me to virtue;
> My heart is sad, a torrent of tears bathes my cheeks,

But example conquers, and thou, O fire of youth!
Soon you dry these noble tears.
A true man must live far from men!

But if the poetic instinct of Kleist leads him thus far away from the narrow circle of social relations, in solitude and among the fruitful inspirations of nature, the image of social life and of its anguish pursues him, and also alas! its chains. What he flees from he carries in himself, and what he seeks remains entirely outside him: never can he triumph over the fatal influence of his time. In vain does he find sufficient flame in his heart and enough energy in his imagination to animate by painting the cold conceptions of the understanding; cold thought each time kills the living creations of fancy, and reflection destroys the secret work of the sensuous nature. His poetry, it must be admitted, is of as brilliant colour and as variegated as the spring he celebrated in verse; his imagination is vivid and active; but it might be said that it is more variable than rich, that it sports rather than creates, that it always goes forward with a changeful gait, rather than stops to accumulate and mould things into shape. Traits succeed each other rapidly, with exuberance, but without concentrating to form an individual, without completing each other to make a living whole, without rounding to a form, a figure. While he remains in purely lyrical poetry, and pauses amidst his landscapes of country life, on the one hand the greater freedom of the lyrical form and, on the other, the more arbitrary nature of the subject prevent us from being struck with this defect; in these sorts of works it is in general rather the feelings of the poet than the object in itself of which we expect the portraiture. But this defect becomes too apparent when he undertakes, as in *Cissides und Paches,* or in his Seneca, to represent men and human actions; because here the imagination sees itself kept in within certain fixed and necessary limits, and because here the effect can only be derived from the object itself. Kleist becomes poor, tiresome, jejune, and insupportably frigid; an example full of lessons for those who, without having an inner vocation, aspire to issue from musical poetry, to rise to the regions of plastic poetry. A spirit of this family, Thomson, has paid the same penalty to human infirmity.

In the sentimental kind, and especially in that part of the sentimental kind which we name elegiac, there are but few modern poets, and still fewer ancient ones, who can be compared to our Klopstock. Musical poetry has produced in this poet all that can be attained out of the limits of the living form, and out of the sphere of individuality, in the region of

ideas. It would, no doubt, be doing him a great injustice to dispute entirely in his case that individual truth and that feeling of life with which
the simple poet describes his pictures. Many of his odes, many separate
traits in his dramas, and in his *Messias* ["Messiah"] represent the object
with a striking truth, and mark the outline admirably; especially, when
the object is his own heart, he has given evidence on many occasions
of a great natural disposition and of a charming simplicity. I mean only
that it is not in this that the proper force of Klopstock consists, and that
it would not perhaps be right to seek for this throughout his work. Viewed
as a production of musical poetry, the *Messias* is a magnificent work; but
in the light of plastic poetry, where we look for determined forms and
forms determined for the intuition, the *Messias* leaves much to be desired.
Perhaps in this poem the figures are sufficiently determined, but they are
not so with intuition in view. It is abstraction alone that created them,
and abstraction alone can discern them. They are excellent types to express ideas, but they are not individuals nor living figures. With regard
to the imagination, which the poet ought to address, and which he ought
to command by putting before it always perfectly determinate forms, it
is left here much too free to represent as it wishes these men and these
angels, these divinities and demons, this paradise and this hell. We see
quite well the vague outlines in which the understanding must be kept
to conceive these personages; but we do not find the limit clearly traced
in which the imagination must be enclosed to represent them. And what
I say here of characters must apply to all that in this poem is, or ought to
be, action and life, and not only in this epopee, but also in the dramatic
poetry of Klopstock. For the understanding all is perfectly determined
and bounded in them—I need only here recall his Judas, his Pilate, his
Philo, his Solomon in the tragedy that bears that name—but for the imagination all this wants form too much, and I must readily confess I do
not find that our poet is at all in his sphere here. His sphere is always the
realm of ideas; and he knows how to raise all he touches to the infinite. It
might be said that he strips away their bodily envelope, to spiritualize
them, from all the objects with which he is occupied, in the same way
that other poets clothe all that is spiritual with a body. The pleasure occasioned by his poems must almost always be obtained by an exercise
of the faculty of reflection; the feelings he awakens in us, and that so
deeply and energetically, flow always from supersensuous sources.
Hence the earnestness, the strength, the elasticity, the depth, that characterize all that comes from him; but from that also issues that perpetual
tension of mind in which we are kept when reading him. No poet—except

perhaps Young, who in this respect exacts even more than Klopstock, without giving us so much compensation—no poet could be less adapted than Klopstock to play the part of favourite author and guide in life, because he never does anything else than lead us out of life, because he never calls to arms anything save spirit, without giving recreation and refreshment to sensuous nature by the calm presence of any object. His muse is chaste, it has nothing of the earthly, it is immaterial and holy as his religion; and we are forced to admit with admiration that if he wanders sometimes on these high places, it never happened to him to fall from them. But precisely for this reason, I confess in all ingenuousness, that I am not free from anxiety for the common sense of those who quite seriously and unaffectedly make Klopstock the favourite book, the book in which we find sentiments fitting all situations, or to which we may revert at all times: perhaps even—and I suspect it—Germany has seen enough results of his dangerous influence. It is only in certain dispositions of the mind, and in hours of exaltation, that recourse can be had to Klopstock, and that he can be felt. It is for this reason that he is the idol of youth, without, however, being by any means the happiest choice that they could make. Youth, which always aspires to something beyond real life, which avoids all stiffness of form, and finds all limits too narrow, lets itself be carried away with love, with delight, into the infinite spaces opened up to them by this poet. But wait till the youth has become a man, and till, from the domain of ideas, he comes back to the world of experience, then you will see this enthusiastic love of Klopstock decrease greatly, without, however, a riper age changing at all the esteem due to this unique phenomenon, to this so extraordinary genius, to these noble sentiments—the esteem that Germany in particular owes to his high merit.

I have said that this poet was great specially in the elegiac style, and it is scarcely necessary to confirm this judgment by entering into particulars. Capable of exercising all kinds of action on the heart, and having graduated as master in all that relates to sentimental poetry, he can sometimes shake the soul by the most sublime pathos, at others cradle it with sweet and heavenly sensations. Yet his heart prefers to follow the direction of a lofty spiritual melancholy; and, however sublime be the tones of his harp and of his lyre, they are always the tender notes of his lute that resound with most truth and the deepest emotion. I take as witnesses all those whose nature is pure and sensuous: would they not be ready to give all the passages where Klopstock is strong and bold; all those fictions, all the magnificent descriptions, all the models of eloquence which abound in the *Messias,* all those dazzling comparisons in which our poet excels—would they not exchange them for the pages breathing tenderness, the "Elegy to Ebert," for example, or that admirable poem entitled "Bardalus," or again, the "Tombs Opened before the Hour," the "Summer's Night," the "Lake of Zurich," and many other pieces of this kind? In the same way the *Messias* is dear to me as a treasure of elegiac feelings and of ideal paintings, though I am not much satisfied with it as the recital of an action and as an epic.

I ought, perhaps, before quitting this department, to recall the merits in this style of Uz, Denis, Gessner—in *Der Tod Abels* ["Death of Abel"]— Jacobi, Gerstenberg, Hölty, von Goeckingk, and several others who all knew how to touch by ideas, and whose poems belong to the sentimental kind in the sense in which we have agreed to understand the word. But my object is not here to write a history of German poetry; I only wished to clear up what I said further back by some examples from our literature. I wished to show that the ancient and the modern poets, the authors of simple poetry and of sentimental poetry, follow essentially different paths to arrive at the same end: that the former move by nature, individuality, a very vivid sensuous element; while the latter do it by means of ideas and a high spirituality, exercising over our minds an equally powerful though less extensive influence.

It has been seen, by the examples which precede, how sentimental poetry conceives and treats subjects taken from nature; perhaps the reader may be curious to know how also simple poetry treats a subject of the sentimental order. This is, as it seems, an entirely new question, and one of special difficulty; for, in the first place, has a subject of the sentimental order ever been presented in primitive and simple periods? And in modern times, where is the simple poet with whom we could make this experiment? This has not, however, prevented genius from setting this problem, and solving it in a wonderfully happy way. A poet in whose mind nature works with a purer and more faithful activity than in any other, and who is perhaps of all modern poets the one who departs the least from the sensuous truth of things, has proposed this problem to himself in his conception of a mind, and of the dangerous extreme of the sentimental character. This mind and this character have been portrayed by the modern poet we speak of, a character which with a burning sensuousness embraces the ideal and flies the real, to soar up to an infinite devoid of being, always occupied in seeking out of himself what he incessantly destroys in himself; a mind that only finds reality in his dreams, and to whom the realities of life are only limits and obstacles; in short, a mind that sees only in its own existence a barrier, and goes on, as it were, logically to break down this barrier in order to penetrate to true reality.

It is interesting to see with what a happy instinct all that is of a nature to feed the sentimental mind is gathered together in Werther: a dreamy and unhappy love, a very vivid feeling for nature, the religious sense coupled with the spirit of philosophic contemplation, and lastly, to omit nothing, the world of Ossian, dark, formless, melancholy. Add to this the aspect under which reality is presented, all is depicted which is least adapted to make it lovable, or rather all that is most fit to make it hated; see how all external circumstances unite to drive back the unhappy man into his ideal world; and now we understand that it was quite impossible for a character thus constituted to save itself, and issue from the circle in which it was enclosed. The same contrast reappears in the *Torquato Tasso* of the same poet, though the characters are very different. Even his last romance presents, like his first, this opposition between the poetic mind and the common sense of practical men, between the ideal and the real, between the subjective mode and the objective mode of seeing and representing things; it is the same opposition, I say, but with what a diversity! Even in *Faust* we still find this contrast, rendered, I admit—as the subject required—much more coarsely on both hands, and material-ized. It would be quite worth while if a psychological explanation were attempted of this character, personified and specified in four such differ-ent ways.

It has been observed further back that a mere disposition to frivolity of mind, to a merry humour, if a certain fund of the ideal is not joined to it, does not suffice to constitute the vocation of a satirical poet, though this mistake is frequently made. In the same way a mere disposition for tender sentiments, softness of heart, and melancholy do not suffice to constitute a vocation for elegy. I cannot detect the true poetical talent, either on one side or the other; it wants the essential, I mean the energetic and fruitful principle that ought to enliven the subject, and produce true beauty. Accordingly, the productions of this latter nature, of the tender nature, do nothing but enervate us; and without refreshing the heart, without occupying the mind, they are only able to flatter in us the sensu-ous nature. A constant disposition to this mode of feeling ends necessarily, in the long run, by weakening the character and makes it fall into a state of passivity from which nothing real can issue, either for external or for internal life. People have, therefore, been quite right to persecute by pitiless raillery this fatal mania of sentimentality and of tearful melancholy which possessed Germany eighteen years since, in consequence of certain excellent works that were ill understood and indiscreetly imitated. People have been right, I say, to combat this perversity, though the indulgence with which men are disposed to receive the parodies of these elegiac caricatures—that are very little better themselves—the complaisance shown to bad wit, to heartless satire and spiritless mirth, show clearly enough that this zeal against false sentimentalism does not issue from quite a pure source. In the balance of true taste one cannot weigh more than the other, considering that both here and there is wanting that which forms the aesthetic value of a work of art, the intimate union of spirit with matter, and the twofold relation of the work with the faculty of perception as well as with the faculty of the ideal.

People have turned Siegwart and his convent story into ridicule, and yet the *Travels into the South of France* are admired; yet both works have an equal claim to be esteemed in certain respects, and as little to be unreservedly praised in others. A true, though excessive, sensuousness gives value to the former of these two romances; a lively and sportive humour, a fine wit, recommends the other: but one totally lacks all sobriety of mind that would befit it, the other lacks all aesthetic dignity. If you consult experience, one is rather ridiculous; if you think of the ideal, the other is almost contemptible. Now, as true beauty must of necessity accord both with nature and with the ideal, it is clear that neither the one nor the other of these two romances could pretend to pass for a fine work. And notwithstanding all this, it is natural, as I know it by my own experience, that the romance of Thümmel should be read with much pleasure. As a fact it only wounds those requirements which have their principle in the ideal, and which consequently do not exist for the greater part of readers; requirements that, even in persons of most delicate feeling, do not make themselves felt at the moments when we read romances. With regard to the other needs of the mind, and especially to those of the senses, this book on the other hand affords unusual satisfaction. Accordingly, it must be, and will be so, that this book will remain justly one of the favourite works of our age, and of all epochs when men only write aesthetic works to please, and people only read to get pleasure.

But does not poetical literature also offer, even in its classical monuments, some analogous examples of injuries inflicted or attempted against the ideal and its superior purity? Are there not some who, by the gross, sensuous nature of their subject, seem to depart strangely from the spiritualism I here demand of all works of art? If this is permitted to the poet, the chaste nurseling of the muses, ought it not to be conceded to the novelist, who is only the half-brother of the poet, and who still touches by so many points? I can the less avoid this question because there are masterpieces, both in the elegiac and in the satirical kind, where the authors seek and preach up a nature quite different from that I am discussing in this Essay, and where they seem to defend it, not so much against bad, as against good, morals. The natural conclusion would be either that this sort of poem ought to be rejected, or that, in tracing here the idea of elegiac poetry, we have granted far too much to what is arbitrary.

The question I asked was whether what was permitted by the poet might not be tolerated in a prose narrator, too? The answer is contained in the question. What is allowed in the poet proves nothing about what must be allowed in one who is not a poet. This tolerancy in fact reposes on the very idea which we ought to make to ourselves of the poet, and only on this idea; what in his case is legitimate freedom is only a licence worthy of contempt as soon as it no longer takes its source in the ideal, in those high and noble inspirations which make the poet.

The laws of decency are strangers to innocent nature; the experience of corruption alone has given birth to them. But when once this experience has been made, and natural innocence has disappeared from manners, these laws are henceforth sacred laws that man, who has a moral sense, ought not to infringe upon. They reign in an artificial world with the same right that the laws of nature reign in the innocence of primitive ages. But by what characteristic is the poet recognized? Precisely by his silencing in his soul all that recalls an artificial world, and by causing nature herself to revive in him with her primitive simplicity. The moment he has done this, he is emancipated by this alone from all the laws by which a depraved heart secures itself against itself. He is pure, he is innocent, and all that is permitted to innocent nature is equally permitted to him. But you who read him or listen to him, if you have lost your innocence, and if you are incapable of finding it again, even for a moment, in a purifying contact with the poet, it is your own fault, and not his: why do not you leave him alone? It is not for you that he has sung!

Here follows, therefore, in what relates to these kinds of freedoms, the rules that we can lay down.

Let us remark in the first place that nature only can justify these licences; whence it follows that you could not legitimately take them up of your own choice, nor with a determination of imitating them; the will, in fact, ought always to be directed according to the laws of morality, and on its part all condescending to the sensuous is absolutely unpardonable. These licences must, therefore, above all, be simplicity. But how can we be convinced that they are actually simple? We shall hold them to be so if we see them accompanied and supported by all the other circumstances which also have their spring of action in nature; for nature can only be recognized by the close and strict consistency, by the unity and uniformity, of its effects. It is only a soul that has on all occasions a horror of all kinds of artifice, and which consequently rejects them even where they would be useful—it is only that soul which we permit to be emancipated from them when the artificial conventionalities hamper and hinder it. A heart that submits to all the obligations of nature has alone the right to profit also by the liberties which it authorizes. All the other feelings of that heart ought consequently to bear the stamp of nature: it will be true, simple, free, frank, sensible, and straightforward; all disguise, all cunning, all arbitrary fancy, all egotistical pettiness will be banished from his character, and you will see no trace of them in his writings.

Second rule: beautiful nature alone can justify freedoms of this kind; whence it follows that they ought not to be a mere outbreak of the appetites; for all that proceeds exclusively from the wants of sensuous nature is contemptible. It is, therefore, from the totality and the fullness of human nature that these vivid manifestations must also issue. We must find humanity in them. But how can we judge that they proceed in fact from our whole nature, and not only from an exclusive and vulgar want of the sensuous nature? For this purpose it is necessary that we should see —that they should represent to us—this whole of which they form a particular feature. This disposition of the mind to experience the impressions of the sensuous is in itself an innocent and an indifferent thing. It does not sit well on a man only because of its being common to animals with him; it augurs in him the lack of true and perfect humanity. It only shocks us in the poem because such a work having the pretension to please us, the author consequently seems to think us capable, us also, of this moral infirmity. But when we see in the man who has let himself be drawn into it by surprise all the other characteristics that human nature in general embraces; when we find in the work where these liberties have been taken the expression of all the realities of human nature, this motive of discontent disappears, and we can enjoy, without anything changing our joy, this simple expression of a true and beautiful nature. Consequently, this same poet who ventures to allow himself to associate us with feelings so basely human, ought to know on the other hand how to raise us to all that is grand, beautiful, and sublime in our nature.

We should, therefore, have found there a measure to which we could subject the poet with confidence, when he trespasses on the ground of decency, and when he does not fear to penetrate as far as that in order freely to paint nature. His work is common, base, absolutely inexcusable from the moment it is frigid, and from the moment it is empty, because that shows a prejudice, a vulgar necessity, an unhealthy appeal to our appetites. His work on the other hand is beautiful and noble, and we ought to applaud it without any consideration for all the objections of frigid decency, as soon as we recognize in it simplicity, the alliance of spiritual nature and of the heart.

Perhaps I shall be told that if we adopt this criterion, most of the recitals of this kind composed by the French, and the best imitations made of them in Germany, would not perhaps find their interest in it; and that it might be the same, at least in part with many of the productions of our most intellectual and amiable poet, without even excepting his masterpieces. I should have nothing to reply to this. The sentence after all is anything but new, and I am only justifying the judgment pronounced long since on this matter by all men of delicate perceptions. But these same principles which, applied to the works of which I have just spoken, seem perhaps in too strict a spirit, might also be found too indulgent when applied to some other works. I do not deny, in fact, that the same reasons which make me hold to be quite inexcusable the dangerous pictures drawn by the Roman Ovid and the German Ovid, those of Crébillon, of Voltaire, of Marmontel, who pretends to write moral tales! —of Lacroix, and of many others—that these same reasons, I say, reconcile me with the elegies of the Roman Propertius and of the German Propertius, and even with some of the decried productions of Diderot. This is because the former of these works are only witty, prosaic, and voluptuous, while the others are poetic, human, and simple.

IDYLL

It remains for me to say a few words about this third kind of sentimental poetry—some few words and no more, for I propose to speak of it at another time with the developments particularly demanded by the theme.

This kind of poetry generally presents the idea and description of an innocent and happy humanity. This innocence and bliss seeming remote from the artificial refinements of fashionable society, poets have removed the scene of the idyll from crowds of worldly life to the simple shepherd's cot, and have given it a place in the infancy of humanity before the beginning of culture. These limitations are evidently accidental; they do not form the object of the idyll, but are only to be regarded as the most natural means to attain this end. The end is everywhere to portray man in a state of innocence, which means a state of harmony and peace with himself and the external world.

But a state such as this is not merely met with before the dawn of civilization; it is also the state to which civilization aspires, as to its last end, if only it obeys a determined tendency in its progress. The idea of a similar state, and the belief of the possible reality of this state, is the only thing that can reconcile man with all the evils to which he is exposed in the path of civilization; and if this idea were only a chimera, the complaints of those who accuse civil life and the culture of the intelligence as an evil for which there is no compensation, and who represent this primitive state of nature that we have renounced as the real end of humanity—their complaints, I say, would have a perfectly just foundation. It is, therefore, of infinite importance for the man engaged in the path of civilization to see confirmed in a sensuous manner the belief that this idea can be accomplished in the world of sense, that this state of innocence can be realized in it; and as real experience, far from keeping up this belief, is rather made incessantly to contradict it, poetry comes here, as in many other cases, in aid of reason, to cause this idea to pass into the condition of an intuitive idea, and to realize it in a particular fact. No doubt this innocence of pastoral life is also a poetic idea, and the imagination must already have shown its creative power in that. But the problem, with this datum, becomes infinitely simpler and easier to solve; and we must not forget that the elements of these pictures already existed in real life, and that it was only requisite to gather up the separate traits to form a whole. Under a fine sky, in a primitive society, when all the relations are still simple, when science is limited to so little, nature is easily satisfied, and man turns to savagery only when he is tortured by want. All nations that have a history have a paradise, an age of innocence, a golden age. Nay, more than this, every man has his paradise, his golden age, which he remembers with more or less enthusiasm, according as he is more or less poetical. Thus experience itself furnishes sufficient traits to this picture which the pastoral idyll executes. But this does not prevent the pastoral idyll from remaining always a beautiful and an encouraging fiction; and poetic genius, in retracing these pictures, has really worked in favour of the ideal. For, to the man who has once departed from simple nature, and who has been abandoned to the dangerous guidance of his reason, it is of the greatest importance to find the laws of nature expressed in a faithful copy, to see their image in a clear mirror, and to reject all the stains of artificial life. There is, however, a circumstance which remarkably lessens the aesthetic value of these sorts of poetry. By the very fact that the idyll is transported to the time that precedes civilization, it also loses the advantages thereof; and by its nature finds itself in opposition to itself. Thus, in a theoretical sense, it takes us back at the same time that in a practical sense it leads us on and ennobles us. Unhappily it places behind us the end towards which it ought to lead us, and consequently it can only inspire us with the sad feeling of a loss, and not the joyous feeling of a hope. As these poems can only attain their end by dispensing with all art, and by simplifying human nature, they have the highest value for the heart, but they are also far too poor for what concerns the mind, and their uniform circle is too quickly traversed. Accordingly, we can only seek them and love them in moments in which we need calm, and not when our faculties aspire after movement and exercise. A morbid mind will find its cure in them, a sound soul will not find its food in them. They cannot vivify, they can only soften. This defect, grounded in the essence of the pastoral idyll, has not been remedied by the whole art of poets. I know that this kind of poem is not without admirers, and that there are readers enough who prefer an Amyntus and a Daphnis to the most splendid masterpieces of the epic or the dramatic muse; but in them it is less the aesthetical taste than the feeling of an individual want that pronounces on works of art; and their judgment, by that very fact, could not be taken into consideration here. The reader who judges with his mind, and whose heart is sensuous, without being blind to the merit of these poems, will confess that he is rarely affected by them, and that they tire him most quickly. But they act with so much the more effect in the exact moment of need. But must the truly beautiful be reduced to await our hours of need? And is it not rather its office to awaken in our soul the want that it is going to satisfy?

The reproaches I here level against the bucolic idyll cannot be understood of the sentimental. The simple pastoral, in fact, cannot be deprived of aesthetic value, since this value is already found in the mere form. To explain myself: every kind of poetry is bound to possess an infinite ideal value, which alone constitutes it a true poetry; but it can satisfy this condition in two different ways. It can give us the feeling of the infinite as to form, by representing the object altogether limited and individualizing it; it can awaken in us the feeling of the infinite as to matter, in freeing its object from all limits in which it is enclosed, by idealizing this object; therefore it can have an ideal value either by an absolute representation or by the representation of an absolute. Simple poetry takes the former road, the other is that of sentimental poetry. Accordingly, the simple poet is not exposed to failure in value so long as he keeps faithfully to nature, which is always completely circumscribed, that is, is infinite as regards form. The sentimental poet, on the contrary, by that very fact, that nature only offers him completely circumscribed objects, finds in it an obstruction when he wishes to give an absolute value to a particular object. Thus the sentimental poet understands his interests badly when he goes along the trail of the simple poet, and borrows his objects from him—objects which by themselves are perfectly indifferent, and which only become poetical by the way in which they are treated. By this he imposes on himself without any necessity the same limits that confine the field on the simple poet, without, however, being able to carry out the limitation properly, or to vie with his rival in absolute definiteness of representation. He ought rather, therefore, to depart from the simple poet, just in the choice of subject; because the latter having the advantage of him on the score of form, it is only by the nature of the objects that he can resume the upper hand.

Applying this to the pastoral idylls of the sentimental poet, we see why these poems, whatever amount of art and genius be displayed in them, do not fully satisfy the heart or the mind. An ideal is proposed in it, and, at the same time, the writer keeps to this narrow and poor medium of pastoral life. Would it not have been better, on the contrary, to choose for the ideal another frame, or for the pastoral world another kind of picture? These pictures are just ideal enough for painting to lose its individual truth in them, and, again, just individual enough for the ideal in them to suffer therefrom. For example, a shepherd of Gessner can neither charm by the illusion of nature nor by the beauty of imitation; he is too ideal a being for that, but he does not satisfy us any more as an ideal by the infinity of the thought; he is a far too limited creature to give us this satisfaction. He will, therefore, please up to a certain point all classes of readers, without exception, because he seeks to unite the simple with the sentimental, and he thus gives a commencement of satisfaction to the two opposite exigencies that may be brought to bear on any particular part of a poem; but the author, in trying to unite the two points, does not fully satisfy either one or the other exigency, as you do not find in him either pure nature or the pure ideal; he cannot rank himself as entirely up to the mark of a stringent critical taste, for taste does not accept anything equivocal or incomplete in aesthetical matters. It is a strange thing that, in the poet whom I have named, this equivocal character extends to the language, which floats undecided between poetry and prose, as if he feared either to depart too far from nature by speaking rhythmical language, or if he completely freed himself from rhythm, to lose all poetic flight. Milton gives a higher satisfaction to the mind, in the magnificent picture of the first human pair, and of the state of innocence in paradise— the most beautiful idyll I know of the sentimental kind. Here nature is noble, inspired, simple, full of breadth, and, at the same time, of depth; it is humanity in its highest moral value, clothed in the most graceful form.

Thus, even in respect to the idyll, as well as to all kinds of poetry, we must once for all declare either for individuality or ideality; for to aspire to give satisfaction to both exigencies is the surest means, unless you have reached the terminus of perfection, to miss both ends. If the modern poet thinks he feels enough of the Greeks' mind to vie with them, notwithstanding all the indocility of his matter, on their own ground, namely that of simple poetry, let him do it exclusively, and place himself apart from all the requirements of the sentimental taste of his age. No doubt it is very doubtful if he come up to his models; between the original and the happiest imitation there will always remain a notable distance; but, by taking this road, he is at all events secure of producing a really poetic work. If, on the other hand, he feels himself carried to the ideal by the instinct of sentimental poetry, let him decide to pursue this end fully; let him seek the ideal in its purity, and let him not pause till he has reached the highest regions without looking behind him to know if the real follows him, and does not leave him by the way. Let him not lower himself to this wretched expedient of spoiling the ideal to accommodate himself to the wants of human weakness, and to turn out mind in order to play more easily with the heart. Let him not take us back to our infancy, to make us buy, at the cost of the most precious acquisitions of the understanding, a repose that can only last as long as the slumber of our spiritual faculties; but let him lead us on to emancipation, and give us this feeling of higher harmony which compensates for all his troubles and secures the happiness of the victor! Let him prepare as his task an idyll that realizes the pastoral innocence, even in the children of civilization, and in all the conditions of the most militant and excited life; of thought enlarged by culture; of the most refined art; of the most delicate social conventionalities—an idyll, in short, that is made, not to bring back man to Arcadia, but to lead him to Elysium.

This idyll, as I conceive it, is the idea of humanity definitely reconciled with itself, in the individual as well as in the whole of society; it is union freely re-established between inclination and duty; it is nature purified, raised to its highest moral dignity; in short, it is no less than the ideal of beauty applied to real life. Thus, the character of this idyll is to reconcile perfectly all the contradictions between the real and the ideal, which formed the matter of satirical and elegiac poetry, and, setting aside their contradictions, to put an end to all conflict between the feelings of the soul. Thus, the dominant expression of this kind of poetry would be calm; but the calm that follows the accomplishment, and not that of indolence— the calm that comes from the equilibrium re-established between the faculties, and not from the suspending of their exercise; from the fullness of our strength, and not from our infirmity; the calm, in short, which is accompanied in the soul by the feeling of an infinite power. But precisely because idyll thus conceived removes all idea of struggle, it will be infinitely more difficult than it was in two previously named kinds of poetry to express movement; yet this is an indispensable condition, without which poetry can never act on men's souls. The most perfect unity is required, but unity ought not to wrong variety; the heart must be satisfied, but without the inspiration ceasing on that account. The solution of this problem is properly what ought to be given us by the theory of the idyll.

Now what are the relations of the two poetries to one another, and their relations to the poetic ideal? Here are the principles we have established.

Nature has granted this favour to the simple poet, to act always as an indivisible unity, to be at all times identical and perfect, and to represent, in the real world, humanity at its highest value. In opposition, it has given a powerful faculty to the sentimental poet, or, rather, it has imprinted an ardent feeling on him: this is to replace out of himself this first unity that abstraction has destroyed in him, to complete humanity in his person, and to pass from a limited state to an infinite state. They both propose to represent human nature fully, or they would not be poets; but the simple poet has always the advantage of sensuous reality over the sentimental poet, by setting forth as a real fact what the other aspires only to reach. Every one experiences this in the pleasure he takes in simple poetry. We there feel that the human faculties are brought into play; no vacuum is felt; we have the feeling of unity, without distinguishing anything of what we experience; we enjoy both our spiritual activity and also the fullness of physical life. Very different is the disposition of mind elicited by the sentimental poet. Here we feel only a vivid aspiration to produce in us this harmony of which we had in the other case the consciousness and reality; to make of ourselves a single and same totality; to realize in ourselves the idea of humanity as a complete expression. Hence it comes that the mind is here all in movement, stretched, hesitating between contrary feelings; whereas it was before calm and at rest, in harmony with itself, and fully satisfied.

But if the simple poet has the advantage over the sentimental poet on the score of reality; if he causes really to live that of which the other can only elicit a vivid instinct, the sentimental poet, in compensation, has this great advantage over the simple poet: to be in a position to offer to this instinct a greater object than that given by his rival, and the only one he could give. All reality, we know, is below the ideal; all that exists has limits, but thought is infinite. This limitation, to which everything is subject in sensuous reality, is, therefore, a disadvantage for the simple poet, while the absolute, unconditional freedom of the ideal profits the sentimental poet. No doubt, the former accomplishes his object, but this object is limited; the second, I admit, does not entirely accomplish his, but his object is infinite. Here I appeal to experience. We pass pleasantly to real life and things from the frame of mind in which the simple poet has placed us. On the other hand, the sentimental poet will always disgust us, for a time, with real life. This is because the infinite character has, in a manner, enlarged our mind beyond its natural measure, so that nothing it finds in the world of sense can fill its capacity. We prefer to fall back in contemplation on ourselves, where we find food for this awakened impulse towards the ideal world; while, in the simple poet, we only strive to issue out of ourselves, in search of sensuous objects. Sentimental poetry is the offspring of retirement and science, and invites to it; simple poetry is inspired by the spectacle of life, and brings back life.

I have styled simple poetry a gift of nature, to show that thought has no share in it. It is a first jet, a happy inspiration, that needs no correction, when it turns out well, and which cannot be rectified if ill turned out. The entire work of the simple genius is accomplished by feeling; in that is its strength, and in it are its limits. If, then, he has not felt at once in poetic manner—that is, in a perfectly human manner—no art in the world can remedy this defect. Criticism may help him to see the defect, but can place no beauty in its stead. Simple genius must draw all from nature; it can do nothing, or almost nothing, by its will; and it will fulfil the idea of this kind of poetry provided nature acts in it by an inner necessity. Now, it is true that all which happens by nature is necessary, and all the productions, happy or not, of the simple genius, which is disassociated from nothing so much as from arbitrary will, are also imprinted with this character of necessity; momentary constraint is one thing, and the internal necessity dependent on the totality of things, another. Considered as a whole, nature is independent and infinite; in isolated operations it is poor and limited. The same distinction holds good in respect to the nature of the poet. The very moment when he is most happily inspired depends on a preceding instant, and consequently only a conditional necessity can be attributed to him. But now the problem that the poet ought to solve is to make an individual state similar to the human whole, and consequently to base it in an absolute and necessary manner on itself. It is therefore necessary that at the moment of inspiration every trace of a temporal need should be banished, and that the object itself, however limited, should not limit the flight of the poet. But it may be conceived that this is only possible in so far as the poet brings to the object an absolute freedom, an absolute fullness of faculties, and in so far as he is prepared by an anterior exercise to embrace all things with all his humanity. Now he cannot acquire this exercise except by the world in which he lives, and of which he receives the impressions immediately. Thus simple genius is in a state of dependence with regard to experience, while the sentimental genius is forced from it. We know that the sentimental genius begins its operation at the place where the other finishes its own; its virtue is to complete by the elements which it derives from itself a defective object, and to transport itself by its own strength from a limited state to one of absolute freedom. Thus the simple poet needs a help from without, while the sentimental poet feeds his genius from his own fund, and purifies himself by himself. The former requires a picturesque nature, a poetical world, a simple humanity which casts its eyes around; for he ought to do his work without issuing from the sensuous sphere. If external aid fails him, if he be surrounded by matter not speaking to mind, one of two things will happen: either, if the general character of the poet-race is what prevails in him, he issues from the particular class to which he belongs as a poet, and becomes sentimental to be at any rate poetic; or, if his particular character as simple poet has the upper hand, he leaves his species, and becomes a common nature, in order to remain at any rate natural. The former of these two alternatives might represent the case of the principal poets of the sentimental kind in Roman antiquity and in modern times. Born at another period of the world, transplanted under another sky, these poets who stir us now by ideas, would have charmed us by individual truth and simple beauty. The other alternative is the almost unavoidable quicksand for a poet who, thrown into a vulgar world, cannot resolve to lose sight of nature.

I mean, to lose sight of actual nature; but the greatest care must be given to distinguish actual nature from true nature, which is the subject of simple poetry. Actual nature exists everywhere; but true nature is so much the more rare because it requires an internal necessity that determines its existence. Every eruption of passion, however vulgar, is real—it may be even true nature; but it is not true human nature, for true human nature requires that the self-directing faculty in us should have a share in the manifestation, and the expression of this faculty is always dignified. All moral baseness is an actual human phenomenon, but I hope not real human nature, which is always noble. All the faults of taste cannot be surveyed that have been occasioned in criticism or the practice of art by this confusion between actual human nature and true human nature. The greatest trivialities are tolerated and applauded under the pretext that they are real nature. Caricatures not to be tolerated in the real world are carefully preserved in the poetic world and reproduced according to nature! The poet can certainly imitate a lower nature, and it enters into the very definition of a satirical poet; but then a beauty by its own nature must sustain and raise the object, and the vulgarity of the subject must not lower the imitator too much. If at the moment he paints he is true human nature himself, the object of his paintings is indifferent; but it is only on this condition we can tolerate a faithful reproduction of reality. Unhappy for us readers when the rod of satire falls into hands that nature meant to handle another instrument, and when, devoid of all poetic talent, with nothing but the ape's mimicry, they exercise it brutally at the expense of our taste!

But vulgar nature has even its dangers for the simple poet; for the simple poet is formed by this fine harmony of the feeling and thinking faculty, which yet is only an idea, never actually realized. Even in the happiest geniuses of this class, receptivity will always more or less carry the day over spontaneous activity. But receptivity is always more or less subordinate to external impressions, and nothing but a perpetual activity of the creative faculty could prevent matter from exercising a blind violence over this quality. Now every time this happens the feeling becomes vulgar instead of poetical.

No genius of the simple class, from Homer down to Bodmer, has entirely steered clear of this quicksand. It is evident that it is most perilous to those who have to struggle against external vulgarity, or who have parted with their refinement owing to a want of proper restraint. The first-named difficulty is the reason why even authors of high cultivation are not always emancipated from platitudes—a fact which has prevented many splendid talents from occupying the place to which they

were summoned by nature. For this reason, a comic poet whose genius
has chiefly to deal with scenes of real life is more liable to the danger of
acquiring vulgar habits of style and expression—a fact evidenced in the
case of Aristophanes, Plautus, and all the poets who have followed in their
track. Even Shakespeare, with all his sublimity, suffers us to fall very low
now and then. Again, Lope de Vega, Molière, Regnard, Goldoni worry us
with frequent trifling. Holberg drags us down into the mire. Schlegel, a
German poet among the most remarkable for intellectual talent, with
genius to raise him to a place among poets of the first order; Gellert, a
truly simple poet; Rabener; and Lessing himself, if I am warranted to
introduce his name in this category—this highly cultivated scholar of
criticism and vigilant examiner of his own genius—all these suffer in
different degrees from the platitudes and uninspired movements of the
natures they chose as the theme of their satire. With regard to more recent
authors of this class, I avoid naming any of them, as I can make no
exceptions in their case.

But not only is simple genius exposed to the danger of coming too near
to vulgar reality; the ease of expression, even this too close approximation
to reality, encourages vulgar imitators to try their hand in poetry. Sentimental poetry, though offering danger enough, has this advantage, to
keep this crowd at a distance, for it is not for the first comer to rise to the
ideal; but simple poetry makes them believe that, with feeling and
humour, you need only imitate real nature to claim the title of poet. Now
nothing is more revolting than platitude when it tries to be simple and
amiable, instead of hiding its repulsive nature under the veil of art. This
occasions the incredible trivialities loved by the Germans under the name
of simple and facetious songs, and which give them endless amusement
round a well-garnished table. Under the pretext of good humour and of
sentiment people tolerate these poverties; but this good humour and this
sentiment ought to be carefully proscribed. The muses of the Pleisse, in
particular, are singularly pitiful; and other muses respond to them, from
the banks of the Seine and the Elbe. If these pleasantries are flat, the
passion heard on our tragic stage is equally pitiful, for, instead of imitating
true nature, it is only an insipid and ignoble expression of the actual.
Thus, after shedding torrents of tears, you feel as you would after visiting
a hospital or reading the "Human Misery" of Saltzmann. But the evil is
worse in satirical poetry and comic romance, kinds which touch closely on
every-day life, and which consequently, as all frontier posts, ought to be
in safer hands. In truth, he less than any other is called on to become the
painter of his century, who is himself the child and caricature of his

century. But as, after all, nothing is easier than to take in hand, among our acquaintances, a comic character—a big, fat man—and draw a coarse likeness of him on paper, the sworn enemies of poetic inspiration are often led to blot some paper in this way to amuse a circle of friends. It is true that a pure heart, a well-made mind, will never confound these vulgar productions with the inspirations of simple genius. But purity of feeling is the very thing that is wanting, and in most cases nothing is thought of but satisfying a want of sense, without spiritual nature having any share. A fundamentally just idea, ill understood, that works of *bel-esprit* serve to recreate the mind contributes to keep up this indulgence, if indulgence it may be called when nothing higher occupies the mind, and reader as well as writer find their chief interest therein. This is because vulgar natures, if overstrained, can only be refreshed by vacuity; and even a higher intelligence, when not sustained by a proportional culture, can only rest from its work amidst sensuous enjoyments, from which spiritual nature is absent.

Poetic genius ought to have strength enough to rise with a free and innate activity above all the accidental hindrances which are inseparable from every confined condition, to arrive at a representation of humanity in the absolute plenitude of its powers; it is not, however, permitted, on the other hand, to emancipate itself from the necessary limits implied by the very idea of human nature; for the absolute only in the circle of humanity is its true problem. Simple genius is not exposed to overstep this sphere, but rather not to fill it entirely, giving too much scope to external necessity, to accidental wants, at the expense of the inner necessity. The danger for the sentimental genius is, on the other hand, by trying to remove all limits, of nullifying human nature absolutely, and not only rising, as is its right and duty, beyond finite and determinate reality, as far as absolute possibility, or in other terms to idealize; but of passing even beyond possibility, or, in other words, dreaming. This fault—over-straining—is precisely dependent on the specific property of the senti-mental process, as the opposite defect, inertia, depends on the peculiar operation of the simple genius. The simple genius lets nature dominate, without restricting it; and as nature in her particular phenomena is always subject to some want, it follows that the simple sentiment will not be always exalted enough to resist the accidental limitations of the present hour. The sentimental genius, on the contrary, leaves aside the real world, to rise to the ideal and to command its matter with free spontaneity. But while reason, according to law, aspires always to the unconditional, so the sentimental genius will not always remain calm enough to restrain itself uniformly and without interruption within the conditions implied by the idea of human nature, and to which reason must always, even in its freest acts, remain attached. He could only confine himself in these conditions by help of a receptivity proportioned to his free activity; but most commonly this activity predominates over receptivity in the sentimental poet, as much as receptivity over activity in the simple poet. Hence, in the productions of simple genius, if sometimes inspiration is wanting, so also in works of sentimental poetry the object is often missed. Thus, though they proceed in opposite ways, they will both fall into a vacuum, for before the aesthetic judgment an object without inspiration, and inspiration without an object, are both negations.

The poets who borrow their matter too much from thought, and rather conceive poetic pictures by the internal abundance of ideas than by the suggestions of feeling, are more or less likely to be addicted to go thus astray. In their creations reason makes too little of the limits of the sensuous world, and thought is always carried too far for experience to follow it. Now, when the idea is carried so far that not only no experience corresponds to it—as is the case in the beau ideal—but also that it is repugnant to the conditions of all possible experience, so that, in order to realize it, one must leave human nature altogether, it is no longer a poetic but an exaggerated thought; that is, supposing it claims to be representable and poetical, for otherwise it is enough if it is not self-contradictory. If thought is contradictory it is not exaggeration, but nonsense; for what does not exist cannot exceed. But when the thought is not an object proposed to the fancy, we are just as little justified in calling it exaggerated. For simple thought is infinite, and what is limitless also cannot exceed. Exaggeration, therefore, is only that which wounds, not logical truth, but sensuous truth, and what pretends to be sensuous truth. Consequently, if a poet has the unhappy chance to choose for his picture certain natures that are merely superhuman and cannot possibly be represented, he can only avoid exaggeration by ceasing to be a poet, and not trusting the theme to his imagination. Otherwise one of two things would happen: either imagination, applying its limits to the object, would make a limited and merely human object of an absolute object—which happened with the gods of Greece—or the object would take away limits from fancy, that is, would render it null and void; and this is precisely exaggeration.

Extravagance of feeling should be distinguished from extravagance of portraiture: we are speaking of the former. The object of the feeling may be unnatural, but the feeling itself is natural, and ought accordingly to be shadowed forth in the language of nature. While extravagant feelings may issue from a warm heart and a really poetic nature, extravagance of portraiture always displays a cold heart, and very often a want of poetic capacity. Therefore this is not a danger for the sentimental poet, but only for the imitator, who has no vocation; it is therefore often found with platitude, insipidity, and even baseness. Exaggeration of sentiment is not without truth, and must have a real object; as nature inspires it, it admits of simplicity of expression, and coming from the heart, it goes to the heart. As its object, however, is not in nature, but artificially produced by the understanding, it has only a logical reality, and the feeling is not purely human. It was not an illusion that Héloïse had for Abélard, Petrarch for Laura, Saint Preux for his Julia, Werther for his Charlotte; Agathon, Phanias, and Peregrinus—in Wieland—for the object of their dreams: the feeling is true, only the object is factitious and outside nature. If their thought had kept to simple sensuous truth, it could not have taken this flight; but on the other hand a mere play of fancy, without inner value, could not have stirred the heart: this is only stirred by reason. Thus this sort of exaggeration must be called to order, but it is not contemptible; and those who ridicule it would do well to find out if the wisdom on which they pride themselves is not want of heart, and if it is not through want of reason that they are so acute. The exaggerated delicacy in gallantry and honour which characterizes the chivalrous romances, especially of Spain, is of this kind; also the refined and even ridiculous tenderness of French and English sentimental romances of the best kind. These sentiments are not only subjectively true, but also objectively they are not without value; they are sound sentiments issuing from a moral source, only reprehensible as overstepping the limits of human truth. Without this moral reality how could they stir and touch so powerfully? The same remark applies to moral and religious fanaticism, patriotism, and the love of freedom when carried up to exaltation. As the object of these sentiments is always a pure idea, and not an external experience, imagination with its proper activity has here a dangerous liberty, and cannot, as elsewhere, be called back to bounds by the presence of a visible object. But neither the man nor the poet can withdraw from the law of nature, except to submit to that of reason. He can only abandon reality for the ideal; for liberty must hold to one or the other of these anchors. But it is far from the real to the ideal; and between the two is found fancy, with its arbitrary conceits and its unbridled freedom. It must needs be, therefore, that man in general, and the poet in particular, when he withdraws by liberty of his understanding from the dominion of feeling, without being moved to it by the laws of reason—that is, when he abandons nature through pure liberty—he finds himself freed from all law, and therefore a prey to the illusions of fantasy.

It is testified by experience that entire nations, as well as individual men, who have parted with the safe direction of nature, are actually in this condition; and poets have gone astray in the same manner. The true genius of sentimental poetry, if its aim is to raise itself to the rank of the ideal, must overstep the limits of the existing nature; but false genius oversteps all boundaries without any discrimination, flattering itself with the belief that the wild sport of the imagination is poetic inspiration. A true poetical genius can never fall into this error, because it only abandons the real for the sake of the ideal, or at all events, it can only do so at certain moments when the poet forgets himself; but his main tendencies may dispose him to extravagance within the sphere of the senses. His example may also drive others into a chase of wild conceptions, because readers of lively fancy and weak understanding only remark the freedom which he takes with existing nature, and are unable to follow him in copying the elevated necessities of his inner being. The same difficulties beset the path of the sentimental genius in this respect, as those which afflict the career of a genius of the simple order. If a genius of this class carries out every work, obedient to the free and spontaneous impulses of his nature, the man devoid of genius who seeks to imitate him is not willing to consider his own nature a worse guide than that of the great poet. This accounts for the fact that masterpieces of simple poetry are commonly followed by a host of stale and unprofitable works in print, and masterpieces of the sentimental class by wild and fanciful effusions— a fact that may be easily verified on questioning the history of literature.

Two maxims are prevalent in relation to poetry, both of them quite correct in themselves, but mutually destructive in the way in which they are generally conceived. The first is that "poetry serves as a means of amusement and recreation," and we have previously observed that this maxim is highly favourable to aridity and platitudes in poetical fictions. The other maxim, that "poetry is conducive to the moral progress of humanity," takes under its shelter theories and views of the most wild and extravagant character. It may be profitable to examine more attentively these two maxims, of which so much is heard, and which are so often imperfectly understood and falsely applied.

We say that a thing amuses us when it makes us pass from a forced state to the state that is natural to us. The whole question here is to know in what our natural state ought to consist, and what a forced state means.

If our natural state is made to consist merely in the free development of all our physical powers, in emancipation from all constraint, it follows that every act of reason by resisting what is sensuous is a violence we undergo, and rest of mind combined with physical movement will be a recreation par excellence. But if we make our natural state consist in a limitless power of human expression and of freely disposing of all our strength, all that divides these forces will be a forced state, and recreation will be what brings all our nature to harmony. Thus, the first of these ideal recreations is simply determined by the wants of our sensuous nature; the second, by the autonomous activity of human nature. Which of these two kinds of recreation can be demanded of the poet? Theoretically, the question is inadmissible, as no one would put the human ideal beneath the brutal. But in practice the requirements of a poet have been especially directed to the sensuous ideal, and for the most part favour, though not the esteem, for these sorts of works is regulated thereby. Men's minds are mostly engaged in a labour that exhausts them, or an enjoyment that sets them asleep. Now labour makes rest a sensible want, much more imperious than that of the moral nature; for physical nature must be satisfied before the mind can show its requirements. On the other hand, enjoyment paralyses the moral instinct. Hence these two dispositions common in men are very injurious to the feeling for true beauty, and thus very few even of the best judge soundly in aesthetics. Beauty results from the harmony between spirit and sense; it addresses all the faculties of man, and can only be appreciated if a man employs fully all his strength. He must bring to it an open sense, a broad heart, a spirit full of freshness. All a man's nature must be on the alert, and this is not the case with those divided by abstraction, narrowed by formulas, enervated by application. They demand, no doubt, a material for the senses, but not to quicken, only to suspend, thought. They ask to be freed from what? From a load that oppressed their indolence, and not a rein that curbed their activity.

After this can one wonder at the success of mediocre talents in aesthetics? Or at the bitter anger of small minds against true energetic beauty? They reckon on finding therein a congenial recreation, and regret to discover that a display of strength is required to which they are unequal. With mediocrity they are always welcome; however little mind they bring, they want still less to exhaust the author's inspiration. They are relieved of the load of thought; and their nature can lull itself in beatific nothings on the soft pillow of platitude. In the temple of Thalia and Melpomene—at least, so it is with us—the stupid savant and the exhausted man of business are received on the broad bosom of the goddess, where their intelligence is wrapt in a magnetic sleep, while their sluggish senses are warmed, and their imagination with gentle motions rocked.

Vulgar people may be excused what happens to the best capacities. Those moments of repose demanded by nature after lengthy labour are not favourable to aesthetic judgment, and hence in the busy classes few can pronounce safely on matters of taste. Nothing is more common than for scholars to make a ridiculous figure, in regard to a question of beauty, beside cultured men of the world; and technical critics are especially the laughing-stock of connoisseurs. Their opinion, from exaggeration, crudeness, or carelessness guides them generally quite awry, and they can only devise a technical judgment, and not an aesthetical one, embracing the whole work, in which feeling should decide. If they would kindly keep to technicalities, they might still be useful, for the poet in moments of inspiration and readers under his spell are little inclined to consider details. But the spectacle which they afford us is only the more ridiculous inasmuch as we see these crude natures—with whom all labour and trouble only develop at the most a particular aptitude—when we see them set up their paltry individualities as the representation of universal and complete feeling, and in the sweat of their brow pronounce judgment on beauty.

We have just seen that the kind of recreation poetry ought to afford is generally conceived in too restricted a manner, and only referred to a simple sensuous want. Too much scope, however, is also given to the other idea, the moral ennobling the poet should have in view inasmuch as too purely an ideal aim is assigned.

In fact, according to the pure ideal, the ennobling goes on to infinity, because reason is not restricted to any sensuous limits, and only finds rest in absolute perfection. Nothing can satisfy while a superior thing can be conceived; it judges strictly and admits no excuses of infirmity and finite nature. It only admits for limits those of thought, which transcends time and space. Hence the poet could no more propose to himself such an ideal of ennobling (traced for him by pure [didactic] reason) any more than the coarse ideal of recreation of sensuous nature. The aim is to free human nature from accidental hindrances, without destroying the essential idea of our humanity, or displacing its limits. All beyond this is exaggeration, and a quicksand in which the poet too easily suffers shipwreck if he mistakes the idea of nobleness. But, unfortunately, he cannot rise to the true ideal of ennobled human nature without going some steps beyond it. To rise so high he must abandon the world of reality, for, like every ideal, it is only to be drawn from its inner moral source. He does not find it in the turmoil of worldly life, but only in his heart, and that only in calm meditation. But in this separation from real life he is likely to lose sight of all the limits of human nature, and seeking pure form he may easily lose himself in arbitrary and baseless conceptions. Reason will abstract itself too much from experience, and the practical man will not be able to carry out, in the crush of real life, what the contemplative mind has discovered on the peaceful path of thought. Thus, what makes a dreamy man is the very thing that alone could have made him a sage; and the advantage for the latter is not that he has never been a dreamer, but rather that he has not remained one.

We must not, then, allow the workers to determine recreation according to their wants, nor thinkers that of nobleness according to their speculations, for fear of either a too low physical poetry, or a poetry too given to hyperphysical exaggeration. And as these two ideas direct most men's judgments on poetry, we must seek a class of mind at once active, but not slavishly so, and idealizing, but not dreamy; uniting the reality of life within as few limits as possible, obeying the current of human affairs, but not enslaved by them. Such a class of men can alone preserve the beautiful unity of human nature, that harmony which all work for a moment disturbs, and a life of work destroys; such alone can, in all that is purely human, give by its feelings universal rules of judgment. Whether such a class exists, or whether the class now existing in like conditions answers to this ideal conception, I am not concerned to inquire. If it does not respond to the ideal it has only itself to blame. In such a class—here regarded as a mere ideal—the simple and sentimental would keep each other from extremes of extravagance and relaxation. For the idea of a beautiful humanity is not exhausted by either, but can only be presented in the union of both.

"On Simple and Sentimental Poetry"
is from a collection of Schiller's essays
entitled ESSAYS AESTHETICAL AND PHILOSOPHICAL.

Percy Bysshe Shelley

1792–1822

Percy Bysshe Shelley was born at Field Place in Sussex, England, on August 4, 1792. His father was a lawyer and member of Parliament. Shelley entered Eton at the age of twelve. His classmates called him "mad Shelley" because of his outspoken atheism. He went to Oxford in 1810 but was expelled at the end of five months for writing a pamphlet that attacked religion.

In 1811 Shelley eloped with Harriet Westbrook, a girl of sixteen. The couple separated in 1815, and the following year Harriet killed herself. After her death Shelley married Mary Wollstonecraft Godwin, the daughter of William Godwin, an essayist and political philosopher.

In 1818 the Shelleys left England for Italy, where the poet lived for the rest of his life. He had already published three long poems: *Queen Mab, Alastor,* and *The Revolt of Islam.*

In the remaining few years of his life, Shelley traveled in Italy. He visited with friends, especially Byron, and continued to write poetry, the subject matter and approach of which were in the Romantic vein of his time. His most famous long poem was *Adonais,* an elegy on the death of Keats.

Shelley thought of himself primarily as a reformer, a champion of beauty who would purify life of evil and ugliness. Matthew Arnold

Notes from the artist: "Shelley and the 'Skylark' drawn to suggest that both the man and the bird, though housed in fragile bodies, possessed great strength and power."

HAIL to thee, blithe spirit!
Bird thou never wert—
That from heaven or near it
Pourest thy full heart
In profuse strains of unpremeditated art.

characterized Shelley's Romanticism by describing him as "a beautiful and ineffectual angel, beating in the void his luminous wings in vain."

The poet's success as a reformer may be questionable, but some of his lyric poems, such as *To a Skylark, Ode to the West Wind,* and *The Cloud,* are ranked with the greatest in English.

Shelley was drowned on July 8, 1822, while sailing with a friend off Leghorn, Italy. His body was recovered and cremated on the beach.

When Shelley set out to defend poetry he did a thorough job of it. In *A Defence of Poetry,* he attempts to prove that poets are philosophers; that they are the creators and protectors of moral and civil laws; and that if it were not for poets, scientists could not have developed either their theories or their inventions.

How is it possible to make such extravagant claims for poetry, which, for many people, is at worst useless and trivial, and at best an impractical delight?

Shelley starts by drawing a distinction between "reason" and "imagination." Imagination, he says, is "the principle of synthesis," reason "the principle of analysis." Imagination involves being, reason involves relations. "Reason is the enumeration of quantities already known; imagination is the perception of the value of those quantities, both separately and as a whole."

"Poetry," he goes on, "in a general sense, may be defined to be 'the expression of the imagination.'" We see immediately that he does not mean only verse. "The distinction between poets and prose-writers," he writes, "is a vulgar error." Bacon was a poet, he says, and so was Plato—not because they wrote beautifully (though they did that), but because they spoke the truth. Any important truth is, for Shelley, primarily poetic. "A poem is the very image of life expressed in its eternal truth."

But poetry is not only writing, either. "The functions of the poetical faculty are twofold; by one it creates new materials of knowledge, and power, and pleasure; by the other it engenders in the mind a desire to reproduce and arrange them." It is because of this that poetry is the creator and supporter of morals and law. But it is also for this reason that poetry underlies, and anticipates, scientific discoveries. Science, Shelley maintains, is analytical; it deals only with relations between things which are already known. Poetry finds new things. It puts together rather than takes apart. It creates rather than breaks down. It produces a one rather than a many. If there were no poets to find new truths, there would be no science to find the relations between them.

Given this exalted sense of the term, it is possible that no one will dispute Shelley's view. Clearly, there are some scientists who are "poets" in Shelley's meaning of the word. Newton was one, Einstein another. Both had vital and vibrant imaginations. And a politician could be a poet, too. Dante had what is sometimes called, by hard-headed realists, a "dream" of world government. That dream, as expressed in *De Monarchia*,[1] will perhaps never come true—exactly or completely. But the fact that Dante had it, Shelley would perhaps contend, is the reason why the world now has a United Nations. Great ideas exist first in the poetic mind. The man of reason, who is also necessary, follows after.

The most famous statement from *A Defence of Poetry* is its concluding sentence: "Poets are the unacknowledged legislators of the world." This statement has been held to be nonsense or "romantic" exaggeration. But a careful reading of the essay will show that it makes sense. It follows from what Shelley has said. Given his view, it is undeniable.

---

[1] See the selection "On World Government" in Vol. 7, pp. 383–399, of this set.

A Defence
of Poetry

According to one mode of regarding those two classes of mental action which are called reason and imagination, the former may be considered as mind contemplating the relations borne by one thought to another, however produced; and the latter, as mind acting upon those thoughts so as to colour them with its own light, and composing from them, as from elements, other thoughts, each containing within itself the principle of its own integrity. The one is the *topoiein*, or the principle of synthesis, and has for its object those forms which are common to universal nature and existence itself; the other is the *to logizein*, or principle of analysis, and its action regards the relations of things simply as relations, considering thoughts not in their integral unity but as the algebraical representations which conduct to certain general results. Reason is the enumeration of quantities already known; imagination is the perception of the value of those quantities, both separately and as a whole. Reason respects the differences, and imagination the similitudes of things. Reason is to the imagination as the instrument to the agent, as the body to the spirit, as the shadow to the substance.

Poetry, in a general sense, may be defined to be "the expression of the imagination": and poetry is connate with the origin of man. Man is an instrument over which a series of external and internal impressions are driven, like the alternations of an ever-changing wind over an Aeolian lyre, which move it by their motion to ever-changing melody. But there is a principle within the human being, and perhaps within all sentient beings which acts otherwise than in a lyre, and produces not melody alone, but harmony, by an internal adjustment of the sounds and motions thus excited to the impressions which excite them. It is as if the lyre could accommodate its chords to the motions of that which strikes them, in a determined proportion of sound; even as the musician can accommodate his voice to the sound of the lyre. A child at play by itself will express its delight by its voice and motions; and every inflection of tone and gesture will bear exact relation to a corresponding antitype in the pleasurable impressions which awakened it; it will be the reflected image of that impression; and as the lyre trembles and sounds after the wind has died away, so the child seeks, by prolonging in its voice and motions the duration of the effect, to prolong also a consciousness of the cause. In relation to the objects which delight a child, these expressions are what poetry is to higher objects. The savage (for the savage is to ages what the child is to years) expresses the emotions produced in him by surrounding objects in a similar manner; and language and gesture, together with plastic or pictorial imitation, become the image of the combined effect of those objects and his apprehension of them. Man in society, with all his passions and his pleasures, next becomes the object of the passions and pleasures of man; an additional class of emotions produces an augmented treasure of expression; and language, gesture, and the imitative arts become at once the representation and the medium, the pencil and the picture, the chisel and the statue, the chord and the harmony. The social sympathies, or those laws from which as from its elements society results, begin to develop themselves from the moment that two human beings coexist; the future is contained within the present as the plant within the seed; and equality, diversity, unity, contrast, mutual dependence become the principles alone capable of affording the motives according to which the will of a social being is determined to action, inasmuch as he is social; and constitute pleasure in sensation, virtue in sentiment, beauty in art, truth in reasoning, and love in the intercourse of kind. Hence men, even in the infancy of society, observe a certain order in their words and actions, distinct from that of the objects and the impressions represented by them, all expression being subject to the laws of that from which it proceeds. But let us dismiss those more general considerations which might involve an inquiry into the principles of society itself, and restrict our view to the manner in which the imagination is expressed upon its forms.

In the youth of the world, men dance and sing and imitate natural objects, observing in these actions, as in all others, a certain rhythm or order. And, although all men observe a similar, they observe not the same order in the motions of the dance, in the melody of the song, in the combinations of language, in the series of their imitations of natural objects. For there is a certain order or rhythm belonging to each of these classes of mimetic representation, from which the hearer and the spectator receive an intenser and purer pleasure than from any other: the sense of an approximation to this order has been called taste by modern writers. Every man in the infancy of art observes an order which approximates more or less closely to that from which this highest delight results: but the diversity is not sufficiently marked as that its gradations should be sensible, except in those instances where the predominance of this faculty of approximation to the beautiful (for so we may be permitted to name the relation between this highest pleasure and its cause) is very great. Those in whom it exists to excess are poets, in the most universal sense of the word; and the pleasure resulting from the manner in which they express the influence of society or nature upon their own minds communicates itself to others, and gathers a sort of reduplication from the community. Their language is vitally metaphorical; that is, it marks the before unapprehended relations of things and perpetuates their apprehension, until words, which represent them, become, through time, signs for portions or classes of thought, instead of pictures of integral thoughts; and then, if no new poets should arise to create afresh the associations which have been thus disorganized, language will be dead to all the nobler purposes of human intercourse. These similitudes or relations are finely said by Bacon to be "the same footsteps of nature impressed upon the various subjects of the world"; and he considers the faculty which perceives them as the storehouse of axioms common to all knowledge. In the infancy of society every author is necessarily a poet, because language itself is poetry; and to be a poet is to apprehend the true and the beautiful, in a word, the good which exists in the relation subsisting, first between existence and perception, and secondly between perception and expression. Every original language near to its source is in itself the chaos of a cyclic poem: the copiousness of lexicography and the distinctions of grammar are the works of a later age, and are merely the catalogue and the form of the creations of poetry.

But poets, or those who imagine and express this indestructible order, are not only the authors of language and of music, of the dance, and architecture, and statuary, and painting; they are the institutors of laws and the founders of civil society, and the inventors of the arts of life, and the teachers, who draw into a certain propinquity with the beautiful and the true that partial apprehension of the agencies of the invisible world which is called religion. Hence all original religions are allegorical or susceptible of allegory, and, like Janus, have a double face of false and true. Poets, according to the circumstances of the age and nation in which they appeared, were called, in the earlier epochs of the world, legislators or prophets: a poet essentially comprises and unites both these characters. For he not only beholds intensely the present as it is, and discovers those laws according to which present things ought to be ordered, but he beholds the future in the present, and his thoughts are the germs of the flower and the fruit of latest time. Not that I assert poets to be prophets in the gross sense of the word, or that they can foretell the form as surely as they foreknow the spirit of events: such is the pretence of superstition, which would make poetry an attribute of prophecy, rather than prophecy an attribute of poetry. A poet participates in the eternal, the infinite, and the one; as far as relates to his conceptions, time and place and number are not. The grammatical forms which express the moods of time, and the difference of persons, and the distinction of place are convertible with respect to the highest poetry without injuring it as poetry; and the choruses of Aeschylus, and the book of Job, and Dante's *Paradiso* would afford, more than any other writings, examples of this fact, if the limits of this essay did not forbid citation. The creations of sculpture, painting, and music are illustrations still more decisive.

Language, colour, form, and religious and civil habits of action are all the instruments and materials of poetry; they may be called poetry by that figure of speech which considers the effect as a synonym of the cause. But poetry in a more restricted sense expresses those arrangements of language, and especially metrical language, which are created by that imperial faculty whose throne is curtained within the invisible nature of man. And this springs from the nature itself of language, which is a more direct representation of the actions and passions of our internal being, and is susceptible of more various and delicate combinations than colour, form, or motion, and is more plastic and obedient to the control of that faculty of which it is the creation. For language is arbitrarily produced by the imagination, and has relation to thoughts alone; but all other materials, instruments, and conditions of art have relations among each other, which limit and interpose between conception and expression. The former is as a mirror which reflects, the latter as a cloud which enfeebles, the light of which both are mediums of communication. Hence the fame of sculptors, painters, and musicians, although the intrinsic powers of the great masters of these arts may yield in no degree to that of those who have employed language as the hieroglyphic of their thoughts, has never equalled that of poets in the restricted sense of the term; as two performers of equal skill will produce unequal effects from a guitar and a harp. The fame of legislators and founders of religion, so long as their institutions last, alone seems to exceed that of poets in the restricted sense;

but it can scarcely be a question whether, if we deduct the celebrity which their flattery of the gross opinions of the vulgar usually conciliates, together with that which belonged to them in their higher character of poets, any excess will remain.

We have thus circumscribed the word poetry within the limits of that art which is the most familiar and the most perfect expression of the faculty itself. It is necessary, however, to make the circle still narrower, and to determine the distinction between measured and unmeasured language; for the popular division into prose and verse is inadmissible in accurate philosophy.

Sounds as well as thoughts have relation both between each other and towards that which they represent, and a perception of the order of those relations has always been found connected with a perception of the order of the relations of thought. Hence the language of poets has ever affected a sort of uniform and harmonious recurrence of sound, without which it were not poetry, and which is scarcely less indispensable to the communication of its influence than the words themselves, without reference to that peculiar order. Hence the vanity of translation; it were as wise to cast a violet into a crucible that you might discover the formal principle of its colour and odour as seek to transfuse from one language into another the creations of a poet. The plant must spring again from its seed, or it will bear no flower—and this is the burden of the curse of Babel.

An observation of the regular mode of the recurrence of harmony in the language of poetical minds, together with its relation to music, produced metre, or a certain system of traditional forms of harmony and language. Yet it is by no means essential that a poet should accommodate his language to this traditional form, so that the harmony, which is its spirit, be observed. The practice is indeed convenient and popular, and to be preferred, especially in such composition as includes much action: but every great poet must inevitably innovate upon the example of his predecessors in the exact structure of his peculiar versification. The distinction between poets and prose-writers is a vulgar error. The distinction between philosophers and poets has been anticipated. Plato was essentially a poet—the truth and splendour of his imagery, and the melody of his language, are the most intense that it is possible to conceive. He rejected the harmony of the epic, dramatic, and lyrical forms, because he sought to kindle a harmony in thoughts divested of shape and action, and he forbore to invent any regular plan of rhythm which would include, under determinate forms, the varied pauses of his style. Cicero sought to imitate the cadence of his periods, but with little success. Bacon

was a poet.[1] His language has a sweet and majestic rhythm, which satisfies the sense no less than the almost superhuman wisdom of his philosophy satisfies the intellect; it is a strain which distends, and then bursts
the circumference of the reader's mind, and pours itself forth together
with it into the universal element with which it has perpetual sympathy.
All the authors of revolutions in opinion are not only necessarily poets
as they are inventors, nor even as their words unveil the permanent
analogy of things by images which participate in the life of truth; but as
their periods are harmonious and rhythmical, and contain in themselves
the elements of verse, being the echo of the eternal music. Nor are those
supreme poets who have employed traditional forms of rhythm on account of the form and action of their subjects less capable of perceiving
and teaching the truth of things than those who have omitted that form.
Shakespeare, Dante, and Milton (to confine ourselves to modern writers) are philosophers of the very loftiest power.

A poem is the very image of life expressed in its eternal truth. There is
this difference between a story and a poem, that a story is a catalogue of
detached facts, which have no other connection than time, place, circumstance, cause, and effect; the other is the creation of actions according
to the unchangeable forms of human nature, as existing in the mind of
the Creator, which is itself the image of all other minds. The one is partial, and applies only to a definite period of time, and a certain combination of events which can never again recur; the other is universal, and
contains within itself the germ of a relation to whatever motives or actions have place in the possible varieties of human nature. Time, which
destroys the beauty and the use of the story of particular facts, stripped
of the poetry which should invest them, augments that of poetry, and
forever develops new and wonderful applications of the eternal truth
which it contains. Hence epitomes have been called the moths of just
history; they eat out the poetry of it. A story of particular facts is as a
mirror which obscures and distorts that which should be beautiful: poetry
is a mirror which makes beautiful that which is distorted.

The parts of a composition may be poetical, without the composition
as a whole being a poem. A single sentence may be considered as a
whole, though it may be found in the midst of a series of unassimilated
portions; a single word even may be a spark of inextinguishable thought.
And thus all the great historians, Herodotus, Plutarch, Livy, were poets;
and although the plan of these writers, especially that of Livy, restrained

---

1. See the *Filum Labyrinthi* and the *Essay on Death* particularly.

them from developing this faculty in its highest degree, they made copious and ample amends for their subjection, by filling all the interstices of their subjects with living images.

Having determined what is poetry, and who are poets, let us proceed to estimate its effects upon society.

Poetry is ever accompanied with pleasure: all spirits upon which it falls open themselves to receive the wisdom which is mingled with its delight. In the infancy of the world, neither poets themselves nor their auditors are fully aware of the excellence of poetry: for it acts in a divine and unapprehended manner, beyond and above consciousness; and it is reserved for future generations to contemplate and measure the mighty cause and effect in all the strength and splendour of their union. Even in modern times, no living poet ever arrived at the fullness of his fame: the jury which sits in judgment upon a poet, belonging as he does to all time, must be composed of his peers: it must be empanelled by time from the selectest of the wise of many generations. A poet is a nightingale, who sits in darkness and sings to cheer its own solitude with sweet sounds; his auditors are as men entranced by the melody of an unseen musician, who feel that they are moved and softened, yet know not whence or why. The poems of Homer and his contemporaries were the delight of infant Greece; they were the elements of that social system which is the column upon which all succeeding civilization has reposed. Homer embodies the ideal perfection of his age in human character; nor can we doubt that those who read his verses were awakened to an ambition of becoming like to Achilles, Hector, and Ulysses: the truth and beauty of friendship, patriotism, and persevering devotion to an object were unveiled to their depths in these immortal creations: the sentiments of the auditors must have been refined and enlarged by a sympathy with such great and lovely impersonations, until from admiring they imitated, and from imitation they identified themselves with the objects of their admiration. Nor let it be objected that these characters are remote from moral perfection, and that they are by no means to be considered as edifying patterns for general imitation. Every epoch, under names more or less specious, has deified its peculiar errors; Revenge is the naked idol of the worship of a semi-barbarous age; and Self-deceit is the veiled image of unknown evil, before which luxury and satiety lie prostrate. But a poet considers the vices of his contemporaries as the temporary dress in which his creations must be arrayed, and which cover without concealing the eternal proportions of their beauty. An epic or dramatic personage is understood to wear them around his soul, as he may the ancient armour or modern uniform around his body; whilst it is easy to conceive a dress more graceful than either. The beauty of the internal nature cannot be so far concealed by its accidental vesture, but that the spirit of its form shall communicate itself to the very disguise, and indicate the shape it hides from the manner in which it is worn. A majestic form and graceful motions will express themselves through the most barbarous and tasteless costume. Few poets of the highest class have chosen to exhibit the beauty of their conceptions in its naked truth and splendour; and it is doubtful whether the alloy of costume, habit, etc., be not necessary to temper this planetary music for mortal ears.

The whole objection, however, of the immorality of poetry rests upon a misconception of the manner in which poetry acts to produce the moral improvement of man. Ethical science arranges the elements which poetry has created, and propounds schemes and proposes examples of civil and domestic life: nor is it for want of admirable doctrines that men hate, and despise, and censure, and deceive, and subjugate one another. But poetry acts in another and diviner manner. It awakens and enlarges the mind itself by rendering it the receptacle of a thousand unapprehended combinations of thought. Poetry lifts the veil from the hidden beauty of the world, and makes familiar objects be as if they were not familiar; it reproduces all that it represents, and the impersonations clothed in its Elysian light stand thenceforward in the minds of those who have once contemplated them as memorials of that gentle and exalted content which extends itself over all thoughts and actions with which it coexists. The great secret of morals is love; or a going out of our own nature, and an identification of ourselves with the beautiful which exists in thought, action, or person, not our own. A man, to be greatly good, must imagine intensely and comprehensively; he must put himself in the place of another and of many others; the pains and pleasures of his species must become his own. The great instrument of moral good is the imagination; and poetry administers to the effect by acting upon the cause. Poetry enlarges the circumference of the imagination by replenishing it with thoughts of ever new delight, which have the power of attracting and assimilating to their own nature all other thoughts, and which form new intervals and interstices whose void for ever craves fresh food. Poetry strengthens the faculty which is the organ of the moral nature of man, in the same manner as exercise strengthens a limb. A poet therefore would do ill to embody his own conceptions of right and wrong, which are usually those of his place and time, in his poetical creations, which participate in neither. By this assumption of the inferior office of interpreting the effect, in which perhaps after all he might acquit himself but imperfectly, he would resign a glory in the participation of the cause. There was little danger that Homer, or any of the eternal poets, should have so far misunderstood themselves as to have abdicated this throne of their widest dominion. Those in whom the poetical faculty, though great, is less intense, as Euripides, Lucan, Tasso, Spenser, have frequently affected a moral aim, and the effect of their poetry is diminished in exact proportion to the degree in which they compel us to advert to this purpose.

Homer and the cyclic poets were followed at a certain interval by the dramatic and lyrical poets of Athens, who flourished contemporaneously with all that is most perfect in the kindred expressions of the poetical faculty; architecture, painting, music, the dance, sculpture, philosophy, and we may add, the forms of civil life. For although the scheme of Athenian society was deformed by many imperfections which the poetry existing in chivalry and Christianity has erased from the habits and institutions of modern Europe; yet never at any other period has so much energy, beauty and virtue been developed; never was blind strength and stubborn form so disciplined and rendered subject to the will of man, or that will less repugnant to the dictates of the beautiful and the true, as during the century which preceded the death of Socrates. Of no other epoch in the history of our species have we records and fragments stamped so visibly with the image of the divinity in man. But it is poetry alone, in form, in action, and in language which has rendered this epoch memorable above all others, and the storehouse of examples to everlasting time. For written poetry existed at that epoch simultaneously with the other arts, and it is an idle inquiry to demand which gave and which received the light, which all, as from a common focus, have scattered over the darkest periods of succeeding time. We know no more of cause and effect than a constant conjunction of events: poetry is ever found to coexist with whatever other arts contribute to the happiness and perfection of man. I appeal to what has already been established to distinguish between the cause and the effect.

It was at the period here adverted to that the drama had its birth; and however a succeeding writer may have equalled or surpassed those few great specimens of the Athenian drama which have been preserved to us, it is indisputable that the art itself never was understood or practised according to the true philosophy of it as at Athens. For the Athenians employed language, action, music, painting, the dance, and religious institutions to produce a common effect in the representation of

the highest idealisms of passion and of power; each division in the art
was made perfect in its kind by artists of the most consummate skill,
and was disciplined into a beautiful proportion and unity one towards
the other. On the modern stage few only of the elements capable of expressing the image of the poet's conception are employed at once. We
have tragedy without music and dancing; and music and dancing without the highest impersonations of which they are the fit accompaniment,
and both without religion and solemnity. Religious institution has indeed
been usually banished from the stage. Our system of divesting the actor's
face of a mask, on which the many expressions appropriated to his dramatic character might be moulded into one permanent and unchanging
expression, is favourable only to a partial and inharmonious effect; it is
fit for nothing but a monologue, where all the attention may be directed
to some great master of ideal mimicry. The modern practice of blending
comedy with tragedy, though liable to great abuse in point of practice,
is undoubtedly an extension of the dramatic circle; but the comedy
should be as in King Lear, universal, ideal, and sublime. It is perhaps
the intervention of this principle which determines the balance in favour
of *King Lear* against the *Oedipus Tyrannus* or the *Agamemnon*, or, if you
will, the trilogies with which they are connected; unless the intense power
of the choral poetry, especially that of the latter, should be considered
as restoring the equilibrium. King Lear, if it can sustain this comparison,
may be judged to be the most perfect specimen of the dramatic art existing in the world; in spite of the narrow conditions to which the poet was
subjected by the ignorance of the philosophy of the drama which has prevailed in modern Europe. Calderón, in his religious Autos, has attempted
to fulfil some of the high conditions of dramatic representations neglected
by Shakespeare; such as the establishing a relation between the drama
and religion, and the accommodating them to music and dancing; but he
omits the observation of conditions still more important, and more is lost
than gained by the substitution of the rigidly defined and ever-repeated
idealisms of a distorted superstition for the living impersonations of the
truth of human passions.

But I digress. The connection of scenic exhibitions with the improvement or corruption of the manners of men has been universally recognized: in other words, the presence or absence of poetry, in its most
perfect and universal form, has been found to be connected with good
and evil in conduct or habit. The corruption which has been imputed
to the drama as an effect begins when the poetry employed in its constitution ends: I appeal to the history of manners whether the periods of

the growth of the one and the decline of the other have not corresponded with an exactness equal to any example of moral cause and effect.

The drama at Athens, or wheresoever else it may have approached to its perfection, ever coexisted with the moral and intellectual greatness of the age. The tragedies of the Athenian poets are as mirrors in which the spectator beholds himself, under a thin disguise of circumstance, stripped of all but that ideal perfection and energy which every one feels to be the internal type of all that he loves, admires, and would become. The imagination is enlarged by a sympathy with pains and passions so mighty that they distend in their conception the capacity of that by which they are conceived; the good affections are strengthened by pity, indignation, terror and sorrow; and an exalted calm is prolonged from the satiety of this high exercise of them into the tumult of familiar life: even crime is disarmed of half its horror and all its contagion by being represented as the fatal consequence of the unfathomable agencies of nature; error is thus divested of its wilfulness; men can no longer cherish it as the creation of their choice. In the drama of the highest order there is little food for censure or hatred; it teaches rather self-knowledge and self-respect. Neither the eye nor the mind can see itself, unless reflected upon that which it resembles. The drama, so long as it continues to express poetry, is a prismatic and many-sided mirror, which collects the brightest rays of human nature and divides and reproduces them from the simplicity of these elementary forms, and touches them with majesty and beauty, and multiplies all that it reflects, and endows it with the power of propagating its like wherever it may fall.

But in periods of the decay of social life, the drama sympathizes with that decay. Tragedy becomes a cold imitation of the form of the great masterpieces of antiquity, divested of all harmonious accompaniment of the kindred arts; and often the very form misunderstood, or a weak attempt to teach certain doctrines, which the writer considers as moral truths; and which are usually no more than specious flatteries of some gross vice or weakness, with which the author, in common with his auditors, are infected. Hence what has been called the classical and domestic drama. Addison's *Cato* is a specimen of the one; and would it were not superfluous to cite examples of the other! To such purposes poetry cannot be made subservient. Poetry is a sword of lightning, ever unsheathed, which consumes the scabbard that would contain it. And thus we observe that all dramatic writings of this nature are unimaginative in a singular degree; they affect sentiment and passion, which, divested of imagination, are other names for caprice and appetite. The period in our own history of the grossest degradation of the drama is the reign of Charles II, when all forms in which poetry had been accustomed to be expressed became hymns to the triumph of kingly power over liberty and virtue. Milton stood alone illuminating an age unworthy of him. At such periods the calculating principle pervades all the forms of dramatic exhibition, and poetry ceases to be expressed upon them. Comedy loves its ideal universality: wit succeeds to humour; we laugh from self-complacency and triumph, instead of pleasure; malignity, sarcasm, and contempt succeed to sympathetic merriment; we hardly laugh, but we smile. Obscenity, which is ever blasphemy against the divine beauty in life, becomes, from the very veil which it assumes, more active if less disgusting: it is a monster for which the corruption of society for ever brings forth new food, which it devours in secret.

The drama being that form under which a greater number of modes of expression of poetry are susceptible of being combined than any other, the connection of poetry and social good is more observable in the drama than in whatever other form. And it is indisputable that the highest perfection of human society has ever corresponded with the highest dramatic excellence; and that the corruption or the extinction of the drama in a nation where it has once flourished is a mark of a corruption of manners, and an extinction of the energies which sustain the soul of social life. But, as Machiavelli says of political institutions, that life may be preserved and renewed, if men should arise capable of bringing back the drama to its principles. And this is true with respect to poetry in its most extended sense: all language, institution and form require not only to be produced but to be sustained: the office and character of a poet participates in the divine nature as regards providence, no less than as regards creation.

Civil war, the spoils of Asia, and the fatal predominance first of the Macedonian, and then of the Roman arms, were so many symbols of the extinction or suspension of the creative faculty in Greece. The bucolic writers, who found patronage under the lettered tyrants of Sicily and Egypt, were the latest representatives of its most glorious reign. Their poetry is intensely melodious; like the odour of the tuberose, it overcomes and sickens the spirit with excess of sweetness; whilst the poetry of the preceding age was as a meadow-gale of June, which mingles the fragrance of all the flowers of the field, and adds a quickening and harmonizing spirit of its own which endows the sense with a power of sustaining its extreme delight. The bucolic and erotic delicacy in written poetry is correlative with that softness in statuary, music, and the kindred arts, and even in manners and institutions, which distinguished the epoch to which I now refer. Nor is it the poetical faculty itself, or any misapplication of it, to which this want of harmony is to be imputed. An equal sensibility to the influence of the senses and the affections is to be found in the writings of Homer and Sophocles: the former, especially, has clothed sensual and pathetic images with irresistible attractions. The superiority in these to succeeding writers consists in the presence of those thoughts which belong to the inner faculties of our nature, not in the absence of those which are connected with the external: their incomparable perfection consists in a harmony of the union of all. It is not what the erotic poets have, but what they have not, in which their imperfection consists. It is not inasmuch as they were poets, but inasmuch as they were not poets, that they can be considered with any plausibility as connected with the corruption of their age. Had that corruption availed so as to extinguish in them the sensibility to pleasure, passion, and natural scenery, which is imputed to them as an imperfection, the last triumph of evil would have been achieved.

For the end of social corruption is to destroy all sensibility to pleasure; and, therefore, it is corruption. It begins at the imagination and the intellect as at the core, and distributes itself thence as a paralysing venom, through the affections into the very appetites, until all become a torpid mass in which hardly sense survives. At the approach of such a period, poetry ever addresses itself to those faculties which are the last to be destroyed, and its voice is heard, like the footsteps of Astraea, departing from the world. Poetry ever communicates all the pleasure which men are capable of receiving: it is ever still the light of life; the source of whatever of beautiful or generous or true can have place in an evil time. It will readily be confessed that those among the luxurious citizens of Syracuse and Alexandria, who were delighted with the poems of Theocritus, were less cold, cruel, and sensual than the remnant of their tribe. But corruption must utterly have destroyed the fabric of human society before poetry can ever cease. The sacred links of that chain have never been entirely disjoined, which descending through the minds of many men is attached to those great minds, whence as from a magnet the invisible effluence is sent forth, which at once connects, animates, and sustains the life of all. It is the faculty which contains within itself the seeds at once of its own and of social renovation. And let us not circumscribe the effects of the bucolic and erotic poetry within the limits of the sensibility of those to whom it was addressed. They may have perceived the beauty of those immortal compositions simply as fragments and isolated portions;

those who are more finely organized, or born in a happier age, may recognize them as episodes to that great poem which all poets, like the co-operating thoughts of one great mind, have built up since the beginning of the world.

The same revolutions within a narrower sphere had place in ancient Rome; but the actions and forms of its social life never seem to have been perfectly saturated with the poetical element. The Romans appear to have considered the Greeks as the selectest treasuries of the selectest forms of manners and of nature, and to have abstained from creating in measured language, sculpture, music, or architecture anything which might bear a particular relation to their own condition, whilst it should bear a general one to the universal constitution of the world. But we judge from partial evidence, and we judge perhaps partially. Ennius, Varro, Pacuvius, and Accius, all great poets, have been lost. Lucretius is in the highest, and Virgil in a very high sense, a creator. The chosen delicacy of expressions of the latter are as a mist of light which conceal from us the intense and exceeding truth of his conceptions of nature. Livy is instinct with poetry. Yet Horace, Catullus, Ovid, and generally the other great writers of the Virgilian age saw man and nature in the mirror of Greece. The institutions also, and the religion of Rome, were less poetical than those of Greece, as the shadow is less vivid than the substance. Hence poetry in Rome seemed to follow, rather than accompany, the perfection of political and domestic society. The true poetry of Rome lived in its institutions; for whatever of beautiful, true, and majestic they contained could have sprung only from the faculty which creates the order in which they consist. The life of Camillus; the death of Regulus; the expectation of the senators, in their godlike state, of the victorious Gauls; the refusal of the republic to make peace with Hannibal after the battle of Cannae were not the consequences of a refined calculation of the probable personal advantage to result from such a rhythm and order in the shows of life to those who were at once the poets and the actors of these immortal dramas. The imagination beholding the beauty of this order created it out of itself according to its own idea; the consequence was empire, and the reward everlasting fame. These things are not the less poetry, *quia carent vate sacro* [because they lack a poet]. They are the episodes of that cyclic poem written by Time upon the memories of men. The Past, like an inspired rhapsodist, fills the theatre of everlasting generations with their harmony.

At length the ancient system of religion and manners had fulfilled the circle of its evolutions. And the world would have fallen into utter anarchy and darkness, but that there were found poets among the authors of the Christian and chivalric systems of manners and religion, who created forms of opinion and action never before conceived; which, copied into the imaginations of men, became as generals to the bewildered armies of their thoughts. It is foreign to the present purpose to touch upon the evil produced by these systems: except that we protest, on the ground of the principles already established, that no portion of it can be attributed to the poetry they contain.

It is probable that the poetry of Moses, Job, David, Solomon, and Isaiah had produced a great effect upon the mind of Jesus and his disciples. The scattered fragments preserved to us by the biographers of this extraordinary person are all instinct with the most vivid poetry. But his doctrines seem to have been quickly distorted. At a certain period after the prevalence of a system of opinions founded upon those promulgated by him, the three forms into which Plato had distributed the faculties of mind underwent a sort of apotheosis, and became the object of the worship of the civilized world. Here it is to be confessed that "Light thickens," and

> . . . the crow makes wing to the rooky wood,
> Good things of day begin to droop and drowse;
> Whiles night's black agents to their preys do rouse.[2]

But mark how beautiful an order has sprung from the dust and blood of this fierce chaos! how the world, as from a resurrection, balancing itself on the golden wings of knowledge and of hope, has reassumed its yet unwearied flight into the heaven of time. Listen to the music, unheard by outward ears, which is as a ceaseless and invisible wind, nourishing its everlasting course with strength and swiftness.

The poetry in the doctrines of Jesus, and the mythology and institutions of the Celtic conquerors of the Roman empire, outlived the darkness and the convulsions connected with their growth and victory, and blended themselves in a new fabric of manners and opinion. It is an error to impute the ignorance of the dark ages to the Christian doctrines or the predominance of the Celtic nations. Whatever of evil their agencies may have contained sprang from the extinction of the poetical principle, connected with the progress of despotism and superstition. Men, from causes too intricate to be here discussed, had become insensible and selfish; their own will had become feeble, and yet they were its slaves, and thence the slaves of the will of others; but fear, avarice, cruelty, and fraud character-

---

2. *Macbeth*, act iii, scene 2, *Great Books of the Western World*, Vol. 27, p. 297 [Ed.].

ized a race amongst whom no one was to be found capable of *creating* in form, language, or institution. The moral anomalies of such a state of society are not justly to be charged upon any class of events immediately connected with them, and those events are most entitled to our approbation which could dissolve it most expeditiously. It is unfortunate for those who cannot distinguish words from thoughts that many of these anomalies have been incorporated into our popular religion.

It was not until the eleventh century that the effects of the poetry of the Christian and chivalric systems began to manifest themselves. The principle of equality had been discovered and applied by Plato in his *Republic* as the theoretical rule of the mode in which the materials of pleasure and of power, produced by the common skill and labour of human beings, ought to be distributed among them. The limitations of this rule were asserted by him to be determined only by the sensibility of each, or the utility to result to all. Plato, following the doctrines of Timaeus and Pythagoras, taught also a moral and intellectual system of doctrine, comprehending at once the past, the present, and the future condition of man. Jesus divulged the sacred and eternal truths contained in these views to mankind, and Christianity, in its abstract purity, became the exoteric expression of the esoteric doctrines of the poetry and wisdom of antiquity. The incorporation of the Celtic nations with the exhausted population of the south impressed upon it the figure of the poetry existing in their mythology and institutions. The result was a sum of the action and reaction of all the causes included in it; for it may be assumed as a maxim that no nation or religion can supersede any other without incorporating into itself a portion of that which it supersedes. The abolition of personal and domestic slavery, and the emancipation of women from a great part of the degrading restraints of antiquity, were among the consequences of these events.

The abolition of personal slavery is the basis of the highest political hope that it can enter into the mind of man to conceive. The freedom of women produced the poetry of sexual love. Love became a religion, the idols of whose worship were ever present. It was as if the statues of Apollo and the Muses had been endowed with life and motion, and had walked forth among their worshippers; so that earth became peopled by the inhabitants of a diviner world. The familiar appearance and proceedings of life became wonderful and heavenly, and a paradise was created as out of the wrecks of Eden. And as this creation itself is poetry, so its creators were poets; and language was the instrument of their art:

Galeotto fù il libro, e chi lo scrisse [Galeotto was the book, and he who wrote it].[3] The Provençal Trouvères, or inventors, preceded Petrarch, whose verses are as spells, which unseal the inmost enchanted fountains of the delight which is in the grief of love. It is impossible to feel them without becoming a portion of that beauty which we contemplate: it were superfluous to explain how the gentleness and elevation of mind connected with these sacred emotions can render men more amiable, more generous and wise, and lift them out of the dull vapours of the little world of self. Dante understood the secret things of love even more than Petrarch. His *Vita Nuova* is an inexhaustible fountain of purity of sentiment and language: it is the idealized history of that period, and those intervals of his life which were dedicated to love. His apotheosis to Beatrice in Paradise, and the gradations of his own love and her loveliness, by which as by steps he feigns himself to have ascended to the throne of the Supreme Cause, is the most glorious imagination of modern poetry. The acutest critics have justly reversed the judgment of the vulgar, and the order of the great acts of the *Divina Commedia,* in the measure of the admiration which they accord to the Hell, Purgatory, and Paradise. The latter is a perpetual hymn of everlasting love. Love, which found a worthy poet in Plato alone of all the ancients, has been celebrated by a chorus of the greatest writers of the renovated world; and the music has penetrated the caverns of society, and its echoes still drown the dissonance of arms and superstition. At successive intervals, Ariosto, Tasso, Shakespeare, Spenser, Calderón, Rousseau, and the great writers of our own age have celebrated the dominion of love, planting as it were trophies in the human mind of that sublimest victory over sensuality and force. The true relation borne to each other by the sexes into which human kind is distributed has become less misunderstood; and if the error which confounded diversity with inequality of the powers of the two sexes has been partially recognized in the opinions and institutions of modern Europe, we owe this great benefit to the worship of which chivalry was the law, and poets the prophets.

The poetry of Dante may be considered as the bridge thrown over the stream of time, which unites the modern and ancient world. The distorted notions of invisible things which Dante and his rival Milton have idealized, are merely the mask and the mantle in which these great

---

3. From the episode of Paolo and Francesca in Dante's *Hell* (see *Great Books of the Western World,* Vol. 21, pp. 7–8). Their love was instigated by their reading the story of Galahad's (Gallehaut's) bringing together Lancelot and Guenevere in the Arthurian romance [Ed.].

poets walk through eternity enveloped and disguised. It is a difficult question to determine how far they were conscious of the distinction which must have subsisted in their minds between their own creeds and that of the people. Dante at least appears to wish to mark the full extent of it by placing Riphaeus, whom Virgil calls *justissimus unus* [the most upright], in Paradise, and observing a most poetical caprice in his distribution of rewards and punishments. And Milton's poem contains within itself a philosophical refutation of that system of which, by a strange and natural antithesis, it has been a chief popular support. Nothing can exceed the energy and magnificence of the character of Satan as expressed in *Paradise Lost*. It is a mistake to suppose that he could ever have been intended for the popular personification of evil. Implacable hate, patient cunning, and a sleepless refinement of device to inflict the extremest anguish on an enemy, these things are evil; and, although venial in a slave, are not to be forgiven in a tyrant; although redeemed by much that ennobles his defeat in one subdued, are marked by all that dishonours his conquest in the victor. Milton's Devil as a moral being is as far superior to his God as one who perseveres in some purpose which he has conceived to be excellent in spite of adversity and torture is to one who in the cold security of undoubted triumph inflicts the most horrible revenge upon his enemy not from any mistaken notion of inducing him to repent of a perseverance in enmity but with the alleged design of exasperating him to deserve new torments. Milton has so far violated the popular creed (if this shall be judged to be a violation) as to have alleged no superiority of moral virtue to his God over his Devil. And this bold neglect of a direct moral purpose is the most decisive proof of the supremacy of Milton's genius. He mingled as it were the elements of human nature as colours upon a single palette, and arranged them in the composition of his great picture according to the laws of epic truth, that is, according to the laws of that principle by which a series of actions of the external universe and of intelligent and ethical beings is calculated to excite the sympathy of succeeding generations of mankind. The *Divina Commedia* and *Paradise Lost* have conferred upon modern mythology a systematic form; and when change and time shall have added one more superstition to the mass of those which have arisen and decayed upon the earth, commentators will be learnedly employed in elucidating the religion of ancestral Europe, only not utterly forgotten because it will have been stamped with the eternity of genius.

Homer was the first and Dante the second epic poet: that is, the second poet, the series of whose creations bore a defined and intelligible relation to the knowledge and sentiment and religion of the age in which he lived, and of the ages which followed it: developing itself in correspondence with their development. For Lucretius had limed the wings of his swift spirit in the dregs of the sensible world; and Virgil, with a modesty that ill became his genius, had affected the fame of an imitator, even whilst he created anew all that he copied; and none among the flock of mock-birds, though their notes are sweet, Apollonius Rhodius, Quintus Calaber, Smyrnaeus, Nonnus, Lucan, Statius, or Claudian, have sought even to fulfil a single condition of epic truth. Milton was the third epic poet. For if the title of epic in its highest sense be refused to the *Aeneid*, still less can it be conceded to the *Orlando Furioso*, the *Gerusalemme Liberata, Os Lusíadas* [the *Lusiad*], or the *Faerie Queene.*

Dante and Milton were both deeply penetrated with the ancient religion of the civilized world; and its spirit exists in their poetry probably in the same proportion as its forms survived in the unreformed worship of modern Europe. The one preceded and the other followed the Reformation at almost equal intervals. Dante was the first religious reformer, and Luther surpassed him rather in the rudeness and acrimony than in the boldness of his censures, of papal usurpation. Dante was the first awakener of entranced Europe; he created a language, in itself music and persuasion, out of a chaos of inharmonious barbarisms. He was the congregator of those great spirits who presided over the resurrection of learning; the Lucifer of that starry flock which in the thirteenth century shone forth from republican Italy, as from a heaven, into the darkness of the benighted world. His very words are instinct with spirit; each is as a spark, a burning atom of inextinguishable thought; and many yet lie covered in the ashes of their birth, and pregnant with a lightning which has yet found no conductor. All high poetry is infinite; it is as the first acorn, which contained all oaks potentially. Veil after veil may be undrawn, and the inmost naked beauty of the meaning never exposed. A great poem is a fountain for ever overflowing with the waters of wisdom and delight; and after one person and one age has exhausted all of its divine effluence which their peculiar relations enable them to share, another and yet another succeeds, and new relations are ever developed, the source of an unforeseen and an unconceived delight.

The age immediately succeeding to that of Dante, Petrarch, and Boccaccio was characterized by a revival of painting, sculpture, and architecture. Chaucer caught the sacred inspiration, and the superstructure of English literature is based upon the materials of Italian invention.

But let us not be betrayed from a defence into a critical history of poetry and its influence on society. Be it enough to have pointed out the effects of poets, in the large and true sense of the word, upon their own and all succeeding times.

But poets have been challenged to resign the civic crown to reasoners and mechanists on another plea. It is admitted that the exercise of the imagination is most delightful, but it is alleged that that of reason is more useful. Let us examine, as the grounds of this distinction, what is here meant by utility. Pleasure or good, in a general sense, is that which the consciousness of a sensitive and intelligent being seeks, and in which, when found, it acquiesces. There are two kinds of pleasure, one durable, universal, and permanent; the other transitory and particular. Utility may either express the means of producing the former or the latter. In the former sense, whatever strengthens and purifies the affections, enlarges the imagination, and adds spirit to sense is useful. But a narrower meaning may be assigned to the word utility, confining it to express that which banishes the importunity of the wants of our animal nature, the surrounding men with security of life, the dispersing the grosser delusions of superstition, and the conciliating such a degree of mutual forbearance among men as may consist with the motives of personal advantage.

Undoubtedly the promoters of utility, in this limited sense, have their appointed office in society. They follow the footsteps of poets, and copy the sketches of their creations into the book of common life. They make space, and give time. Their exertions are of the highest value, so long as they confine their administration of the concerns of the inferior powers of our nature within the limits due to the superior ones. But while the sceptic destroys gross superstitions, let him spare to deface, as some of the French writers have defaced, the eternal truths charactered upon the imaginations of men. Whilst the mechanist abridges, and the political economist combines, labour, let them beware that their speculations, for want of correspondence with those first principles which belong to the imagination, do not tend, as they have in modern England, to exasperate at once the extremes of luxury and want. They have exemplified the saying, "To him that hath, more shall be given; and from him that hath not, the little that he hath shall be taken away." The rich have become richer, and the poor have become poorer; and the vessel of the state is driven between the Scylla and Charybdis of anarchy and despotism. Such are the effects which must ever flow from an unmitigated exercise of the calculating faculty.

It is difficult to define pleasure in its highest sense; the definition involving a number of apparent paradoxes. For, from an inexplicable defect of harmony in the constitution of human nature, the pain of the inferior is frequently connected with the pleasures of the superior portions of our being. Sorrow, terror, anguish, despair itself are often the chosen expressions of an approximation to the highest good. Our sympathy in tragic fiction depends on this principle; tragedy delights by affording a shadow of that pleasure which exists in pain. This is the source also of the melancholy which is inseparable from the sweetest melody. The pleasure that is in sorrow is sweeter than the pleasure of pleasure itself. And hence the saying, "It is better to go to the house of mourning than to the house of mirth." Not that this highest species of pleasure is necessarily linked with pain. The delight of love and friendship, the ecstasy of the admiration of nature, the joy of the perception and still more of the creation of poetry is often wholly unalloyed.

The production and assurance of pleasure in this highest sense is true utility. Those who produce and preserve this pleasure are poets or poetical philosophers.

The exertions of Locke, Hume, Gibbon, Voltaire, Rousseau,[4] and their disciples, in favour of oppressed and deluded humanity, are entitled to the gratitude of mankind. Yet it is easy to calculate the degree of moral and intellectual improvement which the world would have exhibited had they never lived. A little more nonsense would have been talked for a century or two; and perhaps a few more men, women, and children burnt as heretics. We might not at this moment have been congratulating each other on the abolition of the Inquisition in Spain. But it exceeds all imagination to conceive what would have been the moral condition of the world if neither Dante, Petrarch, Boccaccio, Chaucer, Shakespeare, Calderón, Bacon, nor Milton had ever existed; if Raphael and Michelangelo had never been born; if the Hebrew poetry had never been translated; if a revival of the study of Greek literature had never taken place; if no monuments of ancient sculpture had been handed down to us; and if the poetry of the religion of the ancient world had been extinguished together with its belief. The human mind could never, except by the intervention of these excitements, have been awakened to the invention of the grosser sciences, and that application of analytical reasoning to the aberrations of society, which it is now attempted to exalt over the direct expression of the inventive and creative faculty itself.

We have more moral, political, and historical wisdom than we know

---

4. Although Rousseau has been thus classed, he was essentially a poet. The others, even Voltaire, were mere reasoners.

how to reduce into practice; we have more scientific and economical knowledge than can be accommodated to the just distribution of the produce which it multiplies. The poetry, in these systems of thought, is concealed by the accumulation of facts and calculating processes. There is no want of knowledge respecting what is wisest and best in morals, government, and political economy, or at least what is wiser and better than what men now practise and endure. But we let "*I dare not* wait upon *I would*, like the poor cat in the adage." We want the creative faculty to imagine that which we know; we want the generous impulse to act that which we imagine; we want the poetry of life; our calculations have outrun conception; we have eaten more than we can digest. The cultivation of those sciences which have enlarged the limits of the empire of man over the external world has, for want of the poetical faculty, proportionally circumscribed those of the internal world; and man, having enslaved the elements, remains himself a slave. To what but a cultivation of the mechanical arts in a degree disproportioned to the presence of the creative faculty, which is the basis of all knowledge, is to be attributed the abuse of all invention for abridging and combining labour, to the exasperation of the inequality of mankind? From what other cause has it arisen that the discoveries which should have lightened have added a weight to the curse imposed on Adam? Poetry, and the principle of Self, of which money is the visible incarnation, are the God and Mammon of the world.

The functions of the poetical faculty are twofold; by one it creates new materials of knowledge, and power, and pleasure; by the other it engenders in the mind a desire to reproduce and arrange them according to a certain rhythm and order, which may be called the beautiful and the good. The cultivation of poetry is never more to be desired than at periods when, from an excess of the selfish and calculating principle, the accumulation of the materials of external life exceed the quantity of the power of assimilating them to the internal laws of human nature. The body has then become too unwieldy for that which animates it.

Poetry is indeed something divine. It is at once the centre and circumference of knowledge; it is that which comprehends all science, and that to which all science must be referred. It is at the same time the root and blossom of all other systems of thought; it is that from which all spring, and that which adorns all, and that which, if blighted, denies the fruit and the seed, and withholds from the barren world the nourishment and the succession of the scions of the tree of life. It is the perfect and consummate surface and bloom of all things; it is as the odour and the colour of the rose to the texture of the elements which compose it, as the form and splendour of unfaded beauty to the secrets of anatomy and corruption. What were virtue, love, patriotism, friendship—what were the scenery of this beautiful universe which we inhabit; what were our consolations on this side of the grave—and what were our aspirations beyond it, if poetry did not ascend to bring light and fire from those eternal regions where the owl-winged faculty of calculation dare not ever soar? Poetry is not like reasoning, a power to be exerted according to the determination of the will. A man cannot say, "I will compose poetry." The greatest poet even cannot say it; for the mind in creation is as a fading coal, which some invisible influence, like an inconstant wind, awakens to transitory brightness; this power arises from within, like the colour of a flower which fades and changes as it is developed, and the conscious portions of our nature are unprophetic either of its approach or its departure. Could this influence be durable in its original purity and force, it is impossible to predict the greatness of the results; but when composition begins, inspiration is already on the decline, and the most glorious poetry that has ever been communicated to the world is probably a feeble shadow of the original conceptions of the poet. I appeal to the greatest poets of the present day whether it is not an error to assert that the finest passages of poetry are produced by labour and study. The toil and the delay recommended by critics can be justly interpreted to mean no more than a careful observation of the inspired moments, and an artificial connection of the spaces between their suggestions, by the intertexture of conventional expressions; a necessity only imposed by the limitedness of the poetical faculty itself: for Milton conceived the *Paradise Lost* as a whole before he executed it in portions. We have his own authority also for the muse having "dictated" to him the "unpremeditated song." And let this be an answer to those who would allege the fifty-six various readings of the first line of the *Orlando Furioso*. Compositions so produced are to poetry what mosaic is to painting. The instinct and intuition of the poetical faculty is still more observable in the plastic and pictorial arts: a great statue or picture grows under the power of the artist as a child in the mother's womb; and the very mind which directs the hands in formation is incapable of accounting to itself for the origin, the gradations, or the media of the process.

Poetry is the record of the best and happiest moments of the happiest and best minds. We are aware of evanescent visitations of thought and feeling, sometimes associated with place or person, sometimes regarding our own mind alone, and always arising unforeseen and departing unbidden, but elevating and delightful beyond all expression: so that even in the desire and the regret they leave, there cannot but be pleasure, participating as it does in the nature of its object. It is as it were the interpenetration of a diviner nature through our own; but its footsteps are like those of a wind over the sea, which the morning calm erases, and whose traces remain only, as on the wrinkled sand which paves it. These and corresponding conditions of being are experienced principally by those of the most delicate sensibility and the most enlarged imagination; and the state of mind produced by them is at war with every base desire. The enthusiasm of virtue, love, patriotism, and friendship is essentially linked with such emotions; and whilst they last, self appears as what it is, an atom to a universe. Poets are not only subject to these experiences as spirits of the most refined organization, but they can colour all that they combine with the evanescent hues of this ethereal world; a word, a trait in the representation of a scene or a passion will touch the enchanted chord, and reanimate, in those who have ever experienced those emotions, the sleeping, the cold, the buried image of the past. Poetry thus makes immortal all that is best and most beautiful in the world; it arrests the vanishing apparitions which haunt the interlunations of life, and veiling them, or in language or in form, sends them forth among mankind, bearing sweet news of kindred joy to those with whom their sisters abide— abide, because there is no portal of expression from the caverns of the spirit which they inhabit into the universe of things. Poetry redeems from decay the visitations of the divinity in man.

Poetry turns all things to loveliness; it exalts the beauty of that which is most beautiful, and it adds beauty to that which is most deformed; it marries exultation and horror, grief and pleasure, eternity and change; it subdues to union, under its light yoke, all irreconcilable things. It transmutes all that it touches, and every form moving within the radiance of its presence is changed by wondrous sympathy to an incarnation of the spirit which it breathes: its secret alchemy turns to potable gold the poisonous waters which flow from death through life; it strips the veil of familiarity from the world, and lays bare the naked and sleeping beauty, which is the spirit of its forms.

All things exist as they are perceived; at least in relation to the percipient.

> The mind is its own place, and in itself
> Can make a heaven of hell, a hell of heaven.

But poetry defeats the curse which binds us to be subjected to the accident of surrounding impressions. And whether it spreads its own figured curtain, or withdraws life's dark veil from before the scene of things, it equally creates for us a being within our being. It makes us the inhabitant of a world to which the familiar world is a chaos. It reproduces the common universe of which we are portions and percipients, and it purges from our inward sight the film of familiarity which obscures from us the wonder of our being. It compels us to feel that which we perceive, and to imagine that which we know. It creates anew the universe, after it has been annihilated in our minds by the recurrence of impressions blunted by reiteration. It justifies the bold and true word of Tasso: *Non merita nome di creatore, se non Iddio ed il Poeta* [No one deserves the name of creator except God and the Poet].

A poet, as he is the author to others of the highest wisdom, pleasure, virtue and glory, so he ought personally to be the happiest, the best, the wisest, and the most illustrious of men. As to his glory, let time be challenged to declare whether the fame of any other institutor of human life be comparable to that of a poet. That he is the wisest, the happiest, and the best, inasmuch as he is a poet, is equally incontrovertible: the greatest poets have been men of the most spotless virtue, of the most consummate prudence, and, if we would look into the interior of their lives, the most fortunate of men: and the exceptions, as they regard those who possessed the poetic faculty in a high yet inferior degree, will be found on consideration to confirm rather than destroy the rule. Let us for a moment stoop to the arbitration of popular breath, and usurping and uniting in our own persons the incompatible characters of accuser, witness, judge and executioner, let us decide without trial, testimony, or form that certain motives of those who are "there sitting where we dare not soar" are reprehensible. Let us assume that Homer was a drunkard, that Virgil was a flatterer, that Horace was a coward, that Tasso was a madman, that Bacon was a speculator, that Raphael was a libertine, that Spenser was a poet laureate. It is inconsistent with this division of our subject to cite living poets, but posterity has done ample justice to the great names now referred to. Their errors have been weighed and found to have been dust in the balance; if their sins were as scarlet, they are now white as snow: they have been washed in the blood of the mediator and redeemer, time. Observe in what a ludicrous chaos the imputations of real or fictitious crime have been confused in the contemporary calumnies against poetry and poets; consider how little is, as it appears—or appears as it is; look to your own motives, and judge not, lest ye be judged.

Poetry, as has been said, differs in this respect from logic, that it is not subject to the control of the active powers of the mind, and that its birth and recurrence have no necessary connection with the consciousness or will. It is presumptuous to determine that these are the necessary conditions of all mental causation, when mental effects are experienced insusceptible of being referred to them. The frequent recurrence of the poetical power, it is obvious to suppose, may produce in the mind a habit of order and harmony correlative with its own nature and with its effects upon other minds. But in the intervals of inspiration, and they may be frequent without being durable, a poet becomes a man, and is abandoned to the sudden reflux of the influences under which others habitually live. But as he is more delicately organized than other men, and sensible to pain and pleasure, both his own and that of others, in a degree unknown to them, he will avoid the one and pursue the other with an ardour proportioned to this difference. And he renders himself obnoxious to calumny, when he neglects to observe the circumstances under which these objects of universal pursuit and flight have disguised themselves in one another's garments.

But there is nothing necessarily evil in this error, and thus cruelty, envy, revenge, avarice, and the passions purely evil have never formed any portion of the popular imputations on the lives of poets.

I have thought it most favourable to the cause of truth to set down these remarks according to the order in which they were suggested to my mind, by a consideration of the subject itself, instead of observing the formality of a polemical reply; but if the view which they contain be just, they will be found to involve a refutation of the arguers against poetry, so far at least as regards the first division of the subject. I can readily conjecture what should have moved the gall of some learned and intelligent writers who quarrel with certain versifiers; I, like them, confess myself unwilling to be stunned by the Theseids of the hoarse Codri of the day. Bavius and Maevius undoubtedly are, as they ever were, insufferable persons. But it belongs to a philosophical critic to distinguish rather than confound.

The first part of these remarks has related to poetry in its elements and principles: and it has been shown, as well as the narrow limits assigned them would permit, that what is called poetry in a restricted sense has a common source with all other forms of order and of beauty, according to which the materials of human life are susceptible of being arranged, and which is poetry in an universal sense.

The second part will have for its object an application of these principles to the present state of the cultivation of poetry, and a defence of the attempt to idealize the modern forms of manners and opinions, and compel them into a subordination to the imaginative and creative faculty.

For the literature of England, an energetic development of which has ever preceded or accompanied a great and free development of the national will, has arisen as it were from a new birth. In spite of the low-thoughted envy which would undervalue contemporary merit, our own will be a memorable age in intellectual achievements, and we live among such philosophers and poets as surpass beyond comparison any who have appeared since the last national struggle for civil and religious liberty. The most unfailing herald, companion, and follower of the awakening of a great people to work a beneficial change in opinion or institution is poetry. At such periods there is an accumulation of the power of communicating and receiving intense and impassioned conceptions respecting man and nature. The persons in whom this power resides may often, as far as regards many portions of their nature, have little apparent correspondence with that spirit of good of which they are the ministers. But even whilst they deny and abjure, they are yet compelled to serve the power which is seated on the throne of their own soul. It is impossible to read the compositions of the most celebrated writers of the present day without being startled with the electric life which burns within their words. They measure the circumference and sound the depths of human nature with a comprehensive and all-penetrating spirit, and they are themselves perhaps the most sincerely astonished at its manifestations; for it is less their spirit than the spirit of the age. Poets are the hierophants of an unapprehended inspiration; the mirrors of the gigantic shadows which futurity casts upon the present; the words which express what they understand not; the trumpets which sing to battle and feel not what they inspire; the influence which is moved not, but moves. Poets are the unacknowledged legislators of the world.

Walt Whitman

1819–1892

Walt Whitman (Walter Whitman, Jr., in full) came of English, Welsh, and Dutch stock. He was born on the family farm in Huntington, Long Island, New York, May 31, 1819. In the early 1820's, his family moved to Brooklyn, where Whitman got a little schooling. He spent a leisurely youth teaching in country districts on Long Island and working as a newspaper printer and writer.

By 1846 he was editing the *Brooklyn Daily Eagle*. A few months with a New Orleans newspaper gave him a chance to explore the Mississippi Valley en route. In Brooklyn again, he began to meditate the poems for *Leaves of Grass*. This great book became the focus of his life. In 1855, almost singlehanded, he set and printed the first edition. "I greet you at the beginning of a great career," Emerson wrote; but the book went largely unread.

From early 1863 until the end of the Civil War, Whitman served as a volunteer nurse, letter writer, and friend in the national hospitals at Washington, D.C. Later he estimated that he made 600 visits and talked to as many as 100,000 sick or wounded, both Union and Confederate. As the author of "an indecent book," he was discharged from the Department of the Interior in 1865.

His friend W. D. O'Connor defended his name in *The Good Gray Poet* and found him another place in the Attorney General's office. There Whitman worked until he was partly disabled by a cerebral hemorrhage in 1873. Meantime his *Selected Poems* had been brought out in England. He published a fifth enlarged edition of *Leaves of Grass*. A prose work, *Democratic Vistas*, conveyed his vision of America's prospects and liabilities.

Except for trips to Colorado and Canada, he spent most of his later years in Camden, New Jersey. There friends—John Burroughs,

Horace Traubel, Dr. R. M. Bucke, and an English admirer, Mrs. Anne Gilchrist—gathered about him. In his last days he edited the ninth edition of *Leaves of Grass* and his *Complete Prose Works.* Weakened by pneumonia, he died in Camden of a complication of illnesses on March 26, 1892.

Let us imagine for a moment that we are Walt Whitman. The year is 1855. He has sold a house to get money for the first publication of *Leaves of Grass.* He is thirty-six, a calm, big-boned man whose hair is already turning gray. He has written a propaganda novel in favor of temperance, edited a few newspapers, and published some sentimental verses. By common standards he is a nobody, but a very self-reliant nobody, "one full-sized man unconquerable and simple." He lives a ferry ride away from the most energetic city in the bustling new nation of the United States.

This is the man—this nobody, this farmer's son from Long Island —who announces calmly out of the blue, in his first book, that he has elected himself the poet of American democracy, with options on the world and the universe. Even if it were a hoax, this would be the boldest act in the history of American literature. But it is not a hoax. It is a serene act of genius. He gives us the evidence in verse, plus an argument in prose. We cannot help noticing that the claim is not purely literary. It is also philosophical, social, and political. It demands for the poet—for Whitman himself, and for the poets who will come after him—the most exalted position, as lawgiver, seer, creator of the future, and delegate of the "divine average," the free individual.

As if this were not enough, the poems in *Leaves of Grass* break all the rules. They shock the literary reader, who expects meter and rhymed endings. Their frankness violates the provincial conventions of the period. With two or three exceptions, the result is outrage. One reviewer calls Whitman "the poet who brought the slop-pail

Notes from the artist: ". . . Bold, sweeping lines in an abstract pattern swirl around and within the portrait of Whitman in workingman's clothes. The strong, tough lines, like those of Whitman's poetry, might be thought of as Leaves of Grass."

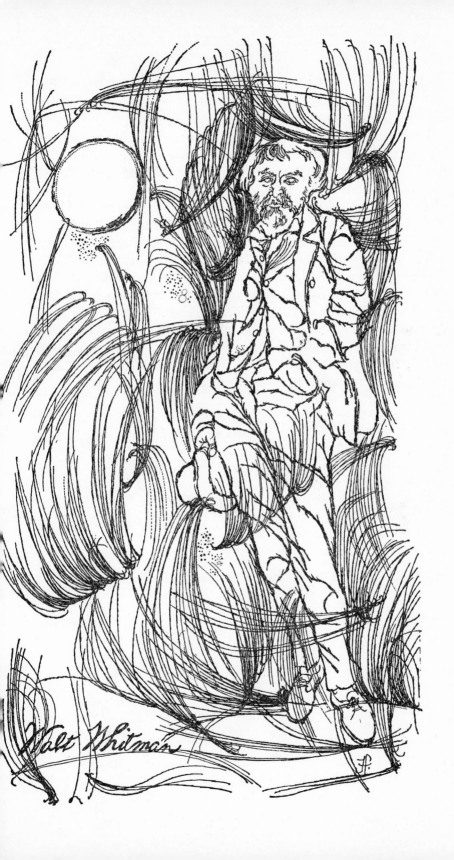

Walt Whitman

into the parlor." And what does Whitman do? He tries to promote the book. When it will not be promoted, he goes calmly about the business of preparing a second, expanded edition.

But the mystery remains. How did this man suddenly produce this book? We know that in the years between his journey to New Orleans and 1855, something has happened to Whitman. We do not know what. Perhaps he does not know himself. Perhaps it is only that all his lines of development have come together for the first time in the bold speeches of his poems. The answer, if we can find it anywhere, may be found in the *Preface* he wrote for *Leaves of Grass*.

It is infused with a sense of mission. In it Whitman speaks in the tone of a man who has experienced a religious conversion. He has fallen in love with the universe and found his true relation to it. His voice is the voice of a great ethical teacher: "Love the earth and sun and the animals, despise riches, give alms to every one that asks, stand up for the stupid and crazy, devote your income and labor to others, hate tyrants, argue not concerning God. . . ." Do these things, he writes, and "your very flesh shall be a great poem. . . ."

Preface to
Leaves of Grass

America does not repel the past, or what the past has produced under its forms, or amid other politics, or the idea of castes, or the old religions—accepts the lesson with calmness—is not impatient because the slough still sticks to opinions and manners in literature, while the life which served its requirements has passed into the new life of the new forms—perceives that the corpse is slowly borne from the eating and sleeping rooms of the house—perceives that it waits a little while in the door—that it was fittest for its days—that its action has descended to the stalwart and well-shaped heir who approaches—and that he shall be fittest for his days.

The Americans of all nations at any time upon the earth, have probably the fullest poetical nature. The United States themselves are essentially the greatest poem. In the history of the earth hitherto, the largest and most stirring appear tame and orderly to their ampler largeness and stir. Here at last is something in the doings of man that corresponds with the broadcast doings of the day and night. Here is action untied from strings, necessarily blind to particulars and details, magnificently moving in masses. Here is the hospitality which forever indicates heroes. Here the performance, disdaining the trivial, unapproached in the tremendous audacity of its crowds and groupings, and the push of its perspective, spreads with crampless and flowing breadth, and showers its prolific and splendid extravagance. One sees it must indeed own the riches of the summer and winter, and need never be bankrupt while corn grows from the ground, or the orchards drop apples, or the bays contain fish, or men beget children upon women.

Other states indicate themselves in their deputies—but the genius of the United States is not best or most in its executives or legislatures, nor in its ambassadors or authors, or colleges or churches or parlors, nor even in its newspapers or inventors—but always most in the common people, south, north, west, east, in all its States, through all its mighty amplitude. The largeness of the nation, however, were monstrous without a corresponding largeness and generosity of the spirit of the citizen. Not swarming states, nor streets and steamships, nor prosperous business, nor farms, nor capital, nor learning, may suffice for the ideal of man—nor suffice the poet. No reminiscences may suffice either. A live nation can always cut a deep mark, and can have the best authority the cheapest—namely, from its own soul. This is the sum of the profitable uses of individuals or states, and of present action and grandeur, and of the subjects of poets. (As if it were necessary to trot back generation after generation to the eastern records! As if the beauty and sacredness of the demonstrable must fall behind that of the mythical! As if men do not make their mark out of any times! As if the opening of the western continent by discovery, and what has transpired in North and South America, were less than the small theatre of the antique, or the aimless sleep walking of the middle ages!) The pride of the United States leaves the wealth and finesse of the cities, and all returns of commerce and agriculture, and all the magnitude of geography or shows of exterior victory, to enjoy the sight and realization of full-sized men, or one full-sized man unconquerable and simple.

The American poets are to enclose old and new, for America is the race of races. The expression of the American poet is to be transcendent and new. It is to be indirect, and not direct or descriptive or epic. Its quality goes through these to much more. Let the age and wars of other nations be chanted, and their eras and characters be illustrated, and that finish the verse. Not so the great psalm of the republic. Here the theme is creative, and has vista. Whatever stagnates in the flat of custom or obedience or legislation, the great poet never stagnates. Obedience does not master him, he masters it. High up out of reach he stands, turning a concentrated light—he turns the pivot with his finger—he baffles the swiftest runners as he stands, and easily overtakes and envelopes them. The time straying toward infidelity and confections and persiflage he withholds by steady faith. Faith is the antiseptic of the soul—it pervades the common people and preserves them—they never give up believing and expecting and trusting. There is that indescribable freshness and unconsciousness about an illiterate person, that humbles and mocks the power of the noblest expressive genius. The poet sees for a certainty how one not a great artist may be just as sacred and perfect as the greatest artist.

The power to destroy or remold is freely used by the greatest poet, but seldom the power of attack. What is past is past. If he does not expose superior models, and prove himself by every step he takes, he is not what is wanted. The presence of the great poet conquers—not parleying, or struggling, or any prepared attempts. Now he has passed that way, see after him! There is not left any vestige of despair, or misanthropy, or cunning, or exclusiveness, or the ignominy of a nativity or color, or delusion of hell or the necessity of hell—and no man thenceforward shall be degraded for ignorance or weakness or sin. The greatest poet hardly knows pettiness or triviality. If he breathes into anything that was before thought small, it dilates with the grandeur and life of the universe. He is a seer—he is individual—he is complete in himself— the others are as good as he, only he sees it, and they do not. He is not one of the chorus—he does not stop for any regulation—he is the president of regulation. What the eyesight does to the rest, he does to the rest. Who knows the curious mystery of the eyesight? The other senses corroborate themselves, but this is removed from any proof but its own, and foreruns the identities of the spiritual world. A single glance of it mocks all the investigations of man, and all the instruments and books of the earth, and all reasoning. What is marvelous? what is unlikely? what is impossible or baseless or vague—after you have once just opened the space of a peach pit, and given audience to far and near, and to the sunset, and had all things enter with electric swiftness, softly and duly, without confusion or jostling or jam?

The land and sea, the animals, fishes and birds, the sky of heaven and the orbs, the forests, mountains and rivers, are not small themes—but folks expect of the poet to indicate more than the beauty and dignity which always attach to dumb real objects—they expect him to indicate the path between reality and their souls. Men and women perceive the beauty well enough—probably as well as he. The passionate tenacity of hunters, woodmen, early risers, cultivators of gardens and orchards and fields, the love of healthy women for the manly form, seafaring persons, drivers of horses, the passion for light and the open air, all is an old varied sign of the unfailing perception of beauty, and of a residence of the poetic in outdoor people. They can never be assisted by poets to perceive —some may, but they never can. The poetic quality is not marshaled in rhyme or uniformity, or abstract addresses to things, nor in melancholy complaints or good precepts, but is the life of these and much else, and is in the soul. The profit of rhyme is that it drops seeds of a sweeter and more luxuriant rhyme, and of uniformity that it conveys itself into its own roots in the ground out of sight. The rhyme and uniformity of perfect poems show the free growth of metrical laws, and bud from them as unerringly and loosely as lilacs and roses on a bush, and take shapes as compact as the shapes of chestnuts and oranges, and melons and pears, and shed the perfume impalpable to form. The fluency and ornaments of the finest poems or music or orations or recitations, are not independent but dependent. All beauty comes from beautiful blood and a beautiful brain. If the greatnesses are in conjunction in a man or woman, it is enough—the fact will prevail through the universe; but the gaggery and gilt of a million years will not prevail. Who troubles himself about his ornaments or fluency is lost. This is what you shall do: Love the earth and sun and the animals, despise riches, give alms to every one that asks, stand up for the stupid and crazy, devote your income and labor to others, hate tyrants, argue not concerning God, have patience and indulgence toward the people, take off your hat to nothing known or unknown, or to any man or number of men—go freely with powerful uneducated persons, and with the young, and with the mothers of families —re-examine all you have been told in school or church or in any book, and dismiss whatever insults your own soul; and your very flesh shall be a great poem, and have the richest fluency, not only in its words, but in the silent lines of its lips and face, and between the lashes of your eyes, and in every motion and joint of your body. The poet shall not spend his time in unneeded work. He shall know that the ground is already ploughed and manured; others may not know it, but he shall. He shall go directly to the creation. His trust shall master the trust of everything he touches—and shall master all attachment.

The known universe has one complete lover, and that is the greatest poet. He consumes an eternal passion, and is indifferent which chance happens, and which possible contingency of fortune or misfortune, and persuades daily and hourly his delicious pay. What balks or breaks others is fuel for his burning progress to contact and amorous joy. Other proportions of the reception of pleasure dwindle to nothing to his proportions. All expected from heaven or from the highest, he is rapport with in the sight of the daybreak, or the scenes of the winter woods, or the presence of children playing, or with his arm round the neck of a man or woman. His love above all love has leisure and expanse—he leaves room ahead of himself. He is no irresolute or suspicious lover—he is sure—he scorns intervals. His experience and the showers and thrills are not for nothing. Nothing can jar him—suffering and darkness cannot—death and fear cannot. To him complaint and jealousy and envy are corpses buried and rotten in the earth—he saw them buried. The sea is not surer of the shore, or the shore of the sea, than he is the fruition of his love, and of all perfection and beauty.

The fruition of beauty is no chance of miss or hit—it is as inevitable as life—it is exact and plumb as gravitation. From the eyesight proceeds another eyesight, and from the hearing proceeds another hearing, and from the voice proceeds another voice, eternally curious of the harmony of things with man. These understand the law of perfection in masses and floods—that it is profuse and impartial—that there is not a minute of the light or dark, nor an acre of the earth and sea, without it—nor any direction of the sky, nor any trade or employment, nor any turn of events. This is the reason that about the proper expression of beauty there is precision and balance. One part does not need to be thrust above another. The best singer is not the one who has the most lithe and powerful organ. The pleasure of poems is not in them that take the handsomest measure and sound.

Without effort, and without exposing in the least how it is done, the greatest poet brings the spirit of any or all events and passions and scenes and persons, some more and some less, to bear on your individual character as you hear or read. To do this well is to compete with the laws that pursue and follow Time. What is the purpose must surely be there, and the clue of it must be there—and the faintest indication is the indication of the best, and then becomes the clearest indication. Past and present and future are not disjoined but joined. The greatest poet forms the consistence of what is to be, from what has been and is. He drags the dead out of their coffins and stands them again on their feet. He says to the past, Rise and walk before me that I may realize you. He learns the lesson—he places himself where the future becomes present. The greatest poet does not only dazzle his rays over character and scenes and passions —he finally ascends, and finishes all—he exhibits the pinnacles that no man can tell what they are for, or what is beyond—he glows a moment on the extremest verge. He is most wonderful in his last half-hidden smile or frown; by that flash of the moment of parting the one that sees it shall be encouraged or terrified afterward for many years. The greatest poet does not moralize or make applications of morals—he knows the soul. The soul has that measureless pride which consists in never acknowledging any lessons or deductions but its own. But it has sympathy as measureless as its pride, and the one balances the other, and neither can stretch too far while it stretches in company with the other. The inmost secrets of art sleep with the twain. The greatest poet has lain close betwixt both, and they are vital in his style and thoughts.

The art of art, the glory of expression and the sunshine of the light of letters, is simplicity. Nothing is better than simplicity—nothing can make up for excess, or for the lack of definiteness. To carry on the heave of impulse and pierce intellectual depths and give all subjects their articulations are powers neither common nor very uncommon. But to speak in literature with the perfect rectitude and insouciance of the movements of animals, and the unimpeachableness of the sentiment of trees in the woods and grass by the roadside, is the flawless triumph of art. If you have looked on him who has achieved it you have looked on one of the masters of the artists of all nations and times. You shall not contemplate the flight of the gray gull over the bay, or the mettlesome action of the blood horse, or the tall leaning of sunflowers on their stalk, or the appearance of the sun journeying through heaven, or the appearance of the moon afterward, with any more satisfaction than you shall contemplate him. The great poet has less a marked style, and is more the channel of thoughts and things without increase or diminution, and is the free channel of himself. He swears to his art, I will not be meddlesome, I will not have in my writing any elegance, or effect, or originality, to hang in the way between me and the rest like curtains. I will have nothing hang in the way, not the richest curtains. What I tell I tell for precisely what it is. Let who may exalt or startle or fascinate or soothe, I will have purposes as health or heat or snow has, and be as regardless of observation. What I experience or portray shall go from my composition without a shred of my composition. You shall stand by my side and look in the mirror with me.

The old red blood and stainless gentility of great poets will be proved by their unconstraint. A heroic person walks at his ease through and out of that custom or precedent or authority that suits him not. Of the traits of the brotherhood of first-class writers, savans, musicians, inventors and artists, nothing is finer than silent defiance advancing from new free forms. In the need of poems, philosophy, politics, mechanism, science, behavior, the craft of art, an appropriate native grand opera, shipcraft, or any craft, he is greatest for ever and ever who contributes the greatest original practical example. The cleanest expression is that which finds no sphere worthy of itself, and makes one.

The messages of great poems to each man and woman are, Come to us on equal terms, only then can you understand us. We are no better than you, what we enclose you enclose, what we enjoy you may enjoy. Did you suppose there could be only one Supreme? We affirm there can be unnumbered Supremes, and that one does not countervail another any more than one eyesight countervails another—and that men can be good or grand only of the consciousness of their supremacy within them. What do you think is the grandeur of storms and dismemberments, and the deadliest battles and wrecks, and the wildest fury of the elements, and the power of the sea, and the motion of Nature, and the throes of human desires, and dignity and hate and love? It is that something in the soul which says, Rage on, whirl on, I tread master here and everywhere— Master of the spasms of the sky and of the shatter of the sea, Master of nature and passion and death, and of all terror and all pain.

The American bards shall be marked for generosity and affection, and for encouraging competitors. They shall be Kosmos, without monopoly or secrecy, glad to pass anything to any one—hungry for equals night and day. They shall not be careful of riches and privilege—they shall be riches and privilege—they shall perceive who the most affluent man is. The most affluent man is he that confronts all the shows he sees by equivalents out of the stronger wealth of himself. The American bard shall delineate no class of persons, nor one or two out of the strata of interests, nor love most nor truth most, nor the soul most, nor the body most—and not be for the Eastern States more than the Western, or the Northern States more than the Southern.

Exact science and its practical movements are no checks on the greatest poet, but always his encouragement and support. The outset and remembrance are there—there the arms that lifted him first, and braced him best—there he returns after all his goings and comings. The sailor and traveler—the anatomist, chemist, astronomer, geologist, phrenologist, spiritualist, mathematician, historian, and lexicographer, are not poets, but they are the lawgivers of poets, and their construction underlies the structure of every perfect poem. No matter what rises or is uttered, they sent the seed of the conception of it—of them and by them stand the visible proofs of souls. If there shall be love and content between the father and the son, and if the greatness of the son is the exuding of the greatness of the father, there shall be love between the poet and the man of demonstrable science. In the beauty of poems are henceforth the tuft and final applause of science.

Great is the faith of the flush of knowledge, and of the investigation of the depths of qualities and things. Cleaving and circling here swells the soul of the poet, yet is president of itself always. The depths are fathomless, and therefore calm. The innocence and nakedness are resumed—they are neither modest nor immodest. The whole theory of the supernatural, and all that was twined with it or educed out of it, departs as a dream. What has ever happened—what happens, and whatever may or shall happen, the vital laws enclose all. They are sufficient for any case and for all cases—none to be hurried or retarded—any special miracle of affairs or persons inadmissible in the vast clear scheme where every motion and every spear of grass, and the frames and spirits of men and women and all that concerns them, are unspeakably perfect miracles, all referring to all, and each distinct and in its place. It is also not consistent with the reality of the soul to admit that there is anything in the known universe more divine than men and women.

Men and women, and the earth and all upon it, are to be taken as they are, and the investigation of their past and present and future shall be unintermitted, and shall be done with perfect candor. Upon this basis philosophy speculates, ever looking towards the poet, ever regarding the eternal tendencies of all toward happiness, never inconsistent with what is clear to the senses and to the soul. For the eternal tendencies of all toward happiness make the only point of sane philosophy. Whatever comprehends less than that—whatever is less than the laws of light and of astronomical motion—or less than the laws that follow the thief, the liar, the glutton and the drunkard, through this life and doubtless afterward—or less than vast stretches of time, or the slow formation of density, or the patient upheaving of strata—is of no account. Whatever would put God in a poem or system of philosophy as contending against some being or influence, is also of no account. Sanity and ensemble characterize the great master—spoilt in one principle, all is spoilt. The great master has nothing to do with miracles. He sees health for himself in being one of the mass—he sees the hiatus in singular eminence. To the perfect shape comes common ground. To be under the general law is great, for that is to correspond with it. The master knows that he is unspeakably great, and that all are unspeakably great—that nothing, for instance, is greater than to conceive children, and bring them up well—that to *be* is just as great as to perceive or tell.

In the make of the great masters the idea of political liberty is indispensable. Liberty takes the adherence of heroes wherever man and woman exist—but never takes any adherence or welcome from the rest more than from poets. They are the voice and exposition of liberty. They out of ages are worthy the grand idea—to them it is confided, and they must sustain it. Nothing has precedence of it, and nothing can warp or degrade it.

As the attributes of the poets of the kosmos concentre in the real body, and in the pleasure of things, they possess the superiority of genuineness over all fiction and romance. As they emit themselves, facts are showered over with light—the daylight is lit with more volatile light—the deep between the setting and rising sun goes deeper many fold. Each precise object or condition or combination or process exhibits a beauty—the multiplication table its—old age its—the carpenter's trade its—the grand opera its—the huge-hulled clean-shaped New York clipper at sea under steam or full sail gleams with unmatched beauty—the American circles and large harmonies of government gleam with theirs—and the commonest definite intentions and actions with theirs. The poets of the kosmos advance through all interpositions and coverings and turmoils and stratagems to first principles. They are of use—they dissolve poverty from its need, and riches from its conceit. You large proprietor, they say, shall not realize or perceive more than any one else. The owner of the library is not he who holds a legal title to it, having bought and paid for it. Any one and every one is owner of the library, (indeed he or she alone is owner,) who can read the same through all the varieties of tongues and subjects and styles, and in whom they enter with ease, and make supple and powerful and rich and large.

These American States, strong and healthy and accomplished, shall receive no pleasure from violations of natural models, and must not permit them. In paintings or moldings or carvings in mineral or wood, or in the illustrations of books or newspapers, or in the patterns of woven stuffs, or anything to beautify rooms or furniture or costumes, or to put upon cornices or monuments, or on the prows or sterns of ships, or to put anywhere before the human eye indoors or out, that which distorts honest shapes, or which creates unearthly beings or places or contingencies, is a nuisance and revolt. Of the human form especially, it is so great it must never be made ridiculous. Of ornaments to a work nothing *outré* can be allowed—but those ornaments can be allowed that conform to the perfect facts of the open air, and that flow out of the nature of the work, and come irrepressibly from it, and are necessary to the completion of the work. Most works are most beautiful without ornament. Exaggerations will be revenged in human physiology. Clean and vigorous childen are jetted and conceived only in those communities where the models of natural forms are public every day. Great genius and the people of these

States must never be demeaned to romances. As soon as histories are properly told, no more need of romances.

The great poets are to be known by the absence in them of tricks, and by the justification of perfect personal candor. All faults may be forgiven of him who has perfect candor. Henceforth let no man of us lie, for we have seen that openness wins the inner and outer world, and that there is no single exception, and that never since our earth gathered itself in a mass have deceit or subterfuge or prevarication attracted its smallest particle or the faintest tinge of a shade—and that through the enveloping wealth and rank of a state, or the whole republic of states, a sneak or sly person shall be discovered and despised—and that the soul has never once been fooled and never can be fooled—and thrift without the loving nod of the soul is only a fetid puff—and there never grew up in any of the continents of the globe, nor upon any planet or satellite, nor in that condition which precedes the birth of babes, nor at any time during the changes of life, nor in any stretch of abeyance or action of vitality, nor in any process of formation or reformation anywhere, a being whose instinct hated the truth.

Extreme caution or prudence, the soundest organic health, large hope and comparison and fondness for women and children, large alimentiveness and destructiveness and causality, with a perfect sense of the oneness of nature, and the propriety of the same spirit applied to human affairs, are called up of the float of the brain of the world to be parts of the greatest poet from his birth out of his mother's womb, and from her birth out of her mother's. Caution seldom goes far enough. It has been thought that the prudent citizen was the citizen who applied himself to solid gains, and did well for himself and for his family, and completed a lawful life without debt or crime. The greatest poet sees and admits these economies as he sees the economies of food and sleep, but has higher notions of prudence than to think he gives much when he gives a few slight attentions at the latch of the gate. The premises of the prudence of life are not the hospitality of it, or the ripeness and harvest of it. Beyond the independence of a little sum laid aside for burial money, and of a few clapboards around and shingles overhead on a lot of American soil owned, and the easy dollars that supply the year's plain clothing and meals, the melancholy prudence of the abandonment of such a great being as a man is, to the toss and pallor of years of money-making, with all their scorching days and icy nights, and all their stifling deceits and underhand dodgings, or infinitesimals of parlors, or shameless stuffing while others starve, and all the loss of the bloom and odor of the earth, and of the flowers and atmosphere, and of the sea, and of the true taste of the women and men you pass or have to do with in youth or middle age, and the issuing sickness and desperate revolt at the close of a life without elevation or naïveté (even if you have achieved a secure 10,000 a year, or election to Congress or the Governorship), and the ghastly chatter of a death without serenity or majesty, is the great fraud upon modern civilization and forethought, blotching the surface and system which civilization undeniably drafts, and moistening with tears the immense features it spreads and spreads with such velocity before the reached kisses of the soul.

Ever the right explanation remains to be made about prudence. The prudence of the mere wealth and respectability of the most esteemed life appears too faint for the eye to observe at all, when little and large alike drop quietly aside at the thought of the prudence suitable for immortality. What is the wisdom that fills the thinness of a year, or seventy or eighty years—to the wisdom spaced out by ages, and coming back at a certain time with strong reinforcements and rich presents, and the clear faces of wedding guests as far as you can look, in every direction, running gaily toward you? Only the soul is of itself—all else has reference to what ensues. All that a person does or thinks is of consequence. Nor can the push of charity or personal force ever be anything else than the profoundest reason, whether it brings argument to hand or no. No specification is necessary—to add or subtract or divide is in vain. Little or big, learned or unlearned, white or black, legal or illegal, sick or well, from the first inspiration down the windpipe to the last expiration out of it, all that a male or female does that is vigorous and benevolent and clean is so much sure profit to him or her in the unshakable order of the universe, and through the whole scope of it forever. The prudence of the greatest poet answers at last the craving and glut of the soul, puts off nothing, permits no letup for its own case or any case, has no particular sabbath or judgment day, divides not the living from the dead, or the righteous from the unrighteous, is satisfied with the present, matches every thought or act by its correlative, and knows no possible forgiveness or deputed atonement.

The direct trial of him who would be the greatest poet is today. If he does not flood himself with the immediate age as with vast oceanic tides —if he be not himself the age transfigured, and if to him is not opened the eternity which gives similitude to all periods and locations and processes, and animate and inanimate forms, and which is the bond of time, and rises up from its inconceivable vagueness and infiniteness in the swimming shapes of today, and is held by the ductile anchors of life, and makes the present spot the passage from what was to what shall be, and commits itself to the representation of this wave of an hour, and this one of the sixty beautiful children of the wave—let him merge in the general run, and wait his development.

Still the final test of poems, or any character or work, remains. The prescient poet projects himself centuries ahead, and judges performer or performance after the changes of time. Does it live through them? Does it still hold on untired? Will the same style, and the direction of genius to similar points, be satisfactory now? Have the marches of tens and hundreds and thousands of years made willing detours to the right hand and the left hand for his sake? Is he beloved long and long after he is buried? Does the young man think often of him? and the young woman think often of him? and do the middle-aged and the old think of him?

A great poem is for ages and ages in common, and for all degrees and complexions, and all departments and sects, and for a woman as much as a man, and a man as much as a woman. A great poem is no finish to a man or woman, but rather a beginning. Has any one fancied he could sit at last under some due authority, and rest satisfied with explanations, and realize, and be content and full? To no such terminus does the greatest poet bring—he brings neither cessation nor sheltered fatness and ease. The touch of him, like Nature, tells in action. Whom he takes he takes with firm sure grasp into live regions previously unattained—thenceforward is no rest—they see the space and ineffable sheen that turn the old spots and lights into dead vacuums. Now there shall be a man cohered out of tumult and chaos—the elder encourages the younger and shows him how—they two shall launch off fearlessly together till the new world fits an orbit for itself, and looks unabashed on the lesser orbits of the stars, and sweeps through the ceaseless rings, and shall never be quiet again.

There will soon be no more priests. Their work is done. A new order shall arise, and they shall be the priests of man, and every man shall be his own priest. They shall find their inspiration in real objects today, symptoms of the past and future. They shall not deign to defend immortality or God, or the perfection of things, or liberty, or the exquisite beauty and reality of the soul. They shall arise in America, and be responded to from the remainder of the earth.

The English language befriends the grand American expression—it is brawny enough, and limber and full enough. On the tough stock of a race who through all change of circumstance was never without the idea of political liberty, which is the animus of all liberty, it has attracted the terms of daintier and gayer and subtler and more elegant tongues. It is the powerful language of resistance—it is the dialect of common sense. It is the speech of the proud and melancholy races, and of all who aspire. It is the chosen tongue to express growth, faith, self-esteem, freedom, justice, equality, friendliness, amplitude, prudence, decision, and courage. It is the medium that shall well-nigh express the inexpressible.

No great literature, nor any like style of behavior or oratory, or social intercourse or household arrangements, or public institutions, or the treatment by bosses of employed people, nor executive detail, or detail of the army and navy, nor spirit of legislation or courts, or police or tuition or architecture, or songs or amusements, can long elude the jealous and passionate instinct of American standards. Whether or no the sign appears from the mouths of the people, it throbs a live interrogation in every freeman's and freewoman's heart, after that which passes by, or this built to remain. Is it uniform with my country? Are its disposals without ignominious distinctions? Is it for the ever-growing communes of brothers and lovers, large, well united, proud, beyond the old models, generous beyond all models? Is it something grown fresh out of the fields, or drawn from the sea for use to me today here? I know that what answers for me, an American, in Texas, Ohio, Canada, must answer for any individual or nation that serves for a part of my materials. Does this answer? Is it for the nursing of the young of the republic? Does it solve readily with the sweet milk of the nipples of the breasts of the Mother of Many Children?

America prepares with composure and good will for the visitors that have sent word. It is not intellect that is to be their warrant and welcome. The talented, the artist, the ingenious, the editor, the statesman, the erudite, are not unappreciated—they fall in their place and do their work. The soul of the nation also does its work. It rejects none, it permits all. Only toward the like of itself will it advance half-way. An individual is as superb as a nation when he has the qualities which make a superb nation. The soul of the largest and wealthiest and proudest nation may well go half-way to meet that of its poets.

---

*The foregoing is Whitman's preface
to the 1882 edition
of* LEAVES OF GRASS.

William Hazlitt

1778–1830

Wil: illiam Hazlitt was born at Maidstone, Kent, April 10, 1778. His father, a Unitarian minister and liberal of Irish stock, knew Franklin and favored the American Revolution. In 1783 he moved his family, first to Ireland, then to Philadelphia and Boston. A little later the Hazlitts returned to England. Young William grew up in the peaceful, flowery countryside at Wem in Shropshire, his mind full of the French Revolution, the great event of his time. All his life he remained a hot libertarian who also idolized Napoleon.

He was sent to a well-taught Unitarian academy at Hackney. Like Henry and William James, he tried painting first. In Paris, he earned his keep making copies of works at the Louvre. Back in England in 1803, he spent two years as a wandering portrait painter. His self-portrait, solidly painted, shows a gaunt-faced, brooding young man, not unhandsome, with lank black hair and big dark eyes.

In 1805 he turned to writing. *On the Principles of Human Action* and three other books of ideas were published in the next few years. He married Sarah Stoddart, a friend of the Lambs, and went to live at Winterslow. Hazlitt was penniless when his second child was born in 1811. He lectured on philosophy in London and got a job as parliamentary reporter on the *Morning Chronicle*. He became the paper's drama critic. A collection of theater articles and two books

Notes from the artist: "Hazlitt and two important figures in his life . . . at the left, Shakespeare, subject of several of Hazlitt's essays; above is Napoleon I, greatly admired by Hazlitt, who was deeply affected by the emperor's defeat at Waterloo."

Wm Hazlitt.

of his "Round Table" essays made his reputation. He praised the Romantic poets. This brought him under attack by the thunderous William Gifford of the *Quarterly Review.* Hazlitt replied with all guns, to the delight of Keats and his other friends.

He wrote on every subject from art exhibitions to prize fights. His three famous lecture series, including *On the English Poets,* were gathered into books. Long separated from his wife, he fell in love with Sarah Walker, the daughter of his London landlord. She played him off against another man. He wrote the story, somewhat disguised, in *Liber Amoris,* a book that English critics found distasteful. Hazlitt married again later, traveled in France and Italy, and wrote a four-volume life of Napoleon. His best-known later work, *The Spirit of the Age,* contained studies of the leading men of his time. He died of cancer of the stomach in London on September 18, 1830.

Up to 1820 the name of Wordsworth was trampled underfoot," said De Quincey; and the same was true of Coleridge. Why? Because they had made a revolution in poetry, and because at that time they supported the French Revolution. Hazlitt met them first in 1798, when he was twenty. A quarter-century later, in *My First Acquaintance with Poets,* he recovers the excitement of that youthful time when a new poetry and a new age were born together.

We see Coleridge, the big, "round-faced man in black," in the character of a Unitarian clergyman, preaching a sermon as vivid as Father Mapple's in Melville.[1] Later, with young Hazlitt, we go on a visit to Coleridge. Walking, of course—what are legs for?—we arrive at Nether Stowey, a "green and hilly" place near the sea. With Dorothy Wordsworth we eat the plain supper of poets and a day or two later get our first view of that other great man, William Wordsworth, "gaunt and Don Quixote-like" in his "brown fustian jacket and striped pantaloons."

Hazlitt and Coleridge held nearly opposite opinions of Swift as a poet. But Coleridge, even in his later falling out with Hazlitt, must have found Hazlitt's essay *On Swift* a generally admirable piece of work. Hazlitt shows a sound understanding of the color and depth of Swift's moralism. He sees that it is central to Swift's work.

---

[1] See *Moby Dick,* in *Great Books of the Western World,* Vol. 48, pp. 30–36.

And he gives us here the best and truest image of Swift as a writer: a jealously irritable father out of patience with "that great baby the world."

In *Of Persons One Would Wish to Have Seen,* Hazlitt leads us up three flights to an evening party at the rooms of Charles Lamb in Mitre-Court, London. The picture has its own snug charm. The host is there, and his sister Mary, here called "Mrs. Reynolds." Others who take part in the conversation are William Ayrton, musician and critic; John Rickman, political economist; Erasmus Phillips, his secretary; Fanny Burney's brother, Captain James Burney, and his son Martin; Barron Field, critic and lawyer; and George Dyer, poet. William Godwin, novelist and political writer, also appears to be present, but silent. The "Eugene Aram" mentioned by Hazlitt was a philologist hanged for murder, later the subject of a novel by Edward Bulwer-Lytton. The "Lord Brooke" of whom Lamb speaks has been named earlier as Fulke Greville, Elizabethan poet and statesman.

Which two persons now dead would *we* like to have seen? We have a century and a half of famous names to add to Hazlitt's list. Lincoln and Jenny Lind? Sun Yat-sen and Vincent Van Gogh? Or Emily Dickinson and Buffalo Bill?

My First Acquaintance
with Poets

My father was a Dissenting Minister, at Wem, in Shropshire; and in the year 1798 (the figures that compose the date are to me like the "dreaded name of Demogorgon") Mr. Coleridge came to Shrewsbury, to succeed Mr. Rowe in the spiritual charge of a Unitarian Congregation there. He did not come till late on the Saturday afternoon before he was to preach; and Mr. Rowe, who himself went down to the coach, in a state of anxiety and expectation, to look for the arrival of his successor, could find no one at all answering the description but a round-faced man, in a short black coat (like a shooting-jacket) which hardly seemed to have been made for him, but who seemed to be talking at a great rate to his fellow-passengers. Mr. Rowe had scarce returned to give an account of his disappointment when the round-faced man in black entered, and dissipated all doubts on the subject by beginning to talk. He did not cease while he stayed; nor has he since, that I know of. He held the good town of Shrewsbury in delightful suspense for three weeks that he remained there, "fluttering the proud Salopians, like an eagle in a dovecote"; and the Welsh mountains that skirt the horizon with their tempestuous confusion agree to have heard no such mystic sounds since the days of

High-born Hoel's harp or soft Llewellyn's lay.

As we passed along between Wem and Shrewsbury, and I eyed their blue tops seen through the wintry branches, or the red rustling leaves of the sturdy oak-trees by the roadside, a sound was in my ears as of a Siren's song; I was stunned, startled with it, as from deep sleep; but I had no notion then that I should ever be able to express my admiration to others in motley imagery of quaint allusion, till the light of his genius shone into my soul, like the sun's rays glittering in the puddles of the road. I was at that time dumb, inarticulate, helpless, like a worm by the wayside, crushed, bleeding, lifeless; but now, bursting from the deadly bands that "bound them,

> With Styx nine times round them,"

my ideas float on winged words, and as they expand their plumes, catch the golden light of other years. My soul has indeed remained in its original bondage, dark, obscure, with longings infinite and unsatisfied; my heart, shut up in the prison-house of this rude clay, has never found, nor will it ever find, a heart to speak to; but that my understanding also did not remain dumb and brutish, or at length found a language to express itself, I owe to Coleridge. But this is not to my purpose.

My father lived ten miles from Shrewsbury, and was in the habit of exchanging visits with Mr. Rowe, and with Mr. Jenkins of Whitchurch (nine miles farther on), according to the custom of Dissenting Ministers in each other's neighborhood. A line of communication is thus established, by which the flame of civil and religious liberty is kept alive, and nourishes its smoldering fire unquenchable, like the fires in the *Agamemnon* of Aeschylus, placed at different stations, that waited for ten long years to announce with their blazing pyramids the destruction of Troy. Coleridge had agreed to come over and see my father, according to the courtesy of the country, as Mr. Rowe's probable successor; but in the meantime, I had gone to hear him preach the Sunday after his arrival. A poet and a philosopher getting up into a Unitarian pulpit to preach the gospel was a romance in these degenerate days, a sort of revival of the primitive spirit of Christianity, which was not to be resisted.

It was in January of 1798, that I rose one morning before daylight, to walk ten miles in the mud, to hear this celebrated person preach. Never, the longest day I have to live, shall I have such another walk as this cold, raw, comfortless one, in the winter of the year 1798. *Il y a des impressions que ni le tems ni les circonstances peuvent effacer. Dussé-je vivre des siècles entiers, le doux tems de ma jeunesse ne peut renaître pour moi, ni s'effacer jamais dans ma mémoire.* ["There are impressions that neither time nor circumstances can erase. Should I live whole centuries, the sweet period of my youth could never be reborn for me, nor could it ever fade from my memory."] When I got there, the organ was playing the 100th Psalm, and when it was done, Mr. Coleridge rose and gave out his text, "And he went up into the mountain to pray, HIMSELF, ALONE." As he gave out this text, his voice "rose like a steam of rich distilled perfumes," and when he came to the two last words, which he pronounced loud, deep, and distinct, it seemed to me, who was then young, as if the sounds had echoed from the bottom of the human heart, and as if that prayer might have floated in solemn silence through the universe. The idea of St. John came into my mind, "of one crying in the wilderness, who had his loins girt about, and whose food was locusts and wild honey." The preacher then launched into his subject, like an eagle dallying with the wind. The sermon was upon peace and war; upon church and state—not their alliance, but their separation—on the spirit of the world and the spirit of Christianity, not as the same, but as opposed to one another. He talked of those who had "inscribed the cross of Christ on banners dripping with human gore." He made a poetical and pastoral excursion—and to show the fatal effects of war, drew a striking contrast between the simple shepherd-boy, driving his team afield, or sitting under the hawthorn, piping to his flock, "as though he should never be old," and the same poor country-lad, crimped, kidnapped, brought into town, made drunk at an alehouse, turned into a wretched drummer-boy, with his hair sticking on end with powder and pomatum, a long cue at his back, and tricked out in the loathsome finery of the profession of blood:

> Such were the notes our once-loved poet sung.

And for myself, I could not have been more delighted if I had heard the music of the spheres. Poetry and Philosophy had met together. Truth and Genius had embraced, under the eye and with the sanction of Religion. This was even beyond my hopes. I returned home well satisfied. The sun that was still laboring pale and wan through the sky, obscured by thick mists, seemed an emblem of the good cause; and the cold dank drops of dew, that hung half melted on the beard of the thistle, had something genial and refreshing in them; for there was a spirit of hope and youth in all nature, that turned everything into good. The face of nature had not then the brand of Jus Divinum on it:

> Like to that sanguine flower inscrib'd with woe.

On the Tuesday following, the half-inspired speaker came. I was called down into the room where he was, and went half-hoping, half-afraid. He received me very graciously, and I listened for a long time without uttering a word. I did not suffer in his opinion by my silence. "For those two hours," he afterwards was pleased to say, "he was conversing with William Hazlitt's forehead!" His appearance was different from what I had anticipated from seeing him before. At a distance, and in the dim light of the chapel, there was to me a strange wildness in his aspect, a

dusky obscurity, and I thought him pitted with the smallpox. His com-
plexion was at that time clear, and even bright—

> As are the children of yon azure sheen.

His forehead was broad and high, light as if built of ivory, with large
projecting eyebrows, and his eyes rolling beneath them, like a sea with
darkened lustre. "A certain tender bloom his face o'erspread," a purple
tinge as we see it in the pale thoughtful complexions of the Spanish
portrait-painters, Murillo and Velasquez. His mouth was gross, voluptuous, open, eloquent; his chin good-humoured and round; but his nose, the
rudder of the face, the index of the will, was small, feeble, nothing—like
what he has done. It might seem that the genius of his face as from a
height surveyed and projected him (with sufficient capacity and huge
aspiration) into the world unknown of thought and imagination, with
nothing to support or guide his veering purpose, as if Columbus had
launched his adventurous course for the New World in a scallop, without
oars or compass. So, at least, I comment on it after the event. Coleridge,
in his person, was rather above the common size, inclining to the corpu-
lent, or like Lord Hamlet, "somewhat fat and pursy." His hair (now, alas!
grey) was then black and glossy as the raven's and fell in smooth masses
over his forehead. This long pendulous hair is peculiar to enthusiasts, to
those whose minds tend heavenward; and is traditionally inseparable
(though of a different colour) from the pictures of Christ. It ought to
belong, as a character, to all who preach Christ crucified, and Coleridge
was at that time one of those!

It was curious to observe the contrast between him and my father, who
was a veteran in the cause, and then declining into the vale of years. He
had been a poor Irish lad, carefully brought up by his parents, and sent to
the University of Glasgow (where he studied under Adam Smith) to
prepare him for his future destination. It was his mother's proudest wish
to see her son a Dissenting Minister. So, if we look back to past generations (as far as eye can reach), we see the same hopes, fears, wishes,
followed by the same disappointments, throbbing in the human heart;
and so we may see them (if we look forward) rising up forever, and
disappearing, like vaporish bubbles, in the human breast! After being
tossed about from congregation to congregation in the heats of the
Unitarian controversy, and squabbles about the American war, he had
been relegated to an obscure village, where he was to spend the last
thirty years of his life, far from the only converse that he loved, the talk
about disputed texts of Scripture, and the cause of civil and religious

liberty. Here he passed his days, repining, but resigned, in the study of the Bible, and the perusal of the Commentators—huge folios, not easily got through, one of which would outlast a winter! Why did he pore on these from morn to night (with the exception of a walk in the fields or a turn in the garden to gather broccoli plants or kidney beans of his own rearing, with no small degree of pride and pleasure)? Here were "no figures nor no fantasies"—neither poetry nor philosophy—nothing to dazzle, nothing to excite modern curiosity; but to his lack-lustre eyes there appeared within the pages of the ponderous, unwieldy, neglected tomes, the sacred name of Jehovah in Hebrew capitals: pressed down by the weight of the style, worn to the last fading thinness of the understanding, there were glimpses, glimmering notions of the patriarchal wanderings, with palm-trees hovering in the horizon, and processions of camels at the distance of three thousand years; there was Moses with the Burning Bush, the number of the Twelve Tribes, types, shadows, glosses on the law and the prophets; there were discussions (dull enough) on the age of Methuselah, a mightly speculation! there were outlines, rude guesses at the shape of Noah's Ark and of the riches of Solomon's Temple; questions as to the date of the creation, predictions of the end of all things; the great lapses of time, the strange mutations of the globe were unfolded with the voluminous leaf, as it turned over; and though the soul might slumber with an hieroglyphic veil of inscrutable mysteries drawn over it, yet it was in a slumber ill-exchanged for all the sharpened realities of sense, wit, fancy, or reason. My father's life was comparatively a dream; but it was a dream of infinity and eternity, of death, the resurrection, and a judgment to come!

No two individuals were ever more unlike than were the host and his guest. A poet was to my father a sort of nondescript; yet whatever added grace to the Unitarian cause was to him welcome. He could hardly have been more surprised or pleased, if our visitor had worn wings. Indeed, his thoughts had wings: and as the silken sounds rustled round our little wainscoted parlor, my father threw back his spectacles over his forehead, his white hairs mixing with its sanguine hue; and a smile of delight beamed across his rugged, cordial face, to think that Truth had found a new ally in Fancy! Besides, Coleridge seemed to take considerable notice of me, and that of itself was enough. He talked very familiarly, but agreeably, and glanced over a variety of subjects. At dinner-time he grew more animated, and dilated in a very edifying manner on Mary Wollstone-craft and Mackintosh. The last, he said, he considered (on my father's speaking of his *Vindiciae Gallicae* as a capital performance) as a clever, scholastic man—a master of the topics—or, as the ready warehouseman of letters, who knew exactly where to lay his hand on what he wanted, though the goods were not his own. He thought him no match for Burke, either in style or matter. Burke was a metaphysician, Mackintosh a mere logician. Burke was an orator (almost a poet) who reasoned in figures, because he had an eye for nature: Mackintosh, on the other hand, was a rhetorician, who had only an eye to commonplaces. On this I ventured to say that I had always entertained a great opinion of Burke, and that (as far as I could find) the speaking of him with contempt might be made the test of a vulgar, democratical mind. This was the first observation I ever made to Coleridge, and he said it was a very just and striking one. I remember the leg of Welsh mutton and the turnips on the table that day had the finest flavor imaginable. Coleridge added that Mackintosh and Tom Wedgwood (of whom, however, he spoke highly) had expressed a very indifferent opinion of his friend Mr. Wordsworth, on which he remarked to them—"He strides on so far before you, that he dwindles in the distance!" Godwin had once boasted to him of having carried on an argument with Mackintosh for three hours with dubious success; Coleridge told him—"If there had been a man of genius in the room, he would have settled the question in five minutes." He asked me if I had ever seen Mary Wollstonecraft, and I said, I had once for a few moments, and that she seemed to me to turn off Godwin's objections to something she advanced with quite a playful, easy air. He replied, that "this was only one instance of the ascendancy which people of imagination exercised over those of mere intellect." He did not rate Godwin very high (this was caprice or prejudice, real or affected), but he had a great idea of Mrs. Wollstonecraft's powers of conversation; none at all of her talent for book-making. We talked a little about Holcroft. He had been asked if he was not much struck *with* him, and he said, he thought himself in more danger of being struck *by* him. I complained that he would not let me get on at all, for he required a definition of even the commonest word, exclaiming, "What do you mean by a *sensation*, Sir? What do you mean by an *idea?*" This, Coleridge said, was barricadoing the road to truth; it was setting up a turnpike gate at every step we took. I forget a great number of things, many more than I remember; but the day passed off pleasantly, and the next morning Mr. Coleridge was to return to Shrewsbury. When I came down to breakfast, I found that he had just received a letter from his friend, T. Wedgwood, making him an offer of £150 a year if he chose to waive his present pursuit, and devote himself entirely to the study of poetry and philosophy. Coleridge seemed to make up his mind to close with this proposal in the act of tying on one of his shoes. It threw an additional damp on his departure. It took the way-ward enthusiast quite from us to cast him into Deva's winding vales, or by the shores of old romance. Instead of living at ten miles' distance, of being the pastor of a Dissenting congregation at Shrewsbury, he was henceforth to inhabit the Hill of Parnassus, to be a Shepherd on the Delectable Mountains. Alas! I knew not the way thither, and felt very little gratitude for Mr. Wedgwood's bounty. I was presently relieved from this dilemma; for Mr. Coleridge, asking for a pen and ink, and going to a table to write something on a bit of card, advanced towards me with undulating step, and giving me the precious document, said that that was his address, *Mr. Coleridge, Nether Stowey, Somersetshire;* and that he should be glad to see me there in a few weeks' time, and, if I chose, would come half-way to meet me. I was not less surprised than the shepherd-boy (this simile is to be found in *Cassandra*), when he sees a thunderbolt fall close at his feet. I stammered out my acknowledgments and acceptance of this offer (I thought Mr. Wedgwood's annuity a trifle to it) as well as I could; and this mighty business being settled, the poet-preacher took leave, and I accompanied him six miles on the road. It was a fine morning in the middle of winter, and he talked the whole way. The scholar in Chaucer is described as going

Sounding on his way.

So Coleridge went on his. In digressing, in dilating, in passing from subject to subject, he appeared to me to float in air, to slide on ice. He told me in confidence (going along) that he should have preached two sermons before he accepted the situation at Shrewsbury, one on Infant Baptism, the other on the Lord's Supper, showing that he could not administer either, which would have effectually disqualified him for the object in view. I observed that he continually crossed me on the way by shifting from one side of the foot-path to the other. This struck me as an odd movement; but I did not at that time connect it with any instabil-ity of purpose or involuntary change of principle, as I have done since. He seemed unable to keep on in a straight line. He spoke slightingly of Hume (whose *Essay on Miracles* he said was stolen from an objection started in one of South's sermons—*Credat Judaeus Apella!* ["Let Apella the Jew believe it."] [1]). I was not very much pleased at this account of Hume, for I had just been reading, with infinite relish, that completest

---

1. Horace, *Satires* V, 100 [Ed.].

of all metaphysical choke-pears, his *Treatise on Human Nature,* to which
the *Essays,* in point of scholastic subtilty and close reasoning, are mere
elegant trifling, light summer reading. Coleridge even denied the excellence of Hume's general style, which I think betrayed a want of taste or
candor. He however made me amends by the manner in which he spoke
of Berkeley. He dwelt particularly on his *Essay on Vision* as a masterpiece of analytical reasoning. So it undoubtedly is. He was exceedingly
angry with Dr. Johnson for striking the stone with his foot, in allusion to
this author's *Theory of Matter and Spirit,* and saying, "Thus I confute
him, Sir." Coleridge drew a parallel (I don't know how he brought about
the connection) between Bishop Berkeley and Tom Paine. He said the
one was an instance of a subtle, the other of an acute mind, than which
no two things could be more distinct. The one was a shop-boy's quality,
the other the characteristic of a philosopher. He considered Bishop Butler
as a true philosopher, a profound and conscientious thinker, a genuine
reader of nature and his own mind. He did not speak of his *Analogy,* but
of his *Sermons at the Rolls' Chapel,* of which I had never heard. Coleridge
somehow always contrived to prefer the *unknown* to the *known.* In this
instance, he was right. The *Analogy* is a tissue of sophistry, of wire-drawn,
theological special pleading; the *Sermons* (with the preface to them) are
in a fine vein of deep, matured reflection, a candid appeal to our observation of human nature, without pedantry and without bias. I told Coleridge
I had written a few remarks, and was sometimes foolish enough to believe
that I had made a discovery on the same subject (the *Natural Disinterestedness of the Human Mind*)—and I tried to explain my view
of it to Coleridge, who listened with great willingness, but I did not
succeed in making myself understood. I sat down to the task shortly
afterwards for the twentieth time, got new pens and paper, determined
to make clear work of it, wrote a few meagre sentences in the skeleton-
style of a mathematical demonstration, stopped half-way down the
second page; and, after trying in vain to pump up any words, images,
notions, apprehensions, facts, or observations, from that gulf of abstraction
in which I had plunged myself for four or five years preceding, gave up
the attempt as labour in vain, and shed tears of helpless despondency on
the blank, unfinished paper. I can write fast enough now. Am I
better than I was then? Oh no! One truth discovered, one pang of regret
at not being able to express it, is better than all the fluency and flippancy
in the world. Would that I could go back to what I then was! Why can we
not revive past times as we can revisit old places? If I had the quaint
muse of Sir Philip Sidney to assist me, I would write a *Sonnet to the Road*

between Wem and Shrewsbury, and immortalize every step of it by some
fond enigmatical conceit. I would swear that the very milestones had
ears, and that Harmer Hill stooped with all its pines, to listen to a poet,
as he passed! I remember but one other topic of discourse in this walk.
He mentioned Paley, praised the naturalness and clearness of his style,
but condemned his sentiments, thought him a mere timeserving casuist,
and said that "the fact of his work on Moral and Political Philosophy being
made a textbook in our Universities was a disgrace to the national character." We parted at the six-mile stone; and I returned homeward,
pensive, but much pleased. I had met with unexpected notice from a
person whom I believed to have been prejudiced against me. "Kind and
affable to me had been his condescension, and should be honoured ever
with suitable regard." He was the first poet I had known, and he certainly answered to that inspired name. I had heard a great deal of his
powers of conversation, and was not disappointed. In fact, I never met
with anything at all like them, either before or since. I could easily credit
the accounts which were circulated of his holding forth to a large party
of ladies and gentlemen, an evening or two before, on the Berkeleian
theory, when he made the whole material universe look like a transpar-
ency of fine words; and another story (which I believe he has somewhere
told himself) of his being asked to a party at Birmingham, of his smoking
tobacco and going to sleep after dinner on a sofa, where the company
found him, to their no small surprise, which was increased to wonder
when he started up of a sudden, and rubbing his eyes, looked about him,
and launched into a three hours' description of the third heaven, of which
he had had a dream, very different from Mr. Southey's *Vision of Judgment,* and also from that other *Vision of Judgment,* which Mr. Murray,
the Secretary of the Bridge Street Junto, took into his especial keeping!

On my way back, I had a sound in my ears—it was the voice of Fancy;
I had a light before me—it was the face of Poetry. The one still lingers
there, the other has not quitted my side! Coleridge, in truth, met me
half-way on the ground of philosophy, or I should not have been won
over to his imaginative creed. I had an uneasy, pleasurable sensation all
the time, till I was to visit him. During those months the chill breath of
winter gave me a welcoming; the vernal air was balm and inspiration to
me. The golden sunsets, the silver star of evening, lighted me on my way
to new hopes and prospects. *I was to visit Coleridge in the spring.* This
circumstance was never absent from my thoughts, and mingled with all
my feelings. I wrote to him at the time proposed, and received an answer
postponing my intended visit for a week or two, but very cordially urging

me to complete my promise then. This delay did not damp, but rather increased, my ardor. In the meantime, I went to Llangollen Vale, by way of initiating myself in the mysteries of natural scenery; and I must say I was enchanted with it. I had been reading Coleridge's description of England in his fine *Ode on the Departing Year*, and I applied it, *con amore*, to the objects before me. That valley was to me (in a manner) the cradle of a new existence: in the river that winds through it, my spirit was baptized in the waters of Helicon!

I returned home, and soon after set out on my journey with unworn heart, and untried feet. My way lay through Worcester and Gloucester, and by Upton, where I thought of Tom Jones and the adventure of the muff. I remember getting completely wet through one day, and stopping at an inn (I think it was Tewkesbury) where I sat up all night to read *Paul and Virginia*. Sweet were the showers in early youth that drenched my body, and sweet the drops of pity that fell upon the books I read! I recollect a remark of Coleridge's upon this very book—that nothing could show the gross indelicacy of French manners and the entire corruption of their imagination more strongly than the behavior of the heroine in the last fatal scene, who turns away from a person on board the sinking vessel, that offers to save her life, because he has thrown off his clothes to assist him in swimming. Was this a time to think of such a circumstance? I once hinted to Wordsworth, as we were sailing in his boat on Grasmere Lake, that I thought he had borrowed the idea of his *Poems on the Naming of Places* from the local inscriptions of the same kind in *Paul and Virginia*. He did not own the obligation, and stated some distinction without a difference, in defense of his claim to originality. Any the slightest variation would be sufficient for this purpose in his mind; for whatever he added or altered would inevitably be worth all that any one else had done, and contain the marrow of the sentiment.—I was still two days before the time fixed for my arrival, for I had taken care to set out early enough. I stopped these two days at Bridgewater; and when I was tired of sauntering on the banks of its muddy river, returned to the inn and read *Camilla*. So have I loitered my life away, reading books, looking at pictures, going to plays, hearing, thinking, writing on what pleased me best. I have wanted only one thing to make me happy; but wanting that, have wanted everything!

I arrived, and was well received. The country about Nether Stowey is beautiful, green and hilly, and near the sea-shore. I saw it but the other day, after an interval of twenty years, from a hill near Taunton. How was the map of my life spread out before me, as the map of the country lay at my feet! In the afternoon, Coleridge took me over to All-Foxden, a romantic old family mansion of the St. Aubins, where Wordsworth lived. It was then in the possession of a friend of the poet's, who gave him the free use of it. Somehow, that period (the time just after the French Revolution) was not a time when nothing was given for nothing. The mind opened and a softness might be perceived coming over the heart of individuals, beneath "the scales that fence" our self-interest. Wordsworth himself was from home, but his sister kept house, and set before us a frugal repast; and we had free access to her brother's poems, the *Lyrical Ballads*, which were still in manuscript, or in the form of *Sybilline Leaves*. I dipped into a few of these with great satisfaction, and with the faith of a novice. I slept that night in an old room with blue hangings, and covered with the round-faced family portraits of the age of George I and II, and from the wooded declivity of the adjoining park that overlooked my window, at the dawn of day, could

> hear the loud stag speak.

In the outset of life (and particularly at this time I felt it so) our imagination has a body to it. We are in a state between sleeping and waking, and have indistinct but glorious glimpses of strange shapes, and there is always something to come better than what we see. As in our dreams the fulness of the blood gives warmth and reality to the coinage of the brain, so in youth our ideas are clothed, and fed, and pampered with our good spirits; we breathe thick with thoughtless happiness, the weight of future years presses on the strong pulses of the heart, and we repose with undisturbed faith in truth and good. As we advance, we exhaust our fund of enjoyment and of hope. We are no longer wrapped in lamb's-wool, lulled in Elysium. As we taste the pleasures of life, their spirit evaporates, the sense palls; and nothing is left but the phantoms, the lifeless shadows of what has been!

That morning, as soon as breakfast was over, we strolled out into the park, and seating ourselves on the trunk of an old ash-tree that stretched along the ground, Coleridge read aloud with a sonorous and musical voice, the ballad of *Betty Foy*. I was not critically or sceptically inclined. I saw touches of truth and nature, and took the rest for granted. But in the *Thorn*, the *Mad Mother*, and the *Complaint of a Poor Indian Woman*, I felt that deeper power and pathos which have been since acknowledged,

> In spite of pride, in erring reason's spite,

as the characteristics of this author; and the sense of a new style and a new spirit in poetry came over me. It had to me something of the effect that arises from the turning up of the fresh soil, or of the first welcome breath of spring:

> While yet the trembling year is unconfirmed.

Coleridge and myself walked back to Stowey that evening, and his voice sounded high

> Of Providence, foreknowledge, will, and fate,
> Fix'd fate, free-will, foreknowledge absolute,

as we passed through echoing grove, by fairy stream or waterfall, gleaming in the summer moonlight! He lamented that Wordsworth was not prone enough to believe in the traditional superstitions of the place, and that there was a something corporeal, a matter-of-factness, a clinging to the palpable, or often to the petty, in his poetry, in consequence. His genius was not a spirit that descended to him through the air; it sprung out of the ground like a flower, or unfolded itself from a green spray, on which the goldfinch sang. He said, however (if I remember right), that this objection must be confined to his descriptive pieces, that his philosophic poetry had a grand and comprehensive spirit in it, so that his soul seemed to inhabit the universe like a palace, and to discover truth by intuition, rather than by deduction. The next day Wordsworth arrived from Bristol at Coleridge's cottage. I think I see him now. He answered in some degree to his friend's description of him, but was more gaunt and Don Quixote-like. He was quaintly dressed (according to the costume of that unconstrained period) in a brown fustian jacket and striped pantaloons. There was something of a roll, a lounge in his gait, not unlike his own *Peter Bell*. There was a severe, worn pressure of thought about his temples, a fire in his eye (as if he saw something in objects more than the outward appearance), an intense, high, narrow forehead, a Roman nose, cheeks furrowed by strong purpose and feeling, and a convulsive inclination to laughter about the mouth, a good deal at variance with the solemn, stately expression of the rest of his face. Chantrey's bust wants the marking traits; but he was teased into making it regular and heavy: Haydon's head of him, introduced into the *Entrance of Christ into Jerusalem*, is the most like his drooping weight of thought and expression. He sat down and talked very naturally and freely, with a mixture of clear, gushing accents in his voice, a deep guttural intonation, and a strong tincture of the northern burr, like the crust on wine. He instantly began to make

havoc of the half of a Cheshire cheese on the table, and said, trium-
phantly, that "his marriage with experience had not been so productive as
Mr. Southey's in teaching him a knowledge of the good things of this
life." He had been to see the *Castle Spectre* by Monk Lewis, while at
Bristol, and described it very well. He said "it fitted the taste of the audience like a glove." This *ad captandum* merit was however by no means a
recommendation of it, according to the severe principles of the new
school, which reject rather than court popular effect. Wordsworth, looking
out of the low, latticed window, said, "How beautifully the sun sets on that
yellow bank!" I thought within myself, "With what eyes these poets see
nature!" and ever after, when I saw the sunset stream upon the objects
facing it, conceived I had made a discovery, or thanked Mr. Wordsworth
for having made one for me! We went over to All-Foxden again the day
following, and Wordsworth read us the story of *Peter Bell* in the open
air; and the comment made upon it by his face and voice was very different from that of some later critics! Whatever might be thought of the
poem, "his face was as a book where men might read strange matters,"
and he announced the fate of his hero in prophetic tones. There is a
chaunt in the recitation both of Coleridge and Wordsworth, which acts as
a spell upon the hearer, and disarms the judgment. Perhaps they have
deceived themselves by making habitual use of this ambiguous accompaniment. Coleridge's manner is more full, animated, and varied; Wordsworth's more equable, sustained, and internal. The one might be termed
more *dramatic*, the other more *lyrical*. Coleridge has told me that he himself liked to compose in walking over uneven ground, or breaking through
the straggling branches of a copsewood; whereas Wordsworth always
wrote (if he could) walking up and down a straight gravel-walk, or in
some spot where the continuity of his verse met with no collateral interruption. Returning that same evening, I got into a metaphysical argument
with Wordsworth, while Coleridge was explaining the different notes of
the nightingale to his sister, in which we neither of us succeeded in
making ourselves perfectly clear and intelligible. Thus I passed three
weeks at Nether Stowey and in the neighborhood, generally devoting the
afternoons to a delightful chat in an arbor made of bark by the poet's
friend Tom Poole, sitting under two fine elm-trees, and listening to the
bees humming round us, while we quaffed our flip. It was agreed, among
other things, that we should make a jaunt down the Bristol Channel, as
far as Linton. We set off together on foot, Coleridge, John Chester,
and I. This Chester was a native of Nether Stowey, one of those who were
attracted to Coleridge's discourse as flies are to honey, or bees in swarming time to the sound of a brass pan. He "followed in the chase like a dog

who hunts, not like one that made up the cry." He had on a brown cloth coat, boots, and corduroy breeches, was low in stature, bow-legged, had a drag in his walk like a drover, which he assisted by a hazel switch, and kept on a sort of trot by the side of Coleridge, like a running footman by a state coach, that he might not lose a syllable or sound that fell from Coleridge's lips. He told me his private opinion, that Coleridge was a wonderful man. He scarcely opened his lips, much less offered an opinion the whole way: yet of the three, had I to choose during that journey, I would be John Chester. He afterwards followed Coleridge into Germany, where the Kantean philosophers were puzzled how to bring him under any of their categories. When he sat down at table with his idol, John's felicity was complete; Sir Walter Scott's, or Mr. Blackwood's, when they sat down at the same table with the King, was not more so. We passed Dunster on our right, a small town between the brow of a hill and the sea. I remember eyeing it wistfully as it lay below us: contrasted with the woody scene around, it looked as clear, as pure, as embrowned and ideal as any landscape I have seen since, of Gaspar Poussin's or Domenichino's. We had a long day's march—(our feet kept time to the echoes of Coleridge's tongue)—through Minehead and by the Blue Anchor, and on to Linton, which we did not reach till near midnight, and where we had some difficulty in making a lodgment. We, however, knocked the people of the house up at last, and we were repaid for our apprehensions and fatigue by some excellent rashers of fried bacon and eggs. The view in coming along had been splendid. We walked for miles and miles on dark brown heaths overlooking the Channel, with the Welsh hills beyond, and at times descended into little sheltered valleys close by the sea-side, with a smuggler's face scowling by us, and then had to ascend conical hills with a path winding up through a coppice to a barren top, like a monk's shaven crown, from one of which I pointed out to Coleridge's notice the bare masts of a vessel on the very edge of the horizon, and within the red-orbed disk of the setting sun, like his own spectre ship in the *Ancient Mariner*. At Linton the character of the sea-coast becomes more marked and rugged. There is a place called the Valley of Rocks (I suspect this was only the poetical name for it), bedded among precipices overhanging the sea, with rocky caverns beneath, into which the waves dash, and where the sea-gull forever wheels its screaming flight. On the tops of these are huge stones thrown transverse, as if an earthquake had tossed them there, and behind these is a fretwork of perpendicular rocks, something like the Giant's Causeway. A thunderstorm came on while we were at the inn, and Coleridge was running out bare-headed to enjoy the commotion of the elements in the Valley of Rocks, but as if in spite, the clouds only muttered a few angry sounds, and let fall a few refreshing drops. Coleridge told me that he and Wordsworth were to have made this place the scene of a prose tale, which was to have been in the manner of, but far superior to, the *Death of Abel*, but they had relinquished the design. In the morning of the second day, we breakfasted luxuriously in an old-fashioned parlor on tea, toast, eggs, and honey, in the very sight of the bee hives from which it had been taken, and a garden full of thyme and wild flowers that had produced it. On this occasion Coleridge spoke of Virgil's *Georgics*, but not well. I do not think he had much feeling for the classical or elegant. It was in this room that we found a little worn-out copy of *The Seasons*, lying in a window-seat, on which Coleridge exclaimed, "*That* is true fame!" He said Thomson was a great poet, rather than a good one; his style was as meretricious as his thoughts were natural. He spoke of Cowper as the best modern poet. He said the *Lyrical Ballads* were an experiment about to be tried by him and Wordsworth, to see how far the public taste would endure poetry written in a more natural and simple style than had hitherto been attempted; totally discarding the artifices of poetical diction, and making use only of such words as had probably been common in the most ordinary language since the days of Henry II. Some comparison was introduced between Shakespeare and Milton. He said "he hardly knew which to prefer. Shakespeare appeared to him a mere stripling in the art; he was as tall and as strong, with infinitely more activity than Milton, but he never appeared to have come to man's estate; or if he had, he would not have been a man, but a monster." He spoke with contempt of Gray, and with intolerance of Pope. He did not like the versification of the latter. He observed that "the ears of these couplet-writers might be charged with having short memories, that could not retain the harmony of whole passages." He thought little of Junius as a writer; he had a dislike of Dr. Johnson; and a much higher opinion of Burke as an orator and politician, than of Fox or Pitt. He, however, thought him very inferior in richness of style and imagery to some of our elder prose writers, particularly Jeremy Taylor. He like Richardson, but not Fielding; nor could I get him to enter into the merits of *Caleb Williams*. In short, he was profound and discriminating with respect to those authors whom he liked, and where he gave his judgment fair play; capricious, perverse, and prejudiced in his antipathies and distastes. We loitered on the "ribbed sea-sands," in such talk as this a whole morning, and, I recollect, met with a curious seaweed, of which John Chester told us the country name! A fisherman gave Coleridge an account of a boy that had been drowned the day before, and that they had tried to save him at the risk of their own lives. He said "he did not know how it was that they ventured, but, Sir, we have a *nature* towards one another." This expression, Coleridge remarked to me, was a fine illustration of that theory of disinterestedness which I (in common with Butler) had adopted. I broached to him an argument of mine to prove that *likeness* was not mere association of ideas. I said that the mark in the sand put one in mind of a man's foot, not because it was part of a former impression of a man's foot (for it was quite new), but because it was like the shape of a man's foot. He assented to the justness of this distinction (which I have explained at length elsewhere, for the benefit of the curious) and John Chester listened; not from any interest in the subject, but because he was astonished that I should be able to suggest anything to Coleridge that he did not already know. We returned on the third morning, and Coleridge remarked the silent cottage smoke curling up the valleys where, a few evenings before, we had seen the lights gleaming through the dark.

In a day or two after we arrived at Stowey, we set out, I on my return home, and he for Germany. It was a Sunday morning, and he was to preach that day for Dr. Toulmin of Taunton. I asked him if he had prepared anything for the occasion? He said he had not even thought of the text, but should as soon as we parted. I did not go to hear him—this was a fault—but we met in the evening at Bridgewater. The next day we had a long day's walk to Bristol, and sat down, I recollect, by a well-side on the road, to cool ourselves and satisfy our thirst, when Coleridge repeated to me some descriptive lines of his tragedy of *Remorse;* which I must say became his mouth and that occasion better than they, some years after, did Mr. Elliston's and the Drury Lane boards—

> Oh, memory! shield me from the world's poor strife,
> And give those scenes thine everlasting life.

I saw no more of him for a year or two, during which period he had been wandering in the Harz Forest, in Germany; and his return was cometary, meteorous, unlike his setting out. It was not till some time after that I knew his friends Lamb and Southey. The last always appears to me (as I first saw him) with a commonplace book under his arm, and the first with a *bon mot* in his mouth. It was at Godwin's that I met him with Holcroft and Coleridge, where they were disputing fiercely which was the best—Man as he was, or man as he is to be. "Give me," says Lamb, "man as he is *not* to be." This saying was the beginning of a friendship between us, which I believe still continues.—Enough of this for the present.

On Swift

Swift's reputation as a poet has been in a manner obscured by the greater splendour, by the natural force and inventive genius of his prose writings; but if he had never written either the *Tale of a Tub* or *Gulliver's Travels*, his name merely as a poet would have come down to us, and have gone down to posterity with well-earned honours. His *Imitations of Horace,* and still more his *Verses on His Own Death,* place him on the first rank of agreeable moralists in verse. There is not only a dry humour, an exquisite tone of irony, in these productions of his pen: but there is a touching, unpretending pathos, mixed up with the most whimsical and eccentric strokes of pleasantry and satire. His *Description of the Morning in London,* and of a *City Shower,* which were first published in the *Tatler,* are among the most delightful of the contents of that very delightful work. Swift shone as one of the most sensible of the poets; he is also distinguished as one of the most nonsensical of them. No man has written so many lackadaisical, slipshod, tedious, trifling, foolish, fantastical verses as he, which are so little an imputation on the wisdom of the writer; and which, in fact, only show his readiness to oblige others, and to forget himself. He has gone so far as to invent a new stanza of fourteen and sixteen syllable lines for Mary the cookmaid to vent her budget of nothings, and for Mrs. Harris to gossip with the deaf old house-keeper. Oh, when shall we have such another Rector of Laracor! The *Tale of a Tub* is one of the most masterly compositions in the language whether for thought, wit, or style. It is so capital and undeniable a proof of the author's talents, that Dr. Johnson, who did not like Swift, would not allow that he wrote it. It is hard that the same performance should stand in the way of a man's promotion to a bishopric, as wanting gravity, and at the same time be denied to be his, as having too much wit. It is a pity the Doctor did not find out some graver author, for whom he felt a critical kindness, on whom to father this splendid but unacknowledged production. Dr. Johnson could not deny that *Gulliver's Travels* were his; he therefore disputed their merits, and said that after the first idea of them was conceived, they were easy to execute; all the rest followed mechanically. I do not know how that may be; but the mechanism employed is something very different from any that the author of *Rasselas* was in the habit of bringing to bear on such occasions. There is nothing more futile as well as invidious than this mode of criticizing a work of original genius. Its greatest merit is supposed to be in the invention; and you say, very wisely, that it is not in the execution. You might as well take away the merit of the invention of the telescope by saying that after its uses were explained and understood any ordinary eyesight could look through it. Whether the excellence of *Gulliver's Travels* is in the conception or the execution is of little consequence; the power is somewhere and it is a power that has moved the world. The power is not that of big words and vaunting commonplaces. Swift left these to those who wanted them; and has done what his acuteness and intensity of mind alone could enable anyone to conceive or to perform. His object was to strip empty pride and grandeur of the imposing air which external circumstances throw around them; and for this purpose he has cheated the imagination of the illusions which the prejudices of sense and of the world put upon it by reducing everything to the abstract predicament of size. He enlarges or diminishes the scale as he wishes to show the insignificance or the grossness of our overweening self-love. That he has done this with mathematical precision, with complete presence of mind and perfect keeping in a manner that comes equally home to the understanding of the man and of the child does not take away from the merit of the work or the genius of the author. He has taken a new view of human nature, such as a being of a higher sphere might take of it; he has torn the scales from off his moral vision; he has tried an experiment upon human life, and sifted its pretensions from the alloy of circumstances. He has measured it with a rule, has weighed it in a balance, and found it, for the most part, wanting and worthless—in substance and in show. Nothing solid, nothing valuable is left in his system but virtue and wisdom. What a libel is this upon mankind! What a convincing proof of misanthropy! What presumption and what *malice prepense*, to show men what they are, and to teach them what they ought to be! What a mortifying stroke aimed at national glory is that unlucky incident of Gulliver's wading across the channel and carrying off the whole fleet of Blefuscu! After that, we have only to consider which of the contending parties was in the right. What a shock to personal vanity is given in the account of Gulliver's nurse Glumdalclitch! Still, notwithstanding the disparagement to her personal charms, her good nature remains the same amiable quality as before. I cannot see the harm, the misanthropy, the immoral and degrading tendency of this. The moral lesson is as fine as the intellectual exhibition is amusing. It is an attempt to tear off the mask of imposture from the world; and nothing but imposture has a right to complain of it. It is, indeed, the way with our quacks in morality to preach up the dignity of human nature, to pamper pride and hypocrisy with the idle mockeries of the virtues they pretend to, and which they have not: but it was not Swift's way to cant morality, or anything else; nor did his genius prompt him to write unmeaning panegyrics on mankind!

The determination with which Swift persisted in a preconcerted theory savoured of the morbid affection of which he died. There is nothing more likely to drive a man mad than the being unable to get rid of the idea of the distinction between right and wrong, and an obstinate, constitutional preference of the true to the agreeable. Swift was not a Frenchman. In this respect he differed from Rabelais and Voltaire. They have been accounted the three greatest wits in modern times; but their wit was of a peculiar kind in each. They are little beholden to each other; there is some resemblance between Lord Peter in the *Tale of a Tub* and Rabelais' Friar John; but in general they are all three authors of a substantive character in themselves. Swift's wit (particularly in his chief prose works) was serious, saturnine, and practical; Rabelais' was fantastical and joyous; Voltaire's was light, sportive, and verbal. Swift's wit was the wit of sense; Rabelais', the wit of nonsense; Voltaire's, of indifference to both. The ludicrous in Swift arises out of his keen sense of impropriety, his soreness and impatience of the least absurdity. He separates, with a severe and caustic air, truth from falsehood, folly from wisdom, "shows vice her own image, scorn her own feature"; and it is the force, the precision, and the honest abruptness with which the separation is made that excites our surprise, our admiration, and laughter. He sets a mark of reprobation on that which offends good sense and good manners, which cannot be mistaken, and which holds it up to our ridicule and contempt ever after. His occasional disposition to trifling was a relaxation from the excessive earnestness of his mind. His better genius was his spleen. It was the biting acrimony of his temper that sharpened his other faculties. The truth of his perceptions produced the pointed coruscations of his wit; his playful irony was the result of inward bitterness of thought; his imagination was the product of the literal, dry, incorrigible tenaciousness of his understanding. He endeavoured to escape from the persecution of realities into the regions of fancy, and invented his Lilliputians and Brobdingnagians, Yahoos, and Houynhyms as a diversion to the more painful knowledge of the world around him: *they* only made him laugh, while men and women made him angry. His feverish impatience made him view the infirmities of that great baby the world with the same scrutinizing glance and jealous irritability that a parent regards the failings of its offspring.

Of Persons
One Would Wish to Have Seen

Lamb it was, I think, who suggested this subject, as well as the defence of Guy Fawkes, which I urged him to execute. As, however, he would undertake neither, I suppose I must do both, a task for which he would have been much fitter, no less from the temerity than the felicity of his pen—

> Never so sure our rapture to create
> As when it touched the brink of all we hate.

Compared with him, I shall, I fear, make but a commonplace piece of business of it; but I should be loth the idea was entirely lost, and besides I may avail myself of some hints of his in the progress of it. I am sometimes, I suspect, a better reporter of the ideas of other people than expounder of my own. I pursue the one too far into paradox or mysticism; the others I am not bound to follow farther than I like, or than seems fair and reasonable.

On the question being started, A[yrton] said, "I suppose the two first persons you would choose to see would be the two greatest names in English literature, Sir Isaac Newton and Mr. Locke?" In this A[yrton], as usual, reckoned without his host. Every one burst out a-laughing at the expression of Lamb's face, in which impatience was restrained by courtesy.

"Yes, the greatest names," he stammered out hastily, "but they were not persons—not persons."

"Not persons?" said A[yrton], looking wise and foolish at the same time, afraid his triumph might be premature.

"That is," rejoined Lamb, "not characters, you know. By Mr. Locke and Sir Isaac Newton, you mean the *Essay on the Human Understanding*, and the *Principia*, which we have to this day. Beyond their contents there is nothing personally interesting in the men. But what we want to see any one *bodily* for is when there is something peculiar, striking, in the individuals, more than we can learn from their writings, and yet are curious to know. I dare say Locke and Newton were very like Kneller's portraits of them. But who could paint Shakespeare?"

"Ay," retorted A[yrton], "there it is; then I suppose you would prefer seeing him and Milton instead?"

"No," said Lamb, "neither. I have seen so much of Shakespeare on the stage and on book-stalls, in frontispieces and on mantel-pieces, that I am quite tired of the everlasting repetition; and as to Milton's face, the impressions that have come down to us of it I do not like: it is too starched and puritanical, and I should be afraid of losing some of the manna of his poetry in the leaven of his countenance and the precisian's band and gown."

"I shall guess no more," said A[yrton]. "Who is it, then, you would like to see 'in his habit as he lived,' if you had your choice of the whole range of English literature?"

Lamb then named Sir Thomas Browne and Fulke Greville, the friend of Sir Philip Sidney, as the two worthies whom he should feel the greatest pleasure to encounter on the floor of his apartment in their nightgown and slippers, and to exchange friendly greetings with them. At this A[yrton] laughed outright, and conceived Lamb was jesting with him; but as no one followed his example, he thought there might be something in it, and waited for an explanation in a state of whimsical suspense. Lamb then (as well as I can remember a conversation that passed twenty years ago—how time slips!) went on as follows: "The reason why I pitch upon these two authors is that their writings are riddles, and they themselves the most mysterious of personages. They resemble the soothsayers of old, who dealt in dark hints and doubtful oracles; and I should like to ask them the meaning of what no mortal but themselves, I should suppose, can fathom. There is Dr. Johnson: I have no curiosity, no strange uncertainty about him; he and Boswell together have pretty well let me into the secret of what passed through his mind. He and other writers like him are sufficiently explicit: my friends whose repose I should be tempted to disturb (were it in my power), are implicit, inextricable, inscrutable.

"When I look at that obscure but gorgeous prose-composition, the *Urn-Burial*, I seem to myself to look into a deep abyss, at the bottom of which are hid pearls and rich treasure; or it is like a stately labyrinth of doubt and withering speculation, and I would invoke the spirit of the author to

lead me through it. Besides, who would not be curious to see the lineaments of a man who, having himself been twice married, wished that
mankind were propagated like trees! As to Fulke Greville, he is like nothing but one of his own 'Prologues spoken by the ghost of an old king of
Ormus,' a truly formidable and inviting personage: his style is apocalypti-
cal, cabalistical, a knot worthy of such an apparition to untie; and for
the unravelling a passage or two, I would stand the brunt of an encounter
with so portentous a commentator!"

"I am afraid, in that case," said A[yrton], "that if the mystery were
once cleared up, the merit might be lost"; and turning to me, whispered
a friendly apprehension that while Lamb continued to admire these old
crabbed authors, he would never become a popular writer. Dr. Donne
was mentioned as a writer of the same period, with a very interesting
countenance, whose history was singular, and whose meaning was often
quite as *uncomeatable,* without a personal citation from the dead, as that
of any of his contemporaries. The volume was produced; and while
some one was expatiating on the exquisite simplicity and beauty of the
portrait prefixed to the old edition, A[yrton] got hold of the poetry, and
exclaiming "What have we here?" read the following:

> Here lies a shee Sunne and a hee Moone here,
> She gives the best light to his Spheare,
> Or each is both, and all, and so
> They unto one another nothing owe.

There was no resisting this, till Lamb, seizing the volume, turned to
the beautiful *Lines to his Mistress,* dissuading her from accompanying
him abroad, and read them with suffused features and a faltering
tongue. . . .

Some one then inquired of Lamb if we could not see from the window
the Temple walk in which Chaucer used to take his exercise; and on his
name being put to the vote, I was pleased to find that there was a general
sensation in his favor in all but A[yrton], who said something about the
ruggedness of the metre, and even objected to the quaintness of the
orthography. I was vexed at this superficial gloss, pertinaciously reducing
everything to its own trite level, and asked "if he did not think it would
be worth while to scan the eye that had first greeted the Muse in that
dim twilight and early dawn of English literature; to see the head round
which the visions of fancy must have played like gleams of inspiration or
a sudden glory; to watch those lips that 'lisped in numbers, for the num-

bers came'—as by a miracle, or as if the dumb should speak? Nor was it alone that he had been the first to tune his native tongue (however imperfectly to modern ears); but he was himself a noble, manly character, standing before his age and striving to advance it; a pleasant humorist withal, who has not only handed down to us the living manners of his time, but had, no doubt, store of curious and quaint devices, and would make as hearty a companion as Mine Host of the Tabard. His interview with Petrarch is fraught with interest. Yet I would rather have seen Chaucer in company with the author of the *Decameron,* and have heard them exchange their best stories together—the *Squire's Tale* against the *Story of the Falcon,* the *Wife of Bath's Prologue* against the *Adventures of Friar Albert.* How fine to see the high mysterious brow which learning then wore, relieved by the gay, familiar tone of men of the world, and by the courtesies of genius! Surely, the thoughts and feelings which passed through the minds of these great revivers of learning, these Cadmuses who sowed the teeth of letters, must have stamped an expression on their features as different from the moderns as their books, and well worth the perusal. Dante," I continued, "is as interesting a person as his own Ugolino, one whose lineaments curiosity would as eagerly devour in order to penetrate his spirit, and the only one of the Italian poets I should care much to see. There is a fine portrait of Ariosto by no less a hand than Titian's; light, Moorish, spirited, but not answering our idea. The same artist's large colossal profile of Peter Aretine [Pietro Aretino] is the only likeness of the kind that has the effect of conversing with 'the mighty dead'; and this is truly spectral, ghastly, necromantic." Lamb put it to me if I should like to see Spenser as well as Chaucer; and I answered, without hesitation, "No; for that his beauties were ideal, visionary, not palpable or personal, and therefore connected with less curiosity about the man. His poetry was the essence of romance, a very halo round the bright orb of fancy; and the bringing in the individual might dissolve the charm. No tones of voice could come up to the mellifluous cadence of his verse; no form but of a winged angel could vie with the airy shapes he has described. He was (to my apprehension) rather a 'creature of the element, that lived in the rainbow and played in the plighted clouds,' than an ordinary mortal. Or if he did appear, I should wish it to be as a mere vision, like one of his own pageants, and that he should pass by unquestioned like a dream or sound—

> That was Arion crown'd:
> So went he playing on the wat'ry plain."

Captain [Burney] muttered something about Columbus, and M[artin Burney] hinted at the Wandering Jew; but the last was set aside as spurious, and the first made over to the New World.

"I should like," said [Mrs. Reynolds], "to have seen Pope talk with Patty Blount; and I *have* seen Goldsmith." Every one turned round to look at [Mrs. Reynolds], as if by so doing they could get a sight at Goldsmith.

"Where," asked a harsh, croaking voice, "was Dr. Johnson in the years 1745–6? He did not write anything that we know of, nor is there any account of him in Boswell during those two years. Was he in Scotland with the Pretender? He seems to have passed through the scenes in the Highlands in company with Boswell, many years after, 'with lack-lustre eye,' yet as if they were familiar to him, or associated in his mind with interests that he durst not explain. If so, it would be an additional reason for my liking him; and I would give something to have seen him seated in the tent with the youthful Majesty of Britain, and penning the Proclamation to all true subjects and adherents of the legitimate Government."

"I thought," said A[yrton], turning short round upon Lamb, "that you of the Lake School did not like Pope?"

"Not like Pope! My dear sir, you must be under a mistake—I can read him over and over forever!"

"Why, certainly, the *Essay on Man* must be allowed to be a masterpiece."

"It may be so, but I seldom look into it."

"Oh! then it's his *Satires* you admire?"

"No, not his *Satires*, but his friendly *Epistles* and his compliments."

"Compliments! I did not know he ever made any."

"The finest," said Lamb, "that were ever paid by the wit of man. Each of them is worth an estate for life—nay, is an immortality. There is that superb one to Lord Cornbury:

> Despise low joys, low gains;
> Disdain whatever Cornbury disdains;
> Be virtuous, and be happy for your pains.

Was there ever more artful insinuation of idolatrous praise? And then that noble apotheosis of his friend Lord Mansfield (however little deserved), when, speaking of the House of Lords, he adds:

> Conspicuous scene! another yet is nigh,
> (More silent far) where kings and poets lie;
> Where Murray (long enough his country's pride)
> Shall be no more than Tully or than Hyde.

And with what a fine turn of indignant flattery he addresses Lord Boling-broke:

> Why rail they then, if but one wreath of mine,
> Oh! all accomplish'd St. John, deck thy shrine?

"Or turn," continued Lamb, with a slight hectic on his cheek and his eyes glistening, "to his list of early friends:

> But why then publish? Granville the polite,
> And knowing Walsh, would tell me I could write;
> Well-natured Garth inflamed with early praise,
> And Congreve loved, and Swift endured my lays;
> The courtly Talbot, Somers, Sheffield read,
> Ev'n mitred Rochester would nod the head;
> And St. John's self (great Dryden's friend before)
> Received with open arms one poet more.
> Happy my studies, if by these approved!
> Happier their author, if by these beloved!
> From these the world will judge of men and books,
> Not from the Burnets, Oldmixons, and Cooks."

Here his voice totally failed him, and throwing down the books, he said, "Do you think I would not wish to have been friends with such a man as this?"

"What say you to Dryden?"

"He rather made a show of himself, and courted popularity in that lowest temple of fame, a coffee-shop, so as in some measure to vulgarize one's idea of him. Pope, on the contrary, reached the very *beau idéal* of what a poet's life should be; and his fame while living seemed to be an emanation from that which was to circle his name after death. He was so far enviable (and one would feel proud to have witnessed the rare spectacle in him) that he was almost the only poet and man of genius who met with his reward on this side of the tomb, who realized in friends, fortune, the esteem of the world, the most sanguine hopes of a youthful ambition, and who found that sort of patronage from the great during his lifetime which they would be thought anxious to bestow upon him after his death. Read Gay's verses to him on his supposed return from Greece, after his translation of Homer was finished, and say if you would not gladly join the bright procession that welcomed him home, or see it once more land at Whitehall stairs."

"Still," said [Mrs. Reynolds], "I would rather have seen him talking with Patty Blount, or riding by in a coronet-coach with Lady Mary Wortley Montagu!"

E[rasmus Phillips], who was deep in a game of piquet at the other end of the room, whispered to M[artin Burney] to ask if Junius would not be a fit person to invoke from the dead. "Yes," said Lamb, "provided he would agree to lay aside his mask."

We were now at a stand for a short time, when Fielding was mentioned as a candidate; only one, however, seconded the proposition. "Richardson?"

"By all means, but only to look at him through the glass-door of his back-shop, hard at work upon one of his novels (the most extraordinary contrast that ever was presented between an author and his works), but not to let him come behind his counter, lest he should want you to turn customer, nor to go upstairs with him, lest he should offer to read the first manuscript of Sir Charles Grandison, which was originally written in eight-and-twenty volumes octavo, or get out the letters of his female correspondents, to prove that Joseph Andrews was low."

There was but one statesman in the whole of English history that anyone expressed the least desire to see—Oliver Cromwell, with his fine, frank, rough, pimply face, and wily policy; and one enthusiast, John Bunyan, the immortal author of the *Pilgrim's Progress*. It seemed that if he came into the room, dreams would follow him, and that each person would nod under his golden cloud, "nigh-sphered in heaven," a canopy as strange and stately as any in Homer.

Of all persons near our own time, Garrick's name was received with the greatest enthusiasm, who was proposed by [Barron] F[ield]. He presently superseded both Hogarth and Handel, who had been talked of, but then it was on condition that he should act in tragedy and comedy, in the play and the farce, *Lear* and *Wildair* and *Abel Drugger*. What a sight for sore eyes that would be! Who would not part with a year's income at least, almost with a year of his natural life, to be present at it? Besides, as he could not act alone, and recitations are unsatisfactory things, what a troop he must bring with him—the silver-tongued Barry, and Quin, and Shuter and Weston, and Mrs. Clive and Mrs. Pritchard, of whom I have heard my father speak as so great a favourite when he was young. This would indeed be a revival of the dead, the restoring of art; and so much the more desirable, as such is the lurking scepticism mingled with our overstrained admiration of past excellence, that though we have the speeches of Burke, the portraits of Reynolds, the writings of Goldsmith, and the conversation of Johnson, to show what people could do at that period, and to confirm the universal testimony to the merits of Garrick; yet, as it was before our time, we have our misgivings, as if he was probably, after all, little better than a Bartlemy-fair actor, dressed out to play Macbeth in a scarlet and laced cocked hat. For one, I should like to have seen and heard with my own eyes and ears. Certainly, by all accounts, if any one was ever moved by the true histrionic estus, it was Garrick. When he followed the Ghost in *Hamlet,* he did not drop the sword, as most actors do, behind the scenes, but kept the point raised the whole way round, so fully was he possessed with the idea, or so anxious not to lose sight of his part for a moment. Once at a splendid dinner party at Lord ———'s, they suddenly missed Garrick, and could not imagine what was become of him, till they were drawn to the window by the convulsive screams and peals of laughter of a young Negro boy, who was rolling on the ground in an ecstasy of delight to see Garrick mimicking a turkey-cock in the courtyard, with his coat-tail stuck out behind, and in a seeming flutter of feathered rage and pride. Of our party only two persons present had seen the British Roscius; and they seemed as willing as the rest to renew their acquaintance with their old favourite.

We were interrupted in the hey-day and mid-career of this fanciful speculation, by a grumbler in a corner, who declared it was a shame to make all this rout about a mere player and farce-writer, to the neglect and exclusion of the fine old dramatists, the contemporaries and rivals of Shakespeare. Lamb said he had anticipated this objection when he had named the author of *Mustapha* and *Alaham;* and, out of caprice, insisted upon keeping him to represent the set, in preference to the wild, hare-brained enthusiast, Kit Marlowe; to the sexton of St. Ann's, Webster, with his melancholy yew-trees and death's-heads; to Dekker, who was but a garrulous proser; to the voluminous Heywood; and even to Beaumont and Fletcher, whom we might offend by complimenting the wrong author on their joint productions. Lord Brooke, on the contrary, stood quite by himself, or, in Cowley's words, was "a vast species alone." Some one hinted at the circumstances of his being a lord, which rather startled Lamb, but he said a *ghost* would perhaps dispense with strict etiquette, on being regularly addressed by his title. Ben Jonson divided our suffrages pretty equally. Some were afraid he would begin to traduce Shakespeare, who was not present to defend himself. "If he grows disagreeable," it was whispered aloud, "there is G[odwin] can match him." At length, his romantic visit to Drummond of Hawthornden was mentioned, and turned the scale in his favor.

Lamb inquired if there was any one that was hanged that I would choose to mention. And I answered, Eugene Aram. The name of the "Admirable Crichton" was suddenly started as a splendid example of *waste* talents, so different from the generality of his countrymen. This choice was mightily approved by a North Briton present, who declared himself descended from that prodigy of learning and accomplishment, and said he had family plate in his possession as vouchers for the fact, with the initals A.C.—*Admirable Crichton!* H——— laughed, or rather roared, as heartily at this as I should think he has done for many years.

The last-named Mitre-courtier then wished to know whether there were any metaphysicians to whom one might be tempted to apply the wizard spell. I replied, there were only six in modern times deserving the name—Hobbes, Berkeley, Butler, Hartley, Hume, Leibniz; and perhaps Jonathan Edwards, a Massachusetts man. As to the French, who talked fluently of having *created* this science, there was not a title in any of their writings that was not to be found literally in the authors I had mentioned. (Horne Tooke, who might have a claim to come in under the head of Grammar, was still living.) None of these names seemed to excite much interest, and I did not plead for the reappearance of those who might be thought best fitted by the abstracted nature of their studies for the present spiritual and disembodied state, and who, even while on this living stage, were nearly divested of common flesh and blood. As A[yrton], with an uneasy, fidgety face, was about to put some question about Mr. Locke and Dugald Stewart, he was prevented by M[artin Burney], who observed, "If J——— was here, he would undoubtedly be for having up those profound and redoubted scholiasts, Thomas Aquinas and Duns Scotus." I said this might be fair enough in him who had read, or fancied he had read, the original works, but I did not see how we could have any right to call up these authors to give an account of themselves in person, till we had looked into their writings.

By this time it should seem that some rumour of our whimsical deliberation had got wind, and had disturbed the *irritabile genus* in their shadowy abodes, for we received messages from several candidates that we had just been thinking of. Gray declined our invitation, though he had not yet been asked; Gay offered to come, and bring in his hand the Duchess of Bolton, the original Polly; Steele and Addison left their cards as Captain Sentry and Sir Roger de Coverley; Swift came in and sat down without speaking a word and quitted the room as abruptly; Otway and Chatterton were seen lingering on the opposite side of the Styx, but

could not muster enough between them to pay Charon his fare; Thomson
fell asleep in the boat, and was rowed back again—and Burns sent a low
fellow, one John Barleycorn, an old companion of his, who had conducted
him to the other world, to say that he had during his lifetime been drawn
out of his retirement as a show, only to be made an exciseman of, and
that he would rather remain where he was. He desired, however, to
shake hands by his representative—the hand, thus held out, was in a
burning fever, and shook prodigiously.

The room was hung round with several portraits of eminent painters.
While we were debating whether we should demand speech with these
masters of mute eloquence, whose features were so familiar to us, it
seemed that all at once they glided from their frames, and seated themselves at some little distance from us. There was Leonardo, with his
majestic beard and watchful eye, having a bust of Archimedes before
him; next him was Raphael's graceful head turned round to the For-
narina; and on his other side was Lucretia Borgia, with calm, golden
locks; Michelangelo had placed the model of St. Peter's on the table
before him; Correggio had an angel at his side; Titian was seated with
his mistress between himself and Giorgione; Guido was accompanied by
his own Aurora, who took a dice-box from him; Claude held a mirror in
his hand; Rubens patted a beautiful panther (led in by a satyr) on the
head; Vandyke appeared as his own Paris, and Rembrandt was hid under
furs, gold chains, and jewels, which Sir Joshua eyed closely, holding his
hand so as to shade his forehead. Not a word was spoken; and as we rose
to do them homage, they still presented the same surface to the view. Not
being *bona fide* representations of living people, we got rid of the splendid
apparitions by signs and dumb show. As soon as they had melted into
thin air, there was a loud noise at the outer door, and we found it was
Giotto, Cimabue, and Ghirlandaio, who had been raised from the dead
by their earnest desire to see their illustrious successors—

> Whose names on earth
> In Fame's eternal records live for aye!

Finding them gone, they had no ambition to be seen after them, and
mournfully withdrew. "Egad!" said Lamb, "these are the very fellows I
should like to have had some talk with, to know how they could see to
paint when all was dark around them."

"But shall we have nothing to say," interrogated G. J——, "to the
Legend of Good Women?"

"Name, name, Mr. J——," cried H—— in a boisterous tone of friendly exultation, "name as many as you please, without reserve or fear of molestation!"

J—— was perplexed between so many amiable recollections, that the name of the lady of his choice expired in a pensive whiff of his pipe; and Lamb impatiently declared for the Duchess of Newcastle. Mrs. Hutchinson was no sooner mentioned, than she carried the day from the Duchess. We were the less solicitous on this subject of filling up the posthumous lists of Good Women, as there was already one in the room as good, as sensible, and in all respects as exemplary, as the best of them could be for their lives! "I should like vastly to have seen Ninon de l'Enclos," said that incomparable person; and this immediately put us in mind that we had neglected to pay honour due to our friends on the other side of the Channel: Voltaire, the patriarch of levity, and Rousseau, the father of sentiment; Montaigne and Rabelais (great in wisdom and in wit); Molière and that illustrious group that are collected round him (in the print of that subject) to hear him read his comedy of the *Tartuffe* at the house of Ninon; Racine, La Fontaine, Rochefoucault, St. Evremont, etc.

"There is one person," said a shrill, querulous voice, "I would rather see than all these—Don Quixote!"

"Come, come!" said H——; "I thought we should have no heroes, real or fabulous. What say you, Mr. Lamb? Are you for eking out your shadowy list with such names as Alexander, Julius Caesar, Tamerlane, or Genghis Khan?"

"Excuse me," said Lamb, "on the subject of characters in active life, plotters and disturbers of the world, I have a crotchet of my own, which I beg leave to reserve."

"No, no! come, out with your worthies!"

"What do you think of Guy Fawkes and Judas Iscariot?" H—— turned an eye upon him like a wild Indian, but cordial and full of smothered glee. "Your most exquisite reason!" was echoed on all sides; and A[yrton] thought that Lamb had now fairly entangled himself.

"Why I cannot but think," retorted he of the wistful countenance, "that Guy Fawkes, that poor, fluttering annual scarecrow of straw and rags, is an ill-used gentleman. I would give something to see him sitting pale and emaciated, surrounded by his matches and his barrels of gunpowder, and expecting the moment that was to transport him to Paradise for his heroic self-devotion; but if I say any more, there is that fellow G[odwin] will make something of it. And as to Judas Iscariot, my reason is different. I would fain see the face of him who, having dipped his hand in the same dish with the Son of Man, could afterwards betray him. I have no conception of such a thing; nor have I ever seen any picture (not even Leonardo's very fine one) that gave me the least idea of it."

"You have said enough, Mr. Lamb, to justify your choice."

"Oh! ever right, Menenius—ever right!"

"There is only one other person I can ever think of after this," continued H————; but without mentioning a name that once put on a semblance of mortality. "If Shakespeare was to come into the room, we should all rise up to meet him; but if that person was to come into it, we should all fall down and try to kiss the hem of his garment!"

As a lady present seemed now to get uneasy at the turn the conversation had taken, we rose up to go. The morning broke with that dim, dubious light by which Giotto, Cimabue, and Ghirlandaio must have seen to paint their earliest works; and we parted to meet again and renew similar topics at night, the next night, and the night after that, till that night overspread Europe which saw no dawn. The same event, in truth, broke up our little congress that broke up the great one. But that was to meet again: our deliberations have never been resumed.

Charles Lamb

1775–1834

Charles Lamb was born in the Inner Temple, London, February 10, 1775. He went to school with Coleridge at Christ's Hospital. They became close friends. In 1792 he took a job at East India House, where James Mill was later his colleague and John Stuart Mill would also be an official. Lamb held his post for thirty-three years.

After an unlucky love affair, he entered an asylum for a while in 1795. During the following year his sister, Mary Lamb, became unbalanced and stabbed her mother to death. In order to prevent her spending the rest of her life in an asylum, Lamb arranged to take care of his sister. He did so until he died. Each time the warning symptoms showed themselves, Mary Lamb, quietly and in tears, would go back to the asylum again.

Lamb's plays, *John Woodvil* and *Mr. H——*, were produced but were not well received. In 1807 he and Mary Lamb published *Tales Founded on the Plays of Shakespeare*. Other children's books and a number of articles for Leigh Hunt's *The Reflector* were written before 1811. Lamb's *Specimens of English Dramatic Poets*, together with Hazlitt's lectures, helped to bring the lesser Elizabethan writers back into favor.

The period of Lamb's weekly literary evenings, described by

---

*Notes from the artist: "An elongated interpretation of Lamb
reminiscent of a sketch made during his lifetime by Charles Pulham.
Next to the portrait is a facsimile of Lamb's poem
Elegy on a Quid of Tobacco."*

Elegy

On a Quid of Tobacco.

It lay before me on the close-grazed grass
  Beside my path, an old Tobacco quid.
And shall I by the mute adviser pass
  Without one serious thought? now Heaven forbid!

Perhaps some idle drunkard threw thee there,
  Some husband, spendthrift of his weekly hire,
One who for wife and children takes no care
  But sits and tipples by the alehouse fire.

Ah luckless was the day he learnt to chew!
  Embryo of ill, the Quid that pleased him first!
Thirsty from that unhappy Quid he grew,
  Then to the alehouse went to quench his thirst.

So great events from causes small arise,
  The forest oak was once an acorn seed,
And many a wretch from drunkenness who dies
  Owes all his evils to the Indian weed.

Let not temptation mortal, e'er come nigh—
  Suspect some ambush in the parsley hid.—
From the first kiss of Love, ye maidens fly!
  Ye youths avoid the first Tobacco Quid.

Charles
Lamb

Hazlitt, began about 1811. He proposed marriage to Fanny Kelly, an actress, but was refused. In 1818 his collected *Works* appeared—a little too early to include his best. In the *London Magazine,* after 1820, he began his most famous series, the *Essays of Elia.* (Elia was a "gay light-hearted foreigner" who had once been Lamb's fellow clerk at South Sea House.)

Lamb was pensioned and moved to the country at Enfield. His sister's malady grew constantly worse. During this period his great joy was the Lambs' adopted daughter, Emma Isola. He died at Edmonton, December 27, 1834, from erysipelas and the effects of a fall on the London Road.

Lamb is the magician of the English familiar essay. At the first touch of his wand, we are friends. Happily we consent to go with him wherever he leads, charmed by the brisk voice, the liveliness of fancy, the literary reference from anywhere and everywhere that lights up each stone on the way. He is amused and amusing. We recall that he once joined the audience in hissing his own play.

My First Play (the first he saw, not the first he wrote) may remind us of our own first visit to a theater. Lamb's recollection centers on a green curtain and the unbearable time it takes to go up on the lighted world of the stage. His gift is that he can make us remember that waiting as it happened to *us,* so that we almost seem to remember what he is telling us about himself.

We too fidget through the little preliminary drama of the weather. Will it stop raining? It does. We have "orders"—that is, passes—to the theater. They are a gift from his godfather the oilman. Lamb wanders off a little to chat happily about this godfather of his, who was a friend of the great Sheridan, and who left Charles a patch of land in Hertfordshire.

Then we are in the theater—a theater doubly magical because it belongs to the late eighteenth century and so is a little strange to us. What is a nonpareil? A kind of apple. The attraction was probably a revival of Thomas Arne's *Artaxerxes*—in effect an opera, with sung speeches. Lamb saw the traditional Harlequin at his tricks. The Rich he mentions was John Rich, father of English pantomime. Later he watches a pantomime of *Robinson Crusoe,* and it was just as he had imagined it.

In *Dream Children,* Lamb tells stories of his own youth to the children he might have had. His grandmother, Mary Field, had been caretaker of just such a great house as he describes, in Hertfordshire. And a girl of that country, Ann Simmons, to whom his first sonnets were written, might well have been the imaginary dead wife Alice of his dreams.

The third essay, *Sanity of True Genius,* makes a point that needs to be repeated in each generation. Art is not daydreaming. It is something willed. A true artist is seldom the servant of his visions. He is their master. They are the materials out of which he constructs his work, as a carpenter uses boards and nails to put up a house.

My First Play

At the north end of Cross-court there yet stands a portal, of some architectural pretensions, though reduced to humble use, serving at present for an entrance to a printing-office. This old doorway, if you are young, reader, you may not know was the identical pit entrance to old Drury—Garrick's Drury—all of it that is left. I never pass it without shaking some forty years from off my shoulders, recurring to the evening when I passed through it to see *my first play*. The afternoon had been wet, and the condition of our going (the elder folks and myself) was that the rain should cease. With what a beating heart did I watch from the window the puddles, from the stillness of which I was taught to prognosticate the desired cessation! I seem to remember the last spurt, and the glee with which I ran to announce it.

We went with orders, which my godfather F. had sent us. He kept the oil shop (now Davies's) at the corner of Featherstone-building, in Holborn. F. was a tall grave person, lofty in speech, and had pretensions above his rank. He associated in those days with John Palmer, the comedian, whose gait and bearing he seemed to copy; if John (which is quite as likely) did not rather borrow somewhat of his manner from my godfather. He was also known to and visited by Sheridan. It was to his house in Holborn that young Brinsley brought his first wife on her elopement with him from a boarding-school at Bath—the beautiful Maria Linley. My parents were present (over a quadrille table) when he arrived in the evening with his harmonious charge. From either of these connections it may be inferred that my godfather could command an order for the then Drury Lane theatre at pleasure—and, indeed, a pretty liberal issue of those cheap billets, in Brinsley's easy autograph, I have heard him say was the sole remuneration which he had received for many years' nightly illumination of the orchestra and various avenues of that theatre—and he was content it should be so. The honour of Sheridan's familiarity—or supposed familiarity—was better to my godfather than money.

F. was the most gentlemanly of oilmen; grandiloquent, yet courteous. His delivery of the commonest matters of fact was Ciceronian. He had two Latin words almost constantly in his mouth (how odd sounds Latin from an oilman's lips!), which my better knowledge since has enabled me to correct. In strict pronunciation they should have been sounded *vice versa*—but in those young years they impressed me with more awe than they would now do, read aright from Seneca or Varro—in his own peculiar pronunciation, monosyllabically elaborated, or anglicized, into something like *verse verse*. By an imposing manner, and the help of these distorted syllables, he climbed (but that was little) to the highest parochial honours which St. Andrew's has to bestow.

He is dead—and thus much I thought due to his memory, both for my first orders (little wondrous talismans!—slight keys, and insignificant to outward sight, but opening to me more than Arabian paradises!) and, moreover, that by his testamentary beneficence I came into possession of the only landed property which I could ever call my own—situate near the roadway village of pleasant Puckeridge, in Hertfordshire. When I journeyed down to take possession, and planted foot on my own ground, the stately habits of the donor descended upon me, and I strode (shall I confess the vanity?) with larger paces over my allotment of three-quarters of an acre, with its commodious mansion in the midst, with the feeling of an English freeholder that all betwixt sky and centre was my own. The estate has passed into more prudent hands, and nothing but an agrarian can restore it.

In those days were pit orders. Beshrew the uncomfortable manager who abolished them!—with one of these we went. I remember the waiting at the door—not that which is left—but between that and an inner door in shelter—O when shall I be such an expectant again!—with the cry of nonpareils, an indispensable playhouse accompaniment in those days. As near as I can recollect, the fashionable pronunciation of the theatrical fruiteresses then was, "Chase some oranges, chase some numparels, chase a bill of the play"—chase *pro* chuse. But when we got in, and I beheld the green curtain that veiled a heaven to my imagination, which was soon to be disclosed—the breathless anticipations I endured! I had seen something like it in the plate prefixed to *Troilus and Cressida*, in Rowe's *Shakespeare*—the tent scene with Diomede—and a sight of that plate can always bring back in a measure the feeling of that evening. The boxes at that time, full of well-dressed women of quality, projected over the pit; and the pilasters reaching down were adorned with a glistening substance (I know not what) under glass (as it seemed), resembling—a homely fancy—but I judged it to be sugar-candy—yet to my raised imagination, divested of its homelier qualities, it appeared a glorified candy! The orchestra lights at length rose, those "fair Auroras"! Once the bell sounded. It was to ring out yet once again—and, incapable of the anticipation, I reposed my shut eyes in a sort of resignation upon the maternal lap. It rang the second time. The curtain drew up—I was not past six years old, and the play was *Artaxerxes!*

I had dabbled a little in the Universal History—the ancient part of it —and here was the court of Persia. It was being admitted to a sight of the past. I took no proper interest in the action going on, for I understood not its import—but I heard the word Darius, and I was in the midst of Daniel. All feeling was absorbed in vision. Gorgeous vests, gardens, palaces, princesses, passed before me. I knew not players. I was in Persepolis for the time, and the burning idol of their devotion almost converted me into a worshipper. I was awe-struck, and believed those significations to be something more than elemental fires. It was all enchantment and a dream. No such pleasure has since visited me but in dreams. Harlequin's Invasion followed; where, I remember, the transformation of the magistrates into reverend beldams seemed to me a piece of grave historic justice, and the tailor carrying his own head to be as sober a verity as the legend of St. Denys.

The next play to which I was taken was the *Lady of the Manor*, of which, with the exception of some scenery, very faint traces are left in my memory. It was followed by a pantomime, called "Lun's Ghost"—a satiric touch, I apprehend, upon Rich, not long since dead—but to my apprehension (too sincere for satire), Lun was as remote a piece of antiquity as Lud—the father of a line of Harlequins—transmitting his dagger of lath (the wooden sceptre) through countless ages. I saw the primeval Motley come from his silent tomb in a ghastly vest of white patchwork, like the apparition of a dead rainbow. So Harlequins (thought I) look when they are dead.

My third play followed in quick succession. It was the *Way of the World*. I think I must have sat at it as grave as a judge; for I remember the hysteric affectations of good Lady Wishfort affected me like some solemn tragic passion. *Robinson Crusoe* followed; in which Crusoe, man Friday, and the parrot were as good and authentic as in the story. The clownery and pantaloonery of these pantomimes have clean passed out of my head. I believe I no more laughed at them than at the same age I should have been disposed to laugh at the grotesque Gothic heads (seeming to me then replete with devout meaning) that gape, and grin, in stone around the inside of the old Round Church (my church) of the Templars.

I saw these plays in the season 1781-2, when I was from six to seven years old. After the intervention of six or seven other years (for at school all play-going was inhibited), I again entered the doors of a theatre. That old Artaxerxes evening had never done ringing in my fancy. I expected the same feelings to come again with the same occasion. But we differ from ourselves less at sixty and sixteen, than the latter does from six. In that interval what had I not lost! At the first period I knew nothing, understood nothing, discriminated nothing. I felt all, loved all, wondered all—

> Was nourished, I could not tell how—

I had left the temple a devotee, and was returned a rationalist. The same things were there materially; but the emblem, the reference, was gone! The green curtain was no longer a veil, drawn between two worlds, the unfolding of which was to bring back past ages, to present a "royal ghost" —but a certain quantity of green baize, which was to separate the audience for a given time from certain of their fellow-men who were to come forward and pretend those parts. The lights—the orchestra lights— came up a clumsy machinery. The first ring, and the second ring, was now but a trick of the prompter's bell—which had been, like the note of the cuckoo, a phantom of a voice, no hand seen or guessed at which ministered to its warning. The actors were men and women painted. I thought the fault was in them; but it was in myself, and the alteration which those many centuries—of six short twelvemonths—had wrought in me. Perhaps it was fortunate for me that the play of the evening was but an indifferent comedy, as it gave me time to crop some unreasonable expectations, which might have interfered with the genuine emotions with which I was soon after enabled to enter upon the first appearance to me of Mrs. Siddons in *Isabella*. Comparison and retrospection soon yielded to the present attraction of the scene; and the theatre became to me, upon a new stock, the most delightful of recreations.

Dream Children,
a Reverie

Children love to listen to stories about their elders, when *they* were children; to stretch their imagination to the conception of a traditionary great-uncle, or grandame, whom they never saw. It was in this spirit that my little ones crept about me the other evening to hear about their great-grandmother Field, who lived in a great house in Norfolk (a hundred times bigger than that in which they and papa lived) which had been the scene—so at least it was generally believed in that part of the country—of the tragic incidents which they had lately become familiar with from the ballad of the Children in the Wood. Certain it is that the whole story of the children and their cruel uncle was to be seen fairly carved out in wood upon the chimney-piece of the great hall, the whole story down to the Robin Redbreasts; till a foolish rich person pulled it down to set up a marble one of modern invention in its stead, with no story upon it. Here Alice put out one of her dear mother's looks, too tender to be called upbraiding. Then I went on to say, how religious and how good their great-grandmother Field was, how beloved and respected by everybody, though she was not indeed the mistress of this great house, but had only the charge of it (and yet in some respects she might be said to be the mistress of it too) committed to her by the owner, who preferred living in a newer and more fashionable mansion which he had purchased somewhere in the adjoining county; but still she lived in it in a manner as if it had been her own, and kept up the dignity of the great house in a sort while she lived, which afterwards came to decay, and was nearly pulled down, and all its old ornaments stripped and carried away to the owner's other house, where they were set up, and looked as awkward as if some one were to carry away the old tombs they had seen lately at the Abbey, and stick them up in Lady C.'s tawdry gilt drawing-room. Here John smiled, as much as to say, "That would be foolish indeed." And then

I told how, when she came to die, her funeral was attended by a concourse of all the poor, and some of the gentry too, of the neighbourhood for many miles round, to show their respect for her memory, because she had been such a good and religious woman; so good indeed that she knew all the Psaltery by heart, ay, and a great part of the Testament besides. Here little Alice spread her hands. Then I told what a tall, upright, graceful person their great-grandmother Field once was; and how in her youth she was esteemed the best dancer—here Alice's little right foot played an involuntary movement, till, upon my looking grave, it desisted—the best dancer, I was saying, in the county, till a cruel disease, called a cancer, came, and bowed her down with pain; but it could never bend her good spirits, or make them stoop, but they were still upright, because she was so good and religious. Then I told how she was used to sleep by herself in a lone chamber of the great lone house; and how she believed that an apparition of two infants was to be seen at midnight gliding up and down the great staircase near where she slept, but she said "those innocents would do her no harm"; and how frightened I used to be, though in those days I had my maid to sleep with me, because I was never half so good or religious as she—and yet I never saw the infants. Here John expanded all his eyebrows and tried to look courageous. Then I told how good she was to all her grandchildren, having us to the great house in the holydays, where I in particular used to spend many hours by myself, in gazing upon the old busts of the twelve Caesars that had been emperors of Rome, till the old marble heads would seem to live again, or I to be turned into marble with them; how I never could be tired with roaming about that huge mansion, with its vast empty rooms, with their worn-out hangings, fluttering tapestry, and carved oaken panels, with the gilding almost rubbed out—sometimes in the spacious old-fashioned gardens, which I had almost to myself, unless when now and then a solitary gardening man would cross me—and how the nectarines and peaches hung upon the walls, without my ever offering to pluck them, because they were forbidden fruit, unless now and then,—and because I had more pleasure in strolling about among the old melancholy-looking yew-trees, or the firs, and picking up the red berries, and the fir-apples, which were good for nothing but to look at—or in lying about upon the fresh grass with all the fine garden smells around me—or basking in the orangery, till I could almost fancy myself ripening too along with the oranges and the limes in that grateful warmth—or in watching the dace that darted to and fro in the fishpond, at the bottom of the garden, with here and there a great sulky pike hanging midway down the water in silent state, as if it mocked at their impertinent friskings—I had more pleasure in these busy-idle diversions than in all the sweet flavours of peaches, nectarines, oranges, and such-like common baits of children. Here John slyly deposited back upon the plate a bunch of grapes, which, not unobserved by Alice, he had meditated dividing with her, and both seemed willing to relinquish them for the present as irrelevant. Then, in somewhat a more heightened tone, I told how, though their great-grandmother Field loved all her grandchildren, yet in an especial manner she might be said to love their uncle, John L——, because he was so handsome and spirited a youth, and a king to the rest of us; and, instead of moping about in solitary corners, like some of us, he would mount the most mettlesome horse he could get, when but an imp no bigger than themselves, and make it carry him half over the county in a morning, and join the hunters when there were any out—and yet he loved the old great house and gardens too, but had too much spirit to be always pent up within their boundaries—and how their uncle grew up to man's estate as brave as he was handsome, to the admiration of everybody, but of their great-grandmother Field most especially; and how he used to carry me upon his back when I was a lame-footed boy—for he was a good bit older than me—many a mile when I could not walk for pain;—and how in after life he became lame-footed too, and I did not always (I fear) make allowances enough for him when he was impatient and in pain, nor remember sufficiently how considerate he had been to me when I was lame-footed, and how when he died, though he had not been dead an hour, it seemed as if he had died a great while ago, such a distance there is betwixt life and death; and how I bore his death as I thought pretty well at first, but afterwards it haunted and haunted me; and though I did not cry or take it to heart as some do, and as I think he would have done if I had died, yet I missed him all day long, and knew not till then how much I had loved him. I missed his kindness, and I missed his crossness, and wished him to be alive again, to be quarrelling with him (for we quarrelled sometimes), rather than not have him again, and was as uneasy without him, as he, their poor uncle, must have been when the doctor took off his limb. Here the children fell a crying, and asked if their little mourning which they had on was not for Uncle John, and they looked up, and prayed me not to go on about their uncle, but to tell them some stories about their pretty dead mother. Then I told how for seven long years, in hope sometimes, sometimes in despair, yet persisting ever, I courted the fair Alice W——n; and as much as children could understand, I explained to them what coyness, and difficulty, and denial, meant in maidens—when suddenly turning to

Alice, the soul of the first Alice looked out at her eyes with such a reality of re-presentment that I became in doubt which of them stood there before me, or whose that bright hair was; and while I stood gazing, both the children gradually grew fainter to my view, receding, and still receding, till nothing at last but two mournful features were seen in the uttermost distance, which, without speech, strangely impressed upon me the effects of speech: "We are not of Alice, nor of thee, nor are we children at all. The children of Alice call Bartrum father. We are nothing; less than nothing, and dreams. We are only what might have been, and must wait upon the tedious shores of Lethe millions of ages before we have existence, and a name"——and immediately awaking, I found myself quietly seated in my bachelor arm-chair, where I had fallen asleep, with the faithful Bridget unchanged by my side—but John L. (or James Elia) was gone forever.

Sanity
of True Genius

So far from the position holding true, that great wit (or genius, in our modern way of speaking) has a necessary alliance with insanity, the greatest wits, on the contrary, will ever be found to be the sanest writers. It is impossible for the mind to conceive of a mad Shakespeare. The greatness of wit, by which the poetic talent is here chiefly to be understood, manifests itself in the admirable balance of all the faculties. Madness is the disproportionate straining or excess of any one of them. "So strong a wit," says Cowley, speaking of a poetical friend,

> ——did Nature to him frame,
> As all things but his judgment overcame;
> His judgment like the heavenly moon did show,
> Tempering that mighty sea below.

The ground of the mistake is that men, finding in the raptures of the higher poetry a condition of exaltation, to which they have no parallel in their own experience, besides the spurious resemblance of it in dreams and fevers, impute a state of dreaminess and fever to the poet. But the true poet dreams being awake. He is not possessed by his subject, but has dominion over it. In the groves of Eden he walks familiar as in his native paths. He ascends the empyrean heaven, and is not intoxicated. He treads the burning marl without dismay; he wins his flight without self-loss through realms of chaos "and old night." Or if, abandoning himself to that severer chaos of a "human mind untuned," he is content awhile to be mad with Lear, or to hate mankind (a sort of madness) with Timon, neither is that madness, nor this misanthropy, so unchecked, but that—never letting the reins of reason wholly go, while most he seems to do so—he has his better genius still whispering at his ear, with the good servant Kent suggesting saner counsels, or with the honest steward Flavius recommending kindlier resolutions. Where he seems most to recede from humanity, he will be found the truest to it. From beyond the scope of Nature if he summon possible existences, he subjugates them to the law of her consistency. He is beautifully loyal to that sovereign directress, even when he appears most to betray and desert her. His ideal tribes submit to policy; his very monsters are tamed to his hand, even as that wild sea-brood, shepherded by Proteus. He tames, and he clothes them with attributes of flesh and blood, till they wonder at themselves, like Indian Islanders forced to submit to European vesture. Caliban, the Witches, are as true to the laws of their own nature (ours with a difference), as Othello, Hamlet, and Macbeth. Herein the great and the little wits are differenced; that if the latter wander ever so little from nature or actual existence, they lose themselves and their readers. Their phantoms are lawless; their visions nightmares. They do not create, which implies shaping and consistency. Their imaginations are not active—for to be active is to call something into act and form—but passive, as men in sick dreams. For the supernatural, or something super-added to what we know of nature, they give you the plainly non-natural. And if this were all, and that these mental hallucinations were discoverable only in the treatment of subjects out of nature, or transcending it, the judgment might with some plea be pardoned if it ran riot, and a little wantonized: but even in the describing of real and everyday life, that which is before their eyes, one of these lesser wits shall more deviate from nature—show more of that inconsequence, which has a natural alliance with frenzy— than a great genius in his "maddest fits," as Withers somewhere calls them. We appeal to any one that is acquainted with the common run of Lane's novels—as they existed some twenty or thirty years back, those scanty intellectual viands of the whole female reading public, till a happier genius arose, and expelled forever the innutritious phantoms— whether he has not found his brain more "betossed," his memory more puzzled, his sense of when and where more confounded, among the improbable events, the incoherent incidents, the inconsistent characters, or no characters, of some third-rate love-intrigue—where the persons shall be a Lord Glendamour and a Miss Rivers, and the scene only alternate between Bath and Bond Street—a more bewildering dreaminess induced upon him than he has felt wandering over all the fairy-grounds of Spenser. In the productions we refer to, nothing but names and places is familiar; the persons are neither of this world nor of any other conceivable one; an endless stream of activities without purpose, of purposes destitute of motive: we meet phantoms in our known walks; *fantasques* only christened. In the poet we have names which announce fiction; and we have absolutely no place at all, for the things and persons of the Fairy Queen prate not of their "whereabout." But in their inner nature, and the law of their speech and actions, we are at home, and upon acquainted ground. The one turns life into a dream: the other to the wildest dreams gives the sobrieties of everyday occurrences. By what subtle art of tracing the mental processes it is effected, we are not philosophers enough to explain, but in that wonderful episode of the cave of Mammon, in which the Money God appears first in the lowest form of a miser, is then a worker of metals, and becomes the god of all the treasures of the world; and has a daughter, Ambition, before whom all the world kneels for favours—with the Hesperian fruit, the waters of Tantalus, with Pilate washing his hands vainly, but not impertinently, in the same stream—that we should be at one moment in the cave of an old hoarder of treasures, at the next at the forge of the Cyclops, in a palace and yet in hell, all at once, with the shifting mutations of the most rambling dream, and our judgment yet all the time awake, and neither able nor willing to detect the fallacy, is a proof of that hidden sanity which still guides the poet in the wildest seeming-aberrations.

It is not enough to say that the whole episode is a copy of the mind's conceptions in sleep; it is, in some sort—but what a copy! Let the most romantic of us, that has been entertained all night with the spectacle of some wild and magnificent vision, recombine it in the morning, and try it by his waking judgment. That which appeared so shifting, and yet so coherent, while that faculty was passive, when it comes under cool examination shall appear so reasonless and so unlinked, that we are ashamed to have been so deluded; and to have taken, though but in sleep, a monster for a god. But the transitions in this episode are every whit as violent as in the most extravagant dream, and yet the waking judgment ratifies them.

"*My First Play*" and "*Dream Children, a Reverie*"
are from a collection of Lamb's essays entitled THE ESSAYS OF ELIA;
"*Sanity of True Genius*" *is from a collection of Lamb's essays
entitled* THE LAST ESSAYS OF ELIA.

Samuel Johnson

1709–1784

Samuel Johnson was born in Lichfield, England, on September 18, 1709. His father, Michael, a bookseller, was sheriff of the city that year. From his father, Samuel inherited his large, powerful, though not entirely healthy, body; and in his father's shop the boy gained an early interest in books.

When he was young, Samuel Johnson suffered from scrofula, a disease which disfigured his face and injured his eyesight. He was educated at Lichfield Grammar School and at Oxford, where he stayed from October, 1728, until December, 1729. For the next few years, Johnson made a meager living teaching, translating, and writing.

In 1735 he married a widow, Mrs. Elizabeth Porter, and set up a school at Edial, near Lichfield. The school failed and in 1737 he left for London, where he was to spend the rest of his life. During the next few years Johnson suffered poverty and enjoyed little success. He earned a living chiefly by writing for the *Gentleman's Magazine*.

In 1744 was published Johnson's *Life of Savage,* a biography of his friend Richard Savage; and his poem *The Vanity of Human Wishes* appeared in 1749. But it was the publication of Johnson's famous *Dictionary of the English Language* in 1755 that made his reputation. The *Dictionary* was an immediate success and was at once accepted as the standard authority. For two of the eight years he spent preparing the dictionary, Johnson supported himself in part by publishing a periodical, *The Rambler* (1750–52). Later, from 1758–60, he also published another periodical, *The Idler.*

In 1762 Johnson was given a government pension which made him financially independent. His remaining years were comparatively easy, but the death of his wife in 1752 had been a great blow to him, and Johnson was never free from the periods of deep depression which had plagued him throughout his life.

At meetings of The Literary Club, which Johnson helped found in 1764, his genius as a conversationalist was displayed. James Boswell recorded these conversations, as well as every quirk and peculiarity of the great man, so that we probably know more about Johnson than about any writer who ever lived.[1]

In 1765, Johnson brought out the long-awaited edition of Shakespeare's plays, which he had been promising for nearly ten years. In 1779–81 was published *Lives of the English Poets,* prefaces written for a large collection of English poetry. He died on December 13, 1784, and was buried in Westminster Abbey.

Shakespeare has been more studied, as well as more read and played, than any English dramatist. Dr. Johnson's critique, in the *Preface* that he wrote to his edition of the plays, reprinted below, is one of a long line of such works. Authors and editors had praised Shakespeare for a hundred years before Johnson's birth; and, of course, the flood of praise and criticism has continued unabated until our time. But there is reason to believe that Johnson's evaluation is the best general study of Shakespeare.

If it is not the best, it is certainly important to read today. Modern criticism of Shakespeare tends to ignore the main point of Johnson's critique. Much contemporary Shakespearean criticism seems to dehumanize Shakespeare, to treat him as difficult, strange, and recondite. It emphasizes the changes that his language has undergone, and points out the intricacy of his images. Doubtless such criticism is valuable. The complexities of Shakespeare should be observed and clarified. His uniquely involuted ironies and ambiguities should be understood.

---

[1] See his *Life of Samuel Johnson,* in *Great Books of the Western World,* Vol. 44.

Notes from the artist: "Johnson and, below, the ever-present Boswell, followed by a coffeehouse waitress, in a fantasy of Fleet Street, scene of some of Johnson's famous verbal jousts."

James Boswell

But one sometimes has the feeling that this criticism misses the forest for the trees. Johnson does not fail to see the forest; he is able to view, and to appreciate, Shakespeare as a whole.

"Nothing can please many," he writes, "and please long, but just representations of general nature." Shakespeare's characters, he goes on, "are not modified by the customs of particular places, unpractised by the rest of the world; by the peculiarities of studies or professions, which can operate but upon small numbers; or by the accidents of transient fashions or temporary opinions: they are the genuine progeny of common humanity, such as the world will always supply, and observation will always find."

"Shakespeare has no heroes," Johnson adds in a later place; "his scenes are occupied only by men who act and speak as the reader thinks that he should himself have spoken or acted on the same occasion."

"This therefore is the praise of Shakespeare," Johnson concludes, "that his drama is the mirror of life; that he who has mazed his imagination, in following the phantoms which other writers raise up before him, may here be cured of his delirious ecstasies, by reading human sentiments in human language, by scenes from which a hermit may estimate the transactions of the world, and a confessor predict the progress of the passions."

Johnson does not praise Shakespeare unreservedly. He has many criticisms which some modern readers consider carping: for example, that Shakespeare is sometimes morally slack, sometimes a poor storyteller, sometimes vulgar, sometimes ignorant, and that he too often indulges in punning. The reader of Johnson's *Preface* will have to decide for himself whether the things that Johnson takes exception to should be condemned or condoned. But he should not forget the chief point. Shakespeare's plays exhibit "the real state of sublunary nature," Johnson writes, "which partakes of good and evil, joy and sorrow, mingled with endless variety of proportion and innumerable modes of combination . . . in which, at the same time, the reveller is hasting to his wine, and the mourner burying his friend; in which the malignity of one is sometimes defeated by the frolic of another; and many mischiefs and many benefits are done and hindered without design."

Shakespeare is the poet of life as we all know it and always will know it. Johnson is saying—and do we wish to dispute him?—that this is the highest praise which can be accorded any artist.

Johnson's *Preface* is useful and interesting for other reasons. It talks sense about the theater, and it talks sense, too, about the business of criticism. The sympathetic reader will not fail to derive delight from Johnson's style. This is the "grand style," so rare in English. The sentences are long and often complex, but they move like stately music to a deeply satisfying close. The combination of Shakespeare and Johnson is a wonderful one.

Preface to Shakespeare

That praises are without reason lavished on the dead, and that the honours due only to excellence are paid to antiquity, is a complaint likely to be always continued by those who, being able to add nothing to truth, hope for eminence from the heresies of paradox; or those who, being forced by disappointment upon consolatory expedients, are willing to hope from posterity what the present age refuses, and flatter themselves that the regard which is yet denied by envy will be at last bestowed by time.

Antiquity, like every other quality that attracts the notice of mankind, has undoubtedly votaries that reverence it, not from reason, but from prejudice. Some seem to admire indiscriminately whatever has been long preserved, without considering that time has sometimes co-operated with chance; all perhaps are more willing to honour past than present excellence; and the mind contemplates genius through the shades of age, as the eye surveys the sun through artificial opacity. The great contention of criticism is to find the faults of the moderns, and the beauties of the ancients. While an author is yet living we estimate his powers by his worst performance, and when he is dead, we rate them by his best.

To works, however, of which the excellence is not absolute and definite, but gradual and comparative; to works not raised upon principles demonstrative and scientific, but appealing wholly to observation and experience, no other test can be applied than length of duration and continuance of esteem. What mankind have long possessed they have often examined and compared; and if they persist to value the possession, it is because frequent comparisons have confirmed opinion in its favour. As among the works of nature no man can properly call a river deep, or a mountain high, without the knowledge of many mountains, and many rivers; so in the productions of genius, nothing can be styled excellent till it has been compared with other works of the same kind. Demonstration immediately displays its power, and has nothing to hope or fear from the flux of years; but works tentative and experimental must be estimated by their proportion to the general and collective ability of man, as it is discovered in a long succession of endeavours. Of the first building that was raised, it might be with certainty determined that it was round or square; but whether it was spacious or lofty must have been referred to time. The Pythagorean scale of numbers was at once discovered to be perfect; but the poems of Homer we yet know not to transcend the common limits of human intelligence, but by remarking that nation after nation, and century after century, has been able to do little more than transpose his incidents, new-name his characters, and paraphrase his sentiments.

The reverence due to writings that have long subsisted arises therefore not from any credulous confidence in the superior wisdom of past ages, or gloomy persuasion of the degeneracy of mankind, but is the consequence of acknowledged and indubitable positions that what has been longest known has been most considered, and what is most considered is best understood.

The Poet, of whose works I have undertaken the revision, may now begin to assume the dignity of an ancient, and claim the privilege of established fame and prescriptive veneration. He has long outlived his century, the term commonly fixed as the test of literary merit. Whatever advantages he might once derive from personal allusions, local customs, or temporary opinions have for many years been lost; and every topic of merriment, or motive of sorrow, which the modes of artificial life afforded him, now only obscure the scenes which they once illuminated. The effects of favour and competition are at an end; the tradition of his friendships and his enmities has perished; his works support no opinion with arguments, nor supply any faction with invectives; they can neither indulge vanity nor gratify malignity; but are read without any other reason than the desire of pleasure, and are therefore praised only as pleasure is obtained; yet, thus unassisted by interest or passion, they have passed through variations of taste and changes of manners, and, as they devolved from one generation to another, have received new honours at every transmission.

But because human judgment, though it be gradually gaining upon certainty, never becomes infallible; and approbation, though long continued, may yet be only the approbation of prejudice or fashion; it is proper to enquire by what peculiarities of excellence Shakespeare has gained and kept the favour of his countrymen.

Nothing can please many, and please long, but just representations of general nature. Particular manners can be known to few, and therefore few only can judge how nearly they are copied. The irregular combinations of fanciful invention may delight awhile, by that novelty of which the common satiety of life sends us all in quest; but the pleasures of sudden wonder are soon exhausted, and the mind can only repose on the stability of truth.

Shakespeare is above all writers, at least above all modern writers, the poet of nature; the poet that holds up to his readers a faithful mirror of manners and of life. His characters are not modified by the customs of particular places, unpractised by the rest of the world; by the peculiarities of studies or professions, which can operate but upon small numbers; or by the accidents of transient fashions or temporary opinions: they are the genuine progeny of common humanity, such as the world will always supply, and observation will always find. His persons act and speak by the influence of those general passions and principles by which all minds are agitated, and the whole system of life is continued in motion. In the writings of other poets a character is too often an individual; in those of Shakespeare it is commonly a species.

It is from this wide extension of design that so much instruction is derived. It is this which fills the plays of Shakespeare with practical axioms and domestic wisdom. It was said of Euripides that every verse was a precept; and it may be said of Shakespeare that from his works may be collected a system of civil and economical prudence. Yet his real power is not shown in the splendour of particular passages, but by the progress of his fable, and the tenor of his dialogue; and he that tries to recommend him by select quotations will succeed like the pedant in Hierocles, who, when he offered his house to sale, carried a brick in his pocket as a specimen.

It will not easily be imagined how much Shakespeare excels in accommodating his sentiments to real life but by comparing him with other authors. It was observed of the ancient schools of declamation that the more diligently they were frequented, the more was the student disqualified for the world, because he found nothing there which he should ever meet in any other place. The same remark may be applied to every stage but that of Shakespeare. The theatre, when it is under any other direction, is peopled by such characters as were never seen, conversing, in a language which was never heard, upon topics which will never arise in the commerce of mankind. But the dialogue of this author is often so evidently determined by the incident which produces it, and is pursued with so much ease and simplicity, that it seems scarcely to claim the merit of fiction, but to have been gleaned by diligent selection out of common conversation, and common occurrences.

Upon every other stage the universal agent is love, by whose power all good and evil is distributed, and every action quickened or retarded. To bring a lover, a lady and a rival into the fable; to entangle them in contradictory obligations, perplex them with oppositions of interest, and harass them with violence of desires inconsistent with each other; to make them meet in rapture and part in agony; to fill their mouths with hyperbolical joy and outrageous sorrow; to distress them as nothing human ever was distressed; to deliver them as nothing human ever was delivered is the business of a modern dramatist. For this probability is violated, life is misrepresented, and language is depraved. But love is only one of many passions; and as it has no great influence upon the sum of life, it has little operation in the dramas of a poet who caught his ideas from the living world, and exhibited only what he saw before him. He knew that any other passion, as it was regular or exorbitant, was a cause of happiness or calamity.

Characters thus ample and general were not easily discriminated and preserved, yet perhaps no poet ever kept his personages more distinct from each other. I will not say with Pope that every speech may be assigned to the proper speaker, because many speeches there are which have nothing characteristical; but perhaps, though some may be equally adapted to every person, it will be difficult to find any that can be properly transferred from the present possessor to another claimant. The choice is right when there is reason for choice.

Other dramatists can only gain attention by hyperbolical or aggravated characters, by fabulous and unexampled excellence or depravity, as the writers of barbarous romances invigorated the reader by a giant and a dwarf; and he that should form his expectations of human affairs from the play, or from the tale, would be equally deceived. Shakespeare has no heroes; his scenes are occupied only by men who act and speak as the reader thinks that he should himself have spoken or acted on the same occasion: Even where the agency is supernatural the dialogue is level with life. Other writers disguise the most natural passions and most frequent incidents; so that he who contemplates them in the book will not know them in the world: Shakespeare approximates the remote, and familiarizes the wonderful; the event which he represents will not happen, but if it were possible, its effects would probably be such as he has assigned; and it may be said that he has not only shown human nature as it acts in real exigencies but as it would be found in trials to which it cannot be exposed.

This therefore is the praise of Shakespeare, that his drama is the mirror of life; that he who has mazed his imagination, in following the phantoms which other writers raise up before him, may here be cured of his delirious ecstasies, by reading human sentiments in human language, by scenes from which a hermit may estimate the transactions of the world, and a confessor predict the progress of the passions.

His adherence to general nature has exposed him to the censure of critics, who form their judgments upon narrower principles. Dennis and Rhymer think his Romans not sufficiently Roman; and Voltaire censures his kings as not completely royal. Dennis is offended that Menenius, a senator of Rome, should play the buffoon; and Voltaire perhaps thinks decency violated when the Danish Usurper is represented as a drunkard. But Shakespeare always makes nature predominate over accident; and if he preserves the essential character, is not very careful of distinctions superinduced and adventitious. His story requires Romans or kings, but he thinks only on men. He knew that Rome, like every other city, had men of all dispositions; and wanting a buffoon, he went into the senate-house for that which the senate-house would certainly have afforded him. He was inclined to show a usurper and a murderer not only odious but despicable; he therefore added drunkenness to his other qualities, knowing that kings love wine like other men, and that wine exerts its natural power upon kings. These are the petty cavils of petty minds; a poet overlooks the casual distinction of country and condition, as a painter, satisfied with the figure, neglects the drapery.

The censure which he has incurred by mixing comic and tragic scenes, as it extends to all his works, deserves more consideration. Let the fact be first stated, and then examined.

Shakespeare's plays are not in the rigorous and critical sense either tragedies or comedies, but compositions of a distinct kind; exhibiting the real state of sublunary nature, which partakes of good and evil, joy and sorrow, mingled with endless variety of proportion and innumerable modes of combination; and expressing the course of the world, in which the loss of one is the gain of another; in which, at the same time, the reveller is hasting to his wine, and the mourner burying his friend; in which the malignity of one is sometimes defeated by the frolic of another; and many mischiefs and many benefits are done and hindered without design.

Out of this chaos of mingled purposes and casualties the ancient poets, according to the laws which custom had prescribed, selected: some the crimes of men, and some their absurdities; some the momentous vicissitudes of life, and some the lighter occurrences; some the terrors of distress, and some the gaieties of prosperity. Thus rose the two modes of imitation, known by the names of tragedy and comedy, compositions intended to promote different ends by contrary means, and considered as so little allied that I do not recollect among the Greeks or Romans a single writer who attempted both.

Shakespeare has united the powers of exciting laughter and sorrow not only in one mind, but in one composition. Almost all his plays are divided between serious and ludicrous characters, and, in the successive evolutions of the design, sometimes produce seriousness and sorrow, and sometimes levity and laughter.

That this is a practice contrary to the rules of criticism will be readily allowed; but there is always an appeal open from criticism to nature. The end of writing is to instruct; the end of poetry is to instruct by pleasing. That the mingled drama may convey all the instruction of tragedy or comedy cannot be denied, because it includes both in its alternations of exhibition and approaches nearer than either to the appearance of life, by showing how great machinations and slender designs may promote or obviate one another, and the high and the low co-operate in the general system by unavoidable concatenation.

It is objected that by this change of scenes the passions are interrupted in their progression, and that the principal event, being not advanced by a due gradation of preparatory incidents, wants at last the power to move, which constitutes the perfection of dramatic poetry. This reasoning is so specious that it is received as true even by those who in daily experience feel it to be false. The interchanges of mingled scenes seldom fail to produce the intended vicissitudes of passion. Fiction cannot move so much but that the attention may be easily transferred; and though it must be allowed that pleasing melancholy be sometimes interrupted by unwelcome levity, yet let it be considered likewise that melancholy is often not pleasing, and that the disturbance of one man may be the relief of another; that different auditors have different habitudes; and that, upon the whole, all pleasure consists in variety.

The players, who in their edition divided our author's works into comedies, histories, and tragedies, seem not to have distinguished the three kinds by any very exact or definite ideas.

An action which ended happily to the principal persons, however serious or distressful through its intermediate incidents, in their opinion constituted a comedy. This idea of a comedy continued long amongst us; and plays were written, which, by changing the catastrophe, were trage- dies to-day, and comedies to-morrow.

Tragedy was not in those times a poem of more general dignity or elevation than comedy; it required only a calamitous conclusion, with which the common criticism of that age was satisfied, whatever lighter pleasure it afforded in its progress.

History was a series of actions, with no other than chronological suc- cession, independent on each other, and without any tendency to intro- duce or regulate the conclusion. It is not always very nicely distinguished from tragedy. There is not much nearer approach to unity of action in the tragedy of Antony and Cleopatra than in the history of Richard the Second. But a history might be continued through many plays; as it had no plan, it had no limits.

Through all these denominations of the drama, Shakespeare's mode of composition is the same; an interchange of seriousness and merriment, by which the mind is softened at one time, and exhilarated at another. But whatever be his purpose, whether to gladden or depress, or to conduct the story, without vehemence or emotion, through tracts of easy and fa- miliar dialogue, he never fails to attain his purpose; as he commands us, we laugh or mourn, or sit silent with quiet expectation, in tranquillity without indifference.

When Shakespeare's plan is understood, most of the criticisms of Rhymer and Voltaire vanish away. The play of Hamlet is opened, with- out impropriety, by two sentinels; Iago bellows at Brabantio's window, without injury to the scheme of the play, though in terms which a modern audience would not easily endure; the character of Polonius is seasonable and useful; and the Grave-diggers themselves may be heard with ap- plause.

Shakespeare engaged in dramatic poetry with the world open before him; the rules of the ancients were yet known to few; the public judg- ment was unformed; he had no example of such fame as might force him upon imitation, nor critics of such authority as might restrain his extrava- gance: He therefore indulged his natural disposition, and his disposition, as Rhymer has remarked, led him to comedy. In tragedy he often writes, with great appearance of toil and study, what is written at last with little felicity; but in his comic scenes, he seems to produce without labour what no labour can improve. In tragedy he is always struggling after some occasion to be comic; but in comedy he seems to repose, or to luxuriate, as in a mode of thinking congenial to his nature. In his tragic scenes there is always something wanting, but his comedy often surpasses expectation or desire. His comedy pleases by the thoughts and the language, and his tragedy for the greater part by incident and action. His tragedy seems to be skill, his comedy to be instinct.

The force of his comic scenes has suffered little diminution from the changes made by a century and a half, in manners or in words. As his personages act upon principles arising from genuine passion, very little modified by particular forms, their pleasures and vexations are communicable to all times and to all places; they are natural, and therefore durable; the adventitious peculiarities of personal habits are only superficial dies, bright and pleasing for a little while, yet soon fading to a dim tinct, without any remains of former lustre; but the discriminations of true passion are the colours of nature; they pervade the whole mass, and can only perish with the body that exhibits them. The accidental compositions of heterogeneous modes are dissolved by the chance which combined them; but the uniform simplicity of primitive qualities neither admits increase, nor suffers decay. The sand heaped by one flood is scattered by another, but the rock always continues in its place. The stream of time, which is continually washing the dissoluble fabrics of other poets, passes without injury by the adamant of Shakespeare.

If there be, what I believe there is, in every nation, a style which never becomes obsolete, a certain mode of phraseology so consonant and congenial to the analogy and principles of its respective language as to remain settled and unaltered; this style is probably to be sought in the common intercourse of life, among those who speak only to be understood, without ambition of elegance. The polite are always catching modish innovations, and the learned depart from established forms of speech, in hope of finding or making better; those who wish for distinction forsake the vulgar, when the vulgar is right; but there is a conversation above grossness and below refinement, where propriety resides, and where this poet seems to have gathered his comic dialogue. He is therefore more agreeable to the ears of the present age than any other author equally remote, and among his other excellencies deserves to be studied as one of the original masters of our language.

These observations are to be considered not as unexceptionably constant, but as containing general and predominant truth. Shakespeare's familiar dialogue is affirmed to be smooth and clear, yet not wholly without ruggedness or difficulty; as a country may be eminently fruitful, though it has spots unfit for cultivation: His characters are praised as natural, though their sentiments are sometimes forced, and their actions improbable; as the earth upon the whole is spherical, though its surface is varied with protuberances and cavities.

Shakespeare with his excellencies has likewise faults, and faults sufficient to obscure and overwhelm any other merit. I shall show them in the proportion in which they appear to me, without envious malignity or superstitious veneration. No question can be more innocently discussed than a dead poet's pretensions to renown; and little regard is due to that bigotry which sets candour higher than truth.

His first defect is that to which may be imputed most of the evil in books or in men. He sacrifices virtue to convenience, and is so much more careful to please than to instruct that he seems to write without any moral purpose. From his writings indeed a system of social duty may be selected, for he that thinks reasonably must think morally; but his precepts and axioms drop casually from him; he makes no just distribution of good or evil, nor is always careful to show in the virtuous a disapprobation of the wicked; he carries his persons indifferently through right and wrong, and at the close dismisses them without further care, and leaves their examples to operate by chance. This fault the barbarity of his age cannot extenuate; for it is always a writer's duty to make the world better, and justice is a virtue independent on time or place.

The plots are often so loosely formed that a very slight consideration may improve them, and so carelessly pursued that he seems not always fully to comprehend his own design. He omits opportunities of instructing or delighting which the train of his story seems to force upon him, and apparently rejects those exhibitions which would be more affecting, for the sake of those which are more easy.

It may be observed that in many of his plays the latter part is evidently neglected. When he found himself near the end of his work, and, in view of his reward, he shortened the labour to snatch the profit. He therefore remits his efforts where he should most vigorously exert them, and his catastrophe is improbably produced or imperfectly represented.

He had no regard to distinction of time or place, but gives to one age or nation, without scruple, the customs, institutions, and opinions of another, at the expense not only of likelihood but of possibility. These faults Pope has endeavoured, with more zeal than judgment, to transfer to his imagined interpolators. We need not wonder to find Hector quoting Aristotle, when we see the loves of Theseus and Hippolyta combined with the Gothic mythology of fairies. Shakespeare, indeed, was not the only violator of chronology, for in the same age Sidney, who wanted not the advantages of learning, has, in his *Arcadia*, confounded the pastoral with the feudal times, the days of innocence, quiet and security, with those of turbulence, violence, and adventure.

In his comic scenes he is seldom very successful when he engages his characters in reciprocations of smartness and contests of sarcasm; their jests are commonly gross, and their pleasantry licentious; neither his gentlemen nor his ladies have much delicacy, nor are sufficiently distinguished from his clowns by any appearance of refined manners. Whether he represented the real conversation of his time is not easy to determine; the reign of Elizabeth is commonly supposed to have been a time of stateliness, formality and reserve; yet perhaps the relaxations of that severity were not very elegant. There must, however, have been always some modes of gaiety preferable to others, and a writer ought to choose the best.

In tragedy his performance seems constantly to be worse, as his labour is more. The effusions of passion which exigence forces out are for the most part striking and energetic; but whenever he solicits his invention, or strains his faculties, the offspring of his throes is tumour, meanness, tediousness, and obscurity.

In narration he affects a disproportionate pomp of diction, and a wearisome train of circumlocution, and tells the incident imperfectly in many words, which might have been more plainly delivered in few. Narration in dramatic poetry is naturally tedious, as it is unanimated and inactive, and obstructs the progress of the action; it should therefore always be rapid, and enlivened by frequent interruption. Shakespeare found it an encumbrance, and instead of lightening it by brevity, endeavoured to recommend it by dignity and splendour.

His declamations or set speeches are commonly cold and weak, for his power was the power of nature; when he endeavoured, like other tragic writers, to catch opportunities of amplification, and instead of enquiring what the occasion demanded, to show how much his stores of knowledge could supply, he seldom escapes without the pity or resentment of his reader.

It is incident to him to be now and then entangled with an unwieldy sentiment, which he cannot well express, and will not reject; he struggles with it awhile, and if it continues stubborn, comprises it in words such as occur, and leaves it to be disentangled and evolved by those who have more leisure to bestow upon it.

Not that always where the language is intricate the thought is subtle, or the image always great where the line is bulky; the equality of words to things is very often neglected, and trivial sentiments and vulgar ideas disappoint the attention, to which they are recommended by sonorous epithets and swelling figures.

But the admirers of this great poet have never less reason to indulge their hopes of supreme excellence than when he seems fully resolved to sink them in dejection, and mollify them with tender emotions by the fall of greatness, the danger of innocence, or the crosses of love. He is not long soft and pathetic without some idle conceit, or contemptible equivocation. He no sooner begins to move than he counteracts himself; and terror and pity, as they are rising in the mind, are checked and blasted by sudden frigidity.

A quibble is to Shakespeare what luminous vapours are to the traveller; he follows it at all adventures; it is sure to lead him out of his way, and sure to engulf him in the mire. It has some malignant power over his mind, and its fascinations are irresistible. Whatever be the dignity or profundity of his disquisition, whether he be enlarging knowledge or exalting affection, whether he be amusing attention with incidents, or enchaining it in suspense, let but a quibble spring up before him, and he leaves his work unfinished. A quibble is the golden apple for which he will always turn aside from his career, or stoop from his elevation. A quibble, poor and barren as it is, gave him such delight that he was content to purchase it, by the sacrifice of reason, propriety and truth. A quibble was to him the fatal Cleopatra for which he lost the world, and was content to lose it.

It will be thought strange that, in enumerating the defects of this writer, I have not yet mentioned his neglect of the unities; his violation of those laws which have been instituted and established by the joint authority of poets and of critics.

For his other deviations from the art of writing I resign him to critical justice, without making any other demand in his favour than that which must be indulged to all human excellence: that his virtues be rated with his failings: But, from the censure which this irregularity may bring upon him, I shall, with due reverence to that learning which I must oppose, adventure to try how I can defend him.

His histories, being neither tragedies nor comedies, are not subject to any of their laws; nothing more is necessary to all the praise which they expect than that the changes of action be so prepared as to be understood, that the incidents be various and affecting, and the characters consistent, natural, and distinct. No other unity is intended, and therefore none is to be sought.

In his other works he has well enough preserved the unity of action. He has not, indeed, an intrigue regularly perplexed and regularly unravelled: he does not endeavour to hide his design only to discover it, for this is seldom the order of real events, and Shakespeare is the poet of nature: But his plan has commonly what Aristotle requires, a beginning, a middle, and an end; one event is concatenated with another, and the conclusion follows by easy consequence. There are perhaps some incidents that might be spared, as in other poets there is much talk that only fills up time upon the stage; but the general system makes gradual advances, and the end of the play is the end of expectation.

To the unities of time and place he has shown no regard; and perhaps a nearer view of the principles on which they stand will diminish their value, and withdraw from them the veneration which, from the time of Corneille, they have very generally received, by discovering that they have given more trouble to the poet than pleasure to the auditor.

The necessity of observing the unities of time and place arises from the supposed necessity of making the drama credible. The critics hold it impossible that an action of months or years can be possibly believed to pass in three hours; or that the spectator can suppose himself to sit in the theatre, while ambassadors go and return between distant kings, while armies are levied and towns besieged, while an exile wanders and returns, or till he whom they saw courting his mistress, shall lament the untimely fall of his son. The mind revolts from evident falsehood, and fiction loses its force when it departs from the resemblance of reality.

From the narrow limitation of time necessarily arises the contraction of place. The spectator, who knows that he saw the first act at Alexandria, cannot suppose that he sees the next at Rome, at a distance to which not the dragons of Medea could, in so short a time, have transported him; he knows with certainty that he has not changed his place, and he knows that place cannot change itself; that what was a house cannot become a plain; that what was Thebes can never be Persepolis.

Such is the triumphant language with which a critic exults over the misery of an irregular poet, and exults commonly without resistance or reply. It is time therefore to tell him by the authority of Shakespeare that he assumes, as an unquestionable principle, a position which, while his breath is forming it into words, his understanding pronounces to be false. It is false that any representation is mistaken for reality; that any dramatic fable in its materiality was ever credible, or, for a single moment, was ever credited.

The objection arising from the impossibility of passing the first hour at

Alexandria, and the next at Rome, supposes that when the play opens, the spectator really imagines himself at Alexandria, and believes that his walk to the theatre has been a voyage to Egypt, and that he lives in the days of Antony and Cleopatra. Surely he that imagines this may imagine more. He that can take the stage at one time for the palace of the Ptolemies may take it in half an hour for the promontory of Actium. Delusion, if delusion be admitted, has no certain limitation; if the spectator can be once persuaded that his old acquaintances are Alexander and Caesar, that a room illuminated with candles is the plain of Pharsalia, or the bank of Granicus, he is in a state of elevation above the reach of reason, or of truth, and from the heights of empyrean poetry, may despise the circumscriptions of terrestrial nature. There is no reason why a mind thus wandering in ecstasy should count the clock, or why an hour should not be a century in that calenture of the brains that can make the stage a field.

The truth is that the spectators are always in their senses, and know, from the first act to the last, that the stage is only a stage, and that the players are only players. They came to hear a certain number of lines recited with just gesture and elegant modulation. The lines relate to some action, and an action must be in some place; but the different actions that complete a story may be in places very remote from each other; and where is the absurdity of allowing that space to represent first Athens, and then Sicily which was always known to be neither Sicily nor Athens, but a modern theatre?

By supposition, as place is introduced, time may be extended; the time required by the fable elapses for the most part between the acts; for, of so much of the action as is represented, the real and poetical duration is the same. If, in the first act, preparations for war against Mithridates are represented to be made in Rome, the event of the war may, without absurdity, be represented, in the catastrophe, as happening in Pontus; we know that there is neither war, nor preparation for war; we know that we are neither in Rome nor Pontus; that neither Mithridates nor Lucullus are before us. The drama exhibits successive imitations of successive actions; and why may not the second imitation represent an action that happened years after the first, if it be so connected with it that nothing but time can be supposed to intervene? Time is, of all modes of existence, most obsequious to the imagination; a lapse of years is as easily conceived as a passage of hours. In contemplation we easily contract the time of real actions, and therefore willingly permit it to be contracted when we only see their imitation.

It will be asked how the drama moves if it is not credited. It is credited with all the credit due to a drama. It is credited, whenever it moves, as a just picture of a real original; as representing to the auditor what he would himself feel if he were to do or suffer what is there feigned to be suffered or to be done. The reflection that strikes the heart is not that the evils before us are real evils but that they are evils to which we ourselves may be exposed. If there be any fallacy, it is not that we fancy the players, but that we fancy ourselves unhappy for a moment; but we rather lament the possibility than suppose the presence of misery, as a mother weeps over her babe when she remembers that death may take it from her. The delight of tragedy proceeds from our consciousness of fiction; if we thought murders and treasons real, they would please no more.

Imitations produce pain or pleasure, not because they are mistaken for realities, but because they bring realities to mind. When the imagination is recreated by a painted landscape, the trees are not supposed capable to give us shade, or the fountains coolness; but we consider how we should be pleased with such fountains playing beside us, and such woods waving over us. We are agitated in reading the history of Henry V, yet no man takes his book for the field of Agincourt. A dramatic exhibition is a book recited with concomitants that increase or diminish its effect. Familiar comedy is often more powerful on the theatre, than in the page; imperial tragedy is always less. The humour of Petruchio may be heightened by grimace; but what voice or what gesture can hope to add dignity or force to the soliloquy of Cato.

A play read affects the mind like a play acted. It is therefore evident that the action is not supposed to be real; and it follows that between the acts a longer or shorter time may be allowed to pass, and that no more account of space or duration is to be taken by the auditor of a drama than by the reader of a narrative, before whom may pass in an hour the life of a hero, or the revolutions of an empire.

Whether Shakespeare knew the unities, and rejected them by design, or deviated from them by happy ignorance, it is, I think, impossible to decide, and useless to enquire. We may reasonably suppose that, when he rose to notice, he did not want the counsels and admonitions of scholars and critics, and that he at last deliberately persisted in a practice which he might have begun by chance. As nothing is essential to the fable but unity of action, and as the unities of time and place arise evidently from false assumptions, and, by circumscribing the extent of the drama, lessen its variety, I cannot think it much to be lamented that they were not

known by him, or not observed: Nor, if such another poet could arise,
should I very vehemently reproach him that his first act passed at
Venice, and his next in Cyprus. Such violations of rules merely positive
become the comprehensive genius of Shakespeare, and such censures are
suitable to the minute and slender criticism of Voltaire:

> *Non usque adeo permiscuit imis*
> *Longus summa dies, ut non, si voce Metelli*
> *Serventur leges, malint a Caesare tolli.*

[Not so far had that long day mixed high with
low that the laws might not rather be broken
by Caesar than kept by Metellus' word.]

Yet when I speak thus slightly of dramatic rules, I cannot but recollect
how much wit and learning may be produced against me; before such
authorities I am afraid to stand, not that I think the present question one
of those that are to be decided by mere authority, but because it is to be
suspected that these precepts have not been so easily received but for
better reasons than I have yet been able to find. The result of my enquiries, in which it would be ludicrous to boast of impartiality, is that the
unities of time and place are not essential to a just drama, that though
they may sometimes conduce to pleasure, they are always to be sacrificed to the nobler beauties of variety and instruction; and that a play,
written with nice observation of critical rules, is to be contemplated as an
elaborate curiosity, as the product of superfluous and ostentatious art, by
which is shown rather what is possible than what is necessary.

He that, without diminution of any other excellence, shall preserve all
the unities unbroken deserves the like applause with the architect who
shall display all the orders of architecture in a citadel without any deduction from its strength; but the principal beauty of a citadel is to exclude the enemy; and the greatest graces of a play are to copy nature and
instruct life.

Perhaps, what I have here not dogmatically but deliberately written
may recall the principles of the drama to a new examination. I am almost
frighted at my own temerity; and when I estimate the fame and the
strength of those that maintain the contrary opinion, am ready to sink
down in reverential silence; as Aeneas withdrew from the defence of
Troy when he saw Neptune shaking the wall, and Juno heading the
besiegers.

Those whom my arguments cannot persuade to give their approbation to the judgment of Shakespeare will easily, if they consider the condition of his life, make some allowance for his ignorance.

Every man's performances, to be rightly estimated, must be compared with the state of the age in which he lived, and with his own particular opportunities; and though to the reader a book be not worse or better for the circumstances of the author, yet as there is always a silent reference of human works to human abilities, and as the enquiry how far man may extend his designs, or how high he may rate his native force, is of far greater dignity than in what rank we shall place any particular perform-ance, curiosity is always busy to discover the instruments, as well as to survey the workmanship, to know how much is to be ascribed to original powers, and how much to casual and adventitious help. The palaces of Peru or Mexico were certainly mean and incommodious habitations if compared to the houses of European monarchs; yet who could forbear to view them with astonishment who remembered that they were built without the use of iron?

The English nation in the time of Shakespeare was yet struggling to emerge from barbarity. The philology of Italy had been transplanted hither in the reign of Henry VIII; and the learned languages had been successfully cultivated by Lilly, Linacre, and More; by Pole, Cheke, and Gardiner; and afterwards by Smith, Clerk, Haddon, and Ascham. Greek was now taught to boys in the principal schools; and those who united elegance with learning read, with great diligence, the Italian and Spanish poets. But literature was yet confined to professed scholars, or to men and women of high rank. The public was gross and dark; and to be able to read and write was an accomplishment still valued for its rarity.

Nations, like individuals, have their infancy. A people newly awakened to literary curiosity, being yet unacquainted with the true state of things, knows not how to judge of that which is proposed as its resem-blance. Whatever is remote from common appearances is always wel-come to vulgar, as to childish, credulity; and of a country unenlightened by learning, the whole people is the vulgar. The study of those who then aspired to plebeian learning was laid out upon adventures, giants, dragons, and enchantments. *The Death of Arthur* was the favourite vol-ume.

The mind, which has feasted on the luxurious wonders of fiction, has no taste of the insipidity of truth. A play which imitated only the common occurrences of the world would, upon the admirers of Palmerin and Guy of Warwick, have made little impression; he that wrote for such an audi-ence was under the necessity of looking round for strange events and fabulous transactions, and that incredibility by which maturer knowledge is offended was the chief recommendation of writings to unskilful curiosity.

Our author's plots are generally borrowed from novels, and it is reasonable to suppose that he chose the most popular, such as were read by many, and related by more; for his audience could not have followed him through the intricacies of the drama had they not held the thread of the story in their hands.

The stories, which we now find only in remoter authors, were in his time accessible and familiar. The fable of *As You Like It*, which is supposed to be copied from Chaucer's Gamelyn, was a little pamphlet of those times; and old Mr. Cibber remembered the tale of Hamlet in plain English prose, which the critics have now to seek in Saxo Grammaticus.

His English histories he took from English chronicles and English ballads; and as the ancient writers were made known to his countrymen by versions, they supplied him with new subjects; he dilated some of Plutarch's lives into plays, when they had been translated by North.

His plots, whether historical or fabulous, are always crowded with incidents, by which the attention of a rude people was more easily caught than by sentiment or argumentation; and such is the power of the marvellous even over those who despise it that every man finds his mind more strongly seized by the tragedies of Shakespeare than of any other writer; others please us by particular speeches, but he always makes us anxious for the event, and has perhaps excelled all but Homer in securing the first purpose of a writer, by exciting restless and unquenchable curiosity and compelling him that reads his work to read it through.

The shows and bustle with which his plays abound have the same original. As knowledge advances, pleasure passes from the eye to the ear, but returns, as it declines, from the ear to the eye. Those to whom our author's labours were exhibited had more skill in pomps or processions than in poetical language, and perhaps wanted some visible and discriminated events, as comments on the dialogue. He knew how he should most please; and whether his practice is more agreeable to nature, or whether his example has prejudiced the nation, we still find that on our stage something must be done as well as said, and inactive declamation is very coldly heard, however musical or elegant, passionate or sublime.

Voltaire expresses his wonder that our author's extravagances are endured by a nation which has seen the tragedy of Cato. Let him be answered that Addison speaks the language of poets, and Shakespeare, of men. We find in Cato innumerable beauties which enamour us of its author, but we see nothing that acquaints us with human sentiments or human actions; we place it with the fairest and the noblest progeny which judgment propagates by conjunction with learning, but Othello is the vigorous and vivacious offspring of observation impregnated by genius. Cato affords a splendid exhibition of artificial and fictitious manners, and delivers just and noble sentiments, in diction easy, elevated and harmonious, but its hopes and fears communicate no vibration to the heart; the composition refers us only to the writer; we pronounce the name of Cato, but we think on Addison.

The work of a correct and regular writer is a garden accurately formed and diligently planted, varied with shades, and scented with flowers; the composition of Shakespeare is a forest, in which oaks extend their branches, and pines tower in the air, interspersed sometimes with weeds and brambles, and sometimes giving shelter to myrtles and to roses; filling the eye with awful pomp, and gratifying the mind with endless diversity. Other poets display cabinets of precious rarities, minutely finished, wrought into shape, and polished unto brightness. Shakespeare opens a mine which contains gold and diamonds in unexhaustible plenty, though clouded by incrustations, debased by impurities, and mingled with a mass of meaner minerals.

It has been much disputed whether Shakespeare owed his excellence to his own native force, or whether he had the common helps of scholastic education, the precepts of critical science, and the examples of ancient authors.

There has always prevailed a tradition that Shakespeare wanted learning, that he had no regular education, nor much skill in the dead languages. Jonson, his friend, affirms, that he had small Latin, and no Greek; who, besides that he had no imaginable temptation to falsehood, wrote at a time when the character and acquisitions of Shakespeare were known to multitudes. His evidence ought therefore to decide the controversy, unless some testimony of equal force could be opposed.

Some have imagined that they have discovered deep learning in many imitations of old writers; but the examples which I have known urged were drawn from books translated in his time; or were such easy coincidences of thought, as will happen to all who consider the same subjects; or such remarks on life or axioms of morality as float in conversation, and are transmitted through the world in proverbial sentences.

I have found it remarked that in this important sentence, "Go before, I'll follow," we read a translation of, *I prae, sequar*. I have been told that when Caliban, after a pleasing dream, says, "I cry'd to sleep again," the author imitates Anacreon, who had, like every other man, the same wish on the same occasion.

There are a few passages which may pass for imitations, but so few that the exception only confirms the rule; he obtained them from accidental quotations, or by oral communication, and as he used what he had, would have used more if he had obtained it.

The *Comedy of Errors* is confessedly taken from the *Menaechmi* of Plautus; from the only play of Plautus which was then in English. What can be more probable than that he who copied that would have copied more; but that those which were not translated were inaccessible?

Whether he knew the modern languages is uncertain. That his plays have some French scenes proves but little; he might easily procure them to be written, and probably, even though he had known the language in the common degree, he could not have written it without assistance. In the story of Romeo and Juliet he is observed to have followed the English translation where it deviates from the Italian; but this on the other part proves nothing against his knowledge of the original. He was to copy, not what he knew himself, but what was known to his audience.

It is most likely that he had learned Latin sufficiently to make him acquainted with construction, but that he never advanced to an easy perusal of the Roman authors. Concerning his skill in modern languages, I can find no sufficient ground of determination; but as no imitations of French or Italian authors have been discovered, though the Italian poetry was then high in esteem, I am inclined to believe that he read little more than English, and chose for his fables only such tales as he found translated.

That much knowledge is scattered over his works is very justly observed by Pope, but it is often such knowledge as books did not supply. He that will understand Shakespeare must not be content to study him in the closet; he must look for his meaning sometimes among the sports of the field, and sometimes among the manufactures of the shop.

There is however proof enough that he was a very diligent reader, nor was our language then so indigent of books but that he might very liberally indulge his curiosity without excursion into foreign literature. Many of the Roman authors were translated, and some of the Greek; the Reformation had filled the kingdom with theological learning; most of the topics of human disquisition had found English writers; and poetry had been cultivated, not only with diligence, but success. This was a stock of knowledge sufficient for a mind so capable of appropriating and improving it.

But the greater part of his excellence was the product of his own genius. He found the English stage in a state of the utmost rudeness; no essays either in tragedy or comedy had appeared, from which it could be discovered to what degree of delight either one or other might be carried. Neither character nor dialogue were yet understood. Shakespeare may be truly said to have introduced them both amongst us, and in some of his happier scenes to have carried them both to the utmost height.

By what gradations of improvement he proceeded is not easily known; for the chronology of his works is yet unsettled. Rowe is of opinion, that "perhaps we are not to look for his beginning, like those of other writers, in his least perfect works; art had so little, and nature so large, a share in what he did that for ought I know," says he, "the performances of his youth, as they were the most vigorous, were the best." But the power of nature is only the power of using to any certain purpose the materials which diligence procures, or opportunity supplies. Nature gives no man knowledge, and when images are collected by study and experience, can only assist in combining or applying them. Shakespeare, however favoured by nature, could impart only what he had learned; and as he must increase his ideas, like other mortals, by gradual acquisition, he, like them, grew wiser as he grew older, could display life better, as he knew it more, and instruct with more efficacy, as he was himself more amply instructed.

There is a vigilance of observation and accuracy of distinction which books and precepts cannot confer; from this almost all original and native excellence proceeds. Shakespeare must have looked upon mankind with perspicacity, in the highest degree curious and attentive. Other writers borrow their characters from preceding writers, and diversify them only by the accidental appendages of present manners; the dress is a little varied, but the body is the same. Our author had both matter and form to provide; for except the characters of Chaucer, to whom I think he is not much indebted, there were no writers in English, and perhaps not many in other modern languages, which showed life in its native colours.

The contest about the original benevolence or malignity of man had not yet commenced. Speculation had not yet attempted to analyse the mind, to trace the passions to their sources, to unfold the seminal principles of vice and virtue, or sound the depths of the heart for the motives of action. All those enquiries which from that time that human nature became the fashionable study have been made sometimes with nice discernment but often with idle subtilty were yet unattempted. The tales, with which the infancy of learning was satisfied, exhibited only the superficial appearances of action, related the events but omitted the causes, and were formed for such as delighted in wonders rather than in truth. Mankind was not then to be studied in the closet; he that would know the world was under the necessity of gleaning his own remarks, by mingling as he could in its business and amusements.

Boyle congratulated himself upon his high birth, because it favoured his curiosity, by facilitating his access. Shakespeare had no such advantage; he came to London a needy adventurer, and lived for a time by very mean employments. Many works of genius and learning have been performed in states of life that appear very little favourable to thought or to enquiry; so many that he who considers them is inclined to think that he sees enterprise and perseverance predominating over all external agency, and bidding help and hindrance vanish before them. The genius of Shakespeare was not to be depressed by the weight of poverty, nor limited by the narrow conversation to which men in want are inevitably condemned; the incumbrances of his fortune were shaken from his mind, "as dewdrops from a lion's mane."

Though he had so many difficulties to encounter, and so little assistance to surmount them, he has been able to obtain an exact knowledge of many modes of life, and many casts of native dispositions; to vary them with great multiplicity; to mark them by nice distinctions; and to show them in full view by proper combinations. In this part of his performances he had none to imitate, but has himself been imitated by all succeeding writers; and it may be doubted whether from all his successors more maxims of theoretical knowledge, or more rules of practical prudence, can be collected than he alone has given to his country.

Nor was his attention confined to the actions of men; he was an exact surveyor of the inanimate world; his descriptions have always some peculiarities, gathered by contemplating things as they really exist. It may be observed that the oldest poets of many nations preserve their reputation, and that the following generations of wit, after a short celebrity, sink into oblivion. The first, whoever they be, must take their sentiments and descriptions immediately from knowledge; the resemblance is therefore just, their descriptions are verified by every eye, and their sentiments acknowledged by every breast. Those whom their fame invites to the same studies copy partly them, and partly nature, till the books of one age gain such authority as to stand in the place of nature to another, and imitation, always deviating a little, becomes at last capricious and casual. Shakespeare, whether life or nature be his subject, shows plainly that he has seen with his own eyes; he gives the image which he receives, not weakened or distorted by the intervention of any other mind; the ignorant feel his representations to be just, and the learned see that they are complete.

Perhaps it would not be easy to find any author, except Homer, who invented so much as Shakespeare, who so much advanced the studies which he cultivated, or effused so much novelty upon his age or country. The form, the characters, the language, and the shows of the English drama are his. "He seems," says Dennis, "to have been the very original of our English tragical harmony, that is, the harmony of blank verse, diversified often by dissyllable and trissyllable terminations. For the diversity distinguishes it from heroic harmony, and by bringing it nearer to common use makes it more proper to gain attention, and more fit for action and dialogue. Such verse we make when we are writing prose; we make such verse in common conversation."

I know not whether this praise is rigorously just. The dissyllable termination, which the critic rightly appropriates to the drama, is to be found, though, I think, not in *Gorboduc* which is confessedly before our author; yet in *Hieronimo*, of which the date is not certain, but which there is reason to believe at least as old as his earliest plays. This however is certain, that he is the first who taught either tragedy or comedy to please, there being no theatrical piece of any older writer of which the name is known, except to antiquaries and collectors of books, which are sought because they are scarce, and would not have been scarce had they been much esteemed.

To him we must ascribe the praise, unless Spenser may divide it with him, of having first discovered to how much smoothness and harmony the English language could be softened. He has speeches, perhaps sometimes scenes, which have all the delicacy of Rowe, without his effeminacy. He endeavours indeed commonly to strike by the force and vigour of his dialogue, but he never executes his purpose better than when he tries to soothe by softness.

Yet it must be at last confessed that as we owe everything to him, he owes something to us; that, if much of his praise is paid by perception and judgment, much is likewise given by custom and veneration. We fix our eyes upon his graces, and turn them from his deformities, and endure in him what we should in another loathe or despise. If we endured without praising, respect for the father of our drama might excuse us; but I have seen, in the book of some modern critic, a collection of anomalies, which show that he has corrupted language by every mode of depravation, but which his admirer has accumulated as a monument of honour.

He has scenes of undoubted and perpetual excellence, but perhaps not one play, which, if it were now exhibited as the work of a contemporary writer, would be heard to the conclusion. I am indeed far from thinking that his works were wrought to his own ideas of perfection; when they were such as would satisfy the audience, they satisfied the writer. It is seldom that authors, though more studious of fame than Shakespeare, rise much above the standard of their own age; to add a little of what is best will always be sufficient for present praise, and those who find themselves exalted into fame are willing to credit their encomiasts, and to spare the labour of contending with themselves.

It does not appear that Shakespeare thought his works worthy of posterity, that he levied any ideal tribute upon future times, or had any further prospect than of present popularity and present profit. When his plays had been acted, his hope was at an end; he solicited no addition of honour from the reader. He therefore made no scruple to repeat the same jests in many dialogues, or to entangle different plots by the same knot of perplexity, which may be at least forgiven him by those who recollect that of Congreve's four comedies two are concluded by a marriage in a mask, by a deception, which perhaps never happened, and which, whether likely or not, he did not invent.

So careless was this great poet of future fame that, though he retired to ease and plenty while he was yet little "declined into the vale of years," before he could be disgusted with fatigue, or disabled by infirmity, he made no collection of his works, nor desired to rescue those that had been already published from the depravations that obscured them, or secure to the rest a better destiny, by giving them to the world in their genuine state.

Of the plays which bear the name of Shakespeare in the late editions, the greater part were not published till about seven years after his death, and the few which appeared in his life are apparently thrust into the world without the care of the author, and therefore probably without his knowledge.

Of all the publishers, clandestine or professed, their negligence and unskilfulness has by the late revisers been sufficiently shown. The faults of all are indeed numerous and gross, and have not only corrupted many passages perhaps beyond recovery, but have brought others into suspicion, which are only obscured by obsolete phraseology, or by the writer's unskilfulness and affectation. To alter is more easy than to explain, and temerity is a more common quality than diligence. Those who saw that they must employ conjecture to a certain degree were willing to indulge it a little further. Had the author published his own works, we should have sat quietly down to disentangle his intricacies, and clear his obscurities; but now we tear what we cannot loose, and eject what we happen not to understand.

The faults are more than could have happened without the concurrence of many causes. The style of Shakespeare was in itself ungrammatical, perplexed and obscure; his works were transcribed for the players by those who may be supposed to have seldom understood them; they were transmitted by copiers equally unskilful, who still multiplied errors; they were perhaps sometimes mutilated by the actors, for the sake of shortening the speeches; and were at last printed without correction of the press.

In this state they remained, not, as Dr. Warburton supposes, because they were unregarded, but because the editor's art was not yet applied to modern languages, and our ancestors were accustomed to so much negligence of English printers that they could very patiently endure it. At last an edition was undertaken by Rowe; not because a poet was to be published by a poet, for Rowe seems to have thought very little on correction or explanation, but that our author's works might appear like those of his fraternity, with the appendages of a life and recommendatory preface. Rowe has been clamorously blamed for not performing what he did not undertake, and it is time that justice be done him, by confessing that though he seems to have had no thought of corruption beyond the printer's errors, yet he has made many emendations, if they were not made before, which his successors have received without acknowledgment, and which, if they had produced them, would have filled pages and pages with censures of the stupidity by which the faults were committed, with displays of the absurdities which they involved, with ostentatious expositions of the new reading, and self congratulations on the happiness of discovering it.

Of Rowe, as of all the editors, I have preserved the preface, and have likewise retained the author's life, though not written with much elegance or spirit; it relates however what is now to be known, and therefore deserves to pass through all succeeding publications.

The nation had been for many years content enough with Mr. Rowe's performance, when Mr. Pope made them acquainted with the true state of Shakespeare's text, showed that it was extremely corrupt, and gave reason to hope that there were means of reforming it. He collated the old copies, which none had thought to examine before, and restored many lines to their integrity; but, by a very compendious criticism, he rejected whatever he disliked, and thought more of amputation than of cure.

I know not why he is commended by Dr. Warburton for distinguishing the genuine from the spurious plays. In this choice he exerted no judgment of his own; the plays which he received were given by Hemings and Condel, the first editors; and those which he rejected, though, according to the licentiousness of the press in those times, they were printed during Shakespeare's life, with his name, had been omitted by his friends, and were never added to his works before the edition of 1664, from which they were copied by the later printers.

This was a work which Pope seems to have thought unworthy of his abilities, being not able to suppress his contempt of "the dull duty of an editor." He understood but half his undertaking. The duty of a collator is indeed dull, yet, like other tedious tasks, is very necessary; but an emendatory critic would ill discharge his duty, without qualities very different from dullness. In perusing a corrupted piece, he must have before him all possibilities of meaning, with all possibilities of expression. Such must be his comprehension of thought, and such his copiousness of language. Out of many readings possible, he must be able to select that which best suits with the state of opinions, and modes of language prevailing in every age, and with his author's particular cast of thought, and turn of expression. Such must be his knowledge, and such his taste. Conjectural criticism demands more than humanity possesses, and he that exercises it with most praise has very frequent need of indulgence. Let us now be told no more of the dull duty of an editor.

Confidence is the common consequence of success. They whose excellence of any kind has been loudly celebrated are ready to conclude that their powers are universal. Pope's edition fell below his own expectations, and he was so much offended, when he was found to have left anything for others to do, that he passed the latter part of his life in a state of hostility with verbal criticism.

I have retained all his notes, that no fragment of so great a writer may be lost; his preface, valuable alike for elegance of composition and justness of remark, and containing a general criticism on his author, so extensive that little can be added, and so exact that little can be disputed, every editor has an interest to suppress, but that every reader would demand its insertion.

Pope was succeeded by Theobald, a man of narrow comprehension and small acquisitions, with no native and intrinsic splendour of genius, with little of the artificial light of learning, but zealous for minute accuracy, and not negligent in pursuing it. He collated the ancient copies, and rectified many errors. A man so anxiously scrupulous might have been expected to do more, but what little he did was commonly right.

In his report of copies and editions he is not to be trusted without examination. He speaks sometimes indefinitely of copies, when he has only one. In his enumeration of editions, he mentions the two first folios as of high, and the third folio as of middle, authority; but the truth is that the first is equivalent to all others, and that the rest only deviate from it by the printer's negligence. Whoever has any of the folios has all, excepting those diversities which mere reiteration of editions will produce. I collated them all at the beginning, but afterwards used only the first.

Of his notes I have generally retained those which he retained himself in his second edition, except when they were confuted by subsequent annotators, or were too minute to merit preservation. I have sometimes adopted his restoration of a comma, without inserting the panegyric in which he celebrated himself for his achievement. The exuberant excrescence of his diction I have often lopped, his triumphant exultations over Pope and Rowe I have sometimes suppressed, and his contemptible ostentation I have frequently concealed; but I have in some places shown him, as he would have shown himself, for the reader's diversion, that the inflated emptiness of some notes may justify or excuse the contraction of the rest.

Theobald, thus weak and ignorant, thus mean and faithless, thus petulant and ostentatious, by the good luck of having Pope for his enemy, has escaped, and escaped alone, with reputation, from this undertaking. So willingly does the world support those who solicit favour, against those who command reverence; and so easily is he praised whom no man can envy.

Our author fell then into the hands of Sir Thomas Hanmer, the Oxford editor, a man, in my opinion, eminently qualified by nature for such studies. He had what is the first requisite to emendatory criticism, that intuition by which the poet's intention is immediately discovered, and that dexterity of intellect which dispatches its work by the easiest means. He had undoubtedly read much; his acquaintance with customs, opinions, and traditions seems to have been large; and he is often learned without show. He seldom passes what he does not understand without an attempt to find or to make a meaning, and sometimes hastily makes what a little more attention would have found. He is solicitous to reduce to grammar what he could not be sure that his author intended to be grammatical. Shakespeare regarded more the series of ideas than of words; and his language, not being designed for the reader's desk, was all that he desired it to be, if it conveyed his meaning to the audience.

Hanmer's care of the metre has been too violently censured. He found the measures reformed in so many passages, by the silent labours of some editors, with the silent acquiescence of the rest, that he thought himself allowed to extend a little further the license, which had already been carried so far without reprehension; and of his corrections in general, it must be confessed that they are often just, and made commonly with the least possible violation of the text.

But, by inserting his emendations, whether invented or borrowed, into the page, without any notice of varying copies, he has appropriated the labour of his predecessors, and made his own edition of little authority. His confidence indeed, both in himself and others, was too great; he supposes all to be right that was done by Pope and Theobald; he seems not to suspect a critic of fallibility, and it was but reasonable that he should claim what he so liberally granted.

As he never writes without careful enquiry and diligent consideration, I have received all his notes, and believe that every reader will wish for more.

Of the last editor it is more difficult to speak. Respect is due to high place, tenderness to living reputation, and veneration to genius and learning; but he cannot be justly offended at that liberty of which he has himself so frequently given an example, nor very solicitous what is thought of notes, which he ought never to have considered as part of his serious employments, and which, I suppose, since the ardour of composition is remitted, he no longer numbers among his happy effusions.

The original and predominant error of his commentary is acquiescence in his first thoughts; that precipitation which is produced by consciousness of quick discernment; and that confidence which presumes to do, by surveying the surface, what labour only can perform, by penetrating the bottom. His notes exhibit sometimes perverse interpretations, and sometimes improbable conjectures; he at one time gives the author more profundity of meaning than the sentence admits, and at another discovers absurdities where the sense is plain to every other reader. But his emendations are likewise often happy and just; and his interpretation of obscure passages learned and sagacious.

Of his notes, I have commonly rejected those against which the gen-

eral voice of the public has exclaimed, or which their own incongruity immediately condemns, and which, I suppose, the author himself would
desire to be forgotten. Of the rest, to part I have given the highest approbation, by inserting the offered reading in the text; part I have left to
the judgment of the reader, as doubtful, though specious; and part I have
censured without reserve, but I am sure without bitterness of malice, and,
I hope, without wantonness of insult.

It is no pleasure to me, in revising my volumes, to observe how much
paper is wasted in confutation. Whoever considers the revolutions of
learning, and the various questions of greater or less importance, upon
which wit and reason have exercised their powers, must lament the un-
successfulness of enquiry, and the slow advances of truth, when he reflects that great part of the labour of every writer is only the destruction
of those that went before him. The first care of the builder of a new system is to demolish the fabrics which are standing. The chief desire of him
that comments an author is to show how much other commentators have
corrupted and obscured him. The opinions prevalent in one age, as
truths above the reach of controversy, are confuted and rejected in another, and rise again to reception in remoter times. Thus the human mind
is kept in motion without progress. Thus sometimes truth and error, and
sometimes contrarieties of error, take each other's place by reciprocal invasion. The tide of seeming knowledge which is poured over one generation retires and leaves another naked and barren; the sudden meteors of
intelligence which for awhile appear to shoot their beams into the regions
of obscurity on a sudden withdraw their lustre, and leave mortals again
to grope their way.

These elevations and depressions of renown, and the contradictions to
which all improvers of knowledge must for ever be exposed, since they
are not escaped by the highest and brightest of mankind, may surely be
endured with patience by critics and annotators, who can rank themselves but as the satellites of their authors. "How canst thou beg for life,"
says Achilles to his captive, "when thou knowest that thou art now to
suffer only what must another day be suffered by Achilles?"

Dr. Warburton had a name sufficient to confer celebrity on those who
could exalt themselves into antagonists, and his notes have raised a
clamour too loud to be distinct. His chief assailants are the authors of
the canons of criticism and of the review of Shakespeare's text; of whom
one ridicules his errors with airy petulance, suitable enough to the levity
of the controversy; the other attacks them with gloomy malignity, as if
he were dragging to justice an assassin or incendiary. The one stings like

a fly, sucks a little blood, takes a gay flutter, and returns for more; the other bites like a viper, and would be glad to leave inflammations and gangrene behind him. When I think on one, with his confederates, I remember the danger of Coriolanus, who was afraid that "girls with spits, and boys with stones, should slay him in puny battle"; when the other crosses my imagination, I remember the prodigy in *Macbeth*,

> An eagle tow'ring in his pride of place,
> Was by a mousing owl hawk'd at and kill'd.

Let me however do them justice. One is a wit, and one a scholar. They have both shown acuteness sufficient in the discovery of faults, and have both advanced some probable interpretations of obscure passages; but when they aspire to conjecture and emendation, it appears how falsely we all estimate our own abilities, and the little which they have been able to perform might have taught them more candour to the endeavours of others.

Before Dr. Warburton's edition, critical observations on Shakespeare had been published by Mr. Upton, a man skilled in languages, and acquainted with books, but who seems to have had no great vigour of genius or nicety of taste. Many of his explanations are curious and useful, but he likewise, though he professed to oppose the licentious confidence of editors, and adhere to the old copies, is unable to restrain the rage of emendation, though his ardour is ill seconded by his skill. Every cold empiric, when his heart is expanded by a successful experiment, swells into a theorist, and the laborious collator at some unlucky moment frolics in conjecture.

Critical, historical and explanatory notes have been likewise published upon Shakespeare by Dr. Grey, whose diligent perusal of the old English writers has enabled him to make some useful observations. What he undertook he has well enough performed, but as he neither attempts judicial nor emendatory criticism, he employs rather his memory than his sagacity. It were to be wished that all would endeavour to imitate his modesty who have not been able to surpass his knowledge.

I can say with great sincerity of all my predecessors, what I hope will hereafter be said of me, that not one has left Shakespeare without improvement, nor is there one to whom I have not been indebted for assistance and information. Whatever I have taken from them it was my intention to refer to its original author, and it is certain that what I have not given to another, I believed when I wrote it to be my own. In some perhaps I have been anticipated; but if I am ever found to encroach upon the remarks of any other commentator, I am willing that the honour, be it more or less, should be transferred to the first claimant, for his right, and his alone, stands above dispute; the second can prove his pretensions only to himself, nor can himself always distinguish invention, with sufficient certainty, from recollection.

They have all been treated by me with candour, which they have not been careful of observing to one another. It is not easy to discover from what cause the acrimony of a scholiast can naturally proceed. The subjects to be discussed by him are of very small importance; they involve neither property nor liberty; nor favour the interest of sect or party. The various readings of copies, and different interpretations of a passage, seem to be questions that might exercise the wit, without engaging the passions. But, whether it be that "small things make mean men proud," and vanity catches small occasions; or that all contrariety of opinion, even in those that can defend it no longer, makes proud men angry; there is often found in commentaries a spontaneous strain of invective and contempt, more eager and venomous than is vented by the most furious controvertist in politics against those whom he is hired to defame.

Perhaps the lightness of the matter may conduce to the vehemence of the agency; when the truth to be investigated is so near to inexistence as to escape attention, its bulk is to be enlarged by rage and exclamation: That to which all would be indifferent in its original state may attract notice when the fate of a name is appended to it. A commentator has indeed great temptations to supply by turbulence what he wants of dignity, to beat his little gold to a spacious surface, to work that to foam which no art or diligence can exalt to spirit.

The notes which I have borrowed or written are either illustrative, by which difficulties are explained; or judicial, by which faults and beauties are remarked; or emendatory, by which depravations are corrected.

The explanations transcribed from others, if I do not subjoin any other interpretation, I suppose commonly to be right; at least I intend by acquiescence to confess that I have nothing better to propose.

After the labours of all the editors, I found many passages which appeared to me likely to obstruct the greater number of readers, and thought it my duty to facilitate their passage. It is impossible for an expositor not to write too little for some, and too much for others. He can only judge what is necessary by his own experience; and how long soever he may deliberate will at last explain many lines which the learned will think impossible to be mistaken, and omit many for which the ignorant will want his help. These are censures merely relative, and must be quietly endured. I have endeavoured to be neither superfluously copious, nor scrupulously reserved, and hope that I have made my author's meaning accessible to many who before were frighted from perusing him, and contributed something to the public, by diffusing innocent and rational pleasure.

The complete explanation of an author not systematic and consequential, but desultory and vagrant, abounding in casual allusions and light hints, is not to be expected from any single scholiast. All personal reflections, when names are suppressed, must be in a few years irrecoverably obliterated; and customs, too minute to attract the notice of law, such as modes of dress, formalities of conversation, rules of visits, disposition of furniture, and practices of ceremony, which naturally find places in familiar dialogue, are so fugitive and unsubstantial that they are not easily retained or recovered. What can be known will be collected by chance, from the recesses of obscure and obsolete papers, perused commonly with some other view. Of this knowledge every man has some, and none has much; but when an author has engaged the public attention, those who can add anything to his illustration communicate their discoveries, and time produces what had eluded diligence.

To time I have been obliged to resign many passages, which, though I did not understand them, will perhaps hereafter be explained, having, I hope, illustrated some which others have neglected or mistaken, sometimes by short remarks, or marginal directions, such as every editor has added at his will, and often by comments more laborious than the matter will seem to deserve; but that which is most difficult is not always most important, and to an editor nothing is a trifle by which his author is obscured.

The poetical beauties or defects I have not been very diligent to observe. Some plays have more, and some fewer, judicial observations, not in proportion to their difference of merit, but because I gave this part of my design to chance and to caprice. The reader, I believe, is seldom pleased to find his opinion anticipated; it is natural to delight more in what we find or make than in what we receive. Judgment, like other faculties, is improved by practice, and its advancement is hindered by submission to dictatorial decisions, as the memory grows torpid by the use of a table book. Some initiation is however necessary; of all skill, part is infused by precept, and part is obtained by habit; I have therefore shown so much as may enable the candidate of criticism to discover the rest.

To the end of most plays, I have added short strictures, containing a general censure of faults, or praise of excellence; in which I know not how much I have concurred with the current opinion; but I have not, by any affectation of singularity, deviated from it. Nothing is minutely and particularly examined, and therefore it is to be supposed that in the plays which are condemned there is much to be praised, and in those which are praised much to be condemned.

The part of criticism in which the whole succession of editors has laboured with the greatest diligence, which has occasioned the most arrogant ostentation, and excited the keenest acrimony, is the emendation of corrupted passages, to which the public attention, having been first drawn by the violence of contention between Pope and Theobald, has been continued by the persecution which, with a kind of conspiracy, has been since raised against all the publishers of Shakespeare.

That many passages have passed in a state of depravation through all the editions is indubitably certain; of these the restoration is only to be attempted by collation of copies or sagacity of conjecture. The collator's province is safe and easy, the conjecturer's perilous and difficult. Yet as the greater part of the plays are extant only in one copy, the peril must not be avoided, nor the difficulty refused.

Of the readings which this emulation of amendment has hitherto produced, some from the labours of every publisher I have advanced into the text; those are to be considered as in my opinion sufficiently supported; some I have rejected without mention, as evidently erroneous; some I have left in the notes without censure or approbation, as resting in equipoise between objection and defence; and some, which seemed specious but not right, I have inserted with a subsequent animadversion.

Having classed the observations of others, I was at last to try what I could substitute for their mistakes, and how I could supply their omissions. I collated such copies as I could procure, and wished for more, but have not found the collectors of these rarities very communicative. Of the editions which chance or kindness put into my hands I have given an enumeration that I may not be blamed for neglecting what I had not the power to do.

By examining the old copies, I soon found that the later publishers, with all their boasts of diligence, suffered many passages to stand unauthorized, and contented themselves with Rowe's regulation of the text, even where they knew it to be arbitrary, and with a little consideration might have found it to be wrong. Some of these alterations are only the ejection of a word for one that appeared to him more elegant or more intelligible. These corruptions I have often silently rectified; for the history of our language, and the true force of our words, can only be preserved by keeping the text of authors free from adulteration. Others, and those very frequent, smoothed the cadence, or regulated the measure; on these I have not exercised the same rigour; if only a word was transposed, or a particle inserted or omitted, I have sometimes suffered the line to stand; for the inconstancy of the copies is such as that some liberties may be easily permitted. But this practice I have not suffered to proceed far, having restored the primitive diction wherever it could for any reason be preferred.

The emendations, which comparison of copies supplied, I have inserted in the text; sometimes where the improvement was slight, without notice, and sometimes with an account of the reasons of the change.

Conjecture, though it be sometimes unavoidable, I have not wantonly nor licentiously indulged. It has been my settled principle that the reading of the ancient books is probably true, and therefore is not to be disturbed for the sake of elegance, perspicuity, or mere improvement of the sense. For though much credit is not due to the fidelity, nor any to the judgment of the first publishers, yet they who had the copy before their eyes were more likely to read it right than we who read it only by imagination. But it is evident that they have often made strange mistakes by ignorance or negligence, and that therefore something may be properly attempted by criticism, keeping the middle way between presumption and timidity.

Such criticism I have attempted to practise, and where any passage appeared inextricably perplexed, have endeavoured to discover how it may be recalled to sense, with least violence. But my first labour is always to turn the old text on every side, and try if there be any interstice through which light can find its way; nor would Huetius himself condemn me, as refusing the trouble of research, for the ambition of alteration. In this modest industry I have not been unsuccessful. I have rescued many lines from the violations of temerity, and secured many scenes from the inroads of correction. I have adopted the Roman sentiment that it is more honourable to save a citizen than to kill an enemy, and have been more careful to protect than to attack.

I have preserved the common distribution of the plays into acts, though I believe it to be in almost all the plays void of authority. Some of those which are divided in the later editions have no division in the first folio, and some that are divided in the folio have no division in the preceding copies. The settled mode of the theatre requires four intervals in the play, but few, if any, of our author's compositions can be properly distributed in that manner. An act is so much of the drama as passes without intervention of time or change of place. A pause makes a new act. In every real, and therefore in every imitative, action, the intervals may be more or fewer, the restriction of five acts being accidental and arbitrary. This Shakespeare knew, and this he practised; his plays were written, and at first printed, in one unbroken continuity, and ought now to be exhibited with short pauses, interposed as often as the scene is changed, or any considerable time is required to pass. This method would at once quell a thousand absurdities.

In restoring the author's works to their integrity, I have considered the punctuation as wholly in my power; for what could be their care of colons and commas who corrupted words and sentences. Whatever could be done by adjusting points is therefore silently performed, in some plays with much diligence, in others with less; it is hard to keep a busy eye steadily fixed upon evanescent atoms, or a discursive mind upon evanescent truth.

The same liberty has been taken with a few particles, or other words of slight effect. I have sometimes inserted or omitted them without notice. I have done that sometimes which the other editors have done always, and which indeed the state of the text may sufficiently justify.

The greater part of readers, instead of blaming us for passing trifles, will wonder that on mere trifles so much labour is expended, with such importance of debate, and such solemnity of diction. To these I answer with confidence that they are judging of an art which they do not understand; yet cannot much reproach them with their ignorance, nor promise that they would become in general, by learning criticism, more useful, happier or wiser.

As I practised conjecture more, I learned to trust it less; and after I had printed a few plays, resolved to insert none of my own readings in the text. Upon this caution I now congratulate myself, for every day increases my doubt of my emendations.

Since I have confined my imagination to the margin, it must not be considered as very reprehensible if I have suffered it to play some freaks in its own dominion. There is no danger in conjecture if it be proposed as conjecture; and while the text remains uninjured, those changes may be safely offered which are not considered even by him that offers them as necessary or safe.

If my readings are of little value, they have not been ostentatiously displayed or importunately obtruded. I could have written longer notes, for the art of writing notes is not of difficult attainment. The work is performed, first by railing at the stupidity, negligence, ignorance, and asinine tastelessness of the former editors, and showing, from all that goes before and all that follows, the inelegance and absurdity of the old reading; then by proposing something which to superficial readers would seem specious, but which the editor rejects with indignation; then by producing the true reading, with a long paraphrase, and concluding with loud acclamations on the discovery, and a sober wish for the advancement and prosperity of genuine criticism.

All this may be done, and perhaps done sometimes without impropriety. But I have always suspected that the reading is right which requires many words to prove it wrong; and the emendation wrong that cannot without so much labour appear to be right. The justness of a happy restoration strikes at once, and the moral precept may be well applied to criticism, *quod dubitas ne feceris* [do nothing that you doubt].

To dread the shore which he sees spread with wrecks is natural to the sailor. I had before my eye so many critical adventures ended in miscarriage that caution was forced upon me. I encountered in every page Wit struggling with its own sophistry, and Learning confused by the multiplicity of its views. I was forced to censure those whom I admired, and could not but reflect, while I was dispossessing their emendations, how soon the same fate might happen to my own, and how many of the readings which I have corrected may be by some other editor defended and established.

> Criticks, I saw, that other's names efface,
> And fix their own, with labour, in the place;
> Their own, like others, soon their place resign'd,
> Or disappear'd, and left the first behind.   POPE.

That a conjectural critic should often be mistaken cannot be wonderful, either to others or himself, if it be considered that in his art there is no system, no principal and axiomatical truth that regulates subordinate positions. His chance of error is renewed at every attempt; an oblique view of the passage, a slight misapprehension of a phrase, a casual inattention to the parts connected, is sufficient to make him not only fail but fail ridiculously; and when he succeeds best, he produces perhaps but one reading of many probable, and he that suggests another will always be able to dispute his claims.

It is an unhappy state, in which danger is hid under pleasure. The allurements of emendation are scarcely resistible. Conjecture has all the joy and all the pride of invention, and he that has once started a happy change is too much delighted to consider what objections may rise against it.

Yet conjectural criticism has been of great use in the learned world; nor is it my intention to depreciate a study that has exercised so many mighty minds, from the revival of learning to our own age, from the Bishop of Aleria to English Bentley. The critics on ancient authors have, in the exercise of their sagacity, many assistances, which the editor of Shakespeare is condemned to want. They are employed upon grammatical and settled languages, whose construction contributes so much to perspicuity that Homer has fewer passages unintelligible than Chaucer. The words have not only a known regimen but invariable quantities, which direct and confine the choice. There are commonly more manuscripts than one; and they do not often conspire in the same mistakes. Yet Scaliger could confess to Salmasius how little satisfaction his emendations gave him. *Illudunt nobis conjecturae nostrae, quarum nos pudet, posteaquam in meliores codices incidimus.* [Our conjectures mock us, when we were ashamed to make them, but later find them in the best editions.] And Lipsius could complain that critics were making faults by trying to remove them, *Ut olim vitiis, ita nunc remediis laboratur* [We are now inconvenienced by corrections, as formerly by errors]. And indeed, where mere conjecture is to be used, the emendations of Scaliger and Lipsius, notwithstanding their wonderful sagacity and erudition, are often vague and disputable, like mine or Theobald's.

Perhaps I may not be more censured for doing wrong than for doing little; for raising in the public, expectations which at last I have not answered. The expectation of ignorance is indefinite, and that of knowledge is often tyrannical. It is hard to satisfy those who know not what to demand, or those who demand by design what they think impossible to be done. I have indeed disappointed no opinion more than my own; yet I have endeavoured to perform my task with no slight solicitude. Not a single passage in the whole work has appeared to me corrupt which I have not attempted to restore; or obscure which I have not endeavoured to illustrate. In many I have failed like others; and from many, after all my efforts, I have retreated, and confessed the repulse. I have not passed over, with affected superiority, what is equally difficult to the reader and to myself, but where I could not instruct him, have owned my ignorance. I might easily have accumulated a mass of seeming learning upon easy scenes; but it ought not to be imputed to negligence that, where nothing was necessary, nothing has been done, or that, where others have said enough, I have said no more.

Notes are often necessary, but they are necessary evils. Let him that is yet unacquainted with the powers of Shakespeare, and who desires to feel the highest pleasure that the drama can give, read every play from the first scene to the last with utter negligence of all his commentators. When his fancy is once on the wing, let it not stoop at correction or explanation. When his attention is strongly engaged, let it disdain alike to turn aside to the name of Theobald and of Pope. Let him read on through brightness and obscurity, through integrity and corruption; let him preserve his comprehension of the dialogue and his interest in the fable. And when the pleasures of novelty have ceased, let him attempt exactness, and read the commentators.

Particular passages are cleared by notes, but the general effect of the work is weakened. The mind is refrigerated by interruption; the thoughts are diverted from the principal subject; the reader is weary, he suspects not why; and at last throws away the book, which he has too diligently studied.

Parts are not to be examined till the whole has been surveyed; there is a kind of intellectual remoteness necessary for the comprehension of any great work in its full design and its true proportions; a close approach shows the smaller niceties, but the beauty of the whole is discerned no longer.

It is not very grateful to consider how little the succession of editors has added to this author's power of pleasing. He was read, admired, studied, and imitated, while he was yet deformed with all the improprieties which ignorance and neglect could accumulate upon him; while the reading was yet not rectified, nor his allusions understood; yet then did Dryden pronounce that "Shakespeare was the man, who, of all modern and perhaps ancient poets, had the largest and most comprehensive soul. All the images of nature were still present to him, and he drew them not laboriously, but luckily: When he describes any thing, you more than see it, you feel it too. Those who accuse him to have wanted learning give him the greater commendation: he was naturally learned: he needed not the spectacles of books to read nature; he looked inwards, and found her there. I cannot say he is every where alike; were he so, I should do him injury to compare him with the greatest of mankind. He is many times flat and insipid; his comic wit degenerating into clenches, his serious swelling into bombast. But he is always great when some great occasion is presented to him: No man can say he ever had a fit subject for his wit, and did not then raise himself as high above the rest of poets,

Quantum lenta solent inter viburna cupressi."

[as cypresses will (rise) among delicate shrubs.]

It is to be lamented that such a writer should want a commentary; that his language should become obsolete, or his sentiments obscure. But it is vain to carry wishes beyond the condition of human things; that which must happen to all has happened to Shakespeare, by accident and time; and more than has been suffered by any other writer since the use of types has been suffered by him through his own negligence of fame, or perhaps by that superiority of mind which despised its own performances when it compared them with its powers, and judged those works unworthy to be preserved which the critics of following ages were to contend for the fame of restoring and explaining.

Among these candidates of inferior fame, I am now to stand the judgment of the public; and wish that I could confidently produce my commentary as equal to the encouragement which I have had the honour of receiving. Every work of this kind is by its nature deficient, and I should feel little solicitude about the sentence were it to be pronounced only by the skilful and the learned.

Dr. Johnson's "Preface to Shakespeare"
first appeared in the 1765 edition
of THE PLAYS OF WILLIAM SHAKESPEARE.

Thomas De Quincey

1785–1859

Born near Manchester, England, in 1785, Thomas De Quincey was the fifth of eight children. He himself would have eight. His father's death left the family with an ample £1,600 a year. Though De Quincey earned his living at writing, he seems to have had a small personal income most of his life. In the public and private schools he went to, he was noted for two things: early brilliance in Latin and Greek and a habit of running away. On one of these excursions he spent a year or more in the rough Soho district of London (an episode mentioned in his *Confessions of an English Opium-Eater*). But afterward he described his growing up as "a youth passed in the divinest happiness."

In his second year at Oxford, he took opium for neuralgic pains and caught the habit. Four times in his life he went deep into the world of the drug; and four times broke out. On a visit to his mother near Bath he met Coleridge. When he left Oxford, De Quincey settled near Coleridge, Wordsworth, and Southey in the Lake District north of Liverpool. There he married Margaret Simpson and edited the *Westmorland Gazette*.

In 1820 he went to London, where he was welcomed by Charles Lamb and his circle. A year later, his *Confessions* were appearing in the *London Magazine* and he was famous—a tiny, neat-boned

---

Notes from the artist: "De Quincey haunted by the dreams of opium. . . .
Poppies grow from his head, and among them is Ann of Oxford Street,
a little girl once befriended by De Quincey and then lost to him.
Around his neck is Death beating the drums, and a crocodile,
recurring images in his dreams. . . .

Thomas McLaury

man, hardly five feet three, handsome with an almost feminine delicacy, and one of the two most celebrated talkers (Coleridge was the other) in an age of great talkers. From that time on, he worked almost entirely for the magazines—*Blackwood's, Tait's,* the *Edinburgh Literary Gazette*—and his writings were not brought together until late in his career.

After his wife died in 1837, he moved his family to Lasswade, near Edinburgh. The children grew up largely in the care of his eldest daughter. De Quincey moved from one rented room to another, each so full of books and papers that he could hardly turn around in it. He loved both solitude and society, and could never get enough of either. He had a great fondness for the human race in all its varieties, and the human race repaid him in kind. His children were enchanted with him. His friends found him a delightful companion. If there had been no creditors in the world, De Quincey might have been that monster of nature, a completely happy man. He died in Edinburgh on December 8, 1859.

We may think of John Stuart Mill as the pure type of the man of ideas, English style. De Quincey, his older contemporary, is a rather more extreme specimen of the English man of letters. True, he spoke of himself as a "philosopher," and wrote little fiction or poetry. Again, he was the author of *The Logic of Political Economy* and, like James Mill and his son, discussed Ricardo's economic theories. But the difference between the man of ideas and the man of letters comes out strongly in his *Literature of Knowledge and Literature of Power.*

If we read it through once, we are struck with its straightforwardness. De Quincey usually likes to stop and make soundings, or curve away from the subject and come back to it. This time he sticks to the point from beginning to end. The point is basic and major. Is it any better or more generally understood now than in De Quincey's time? We may doubt it.

There are, says De Quincey, two types of literature: the literature of knowledge and the literature of power. The function of the one is to teach—that is, convey information or ideas. The function of the other is to move the reader—that is, carry over or call forth emotion or action. The two may run together, and often do; but in function and nature they stand sharply apart.

The literature of knowledge is perishable. It will hold only until more accurate knowledge can be found. De Quincey mentions Sir Isaac Newton's *Principia* as an example of this. In the twentieth century, we have seen even the mechanics of Newton challenged by new theories. But the great works of the literature of power, De Quincey tells us, are "triumphant forever, as long as the languages exist in which they speak or can be taught to speak." Such literature is "moral" and resembles "nature." It nourishes the great truths of human feeling.

Our second essay, *On the Knocking at the Gate in Macbeth,* is De Quincey's interpretation of a great scene from the literature of power—in this case, Shakespeare's *Macbeth*. He tells us that he had always been puzzled by the solemn effect of that knocking after the murder of the "gracious Duncan." Why was it so chilling? He cautions us against trusting what he calls our "understanding," by which he means the habit of seeing things as they are supposed to be rather than as they are. Then he comes back to *Macbeth* and explains how he waited and "clung to the problem" until it could be solved. The solution came to him in the case of a very accomplished English murderer, a "Mr. Williams," in which there was also a knocking at the door. De Quincy understood that we "identify" with the murderer and share his fear of discovery. From that point on, he gives us a superb view of murder as an emotional experience for the murderer. His essay has still another value: it is a perfect little step-by-step example of how the imagination works.

Literature of Knowledge
and Literature of Power

What is it that we mean by literature? Popularly, and amongst the thoughtless, it is held to include everything that is printed in a book. Little logic is required to disturb that definition. The most thoughtless person is easily made aware that in the idea of literature one essential element is some relation to a general and common interest of man, so that what applies only to a local or professional or merely personal interest, even though presenting itself in the shape of a book, will not belong to literature. So far the definition is easily narrowed; and it is as easily expanded. For not only is much that takes a station in books not literature, but, inversely, much that really is literature never reaches a station in books. The weekly sermons of Christendom, that vast pulpit literature which acts so extensively upon the popular mind—to warn, to uphold, to renew, to comfort, to alarm—does not attain the sanctuary of libraries in the ten-thousandth part of its extent. The drama, again, as for instance the finest of Shakespeare's plays in England and all leading Athenian plays in the noontide of the Attic stage, operated as a literature on the public mind, and were (according to the strictest letter of that term) published through the audiences that witnessed their representation some time before they were published as things to be read; and they were published in this scenical mode of publication with much more effect than they could have had as books during ages of costly copying or of costly printing.

Books, therefore, do not suggest an idea coextensive and interchangeable with the idea of literature, since much literature, scenic, forensic, or didactic (as from lecturers and public orators), may never come into books, and much that does come into books may connect itself with no literary interest. But a far more important correction, applicable to the common vague idea of literature, is to be sought, not so much in a better definition of literature, as in a sharper distinction of the two functions which it fulfils. In that great social organ which, collectively, we call literature there may be distinguished two separate offices that may blend and often do so, but capable, severally, of a severe insulation and naturally fitted for reciprocal repulsion. There is, first, the literature of knowledge and, secondly, the literature of power. The function of the first is to teach; the function of the second is to move: the first is a rudder; the second, an oar or a sail. The first speaks to the mere discursive understanding; the second speaks ultimately, it may happen, to the higher understanding, or reason, but always through affections of pleasure and sympathy. Remotely it may travel towards an object seated in what Lord Bacon calls dry light; but proximately, it does and must operate—else it ceases to be a literature of power—on and through that humid light which clothes itself in the mists and glittering iris of human passions, desires, and genial emotions. Men have so little reflected on the higher functions of literature as to find it a paradox if one should describe it as a mean or subordinate purpose of books to give information. But this is a paradox only in the sense which makes it honorable to be paradoxical. Whenever we talk in ordinary language of seeking information or gaining knowledge, we understand the words as connected with something of absolute novelty. But it is the grandeur of all truth which can occupy a very high place in human interests that it is never absolutely novel to the meanest of minds: it exists eternally, by way of germ or latent principle, in the lowest as in the highest, needing to be developed but never to be planted. To be capable of transplantation is the immediate criterion of a truth that ranges on a lower scale. Besides which, there is a rarer thing than truth, namely, power, or deep sympathy with truth. What is the effect, for instance, upon society, of children? By the pity, by the tenderness, and by the peculiar modes of admiration, which connect themselves with the helplessness, with the innocence, and with the simplicity of children, not only are the primal affections strengthened and continually renewed, but the qualities which are dearest in the sight of heaven— the frailty, for instance, which appeals to forbearance, the innocence which symbolizes the heavenly, and the simplicity which is most alien from the worldly—are kept up in perpetual remembrance, and their ideals are continually refreshed. A purpose of the same nature is answered by the higher literature, viz., the literature of power. What do you learn from *Paradise Lost*? Nothing at all. What do you learn from a cookery-book? Something new, something that you did not know before, in every paragraph. But would you therefore put the wretched cookery-book on a higher level of estimation than the divine poem? What you owe to Milton is not any knowledge, of which a million separate items are still but a million of advancing steps on the same earthly level; what you owe is power, that is, exercise and expansion to your own latent capacity of sympathy with the infinite, where every pulse and each separate influx is a step upwards, a step ascending as upon a Jacob's ladder from earth to mysterious altitudes above the earth. All the steps of knowledge, from first to last, carry you further on the same plane, but could never raise you one foot above your ancient level of earth; whereas the very first step in power is a flight, is an ascending movement into another element where earth is forgotten.

Were it not that human sensibilities are ventilated and continually called out into exercise by the great phenomena of infancy, or of real life as it moves through chance and change, or of literature as it recombines these elements in the mimicries of poetry, romance, etc., it is certain that, like any animal power or muscular energy falling into disuse, all such sensibilities would gradually droop and dwindle. It is in relation to these great moral capacities of man that the literature of power, as contradistinguished from that of knowledge, lives and has its field of action. It is concerned with what is highest in man; for the Scriptures themselves never condescended to deal by suggestion or co-operation with the mere discursive understanding: when speaking of man in his intellectual capacity, the Scriptures speak, not of the understanding, but of "the understanding heart," making the heart, *i.e.*, the great intuitive (or non-discursive) organ, to be the interchangeable formula for man in his highest state of capacity for the infinite. Tragedy, romance, fairy tale, or epopee, all alike restore to man's mind the ideals of justice, of hope, of truth, of mercy, of retribution, which else (left to the support of daily life in its realities) would languish for want of sufficient illustration. What is meant, for instance, by poetic justice? It does not mean a justice that differs by its object from the ordinary justice of human jurisprudence, for then it must be confessedly a very bad kind of justice; but it means a justice that differs from common forensic justice by the degree in which it attains its object, a justice that is more omnipotent over its own ends, as dealing, not with the refractory elements of earthly life, but with the elements of its own creation and with materials flexible to its own purest preconceptions. It is certain that, were it not for the literature of power, these ideals would often remain amongst us as mere arid notional forms; whereas, by the creative forces of man put forth in literature, they gain a vernal life of restoration and germinate into vital activities. The commonest novel, by moving in alliance with human fears and hopes, with human instincts of wrong and right, sustains and quickens those affections. Calling them into action, it rescues them from torpor. And hence the pre-eminency, over all authors that merely teach, of the meanest that moves, or that teaches, if at all, indirectly *by* moving. The very highest work that has ever existed in the literature of knowledge is but a provisional work, a book upon trial and sufferance, and *quamdiu bene se gesserit* [as long as it wears well]. Let its teaching be even partially revised, let it be but expanded, nay, even let its teaching be but placed in a better order, and instantly it is superseded. Whereas the feeblest works in the literature of power, surviving at all, survive as finished and unalterable among men. For instance, the *Principia* of Sir Isaac Newton was a book militant on earth from the first. In all stages of its progress it would have to fight for its existence: first, as regards absolute truth; secondly, when that combat was over, as regards its form, or mode of presenting the truth. And as soon as a La Place, or anybody else, builds higher upon the foundations laid by this book, effectually he throws it out of the sunshine into decay and darkness; by weapons won from this book he superannuates and destroys this book, so that soon the name of Newton remains as a mere *nominis umbra* [shadow of a name], but his book, as a living power, has transmigrated into other forms. Now, on the contrary, the *Iliad*, the *Prometheus* of Aeschylus, the *Othello* or *King Lear*, the *Hamlet* or *Macbeth*, and the *Paradise Lost* are not militant but triumphant forever, as long as the languages exist in which they speak or can be taught to speak. They never can transmigrate into new incarnations. To reproduce these in new forms or variations, even if in some things they should be improved, would be to plagiarize. A good steam-engine is properly superseded by a better. But one lovely pastoral valley is not superseded by another, nor a statue of Praxiteles by a statue of Michelangelo. These things are separated, not by imparity, but by disparity. They are not thought of as unequal under the same standard, but as different in kind, and, if otherwise equal, as equal under a different standard. Human works of immortal beauty and works of nature in one respect stand on the same footing: they never absolutely repeat each other, never approach so near as not to differ; and they differ not as better and worse, or simply by more and less; they differ by undecipherable and incommunicable differences, that cannot be caught by mimicries, that cannot be reflected in the mirror of copies, that cannot become ponderable in the scales of vulgar comparison.

On the Knocking at the Gate in Macbeth

Lrom my boyish days I had always felt a great perplexity on one point in *Macbeth*. It was this: the knocking at the gate, which succeeds to the murder of Duncan, produced to my feelings an effect for which I never could account. The effect was that it reflected back upon the murderer a peculiar awfulness and a depth of solemnity; yet, however obstinately I endeavoured with my understanding to comprehend this, for many years I never could see *why* it should produce such an effect.

Here I pause for one moment, to exhort the reader never to pay any attention to his understanding, when it stands in opposition to any other faculty of his mind. The mere understanding, however useful and in-dispensable, is the meanest faculty in the human mind, and the most to be distrusted; and yet the great majority of people trust to nothing else, which may do for ordinary life, but not for philosophical purposes. Of this out of ten thousand instances that I might produce, I will cite one. Ask of any person whatsoever, who is not previously prepared for the demand by a knowledge of the perspective, to draw in the rudest way the commonest appearance which depends upon the laws of that science; as, for instance, to represent the effect of two walls standing at right angles to each other, or the appearance of the houses on each side of a street, as seen by a person looking down the street from one extremity. Now in all cases, unless the person has happened to observe in pictures how it is that artists produce these effects, he will be utterly unable to make the smallest approximation to it. Yet why? For he has actually seen the effect every day of his life. The reason is that he allows his understanding to overrule his eyes. His understanding, which includes no intuitive knowledge of the laws of vision, can furnish him with no reason why a line which is known and can be proved to be a horizontal line should not appear a horizontal line; a line that made any angle with the perpendicular, less than a right angle, would seem to him to indicate that his houses were all tumbling down together. Accordingly, he makes the line of his houses a horizontal line, and fails, of course, to produce the effect demanded. Here, then, is one instance out of many, in which not only the understanding is allowed to overrule the eyes, but where the understanding is positively allowed to obliterate the eyes, as it were; for not only does the man believe the evidence of his understanding in opposition to that of his eyes, but (what is monstrous!) the idiot is not aware that his eyes ever gave such evidence. He does not know that he has seen (and therefore *quoad* his consciousness has *not* seen) that which he *has* seen every day of his life.

But to return from this digression, my understanding could furnish no reason why the knocking at the gate in *Macbeth* should produce any effect, direct or reflected. In fact, my understanding said positively that it could *not* produce any effect. But I knew better; I felt that it did; and I waited and clung to the problem until further knowledge should enable me to solve it. At length, in 1812, Mr. Williams made his debut on the stage of Ratcliffe Highway, and executed those unparalleled murders which have procured for him such a brilliant and undying reputation. On which murders, by the way, I must observe, that in one respect they have had an ill effect, by making the connoisseur in murder very fastidious in his taste, and dissatisfied by anything that has been since done in that line. All other murders look pale by the deep crimson of his; and, as an amateur once said to me in a querulous tone, "There has been absolutely nothing *doing* since his time, or nothing that's worth speaking of." But this is wrong; for it is unreasonable to expect all men to be great artists, and born with the genius of Mr. Williams. Now it will be remembered that in the first of these murders (that of the Marrs), the same incident (of a knocking at the door, soon after the work of extermination was complete) did actually occur, which the genius of Shakespeare has invented; and all good judges, and the most eminent dilettanti, acknowledged the felicity of Shakespeare's suggestion, as soon as it was actually realized. Here, then, was a fresh proof that I was right in relying on my own feeling, in opposition to my understanding; and I again set myself to study the problem; at length I solved it to my own satisfaction, and my solution is this. Murder, in ordinary cases, where the sympathy is wholly directed to the case of the murdered person, is an incident of coarse and vulgar horror; and for this reason, that it flings the interest exclusively upon the natural but ignoble instinct by which we cleave to life; an instinct which, as being indispensable to the primal law of self-preservation, is the same in kind (though different in degree) amongst all living creatures. This instinct, therefore, because it annihilates all distinctions, and degrades the greatest of men to the level of "the poor beetle that we tread on," exhibits human nature in its most abject and humiliating attitude. Such an attitude would little suit the purposes of the poet. What then must he do? He must throw the interest on the murderer. Our sympathy must be with *him* (of course I mean a sympathy of comprehension, a sympathy by which we enter into his feelings, and are made to understand them—not a sympathy of pity or approbation). In the murdered person, all strife of thought, all flux and reflux of passion and of purpose, are crushed by one overwhelming panic; the fear of instant death smites him "with its petrific mace." But in the murderer, such a murderer as a poet will condescend to, there must be raging some great storm of passion—jealousy, ambition, vengeance, hatred—which will create a hell within him; and into this hell we are to look.

In *Macbeth*, for the sake of gratifying his own enormous and teeming faculty of creation, Shakespeare has introduced two murderers: and, as usual in his hands, they are remarkably discriminated; but, though in Macbeth the strife of mind is greater than in his wife, the tiger spirit not so awake, and his feelings caught chiefly by contagion from her—yet, as both were finally involved in the guilt of murder, the murderous mind of necessity is finally to be presumed in both. This was to be expressed; and on its own account, as well as to make it a more proportionable antagonist to the unoffending nature of their victim, "the gracious Duncan," and adequately to expound "the deep damnation of his taking off," this was to be expressed with peculiar energy. We were to be made to feel that the human nature, *i.e.*, the divine nature of love and mercy, spread through the hearts of all creatures, and seldom utterly withdrawn from man—was gone, vanished, extinct; and that the fiendish nature had taken its place. And, as this effect is marvellously accomplished in the dialogues and soliloquies themselves, so it is finally consummated by the expedient under consideration; and it is to this that I now solicit the reader's attention. If the reader has ever witnessed a wife, daughter, or sister in a fainting fit, he may chance to have observed that the most affecting moment in such a spectacle is that in which a sigh and a stirring announce the recommencement of suspended life. Or, if the reader has ever been present in a vast metropolis, on the day when some great national idol was carried in funeral pomp to his grave, and chancing to walk near the course through which it passed, has felt powerfully in the silence and desertion of the streets, and in the stagnation of ordinary business, the deep interest which at that moment was possessing the heart of man—if all at once he should hear the deathlike stillness broken up by the sound of wheels rattling away from the scene, and making known that the transitory vision was dissolved, he will be aware that at no moment was his sense of the complete suspension and pause in ordinary human concerns so full and affecting, as at that moment when the suspension ceases, and the goings-on of human life are suddenly resumed. All action in any direction is best expounded, measured, and made apprehensible, by reaction. Now apply this to the case of *Macbeth*. Here, as I have said, the retiring of the human heart, and the entrance of the fiendish heart was to be expressed and made sensible. Another world has stepped in; and the murderers are taken out of the region of human things, human purposes, human desires. They are transfigured: Lady Macbeth is "unsexed"; Macbeth has forgot that he was born of woman; both are conformed to the image of devils; and the world of devils is suddenly revealed. But how shall this be conveyed and made palpable? In order that a new world may step in, this world must for a time disappear. The murderers, and the murder must be insulated—cut off by an immeasurable gulf from the ordinary tide and succession of human affairs—locked up and sequestered in some deep recess; we must be made sensible that the world of ordinary life is suddenly arrested—laid asleep—tranced—racked into a dread armistice; time must be annihilated; relation to things without abolished; and all must pass self-withdrawn into a deep syncope and suspension of earthly passion. Hence it is, that when the deed is done, when the work of darkness is perfect, then the world of darkness passes away like a pageantry in the clouds: the knocking at the gate is heard; and it makes known audibly that the reaction has commenced; the human has made its reflux upon the fiendish; the pulses of life are beginning to beat again; and the re-establishment of the goings-on of the world in which we live, first makes us profoundly sensible of the awful parenthesis that has suspended them.

O mighty poet! Thy works are not as those of other men, simply and merely great works of art, but are also like the phenomena of nature, like the sun and the sea, the stars and the flowers; like frost and snow, rain and dew, hailstorm and thunder, which are to be studied with entire submission of our own faculties, and in the perfect faith that in them there can be no too much or too little, nothing useless or inert— but that, the further we press in our discoveries, the more we shall see proofs of design and self-supporting arrangement where the careless eye had seen nothing but accident!

Thomas Stearns Eliot

1888–1965

Thomas Stearns Eliot was born in St. Louis, Missouri, on September 26, 1888. His grandfather had founded the city's first Unitarian Church, as well as Washington University. His father was a successful businessman. Tom, a serious, bookish boy, was the youngest of seven children.

Eliot went to Smith Academy in St. Louis and Milton Academy near Boston. He entered Harvard when he was eighteen. A brilliant, hard-working student, he finished his undergraduate work in three years and took a master's degree in the fourth year. The teachers who had the greatest influence on him were George Santayana, Irving Babbitt, and Bertrand Russell.

He spent a year studying at the Sorbonne in Paris, where he wrote his first important poem, *The Love Song of J. Alfred Prufrock.* He returned to Harvard and continued his study of philosophy. In 1914 Eliot won a traveling scholarship and went to Germany. When World War I broke out, he left for England, where, except for a few intervals, he lived the rest of his life.

In England Eliot worked first as a teacher, then as a banker, devoting his evenings to study and writing. Later he became an editor in a publishing firm.

Bertrand Russell introduced him to the Bloomsbury group, who immediately recognized him as a talented writer. Leonard and Virginia Woolf published *The Waste Land,* often said to be the most influential English poem of the twentieth century, at the Hogarth Press in 1922.

In 1927 Eliot became a British citizen and was confirmed in the Anglican Church. In 1928 he published *For Lancelot Andrewes,* a volume of essays in which he first publicly stated his belief in Anglo-

Catholicism. Most of the poems, such as *Ash Wednesday* (1930), and the verse plays he later wrote reflect his religious attitude and his association with a traditional culture. One of his greatest achievements as a poet was *Four Quartets,* published in 1943.

Eliot's first wife, Vivienne Haigh-Wood, died in 1947. In 1957 he married Esmé Valerie Fletcher. He died in London on January 4, 1965.

He was awarded the Nobel Prize for literature in 1948. He received honorary degrees from many of the world's leading universities, as well as Britain's highest honor, the Order of Merit.

In an often quoted statement, Eliot described himself as "classicist in literature, royalist in politics, Anglo-Catholic in religion." Two of these attitudes—classicist and Anglo-Catholic—are illustrated in these essays.

"Dante and Shakespeare divide the modern world between them," Eliot writes. He goes on to indicate what seems to him the difference between them. "Shakespeare," he says, "gives the greatest *width* of human passion; Dante the greatest altitude and greatest depth." The range of Shakespeare is, indeed, wider than that of any poet. Eliot in his essay on Dante attempts to show us, by following Dante in his journey from Hell to Heaven, how the Italian poet plumbs deeper depths, and scales greater heights, than Shakespeare could reach. His argument is persuasive.

Dante, Eliot says, is easy to read. Easy, that is, in the way in which Eliot believes that all good poetry is easy—it can communicate before it is understood. This sounds like a paradox, as indeed it is. Eliot means that Dante's *Divine Comedy* has a first, an immediate, meaning for every reader. It is a story that is comprehensible to all.[1]

The *Divine Comedy* is also, as Eliot points out, an allegory. It is,

[1] See *Great Books of the Western World,* Vol. 21.

Notes from the artist: ". . . a linear portrait of Eliot with a background in medieval style, a scene from Murder in the Cathedral. The two figures below are from Eliot's youth . . . at left, the author as a boy; center, copy of a drawing of George Washington by Eliot when he was seven years old."

MVRDER
IN THE
CATHEDRAL

T. S. Eliot

he says, "one vast metaphor." The *full* understanding of the meaning of the metaphor is, Eliot suggests, unobtainable. The *Divine Comedy* is among the very highest of literary achievements. "The majority of poems one outgrows and outlives, as one outgrows and outlives the majority of human passions: Dante's is one of those which one can only just hope to grow up to at the end of life." Thus Dante is both easy and extraordinarily difficult. These are two criteria of poetic greatness.

Eliot begins the essay *Tradition and the Individual Talent* with another paradox. The truly original poet, he suggests, must have what he calls the historical sense. "This historical sense," Eliot writes, "which is a sense of the timeless as well as of the temporal and of the timeless and of the temporal together, is what makes a writer traditional. And it is at the same time what makes a writer most acutely conscious of his place in time, of his own contemporaneity."

Eliot goes on to say that the great art of the past exists in a kind of order, of which any new, important work must become a part. "Whoever has approved this idea of order, of the form of European, of English literature," he explains, "will not find it preposterous that the past should be altered by the present as much as the present is directed by the past." This startling idea follows from Eliot's conception of order. He does not mean, of course, that the writing of a new work will change any of the lines of Shakespeare. But if the new work is worthy to be placed in the tradition of European poetry, its existence will subtly change our view, our understanding, of Shakespeare. In this sense, Eliot is certainly correct in suggesting that "the poet who is aware of this will be aware of great difficulties and responsibilities."

Having made this point, Eliot turns to a still more important one. "Poetry," he says, "is not a turning loose of emotion, but an escape from emotion; it is not the expression of personality, but an escape from personality." The best poetry, he says, "is an expression of *significant* emotion, emotion which has its life in the poem and not in the history of the poet." Mere individuality is of no interest or importance. Novelty is preferable to repetition, but both are secondary compared to the truest art, which is impersonal.

Dante

I. THE "INFERNO"

In my own experience of the appreciation of poetry I have always found that the less I knew about the poet and his work, before I began to read it, the better. A quotation, a critical remark, an enthusiastic essay, may well be the accident that sets one to reading a particular author; but an elaborate preparation of historical and biographical knowledge has always been to me a barrier. I am not defending poor scholarship; and I admit that such experience, solidified into a maxim, would be very difficult to apply in the study of Latin and Greek. But with authors of one's own speech, and even with some of those of other modern languages, the procedure is possible. At least, it is better to be spurred to acquire scholarship because you enjoy the poetry, than to suppose that you enjoy the poetry because you have acquired the scholarship. I was passionately fond of certain French poetry long before I could have translated two verses of it correctly. With Dante the discrepancy between enjoyment and understanding was still wider.

I do not counsel any one to postpone the study of Italian grammar until he has read Dante, but certainly there is an immense amount of knowledge which, until one has read some of his poetry with intense pleasure—that is, with as keen pleasure as one is capable of getting from any poetry—is positively undesirable. In saying this I am avoiding two possible extremes of criticism. One might say that understanding of the scheme, the philosophy, the concealed meanings, of Dante's verse was *essential* to appreciation; and on the other hand one might say that these things were quite irrelevant, that the poetry in his poems was one thing, which could be enjoyed by itself without studying a framework which had served the author in producing the poetry but could not serve the reader in enjoying it. The latter error is the more prevalent, and is probably the reason why many people's knowledge of the *Comedy* is limited to the *Inferno*, or

371

even to certain passages in it. The enjoyment of the *Divine Comedy* is a continuous process. If you get nothing out of it at first, you probably never will; but if from your first deciphering of it there comes now and then some direct shock of poetic intensity, nothing but laziness can deaden the desire for fuller and fuller knowledge.

What is surprising about the poetry of Dante is that it is, in one sense, extremely easy to read. It is a test (a positive test, I do not assert that it is always valid negatively) that genuine poetry can communicate before it is understood. The impression can be verified on fuller knowledge; I have found with Dante and with several other poets in languages in which I was unskilled, that about such impressions there was nothing fanciful. They were not due, that is, to *mis*understanding the passage, or to reading into it something not there, or to accidental sentimental evocations out of my own past. The impression was new, and of, I believe, the objective "poetic emotion." There are more detailed reasons for this experience on the first reading of Dante, and for my saying that he is easy to read. I do not mean that he writes very simple Italian, for he does not; or that his content is simple or always simply expressed. It is often expressed with such a force of compression that the elucidation of three lines needs a paragraph, and their allusions a page of commentary. What I have in mind is that Dante is, in a sense to be defined (for the word means little by itself), the most *universal* of poets in the modern languages. That does not mean that he is "the greatest," or that he is the most comprehensive—there is greater variety and detail in Shakespeare. Dante's universality is not solely a personal matter. The Italian language, and especially the Italian language in Dante's age, gains much by being the product of universal Latin. There is something much more *local* about the languages in which Shakespeare and Racine had to express themselves. This is not to say, either, that English and French are inferior, as vehicles of poetry, to Italian. But the Italian vernacular of the late Middle Ages was still very close to Latin, as literary expression, for the reason that the men, like Dante, who used it, were trained, in philosophy and all abstract subjects, in mediaeval Latin. Now mediaeval Latin is a very fine language; fine prose and fine verse were written in it; and it had the quality of a highly developed and literary Esperanto. When you read modern philosophy, in English, French, German, and Italian, you must be struck by national or racial differences of thought: modern languages *tend* to separate abstract thought (mathematics is now the only universal language); but mediaeval Latin tended to concentrate on what men of various races and lands could think together. Some of the character of this universal language seems to me to inhere in Dante's Florentine speech; and the localization ("Florentine" speech) seems if anything to emphasize the universality, because it cuts across the modern division of nationality. To enjoy any French or German poetry, I think one needs to have some sympathy with the French or German mind; Dante, none the less an Italian and a patriot, is first a European.

This difference, which is one of the reasons why Dante is "easy to read," may be discussed in more particular manifestations. The style of Dante has a peculiar lucidity—a *poetic* as distinguished from an *intellectual* lucidity. The thought may be obscure, but the word is lucid, or rather translucent. In English poetry words have a kind of opacity which is part of their beauty. I do not mean that the beauty of English poetry is what is called mere "verbal beauty." It is rather that words have associations, and the groups of words *in* association have associations, which is a kind of local self-consciousness, because they are the growth of a *particular* civilization; and the same thing is true of other modern languages. The Italian of Dante, though essentially the Italian of today, is not in this way a modern language. The culture of Dante was not of one European country but of Europe. I am aware, of course, of a directness of speech which Dante shares with other great poets of pre-Reformation and pre-Renaissance times, notably Chaucer and Villon. Undoubtedly there is something in common between the three, so much that I should expect an admirer of any one of them to be an admirer of the others; and undoubtedly there is an opacity, or inspissation of poetic style throughout Europe after the Renaissance. But the lucidity and universality of Dante are far beyond those qualities in Villon and Chaucer, though they are akin.

Dante is "easier to read," for a foreigner who does not know Italian very well, for other reasons: but all related to this central reason, that in Dante's time Europe, with all its dissensions and dirtiness, was mentally more united than we can now conceive. It is not particularly the Treaty of Versailles that has separated nation from nation; nationalism was born long before; and the process of disintegration which for our generation culminates in that treaty began soon after Dante's time. One of the reasons for Dante's "easiness" is the following—but first I must make a digression.

I must explain why I have said that Dante is "easy to read," instead of talking about his "universality." The latter word would have been much easier to use. But I do not wish to be thought to claim a universality for Dante which I deny to Shakespeare or Molière or Sophocles. Dante is no more "universal" than Shakespeare: though I feel that we can come nearer to understanding Dante than a foreigner can come to understanding those others. Shakespeare, or even Sophocles, or even Racine and Molière, are dealing with what is as universally human as the material of Dante; but they had no choice but to deal with it in a more local way. As I have said, the Italian of Dante is very near in feeling to mediaeval Latin: and of the mediaeval philosophers whom Dante read, and who were read by learned men of his time, there were, for instance, St. Thomas who was an Italian, St. Thomas's predecessor Albertus, who was a German, Abelard who was French, and Hugh and Richard of St. Victor who were Scots. For the *medium* that Dante had to use compare the opening of the *Inferno*

> *Nel mezzo del cammin di nostra vita*
> *mi ritrovai per una selva oscura,*
> *che la diritta via era smarrita.*

In the middle of the journey of our life I found myself in a dark wood, having lost the straight path.

with the lines with which Duncan is introduced to Macbeth's castle:

> This castle hath a pleasant seat; the air
> Nimbly and sweetly recommends itself
> Unto our gentle senses.
>   This guest of summer,
> The temple-haunting martlet, does approve
> By his loved masonry that the heaven's breath
> Smells wooingly here: no jutty, frieze,
> Buttress, nor coign of vantage, but this bird
> Hath made his pendant bed and procreant cradle:
> Where they most breed and haunt, I have observed
> The air is delicate.

I do not at all pretend that we appreciate everything, even in one single line of Dante, that a cultivated Italian can appreciate. But I do maintain that more is lost in translating Shakespeare into Italian than in translating Dante into English. How can a foreigner find words to convey in his own language just that combination of intelligibility and remoteness that we get in many phrases of Shakespeare?

I am not considering whether the language of Dante or Shakespeare is superior, for I cannot admit the question: I merely affirm that the differences are such as make Dante easier for a foreigner. Dante's advantages are not due to greater genius, but to the fact that he wrote when Europe was still more or less one. And even had Chaucer or Villon been exact contemporaries of Dante, they would still have been farther, linguistically as well as geographically, from the centre of Europe than Dante.

But the simplicity of Dante has another detailed reason. He not only thought in a way in which every man of his culture in the whole of Europe then thought, but he employed a method which was common and commonly understood throughout Europe. I do not intend, in this essay, to go into questions of disputed interpretations of Dante's allegory. What is important for my purpose is the fact that the allegorical method was a definite method not confined to Italy; and the fact, apparently paradoxical, that the allegorical method makes for simplicity and intelligibility. We incline to think of allegory as a tiresome cross-word puzzle. We incline to associate it with dull poems (at best, *The Romance of the Rose*), and in a great poem to ignore it as irrelevant. What we ignore is, in a case like Dante's, its particular effect towards lucidity of style.

I do not recommend, in first reading the first canto of the *Inferno*, worrying about the identity of the Leopard, the Lion, or the She-Wolf. It is really better, at the start, not to know or care what they do mean. What we should consider is not so much the meaning of the images, but the reverse process, that which led a man having an idea to express it in images. We have to consider the type of mind which by nature and *practice* tended to express itself in allegory: and for a competent poet, allegory means *clear visual images*. And clear visual images are given much more intensity by having a meaning—we do not need to know what that meaning is, but in our awareness of the image we must be aware that the meaning is there too. Allegory is only one poetic method, but it is a method which has very great advantages.

Dante's is a *visual* imagination. It is a visual imagination in a different sense from that of a modern painter of still life: it is visual in the sense that he lived in an age in which men still saw visions. It was a psychological habit, the trick of which we have forgotten, but as good as any of our own. We have nothing but dreams, and we have forgotten that seeing visions—a practice now relegated to the aberrant and uneducated —was once a more significant, interesting, and disciplined kind of dreaming. We take it for granted that our dreams spring from below: possibly the quality of our dreams suffers in consequence.

All that I ask of the reader, at this point, is to clear his mind, if he can, of every prejudice against allegory, and to admit at least that it was not a device to enable the uninspired to write verses, but really a mental habit, which when raised to the point of genius can make a great poet as well as a great mystic or saint. And it is the allegory which makes it possible for the reader who is not even a good Italian scholar to enjoy Dante. Speech varies, but our eyes are all the same. And allegory was not a local Italian custom, but a universal European method.

Dante's attempt is to make us see what he saw. He therefore employs very simple language, and very few metaphors, for allegory and metaphor do not get on well together. And there is a peculiarity about his *comparisons* which is worth noticing in passing.

There is a well-known comparison or simile in the great xvth canto of the *Inferno*, which Matthew Arnold singled out, rightly, for high praise; which is characteristic of the way in which Dante employs these figures. He is speaking of the crowd in Hell who peered at him and his guide under a dim light:

> *e si ver noi aguzzevan le ciglia,*
> *come vecchio sartor fa nella cruna.*

and sharpened their vision (knitted their brows) at us, like an old tailor peering at the eye of his needle.

The purpose of this type of simile is solely to make us see *more definitely* the scene which Dante has put before us in the preceding lines.

> she looks like sleep,
> As she would catch another Antony
> In her strong toil of grace.

The image of Shakespeare's is much more complicated than Dante's, and more complicated than it looks. It has the grammatical form of a kind of simile (the "as if" form), but of course "catch in her toil" is a metaphor. But whereas the simile of Dante is merely to make you see more clearly how the people looked, and is explanatory, the figure of Shakespeare is expansive rather than intensive; its purpose is to *add* to what you see (either on the stage or in your imagination) a reminder of that fascination of Cleopatra which shaped her history and that of the world, and of that fascination being so strong that it prevails even in death. It is more elusive, and it is less possible to convey without close knowledge of the English language. Between men who could make such inventions as these there can be no question of greater or less. But as the whole poem of Dante is, if you like, one vast metaphor, there is hardly any place for metaphor in the detail of it.

There is all the more reason to acquaint oneself well with Dante's poem first part by part, even dwelling specially on the parts that one likes most at first, because we cannot extract the full significance of any part without knowing the whole. We cannot understand the inscription at Hell Gate:

> Giustizia mosse il mio alto Fattore;
> fecemi la divina Potestate,
> la somma Sapienza e il primo Amore.

Justice moved my high Maker; what made me were the divine Power, the supreme Wisdom, and the primal Love—

until we have ascended to the highest Heaven and returned. But we can understand the first Episode that strikes most readers, that of Paolo and Francesca, enough to be moved by it as much as by any poetry, on the first reading. It is introduced by two similes of the same explanatory nature as that which I have just quoted:

> E come gli stornei ne portan l'ali,
> nel freddo tempo, a schiera larga e piena,
> cosi quel fiato gli spiriti mali;

And as their wings bear along the starlings, at the cold season, in large full troop.

> E come i gru van cantando lor lai
> facendo in aer di sè lunga riga;
> cosi vid' io venir, traendo guai,
> ombre portate dalla detta briga;

And as the cranes go chanting their lays, making themselves a long streak in the air, so I saw the wailing shadows come, wailing, carried on the striving wind.

We can see and feel the situation of the two lost lovers, though we do not yet understand the meaning which Dante gives it. Taking such an episode by itself, we can get as much out of it as we get from the reading of a whole single play of Shakespeare. We do not understand Shakespeare from a single reading, and certainly not from a single play. There is a relation between the various plays of Shakespeare, taken in order; and it is a work of years to venture even one individual interpretation of the pattern in Shakespeare's carpet. It is not certain that Shakespeare himself knew what it was. It is perhaps a larger pattern than Dante's, but the pattern is less distinct. We can read with full comprehension the lines:

Noi leggevamo un giorno per diletto
di Lancillotto, come amor lo strinse;
soli eravamo e senza alcun sospetto.
Per più fiate gli occhi ci sospinse
quella lettura, e scolorocci il viso;
ma solo un punto fu quel che ci vinse.
Quando leggemmo il disiato riso
esser baciato da cotanto amante,
questi, che mai da me non fia diviso,
La bocca mi baciò tutto tremante:

One day, for pastime, we read of Lancelot, how love constrained him; we were alone, and without all suspicion. Several times that reading urged our eyes to meet, and changed the colour of our faces; but one moment alone it was that overcame us. When we read how the fond smile was kissed by such a lover, he, who shall never be divided from me, kissed my mouth all trembling.

When we come to fit the episode into its place in the whole *Comedy,* and see how this punishment is related to all other punishments and to purgations and rewards, we can appreciate better the subtle psychology of the simple line of Francesca:

se fosse amico il re dell' universo

if the King of the Universe were our friend. . . .

or of the line

Amor, che a nullo amato amar perdona

Love, which to no loved one permits excuse for loving. . . .

or indeed of the line already quoted:

questi, che mai da me non fia diviso

he, who shall never be divided from me. . . .

Proceeding through the *Inferno* on a first reading, we get a succession of phantasmagoric but clear images, of images which are coherent, in that each reinforces the last; of glimpses of individuals made memorable by a perfect phrase, like that of the proud Farinata degli Uberti:

ed ei s' ergea col petto e colla fronte,
come avesse lo inferno in gran dispitto.

He rose upright with breast and countenance, as though he entertained great scorn of Hell.

and of particular longer episodes, which remain separately in the memory. I think that among those which impress themselves most at the first reading are the episode of Brunetto Latini (Canto xv), Ulysses (Canto xxvi), Bertrand de Born (Canto xxviii), Adamo di Brescia (Canto xxx), and Ugolino (Canto xxxiii).

Although I think it would be a mistake to skip, and find it much better to await these episodes until we come to them in due course, they certainly remain in my memory as the parts of the *Inferno* which first convinced me, and especially the Brunetto and the Ulysses episodes, for which I was unprepared by quotation or allusion. And the two may well be put together: for the first is Dante's testimony of a loved master of arts, the second his reconstruction of a legendary figure of ancient epic; yet both have the quality of *surprise* which Poe declared to be essential to poetry. This *surprise*, at its highest, could by nothing be better illustrated than by the final lines with which Dante dismisses the damned master whom he loves and respects:

> *Poi si rivolse, e parve di coloro*
> *che coronno a Verona il drappo verde*
> *per la campagna; e parve di costoro*
> *quegli che vince e non colui che perde.*

Then he turned, and seemed like one of those who run for the green cloth at Verona through the open field; and of them he seemed like him who wins, and not like him who loses.

One does not need to know anything about the race for the roll of green cloth, to be *hit* by these lines; and in making Brunetto, so fallen, *run like the winner*, a quality is given to the punishment which belongs only to the greatest poetry. So Ulysses, unseen in the hornèd wave of flame,

> *Lo maggior corno della fiamma antica*
> *cominciò a crollarsi mormorando,*
> *pur come quella cui vento affatica.*
> *Indi la cima qua e là menando,*
> *come fosse la lingua che parlasse,*
> *gittò voce di fuori e disse: "Quando*
> *mi dipartì da Circe, che sottrasse*
> *me più d'un anno là presso a Gaeta. . . ."*

The greater horn of the ancient flame began to shake itself murmuring, like a flame struggling against the wind. Then moving to and fro the peak, as though it were the tongue that spoke, threw forth a voice and said: "When I left Circe, who kept me more than a year there near Gaeta. . . ."

is a creature of the pure poetic imagination, apprehensible apart from place and time and the scheme of the poem. The Ulysses episode may strike us first as a kind of excursion, an irrelevance, a self-indulgence on the part of Dante taking a holiday from his Christian scheme. But when we know the whole poem, we recognize how cunningly and convincingly Dante has made to fit in real men, his contemporaries, friends, and enemies, recent historical personages, legendary and Biblical figures, and figures of ancient fiction. He has been reproved or smiled at for satisfying personal grudges by putting in Hell men whom he knew and hated; but these, as well as Ulysses, are transformed in the whole; for the real and the unreal are all representative of types of sin, suffering, fault, and merit, and all become of the same reality and contemporary. The Ulysses episode is particularly "readable," I think, because of its continuous straightforward narrative, and because to an English reader the comparison with Tennyson's poem—a perfect poem at that—is very instructive. It is worth while noticing the greatly superior degree of *simplification* of Dante's version. Tennyson, like most poets, like most even of those whom we can call great poets, has to get his effect with a certain amount of *forcing*. Thus the line about the sea which

> moans round with many voices,

a true specimen of Tennyson-Virgilianism, is too *poetical* in comparison with Dante, to be the highest poetry. (Only Shakespeare can be so "poetical" without giving any effect of overloading, or distracting us from the main issue:

> Put up your bright swords or the dew will rust them.)

Ulysses and his shipmates pass through the pillars of Hercules, that "narrow pass"

> *ov' Ercole segnò li suoi riguardi*
> *acciochè l'uom più oltre non si metta.*

where Hercules set his marks, so that man should pass no farther.

> *"O frati," dissi, "che per cento milia*
> *perigli siete giunti all' occidente,*
> *a questa tanto picciola vigilia*
> *de' vostri sensi, ch' è del rimanente,*
> *non vogliate negar l'esperienza*
> *di retro al sol, del mondo senza gente.*

Considerate la vostra semenza,
fatti non foste a viver come bruti
ma per seguir virtute e conoscenza."

"O brothers!" I said, "who through a hundred thousand dangers have reached the West, deny not, to this so brief vigil of your senses that remains, experience of the world without men that lies behind the sun. Consider your nature, you were made not to live like beasts, but to pursue virtue and knowledge."

They fare forth until suddenly

n'apparve una montagna bruna
per la distanza, e parvemi alta tanto
quanto veduta non n'aveva alcuna.
Noi ci allegrammo, e tosto tornò in pianto,
chè dalla nuova terra un turbo nacque,
e percosse del legno il primo canto.
Tre volte il fe' girar con tutte l'acque,
alla quarta levar la poppa in suso,
e la prora ire in giù, com' altrui piacque,
infin che il mar fu sopra noi richiuso.

there appeared a mountain brown in the distance; and it seemed to me the highest that I had ever seen. We rejoiced, but soon our joy was turned to lamentation: for a storm came up from the new land, and caught the stem of our ship. Three times it whirled her round with all the waters; the fourth time it heaved up the stern and drove her down at the head, as pleased Another; until the sea closed over us.

The story of Ulysses, as told by Dante, reads like a straightforward piece of romance, a well told seaman's yarn; Tennyson's Ulysses is primarily a very self-conscious poet. But Tennyson's poem is flat, it has only two dimensions; there is nothing more in it than what the average Englishman, with a feeling for verbal beauty, can see. We do not need, at first, to know what mountain the mountain was, or what the words mean *as pleased Another,* to feel that Dante's sense has further depths.

It is worth pointing out again how very right was Dante to introduce among his historical characters at least one character who even to him could hardly have been more than a fiction. For the *Inferno* is relieved from any question of pettiness or arbitrariness in Dante's selection of damned. It reminds us that Hell is not a place but a *state;* that man is damned or blessed in the creatures of his imagination as well as in men who have actually lived; and that Hell, though a state, is a state which can only be thought of, and perhaps only experienced, by the projection of sensory images; and that the resurrection of the body has perhaps a deeper meaning than we understand. But these are such thoughts as come only after many readings; they are not necessary for the first poetic enjoyment.

The experience of a poem is the experience both of a moment and of a lifetime. It is very much like our intenser experiences of other human beings. There is a first, or an early moment which is unique, of shock and surprise, even of terror (*Ego dominus tuus* [I am thy God]); a moment which can never be forgotten, but which is never repeated integrally; and yet which would become destitute of significance if it did not survive in a larger whole of experience; which survives inside a deeper and a calmer feeling. The majority of poems one outgrows and outlives, as one outgrows and outlives the majority of human passions: Dante's is one of those which one can only just hope to grow up to at the end of life.

The last canto (xxxiv) is probably the most difficult on first reading. The vision of Satan may seem grotesque, especially if we have fixed in our minds the curly-haired Byronic hero of Milton; it is too like a Satan in a fresco in Siena. Certainly no more than the Divine Spirit can the Essence of Evil be confined in one form and place; and I confess that I tend to get from Dante the impression of a Devil suffering like the human damned souls; whereas I feel that the *kind* of suffering experienced by the Spirit of Evil should be represented as utterly different. I can only say that Dante made the best of a bad job. In putting Brutus, the noble Brutus, and Cassius with Judas Iscariot he will also disturb at first the English reader, for whom Brutus and Cassius must always be the Brutus and Cassius of Shakespeare: but if my justification of Ulysses is valid, then the presence of Brutus and Cassius is also. If any one is repelled by the last canto of the *Inferno,* I can only ask him to wait until he has read and lived for years with the last canto of the *Paradiso,* which is to my thinking the highest point that poetry has ever reached or ever can reach, and in which Dante amply repairs any failure of Canto xxxiv of the *Inferno;* but perhaps it is better, on our first reading of the *Inferno,* to omit the last canto and return to the beginning:

> *Per me si va nella città dolente;*
> *per me si va nell' eterno dolore;*
> *per me si va tra la perduta gente.*
> *Giustizia mosse il mio alto Fattore;*
> *fecemi la divina Potestate,*
> *la somma Sapienza e il primo Amore.*

[Through me is the way into the woeful city; through me is the way into the eternal woe; through me is the way among the lost people. Justice moved my lofty maker: the divine Power, the supreme Wisdom and the primal Love made me.]

II. THE "PURGATORIO" AND THE "PARADISO"

For the science or art of writing verse, one has learned from the *Inferno* that the greatest poetry can be written with the greatest economy of words, and with the greatest austerity in the use of metaphor, simile, verbal beauty, and elegance. When I affirm that more can be learned about how to write poetry from Dante than from any English poet, I do not at all mean that Dante's way is the only right way, or that Dante is thereby *greater* than Shakespeare or, indeed, any other English poet. I put my meaning into other words by saying that Dante can do less *harm* to any one trying to learn to write verse than can Shakespeare. Most great English poets are *inimitable* in a way in which Dante was not. If you try to imitate Shakespeare you will certainly produce a series of stilted, forced, and violent distortions of language. The language of each great English poet is his own language; the language of Dante is the perfection of a common language. In a sense, it is more pedestrian than that of Dryden or Pope. If you follow Dante without talent, you will at worst be pedestrian and flat; if you follow Shakespeare or Pope without talent, you will make an utter fool of yourself.

But if one has learned this much from the *Inferno*, there are other things to be learnt from the two successive divisions of the poem. From the *Purgatorio* one learns that a straightforward philosophical statement can be great poetry; from the *Paradiso*, that more and more rarefied and remote *states of beatitude* can be the material for great poetry. And gradually we come to admit that Shakespeare understands a greater extent and variety of human life than Dante; but that Dante understands deeper degrees of degradation and higher degrees of exaltation. And a further wisdom is reached when we see clearly that this indicates the equality of the two men.

On the one hand, the *Purgatorio* and the *Paradiso* belong, in the way of understanding, together. It is apparently easier to accept damnation as poetic material than purgation or beatitude; less is involved that is strange to the modern mind. I insist that the full meaning of the *Inferno* can only be extracted after appreciation of the two later parts, yet it has sufficient meaning in and by itself for the first few readings. Indeed, the

Purgatorio is, I think, the most difficult of the three parts. It cannot be enjoyed by itself like the *Inferno*, nor can it be enjoyed merely as a sequel to the *Inferno;* it requires appreciation of the *Paradiso* as well; which means that its first reading is arduous and apparently unremunerative. Only when we have read straight through to the end of the *Paradiso*, and re-read the *Inferno*, does the *Purgatorio* begin to yield its beauty. Damnation and even blessedness are more exciting than purgation.

By compensation, the *Purgatorio* has a few episodes which, so to speak, "let us up" (as the counterpart to letting down) more easily than the rest, from the *Inferno*. We must not stop to orient ourselves in the new astronomy of the Mount of Purgatory. We must linger first with the shades of Casella and Manfred slain, and especially Buonconte and La Pia, those whose souls were saved from Hell only at the last moment.

> "*Io fui di Montefeltro, io son Buonconte;*
> *Giovanna o altri non ha di me cura;*
> *perch' io vo tra costor con bassa fronte.*"
> *Ed io a lui: "Qual forza o qual ventura*
> *ti traviò si fuor di Campaldino*
> *che non si seppe mai tua sepoltura?*"
> "*Oh*," *rispos' egli, "a piè del Casentino*
> *traversa un' acqua che ha nome l'Archiano,*
> *che sopra l'Ermo nasce in Apennino.*
> *Dove il vocabol suo diventa vano*
> *arriva' io forato nella gola,*
> *fuggendo a piede e sanguinando il piano.*
> *Quivi perdei la vista, e la parola*
> *nel nome di Maria finii: e quivi*
> *caddi, e rimase la mia carne sola.*"

"I was of Montefeltro, I am Buonconte; neither Giovanna nor any other has care of me, wherefore I go with these, with lowered brow." I said to him: "What force or chance led you so far away from Campaldino that your place of sepulture has always been unknown?" "Oh," said he, "at the foot of Casentino a stream crosses, which is called Archiano, and rises in the Apennines above the Hermitage. There, where its name is lost, came I, jabbed in the throat, fleeing on foot, dripping blood over the plain. There my sight left me, and I ended speech with [crying on] the name of Mary. There I fell, and my flesh alone remained."

When Buonconte ends his story, the third spirit speaks:

> "*Deh, quando tu sarai tornato al mondo,*
> *e riposato della lunga via,*"
> *seguito il terzo spirito al secondo,*

"ricorditi di me, che son la Pia;
Siena mi fe', disfecemi Maremma:
salsi colui che innanellata, pria
disposando, m'avea con la sua gemma."

"O pray, when you return to the world, and are rested from your long
journey," followed the third spirit after the second, "remember me, who
am La Pia. Siena made me, Maremma unmade me: this is known to him
who after due engagement wedded me with his ring."

The next episode that impresses the reader coming fresh from the *Inferno* is the meeting with Sordello the poet (Canto vi), the soul who appeared

altera e disdegnosa
e nel mover degli occhi onesta e tarda!

Proud and disdainful, superb and slow in the movement of his eyes!

E il dolce duca incominciava:
"Mantova" . . . *e l'ombra, tutta in sè romita,*
surse ver lui del loco ove pria stava,
dicendo: "O Mantovano, io son Sordello
della tua terra." E l'un l'altro abbracciava.

The gentle guide [Virgil] began: "Mantua" . . . and the shade, suddenly rapt, leapt towards him from the place where first it was, saying,
"O Mantuan, I am Sordello of thy very soil." And the one embraced the
other.

The meeting with Sordello *a guisa di leon quando si posa*, like a couch-
ant lion, is no more affecting than that with the poet Statius, in Canto
xxi. Statius, when he recognizes his master Virgil, stoops to clasp his
feet, but Virgil answers—the lost soul speaking to the saved:

"Frate,
non far, chè tu se' ombra, ed ombra vedi."
Ed ei surgendo: "Or puoi la quantitate
comprender dell' amor ch' a te mi scalda,
quando dismento nostra vanitate,
trattando l'ombre come cosa salda."

"Brother! refrain, for you are but a shadow, and a shadow is but what
you see." Then the other, rising: "Now can you understand the quantity
of love that warms me towards you, so that I forget our vanity, and treat
the shadows like the solid thing."

The last "episode" at all comparable to those of the *Inferno* is the meeting with Dante's predecessors, Guido Guinizelli and Arnaut Daniel (Canto xxvi). In this canto the Lustful are purged in flame, yet we see clearly how the flame of purgatory differs from that of hell. In hell, the torment issues from the very nature of the damned themselves, expresses their essence; they writhe in the torment of their own perpetually perverted nature. In purgatory the torment of flame is deliberately and consciously accepted by the penitent. When Dante approaches with Virgil these souls in purgatory flame, they crowd towards him:

> *Poi verso me, quanto potevan farsi,*
> *certi si feron, sempre con riguardo*
> *di non uscir dove non fossero arsi.*

Then certain of them made towards me, so far as they could, but ever watchful not to come so far that they should not be in the fire.

The souls in purgatory suffer because they *wish to suffer*, for purgation. And observe that they suffer more actively and keenly, being souls preparing for blessedness, than Virgil suffers in eternal limbo. In their suffering is hope, in the anaesthesia of Virgil is hopelessness; that is the difference. The canto ends with the superb verses of Arnaut Daniel in his Provençal tongue:

> *"Ieu sui Arnaut, que plor e vau cantan;*
> *consiros vei la passada folor,*
> *e vei jausen lo jorn, qu' esper, denan.*
> *Ara vos prec, per aquella valor*
> *que vos guida al som de l'escalina,*
> *sovegna vos a temps de ma dolor."*
> Poi s' ascose nel foco che gli affina.

"I am Arnold, who weeps and goes singing. I see in thought all the past folly. And I see with joy the day for which I hope, before me. And so I pray you, by that Virtue which leads you to the topmost of the stair—be mindful in due time of my pain." Then dived he back into that fire which refines them.

These are the high episodes, to which the reader initiated by the *Inferno* must first cling, until he reaches the shore of Lethe, and Matilda, and the first sight of Beatrice. In the last cantos (xxix–xxxiii) of the *Purgatorio* we are already in the world of the *Paradiso*.

But in between these episodes is the narrative of the ascent of the Mount, with meetings, visions, and philosophical expositions, all important, and all difficult for the uninstructed reader who finds it less exciting than the continuous phantasmagoria of the *Inferno*. The allegory in the *Inferno* was easy to swallow or ignore, because we could, so to speak, grasp the concrete end of it, its solidification into imagery; but as we ascend from Hell to Heaven we are more and more required to grasp the whole from idea to image.

Here I must make a diversion, before tackling a specifically philosophical passage of the *Purgatorio*, concerning the nature of Belief. I wish merely to indicate certain tentative conclusions of my own, which might affect one's reading of the *Purgatorio*.

Dante's debt to St. Thomas Aquinas, like his debt (a much smaller one) to Virgil, can be easily exaggerated; for it must not be forgotten that Dante read and made use of other great mediaeval philosophers as well. Nevertheless, the question of how much Dante took from Aquinas and how much from elsewhere is one which has been settled by others and is not relevant to my present essay. But the question of what Dante "believed" is always relevant. It would not matter, if the world were divided between those persons who are capable of taking poetry simply for what it is and those who cannot take it at all; if so, there would be no need to talk about this question to the former and no use in talking about it to the latter. But most of us are somewhat impure and apt to confuse issues: hence the justification of writing books about books, in the hope of straightening things out.

My point is that you cannot afford to *ignore* Dante's philosophical and theological beliefs, or to skip the passages which express them most clearly; but that on the other hand you are not called upon to believe them yourself. It is wrong to think that there are parts of the *Divine Comedy* which are of interest only to Catholics or to mediaevalists. For there is a difference (which here I hardly do more than assert) between philosophical *belief* and poetic *assent*. I am not sure that there is not as great a difference between philosophical belief and scientific belief; but that is a difference only now beginning to appear, and certainly inapposite to the thirteenth century. In reading Dante you must enter the world of thirteenth-century Catholicism: which is not the world of modern Catholicism, as his world of physics is not the world of modern physics. You are not called upon to believe what Dante believed, for your belief will not give you a groat's worth more of understanding and appreciation; but you are called upon more and more to understand it. If you can read poetry as poetry, you will "believe" in Dante's theology exactly as you believe in the physical reality of his journey; that is, you suspend both belief and disbelief. I will not deny that it may be in practice easier for a Catholic to grasp the meaning, in many places, than for the ordinary agnostic; but that is not because the Catholic believes, but because he has been instructed. It is a matter of knowledge and ignorance, not of belief or scepticism. The vital matter is that Dante's poem is a whole; that you must in the end come to understand every part in order to understand any part.

Furthermore, we can make a distinction between what Dante believes as a poet and what he believed as a man. Practically, it is hardly likely that even so great a poet as Dante could have composed the *Comedy* merely with understanding and without belief; but his private belief becomes a different thing in becoming poetry. It is interesting to hazard the suggestion that this is truer of Dante than of any other philosophical poet. With Goethe, for instance, I often feel too acutely "this is what Goethe the man believed," instead of merely entering into a world which Goethe has created; with Lucretius also; less with the *Bhagavad-Gita,* which is the next greatest philosophical poem to the *Divine Comedy* within my experience. That is the advantage of a coherent traditional system of dogma and morals like the Catholic: it stands apart, for understanding and assent even without belief, from the single individual who propounds it. Goethe always arouses in me a strong sentiment of disbelief in what he believes: Dante does not. I believe that this is because Dante is the purer poet, not because I have more sympathy with Dante the man than Goethe the man.

We are not to take Dante for Aquinas or Aquinas for Dante. It would be a grievous error in psychology. The *belief attitude* of a man reading the *Summa* must be different from that of a man reading Dante, even when it is the same man, and that man a Catholic.

It is not necessary to have read the *Summa* (which usually means, in practice, reading some handbook) in order to understand Dante. But it is necessary to read the philosophical passages of Dante with the humility of a person visiting a new world, who admits that every part is essential to the whole. What is necessary to appreciate the poetry of the *Purgatorio* is not belief, but suspension of belief. Just as much effort is required of any modern person to accept Dante's allegorical method, as is required of the agnostic to accept his theology.

When I speak of understanding, I do not mean merely knowledge of books or words, any more than I mean belief: I mean a state of mind in which one sees certain beliefs, as the order of the deadly sins, in which treachery and pride are greater than lust, and despair the greatest, as *possible*, so that we suspend our judgment altogether.

In the xvith Canto of the *Purgatorio* we meet Marco Lombardo, who discourses at some length on the Freedom of the Will, and on the Soul:

> *Esce di mano a lui, che la vagheggia*
> *prima che sia, a giusa di fanciulla*
> *che piangendo e ridendo pargoleggia,*
> *l'anima semplicetta, che sa nulla,*
> *salvo che, mossa da lieto fattore,*
> *volentier torna a ciò che la trastulla.*
> *Di picciol bene in pria sente sapore;*
> *quivi s'inganna, e retro ad esso corre,*
> *se guida o fren non torce suo amore.*
> *Onde convenne legge per fren porre;*
> *convenne regge aver, che discernesse*
> *della vera cittade almen la torre.*

From the hands of Him who loves her before she is, there issues like a little child that plays, with weeping and laughter, the simple soul, that knows nothing except that, come from the hands of a glad creator, she turns willingly to everything that delights her. First she tastes the flavour of a trifling good; then is beguiled, and pursues it, if neither guide nor check withhold her. Therefore laws were needed as a curb; a ruler was needed, who should at least see afar the tower of the true City.

Later (Canto xvii) it is Virgil himself who instructs Dante in the nature of Love:

> *"Nè creator nè creatura mai,"*
> *cominciò ei, "figiuol, fu senza amore,*
> *o naturale o d'animo; e tu il sai.*
> *Lo natural è sempre senza errore,*
> *ma l'altro puote errar per malo obbietto,*
> *o per poco o per troppo di vigore.*
> *Mentre ch' egli è ne' primi ben diretto,*
> *e ne' secondi sè stesso misura,*
> *esser non può cagion di mal diletto;*
> *ma, quando al mal si torce, o con più cura*
> *o con men che non dee corre nel bene,*
> *contra il fattore adopra sua fattura.*
> *Quinci comprender puoi ch' esser conviene*
> *amor sementa in voi d' ogni virtute,*
> *e d' ogni operazion che merta pene.*

He began: "neither Creator, nor creature, my son, was ever without love, either natural or rational: and you know it. The natural is always without error; but the other may err through mistaking the object, or through excess or deficiency of force. While it is directed towards the primal goods, and in the secondary moderates itself, it cannot be the cause of delight of sin; but when turned to evil, or hurries towards the good with more or less solicitude than is right, then the creature works against the Creator. Accordingly you may understand how Love must be the seed in you both of every virtue and of every act that merits punishment."

I have quoted these two passages at some length, because they are of the sort that a reader might be inclined to skip, thinking that they are only for scholars, not for readers of poetry, or thinking that it is necessary to have studied the philosophy underlying them. It is not necessary to have traced the descent of this theory of the soul from Aristotle's *De Anima* in order to appreciate it as poetry. Indeed, if we worry too much about it at first as philosophy we are likely to prevent ourselves from receiving the poetic beauty. It is the philosophy of that world of poetry which we have entered.

But with the xxvııth canto we have left behind the stage of punishment and the stage of dialectic, and approach the state of Paradise. The last cantos have the quality of the *Paradiso* and prepare us for it; they move straightforward, with no detour or delay. The three poets, Virgil, Statius, and Dante, pass through the wall of flame which separates Purgatory from the Earthly Paradise. Virgil dismisses Dante, who henceforth shall proceed with a higher guide, saying:

> *Non aspettar mio dir più, nè mio cenno.*
> *Libero, dritto e sano è tuo arbitrio,*
> *e fallo fora non fare a suo senno:*
> *per ch'io te sopra te corono e mitrio.*

No more expect my word, or sign. Your Will is free, straight and whole and not to follow its direction would be sin: wherefore I crown and mitre you (king and bishop) over yourself.

I.e., Dante has now arrived at a condition, for the purposes of the rest of his journey, which is that of the blessed: for political and ecclesiastical organization are only required because of the imperfections of the human will. In the Earthly Paradise Dante encounters a lady named Matilda, whose identity need not at first bother us,

> *una donna soletta, che si gia*
> *cantando ed iscegliendo fior da fiore,*
> *ond' era pinta tutta la sua via.*

A lady alone, who went singing and plucking flower after flower, where-
with her path was pied.

After some conversation and explanation by Matilda of the reason and
nature of the place, there follows a "Divine Pageant." To those who dislike—not what are popularly called pageants—but the serious pageants
of royalty, of the church, of military funerals—the "pageantry" which we
find here and in the *Paradiso* will be tedious; and still more to those, if
there be any, who are unmoved by the splendour of the Revelations of
St. John. It belongs to the world of what I call the *high dream*, and the
modern world seems capable only of the *low dream*. I arrived at accept-
ing it, myself, only with some difficulty. There were at least two prejudices, one against pre-Raphaelite imagery, which was natural to one of
my generation, and perhaps affects generations younger than mine. The
other prejudice—which affects this end of the *Purgatorio* and the whole
of the *Paradiso*—is the prejudice that poetry not only must be found
through suffering but can find its material only *in* suffering. Everything
else was cheerfulness, optimism, and hopefulness; and these words stood
for a great deal of what one hated in the nineteenth century. It took me
many years to recognize that the states of improvement and beatitude
which Dante describes are still further from what the modern world
can conceive as cheerfulness, than are his states of damnation. And little
things put one off: Rossetti's *Blessed Damozel*, first by my rapture and
next by my revolt, held up my appreciation of Beatrice by many years.

We cannot understand fully Canto xxx of the *Purgatorio* until we
know the *Vita Nuova*, which in my opinion should be read after the
Divine Comedy. But at least we can begin to understand how skilfully
Dante expresses the recrudescence of an ancient passion in a new emotion, in a new situation, which comprehends, enlarges, and gives a meaning to it.

> sopra candido vel cinta d'oliva
>   donna m'apparve, sotto verde manto,
>   vestita di color di fiamma viva.
> E lo spirito mio, che già cotanto
>   tempo era stato che alla sua presenza
>   non era di stupor, tremando, affranto,
> senza degli occhi aver più conoscenza,
>   per occulta virtù che da lei mosse,
>   d'antico amor sentì la gran potenza.
> Tosto che nella vista mi percosse
>   l'alta virtù, che già m'avea trafitto
>   primo ch'io fuor di puerizia fosse,

*volsemi alla sinistra col rispitto
col quale il fantolin corre alla mamma,
quando ha paura o quando egli è afflito,
per dicere a Virgilio: "Men che dramma
di sangue m' è rimaso, che non tremi;
conosco i segni dell' antica fiamma."*

Olive-crowned over a white veil, a lady appeared to me, clad under a green mantle in colour of living flame. And my spirit, after so many years since trembling in her presence it had been broken with awe, without further knowledge by my eyes, felt, through hidden power which went out from her, the great strength of the old love. As soon as that lofty power struck my sense, which already had transfixed me before my adolescence, I turned leftwards with the trust of the little child who runs to his mama when he is frightened or distressed, to say to Virgil: "Hardly a drop of blood in my body does not shudder: I know the tokens of the ancient flame."

And in the dialogue that follows we see the passionate conflict of the old feelings with the new; the effort and triumph of a new renunciation, greater than renunciation at the grave, because a renunciation of feelings that persist beyond the grave. In a way, these cantos are those of the greatest *personal* intensity in the whole poem. In the *Paradiso* Dante himself, save for the Cacciaguida episode, becomes de- or super-personalized; and it is in these last cantos of the *Purgatorio,* rather than in the *Paradiso,* that Beatrice appears most clearly. But the Beatrice theme is essential to the understanding of the whole, *not* because we need to know Dante's biography—not, for instance, as the Wesendonck history is supposed to cast light upon *Tristan*—but because of Dante's *philosophy* of it. This, however, concerns more our examination of the *Vita Nuova.*

The *Purgatorio* is the most difficult because it is the *transitional* canto: the *Inferno* is one thing, comparatively easy; the *Paradiso* is another thing, more difficult as a whole than the *Purgatorio,* because more a whole. Once we have got the hang of the kind of feeling in it no one part is difficult. The *Purgatorio,* here and there, might be called "dry": the *Paradiso* is never dry, it is either incomprehensible or intensely exciting. With the exception of the episode of Cacciaguida—a pardonable exhibition of family and personal pride, because it provides splendid poetry—it is not episodic. All the other characters have the best credentials. At first, they seem less distinct than the earlier unblessed people; they seem ingeniously varied but fundamentally monotonous variations of insipid blessedness. It is a matter of gradual adjustment of our vision. We have (whether we know it or not) a prejudice against beatitude as material for poetry. The eighteenth and nineteenth centuries knew nothing of it; even Shelley, who knew Dante well and who towards the end of his life was beginning to profit by it, the one English poet of the nineteenth century who could even have begun to follow those footsteps, was able to enounce the proposition that our sweetest songs are those which sing of saddest thought. The early work of Dante might confirm Shelley; the *Paradiso* provides the counterpart, though a different counterpart from the philosophy of Browning.

The *Paradiso* is not monotonous. It is as various as any poem. And take the *Comedy* as a whole, you can compare it to nothing but the *entire* dramatic work of Shakespeare. The comparison of the *Vita Nuova* with the *Sonnets* is another, and interesting, occupation. Dante and Shakespeare divide the modern world between them; there is no third.

We should begin by thinking of Dante fixing his gaze on Beatrice:

> *Nel suo aspetto tal dentro mi fei,*
> *qual si fe' Glauco nel gustar dell' erba,*
> *che il fe' consorto in mar degli altri dei.*
> *Trasumanar significar per verba*
> *non si poria; pero l'esemplo basti* ·
> *a cui esperienza grazia serba.*

Gazing on her, so I became within, as did Glaucus, on tasting of the grass which made him sea-fellow of the other gods. To transcend humanity may not be told in words, wherefore let the instance suffice for him for whom that experience is reserved by Grace.

And as Beatrice says to Dante: *"You make yourself dull with false fancy"*; warns him, that here there are divers sorts of blessedness, as settled by Providence.

If this is not enough, Dante is informed by Piccarda (Canto III) in words which even those who know no Dante know:

> *la sua voluntade è nostra pace.*

His will is our peace.

It is the mystery of the inequality, and of the indifference of that inequality, in blessedness, of the blessed. It is all the same, and yet each degree differs.

Shakespeare gives the greatest *width* of human passion; Dante the greatest altitude and greatest depth. They complement each other. It is futile to ask which undertook the more difficult job. But certainly the "difficult passages" in the *Paradiso* are Dante's difficulties rather than ours: his difficulty in making us apprehend sensuously the various states and stages of blessedness. Thus the long oration of Beatrice about the Will (Canto IV) is really directed at making us *feel* the reality of the condition of Piccarda; Dante has to educate our senses as he goes along. The insistence throughout is upon states of feeling; the reasoning takes only its proper place as a means of reaching these states. We get constantly verses like

> *Beatrice mi guardò con gli occhi pieni*
> *di faville d' amor così divini,*
> *che, vinta, mia virtù diedi le reni,*
> *e quasi mi perdei con gli occhi chini.*

Beatrice looked on me with eyes so divine filled with sparks of love, that my vanquished power turned away, and I became as lost, with downcast eyes.

The whole difficulty is in admitting that this is something that we are meant to feel, not merely decorative verbiage. Dante gives us every aid of images, as when

> *Come in peschiera, ch' è tranquilla e pura,*
> *traggonsi i pesci a a ciò che vien di fuori*
> *per modo che lo stiman lor pastura;*
> *sì vid' io ben più di mille splendori*
> *trarsi ver noi, ed in ciascun s'udia:*
> Ecco che crescerà li nostri amori.

As in a fishpond still and clear, the fishes draw near to anything that falls from without in such a way as to make them think it something to eat, so I saw more than a thousand splendours draw towards us, and in each was heard: Lo! here is one that shall increase our loves.

About the persons whom Dante meets in the several spheres, we need only to enquire enough to consider why Dante placed them where he did.

When we have grasped the strict *utility* of the minor images, such as the one given above, or even the simple comparison admired by Landor:

> *Quale alledetta che in aere si spazia*
> *primo cantando, e poi tace contenta*
> *dell' ultima dolcezza che la sazia,*

Like the lark which soars in the air, first singing, and then ceases, content with the last sweetness that sates her, we may study with respect the more elaborate imagery, such as that of the figure of the Eagle composed by the spirits of the just, which extends from Canto xviii onwards for some space. Such figures are not merely antiquated rhetorical devices, but serious and practical means of making the spiritual visible. An understanding of the rightness of such imagery is a preparation for apprehending the last and greatest canto, the most tenuous and most intense. Nowhere in poetry has experience so remote from ordinary experience been expressed so concretely, by a masterly use of that imagery of *light* which is the form of certain types of mystical experience.

> *Nel suo profondo vidi che s'interna,*
> *legato con amore in un volume,*
> *ciò che per l'universo si squaderna;*
> *sustanzia ed accidenti, e lor costume,*
> *quasi conflati insieme per tal modo,*
> *che ciò ch' io dico è un semplice lume.*
> *La forma universal di questo nodo*
> *credo ch' io vidi, perchè più di largo,*
> *dicendo questo, mi sento ch' io godo.*
> *Un punto solo m'è maggior letargo,*
> *che venticinque secoli alla impresa,*
> *che fe' Nettuno ammirar l'ombra d'Argo.*

Within its depths I saw ingathered, bound by love in one mass, the scattered leaves of the universe: substance and accidents and their relations, as though together fused, so that what I speak of is one simple flame. The universal form of this complex I think I saw, because, as I say this, more largely I feel myself rejoice. One single moment to me is more lethargy than twenty-five centuries upon the enterprise which made Neptune wonder at the shadow of the Argo (passing over him).

One can feel only awe at the power of the master who could thus at every moment realize the inapprehensible in visual images. And I do not know anywhere in poetry more authentic sign of greatness than the power of association which could in the last line, when the poet is speaking of the divine vision, yet introduce the Argo passing over the head of wondering Neptune. Such association is utterly different from that of Marino speaking in one breath of the beauty of the Magdalen and the opulence of Cleopatra (so that you are not quite sure what adjectives apply to which). It is the real right thing, the power of establishing relations between beauty of the most diverse sorts; it is the utmost power of the poet.

O quanto è corto il dire, e come fioco
al mio concetto!

How scant the speech, and how faint, for my conception!

In writing of the *Divine Comedy* I have tried to keep to a few very simple points of which I am convinced. First that the poetry of Dante is the one universal school of style for the writing of poetry in any language. There is much, naturally, which can profit only those who write Dante's own Tuscan language; but there is no poet in any tongue—not even in Latin or Greek—who stands so firmly as a model for all poets. I tried to illustrate his universal mastery in the use of images. In the actual writing I went so far as to say that he is safer to follow, even for us, than any English poet, including Shakespeare. My second point is that Dante's "allegorical" method has great advantages for the writing of *poetry:* it simplifies the diction, and makes clear and precise the images. That in good allegory, like Dante's, it is not necessary to understand the meaning first to enjoy the poetry, but that our enjoyment of the poetry makes us want to understand the meaning. And the third point is that the *Divine Comedy* is a complete scale of the *depths* and *heights* of human emotion; that the *Purgatorio* and *Paradiso* are to be read as extensions of the ordinarily very limited human range. Every degree of the feeling of humanity, from lowest to highest, has, moreover, an intimate relation to the next above and below, and all fit together according to the logic of sensibility.

I have only now to make certain observations on the *Vita Nuova*, which may also amplify what I have suggested about the mediaeval mind expressed in allegory.

NOTE TO SECTION II

The theory of poetic belief and understanding here employed for a particular study is similar to that maintained by Mr. I. A. Richards (see his *Practical Criticism*, pp. 179 ff. and pp. 271 ff.). I say "similar," because my own *general* theory is still embryonic, and Mr. Richards' also is capable of much further development. I cannot therefore tell how far the similarity extends; but for those who are interested in the subject, I should point out one respect in which my view differs from that of Mr. Richards; and then proceed to qualify my own tentative conclusions.

I am in agreement with Mr. Richards' statement on p. 271 (*op. cit.*). I agree for the reason that if you hold any contradictory theory you deny, I believe, the existence of "literature" as well as of "literary criticism." We may raise the question whether "literature" exists; but for certain purposes, such as the purpose of this essay on Dante, we must assume that there is literature and literary appreciation; we must assume that the reader can obtain the full "literary" or (if you will) "aesthetic" enjoyment without sharing the beliefs of the author. *If* there is "literature," *if* there is "poetry," then it must be possible to have full literary or poetic appreciation without sharing the beliefs of the poet. That is as far as my thesis goes in the present essay. It may be argued whether there is literature, whether there is poetry, and whether there is any meaning in the term "full appreciation." But I have assumed for this essay that these things exist and that these terms are understood.

I deny, in short, that the reader must share the beliefs of the poet in order to enjoy the poetry fully. I have also asserted that we can distinguish between Dante's beliefs as a man and his beliefs as a poet. But we are forced to believe that there is a particular relation between the two, and that the poet "means what he says." If we learned, for instance, that *De Rerum Natura* was a Latin exercise which Dante had composed for relaxation after completing the *Divine Comedy,* and published under the name of one Lucretius, I am sure that our capacity for enjoying either poem would be mutilated. Mr. Richards' statement (*Science and Poetry,* p. 76 footnote) that a certain writer has effected "a complete severance between his poetry and *all* beliefs" is to me incomprehensible.

If you deny the theory that full poetic appreciation is possible without belief in what the poet believed, you deny the existence of "poetry" as well as "criticism"; and if you push this denial to its conclusion, you will be forced to admit that there is very little poetry that you can appreciate, and that your appreciation of it will be a function of your philosophy or theology or something else. If, on the other hand, I push *my* theory to the extreme, I find myself in as great a difficulty. I am quite aware of the ambiguity of the word "understand." In one sense, it means to understand without believing, for unless you can understand a view of life (let us say) without believing in it, the word "understand" loses all meaning, and the act of choice between one view and another is reduced to caprice. But if you yourself are convinced of a certain view of life, then you irresistibly and inevitably believe that if any one else comes to "understand" it fully, his understanding *must* terminate in belief. It is possible, and sometimes necessary, to argue that full understanding must identify itself with full belief. A good deal, it thus turns out, hangs on the meaning, if any, of this short word *full.*

In short, both the view I have taken in this essay, and the view which contradicts it, are, if pushed to the end, what I call heresies (not, of course, in the theological, but in a more general sense). Each is true only within a limited field of discourse, but unless you limit fields of discourse, you can have no discourse at all. Orthodoxy can only be found in such contradictions, though it must be remembered that a pair of contradictions may *both* be false, and that not all pairs of contradictions make up a truth.

And I confess to considerable difficulty in analysing my own feelings, a difficulty which makes me hesitate to accept Mr. Richards' theory of "pseudo-
statements." On reading the line which he uses,

> Beauty is truth, truth beauty . . .

I am at first inclined to agree with him, because this statement of equivalence
means nothing to me. But on re-reading the whole Ode, this line strikes me as a
serious blemish on a beautiful poem; and the reason must be either that I fail
to understand it, or that it is a statement which is untrue. And I suppose that
Keats meant something by it, however remote his truth and his beauty may
have been from these words in ordinary use. And I am sure that he would have
repudiated any explanation of the line which called it a pseudo-statement. On
the other hand the line I have often quoted of Shakespeare,

> Ripeness is all,

or the line I have quoted of Dante,

> *la sua voluntade è nostra pace,*

strikes very differently on my ear. I observe that the propositions in these words
are very different in kind, not only from that of Keats, but from each other. The
statement of Keats seems to me meaningless: or perhaps, the fact that it is
grammatically meaningless conceals another meaning from me. The statement
of Shakespeare seems to me to have profound emotional meaning, with, at
least, no literal fallacy. And the statement of Dante seems to me *literally true.*
And I confess that it has more beauty for me now, when my own experience
has deepened its meaning, than it did when I first read it. So I can only conclude that I cannot, in practice, wholly separate my poetic appreciation from
my personal beliefs. Also that the distinction between a statement and a pseudo-
statement is not always, in particular instances, possible to establish. The theory
of Mr. Richards is, I believe, incomplete until he defines the species of religious,
philosophical, scientific, and other beliefs, as well as that of "everyday" belief.

I have tried to make clear some of the difficulties inhering in my own theory.
Actually, one probably has more pleasure in the poetry when one shares the beliefs of the poet. On the other hand there is a distinct pleasure in enjoying
poetry as poetry when one does *not* share the beliefs, analogous to the pleasure
of "mastering" other men's philosophical systems. It would appear that "literary
appreciation" is an abstraction, and pure poetry a phantom; and that both in
creation and enjoyment much always enters which is, from the point of view of
"Art," irrelevant.

III. THE "VITA NUOVA"

All of Dante's "minor works" are important, because they are works of
Dante; but the *Vita Nuova* has a special importance, because it does

more than any of the others help us to a fuller understanding of the *Divine Comedy*. I do not suggest that the others may be neglected; the *Convivio* is important, and also the *De Volgari Eloquio:* and every part of Dante's writings can give us some light on other parts. But the *Vita Nuova* is a youthful work, in which some of the method and design, and explicitly the intention, of the *Divine Comedy* are shown. Because it is an immature work, it requires some knowledge of the masterpiece to understand; and at the same time helps particularly towards understanding of the *Comedy*.

A great deal of scholarship has been directed upon examination of the early life of Dante, in connexion with the *Vita Nuova*. Critics may be roughly divided into those who regard it as primarily biographical, and those who regard it as primarily allegorical. It is much easier for the second group to make a good case than for the first. If this curious medley of verse and prose is biographical, then the biography has unquestionably been manipulated almost out of recognition to fit into conventional forms of allegory. The imagery of much of it is certainly in a very ancient tradition of vision literature: just as the scheme of the *Divine Comedy* has been shown to be closely similar to similar supernatural peregrination stories in Arabic and in old Persian literature—to say nothing of the descents of Ulysses and Aeneas—so there are parallels to the visions of the *Vita Nuova* such as the *Shepherd of Hermas* in Greek. And as the book is obviously not a literal statement, whether of vision or delusion, it is easy to make out a case for its being an entire allegory: for asserting, that is, that Beatrice is merely a personification of an abstract virtue, intellectual or moral.

I wish to make clear that my own opinions are opinions founded only upon reading the text. I do not think that they are such as can either be verified or refuted by scholars; I mean to restrict my comments to the unprovable and the irrefutable.

It appears likely, to any one who reads the *Vita Nuova* without prejudice, that it is a mixture of biography and allegory; but a mixture according to a recipe not available to the modern mind. When I say the "modern mind," I mean the minds of those who have read or could have read such a document as Rousseau's *Confessions*. The modern mind can understand the "confession," that is, the literal account of oneself, varying only in degree of sincerity and self-understanding, and it can understand "allegory" in the abstract. Nowadays "confessions," of an insignificant sort, pour from the press; every one *met son cœur à nu* [bares his heart], or pretends to; "personalities" succeed one another in interest. It is difficult to conceive an age (of many ages) when human beings cared somewhat about the salvation of the "soul," but not about each other as "personalities." Now Dante, I believe, had experiences which seemed to him of some importance; not of importance because they had happened to him and because he, Dante Alighieri, was an important person who kept press-cutting bureaux busy; but important in themselves; and therefore they seemed to him to have some philosophical and impersonal value. I find in it an account of a particular kind of experience: that is, of something which had actual experience (the experience of the "confession" in the modern sense) *and* intellectual and imaginative experience (the experience of thought and the experience of dream) as its materials; and which became a third kind. It seems to me of importance to grasp the simple fact that the *Vita Nuova* is neither a "confession" nor an "indiscretion" in the modern sense, nor is it a piece of Pre-Raphaelite tapestry. If you have that sense of intellectual and spiritual realities that Dante had, then a form of expression like the *Vita Nuova* cannot be classed either as "truth" or "fiction."

In the first place, the type of sexual experience which Dante describes as occurring to him at the age of nine years is by no means impossible or unique. My only doubt (in which I found myself confirmed by a distinguished psychologist) is whether it could have taken place so *late* in life as the age of nine years. The psychologist agreed with me that it is more likely to occur at about five or six years of age. It is possible that Dante developed rather late, and it is also possible that he altered the dates to employ some other significance of the number nine. But to me it appears obvious that the *Vita Nuova* could only have been written around a personal experience. If so, the details do not matter: whether the lady was the Portinari or not, I do not care; it is quite as likely that she is a blind for some one else, even for a person whose name Dante may have forgotten or never known. But I cannot find it incredible that what has happened to others should have happened to Dante with much greater intensity.

The same experience, described in Freudian terms, would be instantly accepted as fact by the modern public. It is merely that Dante, quite reasonably, drew other conclusions and used another mode of expression, which arouses incredulity. And we are inclined to think—as Remy de Gourmont, for once misled by his prejudices into the pedantic attitude, thought—that if an author like Dante follows closely a form of vision that has a long history, it proves that the story is mere allegory (in the modern sense) or fake. I find a much greater difference in sensibility between the *Vita Nuova* and the *Shepherd of Hermas* than Gourmont did. It is not

at all the simple difference between the genuine and the fraud; it is a difference in mind between the humble author of early Christian times and
the poet of the thirteenth century, perhaps as great as that between the
latter and ourselves. The similarities might prove that a certain *habit* in
dream-imagery can persist throughout many changes of civilization.
Gourmont would say that Dante borrowed; but that is imputing our own
mind to the thirteenth century. I merely suggest that possibly Dante, in
his place and time, was following something more essential than merely a
"literary" tradition.

The attitude of Dante to the fundamental experience of the *Vita Nuova*
can only be understood by accustoming ourselves to find meaning in *final
causes* rather than in origins. It is not, I believe, meant as a description of
what he *consciously* felt on his meeting with Beatrice, but rather as a description of what that meant on mature reflection upon it. The final cause
is the attraction towards God. A great deal of sentiment has been spilt,
especially in the eighteenth and nineteenth centuries, upon idealizing
the reciprocal feelings of man and woman towards each other, which
various realists have been irritated to denounce: this sentiment ignoring
the fact that the love of man and woman (or for that matter of man and
man) is only explained and made reasonable by the higher love, or else
is simply the coupling of animals.

Let us entertain the theory that Dante, meditating on the astonishment
of an experience at such an age, which no subsequent experience abolished or exceeded, found meanings in it which we should not be likely to
find ourselves. His account is then just as reasonable as our own; and he
is simply prolonging the experience in a different direction from that
which we, with different mental habits and prejudices, are likely to take.

We cannot, as a matter of fact, understand the *Vita Nuova* without
some saturation in the poetry of Dante's Italian contemporaries, or even
in the poetry of his Provençal predecessors. Literary parallels are most
important, but we must be on guard not to take them in a purely literary
and literal way. Dante wrote more or less, at first, like other poets, not
simply because he had read their works, but because his modes of feeling and thought were much like theirs. As for the Provençal poets, I
have not the knowledge to read them at first hand. That mysterious people had a religion of their own which was thoroughly and painfully extinguished by the Inquisition; so that we hardly know more about them
than about the Sumerians. I suspect that the difference between this unknown, and possibly maligned, Albigensianism and Catholicism has some
correspondence with the difference between the poetry of the Provençal

school and the Tuscan. The system of Dante's organization of sensibility —the contrast between higher and lower carnal love, the transition from Beatrice living to Beatrice dead, rising to the Cult of the Virgin, seems to me to be his own.

At any rate, the *Vita Nuova*, besides being a sequence of beautiful poems connected by a curious vision-literature prose, is, I believe, a very sound psychological treatise on something related to what is now called "sublimation." There is also a practical sense of realities behind it, which is antiromantic: not to expect more from *life* than it can give or more from *human* beings than they can give; to look to *death* for what life cannot give. The *Vita Nuova* belongs to "vision literature"; but its philosophy is the Catholic philosophy of disillusion.

Understanding of the book is greatly advanced by acquaintance with Guido Guinicelli, Cavalcanti, Cino, and others. One ought, indeed, to study the development of the art of love from the Provençal poets onwards, paying just attention to both resemblances and differences in spirit; as well as the development of verse form and stanza form and vocabulary. But such study is vain unless we have first made the conscious attempt, as difficult and hard as rebirth, to pass through the looking-glass into a world which is just as reasonable as our own. When we have done that, we begin to wonder whether the world of Dante is not both larger and more solid than our own. When we repeat

Tutti li miei penser parlan d'Amore

[All my thoughts speak of love]

we must stop to think what *amore* means—something different from its Latin original, its French equivalent, or its definition in a modern Italian dictionary.

It is, I repeat, for several reasons necessary to read the *Divine Comedy* first. The first reading of the *Vita Nuova* gives nothing but Pre-Raphaelite quaintness. The *Comedy* initiates us into the world of mediaeval imagery, in the *Inferno* most apprehensible, in the *Paradiso* most rarefied. It initiates us also into the world of mediaeval thought and dogma: far easier for those who have had the college discipline of Plato and Aristotle, but possible even without that. The *Vita Nuova* plunges us direct into mediaeval sensibility. It is not, for Dante, a masterpiece, so that it is safer for us to read it, the first time, for the light it can throw on the *Comedy* than for itself.

Read in this way, it can be more useful than a dozen commentaries.

The effect of many books about Dante is to give the impression that it is more necessary to read about him than to read what he has written. But the next step after reading Dante again and again should be to read some of the books that he read, rather than modern books about his work and life and times, however good. We may easily be distracted by following up the histories of Emperors and Popes. With a poet like Shakespeare, we are less likely to ignore the text for the commentary. With Dante there is just as much need for concentrating on the text, and all the more because Dante's mind is more remote from the ways of thinking and feeling in which we have been brought up. What we need is not information but knowledge: the first step to knowledge is to recognize the differences between his form of thought and feeling and ours. Even to attach great importance to Thomism, or to Catholicism, may lead us astray, in attracting us too much to such differences as are entirely capable of intellectual formulation. The English reader needs to remember that even had Dante not been a good Catholic, even had he treated Aristotle or Thomas with sceptical indifference, his mind would still be no easier to understand; the forms of imagination, phantasmagoria, and sensibility would be just as strange to us. We have to learn to accept these forms: and this *acceptance* is more important than anything that can be called belief. There is almost a definite moment of acceptance at which the New Life begins.

What I have written is, as I promised, not an "introduction" to the study but a brief account of my own introduction to it. In extenuation, it may be observed that to write in this way of men like Dante or Shakespeare is really less presumptuous than to write of smaller men. The very vastness of the subject leaves a possibility that one may have something to say worth saying; whereas with smaller men, only minute and special study is likely to justify writing about them at all.

Tradition and
the Individual Talent

In English writing we seldom speak of tradition, though we occasionally apply its name in deploring its absence. We cannot refer to "the tradition" or to "a tradition"; at most, we employ the adjective in saying that the poetry of So-and-so is "traditional" or even "too traditional." Seldom, perhaps, does the word appear except in a phrase of censure. If otherwise, it is vaguely approbative, with the implication, as to the work approved, of some pleasing archaeological reconstruction. You can hardly make the word agreeable to English ears without this comfortable reference to the reassuring science of archaeology.

Certainly the word is not likely to appear in our appreciations of living or dead writers. Every nation, every race, has not only its own creative, but its own critical turn of mind; and is even more oblivious of the shortcomings and limitations of its critical habits than of those of its creative genius. We know, or think we know, from the enormous mass of critical writing that has appeared in the French language the critical method or habit of the French; we only conclude (we are such unconscious people) that the French are "more critical" than we, and sometimes even plume ourselves a little with the fact, as if the French were the less spontaneous. Perhaps they are; but we might remind ourselves that criticism is as inevitable as breathing, and that we should be none the worse for articulating what passes in our minds when we read a book and feel an emotion about it, for criticizing our own minds in their work of criticism. One of the facts that might come to light in this process is our tendency to insist, when we praise a poet, upon those aspects of his work in which he least resembles any one else. In these aspects or parts of his work we pretend to find what is individual, what is the peculiar essence of the man. We dwell with satisfaction upon the poet's difference from his predecessors, especially his immediate predecessors; we endeavour to find something that can be isolated in order to be enjoyed. Whereas if we approach a poet without this prejudice we shall often find that not only the best, but the most individual parts of his work may be those in which the dead poets, his ancestors, assert their immortality most vigorously. And I do not mean the impressionable period of adolescence, but the period of full maturity.

Yet if the only form of tradition, of handing down, consisted in following the ways of the immediate generation before us in a blind or timid adherence to its successes, "tradition" should positively be discouraged. We have seen many such simple currents soon lost in the sand; and novelty is better than repetition. Tradition is a matter of much wider significance. It cannot be inherited, and if you want it you must obtain it by great labour. It involves, in the first place, the historical sense, which we may call nearly indispensable to any one who would continue to be a poet beyond his twenty-fifth year; and the historical sense involves a perception, not only of the pastness of the past, but of its presence; the historical sense compels a man to write not merely with his own generation in his bones, but with a feeling that the whole of the literature of Europe from Homer and within it the whole of the literature of his own country has a simultaneous existence and composes a simultaneous order. This historical sense, which is a sense of the timeless as well as of the temporal and of the timeless and of the temporal together, is what makes a writer traditional. And it is at the same time what makes a writer most acutely conscious of his place in time, of his own contemporaneity.

No poet, no artist of any art, has his complete meaning alone. His significance, his appreciation is the appreciation of his relation to the dead poets and artists. You cannot value him alone; you must set him, for contrast and comparison, among the dead. I mean this as a principle of aesthetic, not merely historical, criticism. The necessity that he shall conform, that he shall cohere, is not one-sided; what happens when a new work of art is created is something that happens simultaneously to all the works of art which preceded it. The existing monuments form an ideal order among themselves, which is modified by the introduction of the new (the really new) work of art among them. The existing order is complete before the new work arrives; for order to persist after the supervention of novelty, the *whole* existing order must be, if ever so slightly, altered; and so the relations, proportions, values of each work of art towards the whole are readjusted; and this is conformity between the old and the new. Whoever has approved this idea of order, of the form of European, of English literature will not find it preposterous that the past should be altered by the present as much as the present is directed by the past. And the poet who is aware of this will be aware of great difficulties and responsibilities.

In a peculiar sense he will be aware also that he must inevitably be judged by the standards of the past. I say judged, not amputated, by them; not judged to be as good as, or worse or better than, the dead; and certainly not judged by the canons of dead critics. It is a judgment, a comparison, in which two things are measured by each other. To conform merely would be for the new work not really to conform at all; it would not be new, and would therefore not be a work of art. And we do not quite say that the new is more valuable because it fits in; but its fitting in is a test of its value—a test, it is true, which can only be slowly and cautiously applied, for we are none of us infallible judges of conformity. We say: it appears to conform, and is perhaps individual, or it appears individual, and many conform; but we are hardly likely to find that it is one and not the other.

To proceed to a more intelligible exposition of the relation of the poet to the past: he can neither take the past as a lump, an indiscriminate bolus, nor can he form himself wholly on one or two private admirations, nor can he form himself wholly upon one preferred period. The first course is inadmissible, the second is an important experience of youth, and the third is a pleasant and highly desirable supplement. The poet must be very conscious of the main current, which does not at all flow invariably through the most distinguished reputations. He must be quite aware of the obvious fact that art never improves, but that the material of art is never quite the same. He must be aware that the mind of Europe —the mind of his own country—a mind which he learns in time to be much more important than his own private mind—is a mind which changes, and that this change is a development which abandons nothing *en route*, which does not superannuate either Shakespeare, or Homer, or the rock drawing of the Magdalenian draughtsmen. That this development, refinement perhaps, complication certainly, is not, from the point of view of the artist, any improvement. Perhaps not even an improvement from the point of view of the psychologist or not to the extent which we imagine; perhaps only in the end based upon a complication in economics and machinery. But the difference between the present and the past is that the conscious present is an awareness of the past in a way and to an extent which the past's awareness of itself cannot show.

Some one said: "The dead writers are remote from us because we *know* so much more than they did." Precisely, and they are that which we know.

I am alive to a usual objection to what is clearly part of my program for the *métier* of poetry. The objection is that the doctrine requires a ridiculous amount of erudition (pedantry), a claim which can be rejected by appeal to the lives of poets in any pantheon. It will even be affirmed that much learning deadens or perverts poetic sensibility. While, however, we persist in believing that a poet ought to know as much as will not encroach upon his necessary receptivity and necessary laziness, it is not desirable to confine knowledge to whatever can be put into a useful shape for examinations, drawing-rooms, or the still more pretentious modes of publicity. Some can absorb knowledge, the more tardy must sweat for it. Shakespeare acquired more essential history from Plutarch than most men could from the whole British Museum. What is to be insisted upon is that the poet must develop or procure the consciousness of the past and that he should continue to develop this consciousness throughout his career.

What happens is a continual surrender of himself as he is at the moment to something which is more valuable. The progress of an artist is a continual self-sacrifice, a continual extinction of personality.

There remains to define this process of depersonalization and its relation to the sense of tradition. It is in this depersonalization that art may be said to approach the condition of science. I, therefore, invite you to consider, as a suggestive analogy, the action which takes place when a bit of finely filiated platinum is introduced into a chamber containing oxygen and sulphur dioxide.

Honest criticism and sensitive appreciation are directed not upon the poet but upon the poetry. If we attend to the confused cries of the newspaper critics and the susurrus of popular repetition that follows, we shall hear the names of poets in great numbers; if we seek not Blue-book knowledge but the enjoyment of poetry, and ask for a poem, we shall seldom find it. I have tried to point out the importance of the relation of the poem to other poems by other authors, and suggested the conception of poetry as a living whole of all the poetry that has ever been written. The other aspect of this Impersonal theory of poetry is the relation of the poem to its author. And I hinted, by an analogy, that the mind of the mature poet differs from that of the immature one not precisely in any valuation of "personality," not being necessarily more interesting, or having "more to say," but rather by being a more finely perfected me-

dium in which special, or very varied, feelings are at liberty to enter into
new combinations.

The analogy was that of the catalyst. When the two gases previously
mentioned are mixed in the presence of a filament of platinum, they
form sulphurous acid. This combination takes place only if the platinum
is present; nevertheless the newly formed acid contains no trace of
platinum, and the platinum itself is apparently unaffected; has remained inert, neutral, and unchanged. The mind of the poet is the shred
of platinum. It may partly or exclusively operate upon the experience of
the man himself; but, the more perfect the artist, the more completely
separate in him will be the man who suffers and the mind which creates;
the more perfectly will the mind digest and transmute the passions which
are its material.

The experience, you will notice, the elements which enter the presence of the transforming catalyst, are of two kinds: emotions and feelings. The effect of a work of art upon the person who enjoys it is an experience different in kind from any experience not of art. It may be
formed out of one emotion, or may be a combination of several; and various feelings, inhering for the writer in particular words or phrases or images, may be added to compose the final result. Or great poetry may be
made without the direct use of any emotion whatever: composed out of
feelings solely. Canto xv of the *Inferno* (Brunetto Latini) is a working
up of the emotion evident in the situation; but the effect, though single
as that of any work of art, is obtained by considerable complexity of
detail. The last quatrain gives an image, a feeling attaching to an image,
which "came," which did not develop simply out of what precedes, but
which was probably in suspension in the poet's mind until the proper
combination arrived for it to add itself to. The poet's mind is in fact a
receptacle for seizing and storing up numberless feelings, phrases,
images, which remain there until all the particles which can unite to
form a new compound are present together.

If you compare several representative passages of the greatest poetry
you see how great is the variety of types of combination, and also how
completely any semi-ethical criterion of "sublimity" misses the mark.
For it is not the "greatness," the intensity, of the emotions, the com-
ponents, but the intensity of the artistic process, the pressure, so to speak,
under which the fusion takes place, that counts. The episode of Paolo
and Francesca employs a definite emotion, but the intensity of the
poetry is something quite different from whatever intensity in the supposed experience it may give the impression of. It is no more intense,

furthermore, than Canto xxvi, the voyage of Ulysses, which has not the direct dependence upon an emotion. Great variety is possible in the process of transmutation of emotion: the murder of Agamemnon, or the agony of Othello, gives an artistic effect apparently closer to a possible original than the scenes from Dante. In the *Agamemnon,* the artistic emotion approximates to the emotion of an actual spectator; in *Othello* to the emotion of the protagonist himself. But the difference between art and the event is always absolute; the combination which is the murder of Agamemnon is probably as complex as that which is the voyage of Ulysses. In either case there has been a fusion of elements. The ode of Keats contains a number of feelings which have nothing particular to do with the nightingale, but which the nightingale, partly, perhaps, because of its attractive name, and partly because of its reputation, served to bring together.

The point of view which I am struggling to attack is perhaps related to the metaphysical theory of the substantial unity of the soul: for my meaning is, that the poet has, not a "personality" to express, but a particular medium, which is only a medium and not a personality, in which impressions and experiences combine in peculiar and unexpected ways. Impressions and experiences which are important for the man may take no place in the poetry, and those which become important in the poetry may play quite a negligible part in the man, the personality.

I will quote a passage which is unfamiliar enough to be regarded with fresh attention in the light—or darkness—of these observations:

> And now methinks I could e'en chide myself
> For doating on her beauty, though her death
> Shall be revenged after no common action.
> Does the silkworm expend her yellow labours
> For thee? For thee does she undo herself?
> Are lordships sold to maintain ladyships
> For the poor benefit of a bewildering minute?
> Why does yon fellow falsify highways,
> And put his life between the judge's lips,
> To refine such a thing—keeps horse and men
> To beat their valours for her? . . .

In this passage (as is evident if it is taken in its context) there is a combination of positive and negative emotions: an intensely strong attraction towards beauty and an equally intense fascination by the ugliness which is contrasted with it and which destroys it. This balance of contrasted emotion is in the dramatic situation to which the speech is pertinent, but that situation alone is inadequate to it. This is, so to speak, the structural emotion, provided by the drama. But the whole effect, the dominant tone, is due to the fact that a number of floating feelings, having an affinity to this emotion by no means superficially evident, have combined with it to give us a new art emotion.

It is not in his personal emotions, the emotions provoked by particular events in his life, that the poet is in any way remarkable or interesting. His particular emotions may be simple, or crude, or flat. The emotion in his poetry will be a very complex thing, but not with the complexity of the emotions of people who have very complex or unusual emotions in life. One error, in fact, of eccentricity in poetry is to seek for new human emotions to express; and in this search for novelty in the wrong place it discovers the perverse. The business of the poet is not to find new emotions, but to use the ordinary ones and, in working them up into poetry, to express feelings which are not in actual emotions at all. And emotions which he has never experienced will serve his turn as well as those familiar to him. Consequently, we must believe that "emotion recollected in tranquillity" is an inexact formula. For it is neither emotion, nor recollection, nor, without distortion of meaning, tranquillity. It is a concentration, and a new thing resulting from the concentration, of a very great number of experiences which to the practical and active person would not seem to be experiences at all; it is a concentration which does not happen consciously or of deliberation. These experiences are not "recollected," and they finally unite in an atmosphere which is "tranquil" only in that it is a passive attending upon the event. Of course this is not quite the whole story. There is a great deal, in the writing of poetry, which must be conscious and deliberate. In fact, the bad poet is usually unconscious where he ought to be conscious, and conscious where he ought to be unconscious. Both errors tend to make him "personal." Poetry is not a turning loose of emotion, but an escape from emotion; it is not the expression of personality, but an escape from personality. But, of course, only those who have personality and emotions know what it means to want to escape from these things.

[*Ho de nous isos theioteron ti kai apathes estin.*]

[But the mind is in a way more godlike and suffers fewer changes.]

This essay proposes to halt at the frontier of metaphysics or mysticism, and confine itself to such practical conclusions as can be applied by the responsible person interested in poetry. To divert interest from the poet to the poetry is a laudable aim: for it would conduce to a juster estimation of actual poetry, good and bad. There are many people who appreciate the expression of sincere emotion in verse, and there is a smaller number of people who can appreciate technical excellence. But very few know when there is an expression of *significant* emotion, emotion which has its life in the poem and not in the history of the poet. The emotion of art is impersonal. And the poet cannot reach this impersonality without surrendering himself wholly to the work to be done. And he is not likely to know what is to be done unless he lives in what is not merely the present, but the present moment of the past, unless he is conscious, not of what is dead, but of what is already living.

Date Due